BUILDING ORACLE WEB SITES

ISBN 0-13-079841-X

90000

9 780130 798411

PRENTICE HALL PTR

BUILDING A WEB SITE SERIES

Prentice Hall PTR
Building a Web Site Series

BUILDING ORACLE WEB SITES
James J. Hobuss

BUILDING SYBASE WEB SITES
James J. Hobuss

BUILDING ACCESS WEB SITES
James J. Hobuss

BUILDING ORACLE WEB SITES

James J. Hobuss

To join a Prentice Hall PTR Internet mailing list, point to:
http://www.prenhall.com/mail_lists/

Prentice Hall PTR
Upper Saddle River, New Jersey 07458

Library of Congress Cataloging-in-Publication Data

Hobuss, James J., 1955–
    Building Oracle web sites / James J. Hobuss.
       p.   cm.
    Includes index.
    ISBN 0-13-079841-X
    1. Internet programming.   2. Oracle (Computer file)   3. Web sites-
-Design.   4. Database design.   I. Title.
QA76.625.H64   1998
005.75'85--dc21   97-43175
                                                     CIP

Acquistions editor: Jeffrey M. Pepper
Cover designer: Design Source
Cover design director: Jerry Votta
Manufacturing manager: Alexis R. Heydt
Marketing manager: Miles Williams
Compositor/Production services: Pine Tree Composition, Inc.

 © 1998 by Prentice Hall PTR
Prentice-Hall, Inc.
A Simon & Schuster Company
Upper Saddle River, New Jersey 07458

Prentice Hall books are widely-used by corporations and
government agencies for training, marketing, and resale.

The publisher offers discounts on this book when ordered in
bulk quantities. For more information contact:

    Corporate Sales Department
    Phone: 800-382-3419
    Fax: 201-236-7141
    E-mail: corpsales@prenhall.com

Or write:

    Prentice Hall PTR
    Corp. Sales Dept.
    One Lake Street
    Upper Saddle River, New Jersey 07458

Printed in the United States of America
10 9 8 7 6 5 4 3 2 1

ISBN: 0-13-079841-X

Prentice-Hall International (UK) Limited, *London*
Prentice-Hall of Australia Pty. Limited, *Sydney*
Prentice-Hall Canada Inc., *Toronto*
Prentice-Hall Hispanoamericana, S.A., *Mexico*
Prentice-Hall of India Private Limited, *New Delhi*
Prentice-Hall of Japan, Inc., *Tokyo*
Simon & Schuster Asia Pte. Ltd., *Singapore*
Editora Prentice-Hall do Brasil, Ltda., *Rio de Janeiro*

Once again, and always, this book is dedicated to my wife, Robin, for her unending support, encouragement, and love, which is continually demonstrated, freely and completely given (quite undeserving) creating limitless boundaries and a world as close to nirvana as this beating heart will ever know; my sons, Andrew James Robert Hobuss and Joel James Vincent Hobuss, for motivating me in ways that they are too young to understand but hopefully will know when they are including their children's names in the dedications of their books; Mark Rife, whose expertise in Oracle 8 and his involvement in writing many of the chapters in this book made it possible to bring it to you in this form; my best friend during my formative years, Chris Colliver, for being a great guy; that old man in a trolley on the way to see Jesus Christ Superstar in Melbourne, Australia, who shared his wisdom with me and gave me a tidbit of advice which has served to guide me for all these years and will serve me the rest of my life.

James J. Hobuss

Contents

Introduction

I f you are reading this Introduction while browsing in a bookstore, go ahead and buy the book. You won't be disappointed. If you are reading this after purchasing the book, good for you. I'll tell you why, and the reason may surprise you. Does it intrigue you that one of the reasons is *not* to add $1.45 to my semi-annual royalty statement from the publisher?

This book will show you the skills and describe the techniques you need to know to become successful designing, developing, and implementing production Web applications that use Oracle 8 databases.

I trust you're not surprised to learn that you are not alone in the migration of developers to building Web database applications. Your ability to be successful in large part is determined by your skillset and how you apply those skills to solve business computing problems. Learn what is in these pages and you will have the basis to be successful. How you apply those skills is up to you.

The book assumes you have at least a beginner's understanding of the Oracle 8 database engine. It is designed to introduce you to the process of designing, developing, and implementing an Internet database application using the Oracle 8 database design. Key topics are the planning, design, and implementation of enterprise-quality Internet/intranet applications that include database connectivity to Oracle Corporation's Oracle 8 databases with production-level security and performance. All technical terms used in the book are defined and there are abundant screen images, tips, and callouts. Also included in this book are abundant examples of Web page construction and program code with database access.

The layout of this book is designed to be informative and valuable if you like to read a book from the front cover to the back. If you are the type of person that likes to read only those topics that interest you, then you will be pleased to learn that with 21 chapters in this book, plus three appendices, you can pick and choose which chapters to read without missing anything. The following is a brief description of each of the chapters in this book:

Section 1: Planning

Chapter 1: The Web Connection.   Before you plunge into the issues specific to the design, development, and implementation of Web database applications, it is valuable that you understand a few things about the origins of the Web. That's what this chapter is about. With this as a foundation, hopefully you can make better sense out of all the Web-hype that so pervades the computer industry.

Chapter 2: Web Commerce.   This chapter introduces you to some of the reasons why companies are turning to the Web as the production platform for database applications. You will learn the role that the database plays in these applications. Following this is a list of some of the things you should consider, outside of the technical issues that you'll learn about in the remainder of this book, when doing business on the Web.

Chapter 3: Choosing a CGI Programming Language.   Choosing a CGI programming language to use to develop a Web database application is becoming increasingly more difficult. Now, you have a myriad of languages, derivatives of languages, dialects of languages, development suites, programming suites, and various iterations of each of these to choose from. To attempt to write about each of the current products would be futile. New languages and tools pop up all the time. This chapter focuses on the most popular languages available to build Web database applications.

Chapter 4: Overview of Java and JavaScript.   The release of Java from Sun Microsystems preceded slightly the release of JavaScript. Partly because of this, some people view these two languages as being an either/or decision. This is not the case. They do share similar syntax and use objects similarly, but the languages were developed to solve different sets of problems. The two languages are not very much related to each other and their intended use is quite a bit different, as you will learn in this chapter.

Chapter 5: Application Development Suites.   This chapter presents information on a number of application development suites. The major features of the products are described along with contact information. I have reviewed only a subset of these products, so it would be unfair (and therefore I won't do it) to recommend one product over the other. Most vendors will supply you with evaluation copies of the their products, and in many cases, you can download these evaluation copies directly from the Web. Most of the products described here are also included on the companion CD-ROM.

Chapter 6: Overview of HTML.   If you are new to the Web, this chapter gives you a good introduction to HyperText Markup Language (HTML), how to read it, write it, and how to use it. If you are an experienced Web developer or user, you too will find useful information in this chapter on topics such as the structure of HTML, advanced HTML topics, good HTML coding practices, and the future of HTML.

Chapter 7: Overview of CGI.   In this chapter, you'll learn about the Common Gateway Interface (CGI) and the role it has in Web database application development. Being one of the most important links that connect Web pages to databases, CGI plays a critical role in Web database design and use. You'll learn about the CGI standard as it applies to UNIX and Windows operating systems. Simple programs are used to communicate and demonstrate CGI capabilities.

Section 2: Internet Database Design

Chapter 8: Web Application Design and Development.   This chapter takes the fundamental concepts of Client Server database application development and applies them to the unique attributes of the Web. We begin by discussing what those concepts are, progress through describing the architectural components of the Web, and end with the application of those concepts to the Web architecture.

Chapter 9: New Features and Creating Database Objects in Oracle.   Beginning with this chapter and continuing into chapters 10, 11, and 12, you are introduced to Oracle Corporations Oracle 8 product. This chapter provides an overview of the product and some of the features (most of which are new) specific to Web database application development. It continues on with specific information on DDL, SQL, and the facilities in Oracle 8 to define databases and database objects.

Chapter 10: Oracle 8 Queries.   You will learn how to build and execute simple queries in Oracle 8. You will also learn how to use an external data source, including Open DataBase Connectivity (ODBC), in your Oracle 8 tables and queries. This information will assist you if you are using a development tool besides Oracle 8 to build your front-end Web database application.

Chapter 11: Designing Advanced Oracle 8 Queries.   In this chapter you will go deeper into the facilities in Oracle 8 to create advanced queries. This includes using multiple aggregate functions, applying criteria in the query, parameter queries, nested queries, and optimizing performance of queries. The information discussed in this chapter is valuable to any developer using Oracle 8 as their back-end RDBMS, regardless of what front-end design and HTML tool is being used.

Chapter 12: Exploiting Oracles Stored Code and Object-Oriented Features.   The information discussed in this chapter is valuable to any developer using Oracle as their back-end RDBMS, regardless of the front-end design and HTML tool being used. Two additional SQL topics, dates and views, are discussed. PL/SQL, Oracle's procedural language is described, as well as the ability to store code within the database. Oracle transactional logic and locking are explained. Finally, performance and tuning of SQL statements are covered.

Section 3: Interfacing with the Internet User

Chapter 13: HTML Forms and Database Access.   This chapter gives you a thorough introduction into the markups (controls) available to construct and transmit an HTML form. These markups, and the actions and attributes you code to the controls on the form, are the input mechanism into your Web database application.

Chapter 14: Accessing Oracle Databases Using CGI Programs.   This chapter begins with a review of CGI basics you learned in previous chapters in this book. You will learn about CGI input and output processing, and some of the different ways that exist in which a client can make a request to the server when an HTML form is submitted. Then, you will see how CGI programs can be used to generate HTML. Later in this chapter you will learn among other things, how to write a CGI program to perform whatever type of database access required by your Web database application.

Chapter 15: MIME and Advanced Data Presentation.   The earlier chapters in this book present material on the tools available for Web database application development, Oracle Corporation's Oracle 8 product, using the Oracle 8 product to build database components, Web database application architecture, and HTML and CGI programming and processing. The chapters include a number of examples of how data can be formatted and displayed. In this chapter, you'll learn how to incorporate multimedia components in your Web database applications.

Chapter 16: Managing Web Database Access and the Application State.   As you may or may not know, the Web is an inherently "stateless" environment—it is nonconversational in nature. From one transaction to the next, unless you specifically build a mechanism to allow the application to keep track of where it is in a series of processes, it will lose track of where it's been. Often, when an application loses track of where it's been, it doesn't know where it needs to go.

This chapter describes three different techniques that you could use to keep track of the "application state." Those three techniques are:

Hidden Fields on Forms

Database Tables

Cookies

Chapter 17: Improving Performance of Web Database Applications.   It is no longer enough to merely build a Web application that has database access to satisfy a business need. With ODBC and the tools available to integrate Web and database technologies, the "art" in Web database application development is no longer in marrying the two toolsets. Rather, the "art" lies in crafting an application that not only meets the business needs *but* is efficient as well.

This chapter describes some techniques you can use to build efficiency into your Web database applications. It is segmented into two major sections; Application Optimization and Database Optimization.

Section 4: Advanced Topics in Internet Database Publishing

Chapter 18: Migrating Data from Enterprise Data Stores to Server-Based Databases. In this chapter you will learn about some of the techniques used to migrate data from enterprise data stores to server-based Web databases. Specifically you'll learn about the features in Oracle 8 that facilitate this process, such as replication and synchronization.

You'll first read about how to determine what to migrate from your corporate databases to Web servers. This is not simply a process of "copying" a database from one location to another. Next, you'll learn about some of the features in Oracle 8 that you can incorporate in your overall data strategy that facilitate deployment of corporate databases to be accessed by Web applications. Finally you will read about backup and recovery principals that you can apply to your Web databases.

Chapter 19: Using Firewalls and Security Components to Protect Your Data. This chapter introduces you to the issues of Web-based security and describes some of the things that you can do to secure your Web applications, including your Web-accessible Oracle 8 databases. It is not intended to be a primer on the subject. It is intended to introduce you to the issues and components that you need to be aware of to safeguard your investment in your Web site and your data.

Chapter 20: Designing an Internet Course Delivery System. This is the first of two "summation" chapters. In this chapter, you will take what was learned in the previous chapters and see how it is applied to the design of a Web database application. Specifically, recall that in Chapter 8 you learned how to design a Web database application to take into account the unique considerations of a Web-based database application. You saw how the information contained in that chapter, plus various other pieces of information from the other chapters in this book, are applied to the actual design of a Web database application. Then, in Chapter 21, this will be taken to the next logical step, which is the actual construction of a Web database application.

Chapter 21: Building a Simple Class Registration System. This chapter focuses on how to use HTML and a Web database application development suite to construct a Web database application that includes both Internet and Intranet access. The company profiled in this chapter is A Better Computer (ABC) Company, a fictitious corporation that provides, among other things, computer training. The Web application profiled in this chapter contains, among other things, a query facility so that Web visitors can see what training classes are held in cities near them. This is the Internet component to the database that is profiled in this chapter. The Intranet component presented in this chapter is the facility used by ABC employees to update the Oracle 8 database that maintains the data that describes the course offerings and availability of ABC Company.

Appendices

Appendix A: **CD-ROM Contents**

Appendix B: **Frequently Asked Questions**

Appendix C: **WWW Database Development Resources**

In addition to the content of the book and the material contained in the chapters, this book also includes a companion CD-ROM. Evaluation copies of many products referenced in the book and that relate to the topic of the book are included on the enclosed CD-ROM.

Finally, I welcome your comments on the book. Feel free to e-mail me at: jhobuss@teleport.com.

About the Author

J im Hobuss has been either building computer applications or managing the activities specific to building computer applications since 1977. After leaving a successful career in which he was the Development Center Manager for a major Northwest Bank (soon to be an acquisition of an even larger mid-West Bank) in 1991, he built a successful high technology training and consulting company. From 1991 through 1996, Jim built his company into a successful enterprise, finally disposing of it in 1996 to enter a phase of semi-retirement at the ripe age of 40! Finding himself at least 20 years away from official retirement and (pensions!), Jim is currently enjoying a more leisurely lifestyle (family, golf, and the hot tub) and spends much of his working-time consulting, writing, and speaking at industry events.

Jim has previously written three books. The first, titled *Application Development Center: Implementation and Management*, is popular with IS executives and management who are charged with the responsibility of implementing new technologies in application development departments. The second, titled *Application Development Using PowerBuilder*, is a very successful book written for developers using PowerBuilder to create client/server applications. The third book, titled *Access Database Publishing on the Internet* is a bestseller. He has written countless articles that have appeared in magazines ranging from *Systems Builder* to *Journal of Information Systems Management*. He also writes a monthly column for *Exploring Sybase SQL Server* journal. You can e-mail Jim at: jhobuss@tele port.com.

CHAPTER 1

The Web Connection

C hances are that you bought this book because you have either an interest or a mandate to develop a Web database application. I have the knowledge to help you do that. We have forged a "Web Connection." The Web has brought us together with what started as an exchange of commerce and continues on now as an exchange of information. For the purposes of this book, I'll define the Web as the whole constellation of server computers that allow text, graphics, sound files, etc. to be mixed together and transmitted to other computers that have the capability to receive them.

Of all the options to consider when building a Web site, this book will present those for incorporating a database using Oracle Corporations Oracle 8 product. Of course this Relational Data Base Management System (RDBMS) cannot be used by itself to create a Web site; other components are required. These additional components are discussed in detail, and you will see how these other components interface with Oracle 8.

Before you plunge into the issues specific to the design, development, and implementation of Web database applications, it is helpful to understand a few things about the origins of the Web. That's what this chapter is about.

Internet Background

A few years ago the Web was an unknown, preceded by the Internet—the Internet being a collection of interconnected networks all using the Transmission Control Protocols/Internet Protocols (TCP/IP), or gateway facilities. The Internet itself was preceded by ARPANET.

Believe it or not, the Internet was not an Al Gore (Vice President of the United States between 1992 and 2000) initiative. Those of you reading this probably remember Al Gore's 1992 Democratic National Convention pledge to develop an "information superhighway" during Presidential candidate Bill Clinton's first term. This was a safe statement for Al Gore to make, considering the momentum that had been building for this during the past 30 years.

ARPANET was established by the U.S. Department of Defense (DOD) beginning in the late 1960s as a result of the cold war the United States was engaged in with the Soviet Union. Government officials wanted to create a communications and networking facility through which governmental and academic computer systems could communicate even in the event of a nuclear strike against the United States.

The DOD certainly succeeded in its objective for ARPANET. In 1988, a hacker-initiated virus called the "Internet-worm" was unleashed that disabled or negatively affected a little over 6,000 of the total number of servers comprising the Internet. What a nuclear bomb could never do was almost accomplished without so much as a pop from a cap gun.

Having succeeded in accomplishing the DOD's objective, the Internet remained a largely academic, scientific and military communications vehicle until about 1988, when the backbone speed of the communications supporting the Internet was upgraded to 1.544 mbps, thanks in large measure to the commercial availability of T1 data communication facilities.

The achievement of implementing a backbone Internet communication speed of 1,544,000 bits per second (1.544 mbps) in 1988 was astounding, especially when you consider that currently most analog telephone lines can achieve, at best, 28,800 bits per second transmission speed of data. Then, in 1990, two events occurred that solidified the commercial application of the Internet. First, a researcher named Tim Berners-Lee published a paper referring (for the first time ever) to the World Wide Web, or WWW. Second, and in large measure due to the end of the cold war as seen during the Reagan/Bush U.S. Presidential administrations, the DOD canceled the ARPANET program and turned the Internet over to commercialization.

Mr. Berners-Lee might have done more harm than good by coining the phrase "World Wide Web" or Web to describe the Internet. The two are often used interchangeably when they should not be. As you will learn later in this chapter, the Web and Internet are not synonymous. The Internet is a global network, and the Web is a set of communications applications and software that execute on the Internet.

Even though the computers that attached to the early Internet did so using TCP/IP protocols, computers on non-TCP/IP networks can now access the Internet via gateway systems that perform the necessary protocol translations.

A Chronological History of the Internet

The initial ARPANET configuration linked together the following four sites:

- Stanford Research Institute (SRI)
- University of California at Santa Barbara (UCSB)
- University of California at Los Angeles (UCLA)
- University of Utah (UU)

The following timeline provides a thumbnail overview of the events triggering the growth of the Web up through today.

1969 United States Department of Defense (DOD) commissions the establishment of ARPA, and the communications facility known as ARPANET.

1970 ARPANET begins using Network Control Protocol (NCP) for inter-site communications.

1972 Telnet specification RFC-318 was proposed to establish a common format for one Internet site to establish communications with another.

1973 Bob Metcalfe, now a columnist and founder of the 3COM corporation, outlined the facilities of Ethernet networking in his Ph.D. thesis at Harvard University. This is also the year that File Transfer Protocol (FTP) specification number RFC 454 was proposed.

1973 was also the year that Bill Gates and I graduated from High School.

1974 TCP/IP communications protocol was proposed by Vint Cerf and Bob Kahn. It remains today as the defining way in which devices on the Internet communicate with each other.

1976 Bell Labs developed the UUCP (Unix-to-Unix CoPy) protocol that allows devices connected to the Internet to share and transfer information in a consistent manner.

1979 Relational Software Incorporated, Oracle Corporation's predecessor, ships the first commercial release of its RDBMS, Oracle version 2. From the very beginning, Oracle is a portable RDBMS, running on several operating systems including UNIX and VMS.

1982 DOD specifies TCP/IP as the standard ARPANET protocol.

1984 The number of Internet host sites reaches 1,000 and is the year that Domain Name Services are established. A Domain Name Service is a method by which each site that attaches to the Internet is assigned a unique name.

1986 Oracle Corporation releases version 5.1 of Oracle, the first version of a SQL-based RDBMS that supports a client-server architecture.

1987   The number of Internet host sites reaches 10,000.

1988   The Internet worm disables or infects more than 6,000 of all Internet host sites.

1989   The number of Internet host sites reaches 100,000.

1900   With the end of the Cold War, the DOD terminates the ARPANET initiative and allows the Internet to commercialize.

1991   Brewster Kahle of Thinking Machines develops the first Wide Area Information Server. Paul Lindner and Mark McCahill of the University of Minnesota write Gopher (named for the school's mascot). Gopher is a method of making menus of materials available over the Internet. Gopher was the predecessor to Hypertext.

1992   The number of Internet host sites reaches 1,000,000. Researchers at the University of Nevada release Veronica, a frequently updated database of the names of almost every menu item on almost all the Gopher servers. At year end, Oracle releases the Oracle 7 server, enhancing its popularity as the enterprise database of choice. Oracle's revenues reach an industry-leading $1.5 billion by 1995. This is also the year that U.S. Vice President Al Gore begins discussing the "Information Superhighway." Also, this is the year that Veronica is released. Veronica stands for Very Early Rodent Oriented Net-wide Index to Computerized Archives. It is a constantly updated database of the name of almost every menu item on almost every Gopher server.

1993   NSF creates InterNIC to facilitate the creation and registration of Internet services. Marc Andreessen, now of Netscape Corporation, releases Mosaic while employed by the National Center for Supercomputing Applications NCSA. Mosaic was the first Web browser available for all the major operating systems with the same graphical Interface. Mosaic was the "killer application" that launched the popularity of the Web.

1994   The first commercial application is developed and delivered over the Internet by Pizza Hut Corporation. With this application, you could order a pizza (and specify the toppings!) from your Web browser and have it delivered to your home from your nearest Pizza Hut franchise. The term "spam" (as opposed to the processed meat product developed and sold by the Hormel Corporation) became popular to describe an inappropriate attempt to use a mailing list.

A bit of trivia that you may be quizzed on later: In the 1970s, my father, Orville Hobuss, while working on a contract for the American Can Company, designed the machine that made Spam cans.

1995   Compuserve, America Online, and Prodigy all begin offering Internet connectivity through their online services. They become so successful with this that most of their subscribers think that Compuserve, America Online, and Prodigy are the Internet. This is also the year that Marc Andreessen issued an Initial Public Offering (IPO) for Netscape Communications Corporation that ranks it as the #3 highest initial public offering share price of all time. Also, major software companies (e.g., Microsoft, Lotus, WordPerfect) announce plans to port their applications to the Internet. Oracle Corporation markets Web Server version 1.0, the company's first industrial-strength product for serving data from Oracle databases to the Web.

1996 America Online is swamped with customer complaints about not being able to connect to their service after it begins offering unlimited-access Internet connections. It discovers that many customers are not terminating their connections when done using their computers.

1997 The number of host sites reaches 10,000,000. Oracle Corp releases Oracle 8, a Relational Data Base Management System (RDBMS) product with extensive Web database application development and deployment tools. This version, in beta testing for two years, solidifies Oracle's position as the database leader.

The Internet Today

The Internet today is a global information resource accumulation and dissemination facility that dwarfs the expectations of its creators. On the Internet today you can find the latest research in AIDS treatments, schedule a vacation down to reservations at restaurants and hotels, view the world's great art works, add your résumé to a confidential job search site, and find and communicate with your high school buddies. Web sites that deal with subjects as diverse as the effects of ribonucleic acids on the upper gastrointestinal tract or the current box office smash hit are popping up at an ever-increasing rate. The number of new Web sites and growth of the Internet are astounding.

An average of 11,000 new sites are added each day, and an estimated 300,000 Web servers (each Web server can host a minimum of one and an unlimited maximum number of Web sites) are expected to be shipped in 1998. It is expected that by 1998 there will be over 22,000,000 Web sites.

With all this information available, one of the critical issues to users becomes one of finding the information being sought. To help, there are a growing number of *search engine* tools available. Search engines browse information stored in a site's Web pages for key words that you supply and display a summary page of the results of the search. Many of these search engines, with names like WebCrawler, HotBot, and Yahoo, display their results page as hypertext links so all you have to do is click on the link and your Browser will automatically go to the site that satisfies your search request. You will learn how to capitalize on the capabilities of search engines later in this book.

What Is the Web?

The Web is *not* the Internet, and the Internet is *not* the Web. Although the terms are used synonymously, they are not interchangeable. They are closely related and frequently discussed in the same sentence. You may find instances in this book where the two terms appear to be used interchangeably.

The Internet is a global network. It is the communications infrastructure by which our computers communicate with other computers attached to them.

The Web is a set of communications applications and software that executes on the Internet. The Internet is to our highway system what the Web is to automobiles, motorcycles, and trucks.

Web applications share some common characteristics:

- Understand and use HTML as their display vehicle
- Use the bi-directional client/server model of data communications and information collection
- Provide facilities to access a variety of protocols, including HyperText Transfer Protocol (HTTP), FTP, Telnet, and Gopher
- Use Uniform Resource Locators (URLs) for document and resource addressing

Intranets

Recently a new term has become popular when describing a segment of the Internet: "intranet." An intranet is a private network inside a company or organization using the same kinds of software that you'd find on the public Internet, but it is targeted for internal use only. Because of their secure nature (they can only be accessed by employees of the company with that intranet), Intranets were the first vehicle for development and deployment of Web database applications.

Intranets, like Internets, are not defined by physical or geographical boundaries. Anyone with a Web browser can access a corporate intranet site from anywhere in the world, although only those people who have security permissions are allowed to enter. An intranet site is usually identified in the same way that an Internet site is identified: by an URL.

An URL is a Uniform Resource Locator that is "supposedly" a unique way of identifying an Internet service. The fact is that increasingly, as the use of the Web explodes, duplicate URLs are popping up. An URL is composed of six parts:

1. A service identifier followed by a colon. HTTP is an example of this.
2. A required string of two characters: "//."
3. An optional path to the resource's filename
4. An optional designator of the type of resource
5. An optional internal marker to identify the resource
6. An optional search/selection specification.

By way of example, I once maintained a working relationship with a PC-based COBOL tools provider named Micro Focus LTD. Its Internet URL is http://www.microfocus.com. It also had developed a very extensive intranet facility that employees all over the world could access through their local Internet Service Provider. Micro Focus LTD., in a very short time, built a large information distribution system that provided the following capabilities:

- Disseminate corporate human resources information
- Disseminate sales activities and status of orders
- Collect and disseminate problem tracking information
- Disseminate marketing information

The statistics describing the popularity of the Web are staggering, and I'll add one more to the caldron. Zona Research estimates that corporate spending on intranet development projects will outpace spending on Internet projects by a factor of 4:1 by 1998, a whopping $7.8 billion.

Benefits of Intranets

Intranets are expanding the reach and scope of ways in which corporations collect and disseminate information. Because intranets offer many advantages over traditional groupware tools such as IBM Notes, their acceptance is expected to continue to escalate.

By using corporate intranets, companies gain the following benefits:

Centralize Information for Dissemination Globally. Because of intranets, employees can go to a single location (the intranet URL) to obtain corporate information. If those employees are located in remote areas and they have access to a local Internet Service Provider, they can attach to their corporate intranet site for the price of a local telephone call.

Very Productive Application Development Environment. Once the architectural components are in place, the tools have been purchased and employees have been trained, developing an application for deployment over an intranet is a very quick process.

Organization of Information. Not only do intranets help to centralize and disseminate internal information, but they can also organize information existing outside the corporation. Via hypertext links, an intranet can provide point-and-click attachment to any external Internet site via that site's URL. This could include directions to home offices, product descriptions and more.

Categorization and Analysis of Captured Data. Because of the list nature of Web pages, data is easy to organize and disseminate in meaningful ways. Lists of one sort or another were one of the very first ways in which data was presented on Web pages and remains to this day the most popular data dissemination format. This is especially true for Web database applications that display the results of queries in tables, which are bi-level lists.

Reduced Network Cost. Once TCP/IP communications are established to a Web site and the user has a Web browser, there are no additional network costs associated with connecting to either the Internet or an intranet. Network cards are not required and

Ethernet or Token Ring cabling is not required. The cost to establish and maintain an intranet connection is significantly less than the cost to establish and maintain a connection to a LAN or WAN.

Secure and Accessible Environments.   By use of security firewalls and taking advantage of global information access, any person at any location around the world that has sufficient security and access rights can query, update, and use a corporations intranet site and the information contained therein.

The items listed below are some of the many uses companies find for intranets:

- Install approved software
- Computer-based training
- Corporate policy manual
- Production status for all current and new products
- Current sick leave and vacation allotments
- EEO guidelines and affirmation statements
- Employee and corporate 401(K) information
- Internal job postings
- Job satisfaction surveys
- New employee orientation manuals
- Corporate financial statements, especially if your company's stock is traded publicly
- Corporate newsletters
- Departmental newsletters
- Merger and acquisition information (a sign of the times: your company is either being bought or is buying)
- Inventory
- Marketing materials
- Pricing policies
- Sales leads
- Sales materials
- White papers
- Project schedules and task breakdowns
- Personnel assignments
- Team meeting scheduling and status reporting
- Goal reporting
- Problem reporting and tracking
- Personnel assignments
- Help desk
- Service call and history reporting

What Is a Web Database and Why Have One?

Web databases are not too much different from non-Web databases; in fact, in most cases they are the same. A Web database is a collection of data that is accessed via a query language or programming an Application Programming Interface (API). Whereas non-Web databases are accessed via front-end interfaces built with such tools as Oracle PowerObjects, Microsoft Access 97, Sybase PowerBuilder, etc., Web databases are accessed indirectly from HTML forms.

As you'll learn later, HTML specifications do not provide for direct database access from within a HTML page. Rather, special tags, or commands, embedded within the HTML page, trigger another program that actually reads the Web database. The results are then formatted into an HTML page for display back to the person that requested the information.

Most commercial Web database applications today provide at least query-only Web database access capabilities. As companies become more comfortable with commerce transactions over the Internet and as security issues become a thing of the past, more applications will be written that provide update capabilities to the Web databases. The technology certainly exists to provide this capability today.

What Is a Web Database?

A Web database is part of an application that is deployed over either the Internet (for external users access) or a corporate intranet (for internal use only). Each of the major relational database engines are supported on the Web:

Oracle

Microsoft Access 97

Sybase

Informix

DB2

Chapter 20 discusses how one company took an existing customer and accounting database and, with minor changes, deployed that same database in an application that was delivered over the Internet via Web browsers, thus creating a Web database application.

Although the development and deployment of database applications over the Web is still in its infancy, there are a number of recognizable advantages to not only your company and your users, but to you as well. This section will explore those advantages.

Intranet Database Application Benefits to the Organization

Although the installation of the architectural components to deliver a Web database application are *usually* expensive, there are a number of advantages to the company that undertakes to develop and deliver a Web database application. These are:

- The potential to spend less money by purchasing less expensive client machines as Web applications become more prolific
- Development of computing skill sets in employees needed by businesses in the 21st century
- Greater job satisfaction for employees, resulting in decreased turnover
- Increased productivity in the development staff
- Interface with more potential customers at less cost per customer than any other means
- Ability to market products and services globally without having to suffer the burden of establishing overseas offices
- Increased opportunity to develop systems that meet more of the needs of the company due to the rapid application development nature of HTML and GUI development tools
- Easy maintenance of Web database applications due to the smooth integration of HTML and CGI programs

Common Gateway Interface, or CGI, defines how a Web server and an external program (also called a CGI program) communicate together. It is a very popular method for building database access into Web applications.

Tip: I use the phrase *"usually expensive"* with emphasis on the word *usually*. It does not have to be an expensive proposition to develop a Web presence and deliver a Web database application. For the price of a Pentium-based machine, Operating System, modem, RDBMS software, and access to a local Internet Service Provider, you can build a Web database application. The other necessary components, such as application development tools, Web server, application server, and CGI programming language are all available as shareware on the Web.

As you may already know, HTML has no facilities to directly query a database. Through CGI, this capability exists. By utilizing CGI scripts, a request can be sent from within HTML, and processed by the Web Server, to query the database for specific information, and then display the result set in dynamically built HTML code. With this capability, there is no need to have to manually change a Web page whenever data on that page changes. Simply place the data in a database, and build a CGI script to access the data and display it dynamically. Whenever a request is made to view the page that contains the CGI script, the Web server initiates a request to the database and formats the most-current data into a dynamic Web page.

Advantages of Web Database Applications for the User

There are two groups of users of Web database applications. These are employees of the corporation you work for who access a Web database application deployed over the intranet, and everyone else. The advantages of Web database applications to intranet users are:

- Graphical user interfaces to corporate data
- Access to up-to-date company information
- Greater opportunity to interact with other people, departments, and technologies within the company
- Ability to customize their browsers to meet their specific needs
- Integration of the Web database application with other applications running on their machines

  The advantages to everyone else accessing Web database applications are:

- A broader reach than conventional advertising or marketing
- An automated sales force
- Access to company information from the comforts of home (or their workplace)
- Ability to interface with the company data without having to purchase expensive equipment or software

Moving On

This chapter introduced you to the Internet, the Web, and intranets. You took a brief tour of the history of the Internet, learning some of the milestones that shaped its course. At the end of the chapter you read about many of the benefits and advantages available to companies, users and application developers that build and use Web database applications.

In the next chapter you'll read about why it makes sense in today's environment to build and deploy a Web database application as well as the role of databases and RDBMS products in the whole process. Finally, you'll read about some of the ways that other companies are using Web database applications they build.

CHAPTER 2

Web
Commerce

Web database application development is about Web commerce: It is about making or saving money. Period. In the movie *Jerry Maguire*, football player Rod Tidwell said to Maguire, his agent, "Show me the money!" To find a purpose for developing and deploying a Web database application you need do nothing more than follow the money. Companies are building them for one of two purposes:

- To sell more products or services and thus make more money: the primary use of Web database applications deployed over the Internet
- To save money by using a more efficient information collection and delivery mechanism from what has been available in the past: the primary use of Web database applications deployed over an *intranet*

This chapter introduces you to some of the reasons companies are turning to the Web as the production platform for database applications. You will learn the role that the database plays in these applications. Following this is a list of some of the things you should consider, outside of the technical issues that you'll learn about in the remainder of this book, when doing business on the Web.

Today's Competitive Business Environment

It has been a very long time since a manager in a business found success in managing a portion of the business she or he had been responsible for by saying, "Well, that's the way we *used* to do it." Sure, Coca-Cola is making Coke with the same recipe it has used for a century, and Hormel & Sons is still making Spam, but that's not what this chapter is about. Even though these companies' products are the same as they have been for years, the way in which both of these companies (and nearly all others) go about running their business is much different now. If you want proof of this, check out their Web sites.

For Coca–Cola, `http://www.cocacola.com`

For Hormel & Sons, `http://www.hormel.com`

Even though companies may still be producing the same products or offering the same services that have been available for years, they have changed the way they do business to remain competitive. Building and deploying Web database applications is an extension of this.

I remember an article written by Jim Seymour of *PC Magazine* published in 1995, in which the theme of the article was: Companies are trying to figure out how to make money on the Web. Mr. Seymour wrote that there existed a deep-rooted sense that it was somehow possible to reap financial benefit by building and deploying a Web presence, but the process of actually knowing how to do this was unknown. Static pages of information were expensive to create and tedious (and expensive) to maintain. Most of the organizations that were the pioneers in establishing a Web presence found reasons other than financial to justify the expense. You could hear such comments as: "Everybody is either doing it or going to do it, so we want to be one of the first," or "We know it's going to be expensive, but we want to get familiar with the issues quickly."

With the advent of HyperText Markup Language (HTML) pages that are able to access corporate databases via Common Gateway Interface (CGI) programs and proprietary extensions to HTML specifications, the Web became significantly more viable as a place to conduct business.

There are a number of factors that precipitate the movement of businesses to build Web database applications. These are:

Changing Marketplace—The rapidly changing marketplace forces companies to respond more quickly to business opportunities. One of the quickest ways to build and deploy a database application is over the Internet, using the latest generation of application development tools.

Cost Containment—The profit margins that companies operate in are continually being squeezed. There are two things that corporate management can do to contain costs and thus maintain their profit margins: reduce costs or increase productivity. Both of these are available with a database application deployed over the Internet.

Increased Services—Customers are more astute now than in the past, and they demand more from the company they purchase their goods from. Web database applications provide a means of offering these services in a very cost-efficient and easy-to-deploy manner.

Organizational Change—Changes in the organizational structure of companies is leading to new ways of doing business: business models. As corporations continue a trend that began in the early 1980s of downsizing and removing hierarchical layers, collaborative product development led to more creative ways of marketing and selling products and services. One of the new ways to do this is with Web database applications accessible by customers.

Direct Sales—Rather than rely solely on distributors or other retailers, an inexpensive sales channel is at your fingertips. Customers can come to your Web site or you can send mail to them without the expense of a direct mail campaign.

Shrinking Product Life Cycles—Due primarily to a more competitive marketplace, companies are releasing new products and new versions of existing products on an ever-accelerated schedule. Marketing and selling activities necessary to sell these products are being accelerated accordingly. Applications developed for deployment over the Internet represent a means to provide this accelerated marketing and sales support.

Why Do Business on the Web?

A few years ago, "doing business on the Web" meant having a series of very static Web pages that described the company, provided phone numbers and addresses, and perhaps a brief description or two about the company's products and/or services. While businesses were trying to figure out *what* to say on the Web, technology was taking care of figuring out *how* to say it.

With the advent of HTML editors, application development tools and suites, and access to Relational Data Base Management Systems (RDBMSs), the use of the Web as a place to conduct business is secured.

A Relational Data Base Management System stores and presents its data in tabular formats and provides for the manipulation of data stored in sets of data, as opposed to individual records. The Web site gives users the opportunity to access the information without travel expense or hastle at any time of the day.

The company with a Web site can:

- Expand reach
- Enhance corporate image
- Improve customer service
- Generate leads
- Create a product/service delivery channel
- Reduce operating expenses
- Test market
- Obtain almost instant feedback from customers to test marketing

Expand Reach

On the Web, you can make a sales presentation or put promotional material in the hands of interested people at any hour of the day or night. Orders can be taken and product queued for shipment before your first cup of coffee in the morning. You no longer have to pony up the $3,000 to $4,000 it costs to send a salesperson around the world to meet with customers, although this is not to say that business travel for sales purposes can be eliminated by the Web.

What this *is* saying is that with the Web, and the Internet, your company has the ability to interact with customers and potential customers in a format where geography and time have no relevance. When you do business on the Web, you have increased the accessibility to your customers, and from your customers.

Enhance Corporate Image

A corporation's image with customers is a very valuable asset. On the financial statements of most large corporations (and the financial statements of smaller corporations that want to boost their financials) a line item titled "Goodwill" appears. A company has a very direct, immediate, inexpensive and significant opportunity to project and enhance its image via its Web presence.

In addition to the marketing and sales opportunities that doing business on the Web presents, there is a lot of opportunity to conduct public relations activities on the Web, thereby enhancing corporate image. This includes: corporate mission statements, goals, philosophies, charities it donates to and testimonials of what a great company it is to do business with and work for.

Improve Customer Service

Customers are demanding more from the companies they do business with. This includes:

- More product choices
- Less-expensive products and services
- Increased customer service

Regarding the last item, the Web provides a tremendous opportunity to provide customer service that is not only very responsive but is very inexpensive to implement. Companies that develop and sell Web-based customer support products are becoming increasingly popular.

Web-based customer service means not only that customers have access to product support over the Web, but it also means that they can perform the following:

- Receive an online and interactive status of past-reported problems
- Browse a support database for similar problems/resolutions
- Access information around the clock
- Submit a question to a company technical support person
- Download patches to software and free utility programs
- Look at Frequently Asked Questions (FAQs)
- Submit a request for future enhancements to the product(s)

The company offering Web-based customer service has the following advantages:
- Ability to track problem areas in product to help determine where to place R&D dollars

- No need to staff phones around the clock
- Customers can have their requests and needs satisfied without interacting with staff
- Ability to monitor the performance of product support technicians

Generate Leads

When people browse your Web site, you can track and extract their login IDs. You know they are at least candidate customers, and with their login IDs you can send follow-up sales/marketing material. If people download something from your Web site that they can access and retrieve for free, then you know you have a qualified lead. You can follow up on that lead with whatever you decide. The point is that it has cost you very little to generate this lead.

Create a Product/Service Delivery Channel

Before the Web, companies had a number of choices in terms of how they delivered products and services. How they managed these choices was a big determinant in the success of the company. The careers of many sales executives were made or broken over how sales and delivery channels were set up and managed.

The Web represents a new delivery channel for product and services. It is not the only one for most companies, but it is one that deserves attention. In the coming years, as companies become more adept at doing business on the Web, we will see the recognition that the Web is a viable and significant delivery channel of products and services.

Increasingly, you can find companies that only do business over the Web. They do not have storefronts, and they have no direct face-to-face interaction with customers. One of these is a company that describes itself as the world's largest selection of books. The company's Web page address is `http://www.amazon.com`. The Web site is the only place you can order a book from its inventory.

Reduce Operating Expenses

Companies are operating with profit margins that are thinner today than ever before. Doing business on the Web allows companies to reduce their operating expenses by:

- Maintaining current sales volumes while decreasing sales staff size and expenses, or increasing sales volumes without increasing staff size
- Reducing the number of support staff
- Reducing the cost of marketing and advertising by taking advantage of the Web as a communication vehicle for this
- Reducing public relations costs
- Measuring and tracking the profitability of products and services, culling out the unprofitable ones

Test Market

The Web is a great place for a company to *test market* in a number of ways, including new products, new services and new marketing campaigns.

The reasons the Web is a great place to conduct a marketing test are its reach and economics. As already discussed in this chapter, doing business on the Web represents an opportunity to reach customers that may never have been contacted before and in a way that is extremely inexpensive.

What to Consider When Creating Your Web Site

Establishing a Web presence and publishing a Web database application, being somewhere between rocket science and kindergarten, requires a certain amount of technical expertise. That's what the remainder of this book will teach you. The information in these sections are some of the things you need to consider, outside of the technical details, when doing business on the Web.

Customer Feedback. Can you find a site that does not allow for customer feedback? I don't think so. You too should build adequate interfaces and hot links to a customer feedback form. You should also make sure that someone within your company is promptly reading and addressing those customer feedback forms when they do come in. Don't let them become a black hole in your Web universe.

Easy Navigation. Make sure your site is not only easy to use but easy to navigate. You want to use abundant links to other pages and sites in a format through which are easy to maneuver.

Maintenance. Make a commitment to maintain your Web site frequently. Forget about using those "Under Construction" labels, as they are now considered to be the same thing as saying, *I spent a little bit of time putting this puppy out there but got distracted before I could finish it. Here, take a look at my work-in-progress.* If you do not frequently maintain your Web site and modify the way it looks or the information on it, you will find that people stop revisiting it—why should they return if they have reason to believe the information they will see is the same information they have already seen?

Monitor Access. There are various tools and freeware products available that let you monitor who is accessing your site, what pages are on your site and how long they stay there. There are even products that will extract that person's ID for later follow-up. This information will become invaluable to you to monitor the effectiveness of your Web site and to see where people spend the most time.

Visibility. Make sure to take advantage of links and techniques that will drive people to your site. In particular you should make sure that the most popular search engines and robots will find your site.

Security. I'm sure that you've heard and read about some of the concerns about commerce transaction over the Internet and the supposed lack of security in them. Although much of this is hype, some of it is valid. You must recognize and appreciate that if you have a retail concern and expect to take orders over the Web, your customers will want to know that their financial information is secure. Many of them read the same magazines that you do, and watch the same television shows. They have an understanding of some of the dangers in performing financial transaction on the Web.

Select Your Internet Service Provider Carefully. If you do not establish your own Web site, be very careful of who you use as an Internet Service Provider (ISP). Make sure that it will allow you to build and install an application on its servers that has the components you need.

My first ISP provided very reasonable rates with unlimited duration on connections. Unfortunately, it would not allow me to place a Common Gateway Interface (CGI) program in its cgi-bin directory. Without this I could not implement my first Web database application. The solution was to switch service providers. This was not an easy solution, as I had invested a lot of resources and time in building a Web presence through the ISP, and required more time and resources to move to the new ISP. I learned then the value of the consideration mentioned above. And yes, my new ISP let me have access to a cgi-bin directory to place the CGI programs I'd written.

Target Marketing. The Web is often used as a marketing vehicle. As is the case with any product or marketing approach, you must develop a thorough understanding of who your target market is and develop a Web presence to address and interest that market. Merely setting up a Web site and building and deploying a Web database application is no guarantee of success. When designing and building your Web site and Web database application, you must know what purpose there is for the existence of that entity.

Web Site Life Cycle. Your Web site and the database applications you deploy over the Web have life cycles. In most cases these life cycles are much shorter than traditional mainframe or PC-based database applications. Recognize this fact when doing your cost-benefit analysis and resource planning.

The Role of Databases in Web Applications

In the last section you saw some of the things to consider when doing business on the Web. Certainly, databases play an important role in all of the items listed. Before the advent of technology to integrate Web applications with corporate databases, many of the items listed in the last section were unavailable. Although I'm sure you can think of one or more ways that your company can make use of a database in its Web applications, the following list is a good introduction.

- Inter-business agreement and document processing, such as ordering, purchasing, invoicing, and automated payment processing.
- Demographics, such as customer, supplier and business partner profiles that are accumulated and used to improve and customize customer services.
- Customer status and account management used to manage purchase history and predict future purchase patterns.
- Establishment and maintenance of customer profiles for use in finely tailored advertising and sales campaigns.
- Inventory management and status to reduce cash reserves held in inventory, to produce online and interactive catalogs, to interface with inventory control systems, and to provide virtual shopping malls.

- Sales tracking and call management to monitor, track and increase the effectiveness of the sales force and various marketing campaigns.
- Technical product specifications that are available by customers and field staff to search for product specifications, parts lists, troubleshooting information and pricing.

There are many, many types of Web database applications, with more coming online every day. The few listed here are just a sample of the many that exist.

Advertising.   Advertising of a company's products and services is one of the traditional types of Web application. With the advent of the technology that allows database queries, a resurgence exists in this type of application. In addition to companies providing advertising on their own products and services, increasingly companies are setting up on the Internet with the only purpose of providing advertising for other companies. These electronic bulletin boards are becoming as popular as home shopping networks are on the television.

Customer Services.   Companies have learned that it is not only cost-effective to offer customer services via Web database applications, but it also promotes customer goodwill. A Web customer service database application gives the user the ability to interact with the information stored in the database in ways that were unavailable via conventional (human) customer service representatives. It is interesting that one of the first classifications of companies that began offering customer service applications that accessed a database of archived information were ISPs. As a result of their pioneering efforts, companies such as FedEx and Microsoft Corporation have recently established customer service Web database applications.

Financial Services.   Banks and other financial institutions are quickly building Web applications that access corporate databases as a way to provide improved financial services. One of the first companies with the most extensive array of services offered is the home page for Charles Schwab & Company. Its URL is: http://www.schwab.com. In addition to being one of the first brokerages to offer financial services over the Web, it also did a very good job of leveraging its investment made in building order entry and processing applications and databases by building Web interfaces into the existing databases. This allowed the company to create a series of Web database applications for a quite modest investment.

Information Collection and Dissemination.   Increasingly, companies are providing search capabilities within their Web applications. These search capabilities allow the user to enter a key word, or series of key words, and the search engine initiates a search of all known sources of information, including databases, for the supplied parameter(s). The results are displayed for follow-up by the user. In addition to this information dissemination capability, some companies are providing the ability to collect information and store it in databases via surveys and online questionnaires, an information collection function. The results of the information provided by the survey/questionnaire participants are stored in databases for later analysis or follow-up.

Job Recruitment.   Another application for Web databases that is becoming increasingly popular is job recruitment. Although smaller companies include this function in their Web applications via static, non-database applications, larger companies have sufficient numbers of openings that it is cost-effective for them to use a database in this Web application. A good example of this type of Web database application is the home page for EDP Markets, a national high-technology recruiting firm. Its URL is `http://www.edpmarkets.com`.

Luxury Products.   Do you have the time to fly to Boston, Massachusetts to view the yachts for sale in the various marinas? Do you want to invest your money and time in flying to the other side of the country to visit automobile dealerships, looking for the pearl-white Rolls Royce that you can now afford? I'm sure if you're in the market for one of these luxury products, you actually do have the money to fly around and find what you're looking for. But do you have the time? Web database applications allow the selling party (or business) the greatest exposure of their product while also respecting the time of the prospective purchaser.

Real Estate.   It is difficult to find a real estate company that does not have a Web database application that shows its listing to customers. A few years ago these same firms were limited to static Web pages giving their contact information and possibly some marketing/sales promotional material. Now, these same companies are deploying database applications that display their listings in dynamic and interactive Web pages.

Specialized Product Sales.   Specialized product sales are an increasingly popular form of Web database application, especially for the firm selling specialized products. There is virtually (pardon the pun) no limit to the reach that such an application has for the specialty firm. A good example of a specialty firms use of a Web database application to advertise its business and promote sales is the Virtual Vineyards company. Its URL is: `http://www.virtualvin.com`.

Virtual Shopping Malls.   This is one of the best-known applications of Web database application technology. I think it is so popular because it works so well: it is an application that is perfectly suited for the Internet. Virtual shopping malls provide the electronic equivalent of a shopping mall by allowing a user to browse through the products of a store in a virtual mall of stores. This same concept can be downsized to the individual store level, with each department in a store showcasing its goods in a virtual shopping environment. A good example of this is what Sears Roebuck and Company has done with its home page, which is at: `http://www.sears.com`. Hint: Check out the Craftsman section. It'd make Tim "the Toolman" Taylor of *Home Improvement* envious.

Moving On

In this chapter you learned some of the reasons companies are turning to the Web as the production platform of database applications. You read about the role that the database plays in these applications. Finally, you read about some of the things you should consider, outside of the technical issues that you'll learn about in the remainder of this book, when doing business on the Web.

Chapter 3 introduces you to some of the options you have available to you when choosing a programming language to use to develop your Web database application. Although your choice for a RDBMS product is made (the selection you made is in the title of this book), you have a number of options when it comes to programming languages.

CHAPTER 3

Choosing a CGI Programming Language

Choosing a programming language to use to develop a Web database application is becoming increasingly more difficult. Now, you have a myriad of languages, derivatives of languages, dialects of languages, development suites, programming suites, and various iterations of each of these to choose from. To attempt to write about each of the current products would be futile. From the time this manuscript was finished until it was published, new versions of languages and tools would have appeared on the market. This chapter then will focus on the most popular languages available to build Web database applications. In the next chapter, we'll look at some of the newest tools—the Web development and programming suites.

It is perhaps beneficial at this point to describe a few terms and abbreviations that are used throughout the remainder of the book. The first is Structured Query Language—(SQL). SQL is a specialized programming language that is used for sending queries to databases. The American National Standards Institute (ANSI) has declared a set of specifications in their ANSI SQL89 standard that attempt to standardize the language across software products. The next abbreviation is Open DataBase Connectivity (ODBC). This is an application programming interface that enables applications written in any ODBC-compliant language to access any ODBC-compliant database. ODBC provides a very high degree of database independence through a standard SQL syntax. Finally, Java DataBase Connectivity (JDBC) is a database connectivity Application Programming Interface (API) that provides the necessary means for a Web application to access a database directly, without having the overhead of ODBC. Because JDBC represents a more direct method of communication between a program and a database, it is frequently a quicker form of database access.

Before we get into the specifics of the various languages to consider, it's beneficial to digress for a bit and talk about the factors that should be addressed when making a decision about which language to use.

Which Language to Use?

The decision of which programming language to use to develop your Web application is not much different from the decision of which programming language to use to develop any other application. It helps to view a Web database application as just another application development project. It has its own unique set of factors that must be evaluated, but the same statement can be made about any development project. For example, consider the following:

- Your company has told you that you are now responsible for developing an order-entry system to replace the one that has been running on the mainframe for 25 years.
- Your boss tells you that you must develop a statistical reporting system to analyze the data that the company's automated tele-sales system is generating.
- Your spouse tells you that she or he'd like you to write an application interface program to transfer the information stored in your home inventory application over to the retirement planning system that you just purchased.
- You have a brilliant idea for an application that you want to write in your free time and make enough money from so you can retire (at the age of 42) in the Caribbean on a 45-foot sailboat. The application is a replacement for many of the functions on the Windows Control panel and allows users to adjust many of their system settings by clicking a button and without the need of having to reboot the machine to get the changes to take effect.

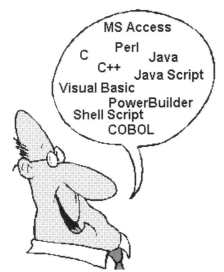

Figure 3–1:   Some of the programming language choices.

There are a number of items to consider in each of the above scenarios to determine which is the best programming language to use. In the following sections we'll take a look at each of these in greater detail. These items are:

- Skillset of developers
- Scope of the project
- Application interfaces
- Availability of support tools
- Database interfaces
- Platforms application will run on

A new language that you invest in either learning for yourself or having your staff learn is often a wise investment that transcends solving the immediate need. When I learned PowerBuilder to meet a need on the project I was working on, there was no way of knowing that this would lead to future consulting contracts, a book deal, and a training company hiring me to develop a PowerBuilder training course for them. Sure, it would be easy for someone to say now that investment in learning a language like PowerBuilder is a wise use of resources. However, this was back when PowerBuilder was at version 1.0, when very few people had heard of it!

Skillset of Developers

The decision to develop a new Web database application, does not necessarily mean that it requires a set of skills foreign to current staff. To the contrary, many of the languages that we'll review in this chapter probably already exist in your skillset. For example, COBOL, Visual Basic, PowerBuilder, and of course Oracle can all be used to develop powerful Web database applications.

So, what are the skills necessary in developers of Web applications? These are briefly described here. Once listed, you should see that they are not too unique from the skills required for most development projects.

- Language proficiency
- System and program analysis
- Database design
- Database implementation and tuning
- Graphical User Interface (GUI) design
- Open DataBase Connectivity (ODBC) or Java DataBase Connectivity (JDBC) experience
- Web page and HTML

ODBC experience is becoming quite common while JDBC is relatively new and there-fore finding someone with experience in this may prove difficult.

The DataBase Administrator (DBA), programming, and language skills that exist in the team members of your Web database development project is very important to help you select the correct programming language. A lack of awareness of either the existence of skills or quality of skills could mean failure of the project.

Scope of the Project

Each of the development scenarios presented earlier in this chapter represents a different degree of scope. The projects that you work on all have differing degrees of scope. Some of the factors that should be considered when evaluating the scope of the project are:

- Interfaces to other computer applications (i.e., inventory, accounting, etc.)
- Relationship to new technology (i.e., voice response system, new Operating Systems, etc.)
- Project timeframe (i.e., compressed and accelerated, or flexible and adequate)
- Project team member composition (i.e., are required skills spread among a large number of team members or is each team member expected to have a large number of skills?)
- Existence of data files (i.e., do data files exist, or do they need to be created? If they need to be created, does any of the information currently exist in another format, or does it have to be entered?)

An awareness of the scope of the project and the range of functions and capabilities of the various programming languages is vitally important to selecting the correct language for a particular development task.

Application Interfaces

There exists a direct relationship between the complexity of a computer system and the number of interfaces that system has with other applications. It is a rare event in today's computing environment when a computer system is built with no interfaces of any kind to other applications. The presence of ODBC and JDBC demonstrate the need to refine and facilitate the interfacing of computer applications with data files.

There is a difference between a computer system interfacing with another computer system, and interfacing with the data files used by another computer system. An example of the former is a computer application using the subroutines (header files, copybooks, DLLs, etc.) that were written for another computer system. An example of the latter is a computer application that is a report writer that reads the data files created from another application.

In the case of a Web database application, most of these applications will interface to either existing or newly created databases supplied by another vendor. That vendor could be Oracle with their Oracle 8 product, Microsoft with their Access 97 product, Sybase with their Sybase System 11 product, IBM with their DB2 product, or any of a number of other RDBMSs. A recognition of the nature and scope of interfaces to other systems and data files is critical to selecting a correct language in which to develop a Web database application.

Availability of Support Tools

Programming languages never are the complete toolset used by programmers. With Oracle 8, you get a very high quality and robust database engine. With Developer/2000 and PowerObjects, both programming tools available from Oracle Corporation, you get development tools that can be used to construct CGI programs that give direct, efficient, responsive access to Oracle 8 databases. However, you might find that the use of one of the development programming languages in concert with the Oracle 8 database is not your configuration. In this case, you will need to consider the availability of support tools for that language.

The particular language choice is only the first step in determining the complete suite of tools to be used in a Web database application development project. Additionally, once the language is selected and attention turns to what tools to use in support of the language, you must once again assess the skillset of the team members in using those other tools. In fact, many would argue that the entire set of tools to be used in a development project, the language as well as support tools, should be considered as a whole before a language decision is made.

Regardless of which approach you use to assess the skills of your developers against the requirements of the task, it is a very valuable investment of time to address the issue of support tool requirements and availability.

Some of the languages included in this chapter could be argued as being development suites, meaning encompassing more support tools than just a programming language. Examples of this are PowerBuilder and Visual Basic. It is my belief that the tools and utilities in neither PowerBuilder nor Visual Basic are comprehensive enough to be the only tool used by developers in Web database application development activities. People still have need of functions such as testing tools, source code protection (assuming you don't want to use the facilities shipping in PowerBuilder v 5.0), advanced RDBMS capabilities, HTML utilities, etc.

Matching the requirements of the development project against the capabilities and limitations of the language(s) you select to write the code is an important step to determine the nature and type of support tools needed to create a complete set of tools. For example, most RDBMS products have limited data modeling capabilities—which is something you derive tremendous benefit from, especially when designing and normalizing a new database. Recognizing that the RDBMS product you are using (with the exception of

Designer/2000) has limited data modeling capabilities and assuming your project requires data modeling steps allows you to provide for this need in one of the many tools available that do this. For example, EasyCASE, DBArtisan, or ER/1 are all products that allow you to easily perform data modeling functions, and, demo copies of the latter two are available on the CD-ROM accompanying this book. And, if you find that a design methodology you are using at your company is not supported within Designer/2000, and is supported in one of the other data modeling tools, then the decision to use one of these other tools is easy to make.

Another example of a support tool you may want to consider is an HTML editor. Although many programming languages have interfaces to HTML, they do not provide extensive editing and formatting capabilities that you'd need in an HTML editor. Fortunately, support tools provide this function, and one of the best is available on the accompanying CD-ROM—HTML Assistant Pro '97.

Database Interfaces

The type and number of databases your Web database application will access and interface with is an important factor in determining what language you select. For example, a decision to have your Web application access an Oracle 8 database would cause you to consider using Oracle Developer/2000 as your application development language. If you are also accessing a Microsoft Access 97 database, then you may want to consider Microsoft Access 97 as your application development language. Likewise, a Web application that accesses a Sybase System 11 database would cause you to consider using PowerBuilder as your application development language. And, with the power of ODBC, your development language choice is not limited to one provided by the database vendor. In other words, it is common to find a Visual Basic or PowerBuilder program accessing an Oracle 8 database.

However, all of the above three listed databases (Oracle 8, MS Access 97, Sybase System 11) can be accessed by the programming languages written by any of the other vendors. For example, an Oracle 8 database can be accessed from a PowerBuilder program. In fact, most RDBMS vendors have ODBC interfaces to development languages. This is the benefit of ODBC—a database supported by one vendor is accessible by a programming language supported by another vendor.

Although ODBC provides great flexibility in matching RDBMS with programming languages, there is a penalty. As ODBC is actually a set of drivers that translate the SQL commands or response codes from one vendor to equivalents that can be recognized by another vendor, there is a performance degradation to do so. A Web application written in Oracle PowerObjects that accesses an Oracle 8 database via ODBC will execute those database calls slower than if the application was written in PowerObjects and reading Oracle 8 databases directly, without having to process through ODBC. You need to be aware of the RDBMS your application is accessing to make an informed decision about programming languages. Sometimes it is more advantageous to select a programming language that requires use of ODBC to access a database than to use a language that accesses the database directly.

Platforms Application Will Run On

It is well known that the Web is universal. It is very hard to find an Operating System that does not allow Web access. This is one of the major benefits of doing business on the Web—it is pretty much platform independent. However, if you are writing an application where components of that application are distributed to a client's machine, then you must be aware of the platforms that run on those machines.

It is not uncommon to write a Web database application where components of that application are distributed to a client machine. An example of this is a parts manufacturer that maintains a price list of the parts in inventory on its Web site that customers can access and download to feed into their own inventory system. You could write a small application and distribute that application to each client that performs the data migration and population activities. An awareness of the operating systems that the various clients use is very important in picking the correct programming language in which to write this application. This is particularly true if the language creates intermediate, or p-code, modules that require an interpreter to execute.

This is especially true in intranet applications, where the Web server is only accessible to (or accessed by) employees or authorized users once they pass a security checkpoint. In such cases, it makes good sense to distribute parts of the application to these client machines as security and is much less of a serious concern when an approved person is accessing the intranet. This "distribution" of application components is most often done to improve the overall performance of the application.

Now that you've read about many of the issues, the following is a description of some of the major programming languages to choose from. Keep in mind the information above when reading the following sections. Each section presents information specific to a popular Web programming language.

C

C and C++ are probably the two most common languages for PC application development. It is expected then that individuals and companies that have invested in building skills in these languages leverage that investment to building Web applications. C compilers are now available on all platforms that support Web browsers, making C as portable a programming language as is needed for Web application development. The limitation of C, as is the limitation with most programming languages, is that the object and execution modules created are platform dependent.

One of the issues specific to C is that programs written in C tend to be much larger (translated: more lines of code) than many of the other programming languages. The most basic of operations (i.e., writing a line of output) takes many lines of code to write.

Oracle Corporation offers a precompiler for C, called Pro*C. Pro*C translates SQL and PL/SQL calls into code understandable by the C compiler. This allows developers to embed SQL and PL/SQL within their applications.

Pro*C programming, like C programming, can be extremely complex. But, Pro*C code can be extremely efficient, because the database calls are compiled at a very low-level. Consider using Pro*C for your Web-based database application if you need absolute speed or have complicated requirements, but be sure you have adequate C and Pro*C resources.

Presently, there is no standard CGI interface to C. As a result, a number of routines and libraries offering their idea of how this should be done are available. Although these are listed here, they are briefly described below: CGIHTML, LIBCGI, and CGIC.

CGIHTML

Perhaps the most flexible of the three, this approach provides for the use of a skeleton program in which application specific variables and functions are added. This approach is promoted by Eugene Kim, of Harvard University. His CGIHTML home page, as well as sample program and header files, can be found at: `http://www.eekim.com/software/cgihtml`. A *Developers Guide* to his approach can be found at:

`http://www.eekim.com/pubs/cgibook`.

LIBCGI

LIBCGI is a tool that allows you to link your program with the CGI specifications. The programming interface is fairly simple, and the tools are quite efficient. This efficiency does not come without a price however. Some of the more complex data handling routines must be written by hand. For Web database applications, this could spell T-R-O-U-B-L-E.

CGIC

CGIC is a library of routines that handle CGI tasks at a very high level. Its author is Tom Boutell. You can find a copy of the library, as well as accompanying documentation at:

`http://www.boutell.com/cgic/`.

CGIC is very easy to use and quite powerful. Because it handles CGI tasks at such a high level, working at a very granular level will stretch the utility of this to its limits. One of the most valuable features of this routine is the way in which it provides a way to capture CGI situations that occur for playback in a debugging environment.

The bottom line is this. If you have a large investment in C skills and a relatively small to medium Web database application to develop, then C is a possible candidate for you. However, the network programming interface, string handling capabilities, and database access components are not nearly as refined and easy to use as many of the other languages. If you can live with the loss in productivity when writing C code, you will appreciate the gain in performance that compiled C code provides over other languages like PERL, PowerBuilder, Visual Basic, etc.

Useful C Language URLs

The following table presents a list of useful URLs if you are using C to build your Web database applications.

Table 3–1   Useful C URLs

URL	Description
http://www.tardis.ed.ac.uk	Tardis is a limited-access UNIX service hosted by the University of Edinburgh with extensive information and resources for LibCGI
http://website.ora.com	A site with great potential for people looking for CGI tools and libraries
http://wsk.eit.com	An extensive selection of CGI and C development programs and libraries
http://www.compusult.nf.ca	C language CGI programmers will want to look at this site and the author's CGIC library
http://www.camtech.com. au/jemtek/cgi/lib	A set of C development libraries for CGI

The following books should be of value if you want to learn more about the C language.

Advanced C Programming

By:	Steve Oualline
Publisher:	Prentice Hall
ISBN:	0-13-663170-3

Expert C Programming Deep C Secrets

By:	Pete Van Der Linden
Publisher:	Prentice Hall
ISBN:	0-13-177429-8

Variations in C Programming Techniques for Developers

By:	Steve Schustack
Publisher:	Microsoft Press
ISBN:	0-91-484548-9

C++

C++ is a very popular programming language that combines much of its syntax and constructs from C while incorporating object-oriented programming capabilities. As a language, it is more difficult than Visual Basic to learn, primarily because of the OO components that are foreign to most people. Of the languages reviewed in this chapter, C++ is the most similar to Java. In fact, the transition from C++ to Java is much easier for most people than any other language.

One of the positive features of C++ is that most database vendors supply an API library that can be called from C++ programs. This feature improves the performance of database calls from C++ programs. Until the bandwidth of the Web and the processing capabilities of computers accessing the Web are sufficient to make performance a "non-issue," the performance of C++ will continue to make it a very popular language to use to develop Web database applications.

There are an abundance of C++ programmers available. For those that have no or very little Web database application experience, most will be anxious to tackle such a project to build their skills. This means that a high quality C++ programmer that has little or no Web experience will probably cost you less (and subsequently earn less) than a seasoned Java, JavaScript, or J++ programmer.

Oracle's Pro*C compiler, mentioned above, has recently added support for C++. The bottom line on C++ is this: It is a language to consider developing your Web database application in if you have skills available in the language. Also, if performance is a critical component of your application, then C++ is an ideal candidate for you. If you have existing code, you can probably adapt it to the Web a lot more simply that building an application from scratch in another language. Its easy migration to Java makes C++ an ideal platform to develop your first (or pilot) application in before investing in Java, building Java skills, purchasing Java support tools, and dealing with the issues that inherently come from a new language that is rapidly evolving.

Useful C++ Language URLs

The following books should be of interest if you want to learn more about the C++ language.

Advanced C++ Programming Styles

By: James Coplien
Publisher: Addison Wesley Publishing Co
ISBN: 0-20-154855-0

Apprentice C++ Programmer

By: Peter Lee
Publisher: Wadsworth Publishing Company
ISBN: 0-53-495339-5

How to Program C++

By: H. M. Deitel
Publisher: Prentice Hall
ISBN: 0-13-117334-0

The following table presents a list of useful URLs if you are using C++ to build your Web database applications.

Table 3–2   Useful C++ URLs

URL	Description
http://www.internetdatabase.com	Internet Resources Database is self-billed as being the ultimate guide to all Internet resources for your PC

PERL

PERL is a language that has evolved considerably the last few years. It is a compiled scripting language written by Larry Wall. PERL, which stands for Practical Extraction and Reporting Language, is a shell-like language that allows programmers to develop Web server scripts to perform common and repetitive functions. Programmers with C or PASCAL experience are finding learning PERL to be an easy transition. This is because expression syntax corresponds quite closely to C expression syntax.

PERL is an interpreted language optimized for scanning arbitrary text files, extracting information from those text files, and printing reports based on that information. It's also a good language for many system management tasks. It is for this reason that system programmers love PERL.

The language is intended to be practical (easy to use, efficient, complete) rather than beautiful (tiny, elegant, minimal). PERL combines some of the best features of C, so people familiar with those languages should have little difficulty with it. PERL is a UNIX utility, but unlike most UNIX utilities, PERL does not arbitrarily limit the size of your data unless you have memory constraints on your machine.

PERL is an excellent text scanning and extraction language because it uses sophisticated pattern matching techniques to scan large amounts of data very quickly. Although optimized for scanning text, PERL is also very efficient working with binary data.

The bottom line on PERL is this. It is gaining in popularity as a scripting language with both system programmers and application programmers. It has the power, speed, and application support to be one of the languages that survives when others will whither. PERL is the language of choice if your Web application calls for parsing or manipulating large amounts of text or binary data.

Useful PERL Language URLs

The following table presents a list of useful URLs if you are using PERL in the construction of your Web database applications.

Table 3–3   Useful PERL URLs

URL	Description
`http://www.cis.ufl.edu/perl`	An archive library of useful PERL information maintained by the University of Florida
`http://www.perl.com`	A mega-site built and maintained by Tom Christiansen that boosts over 14,000 files spanning 300+ megabytes of information specific to PERL
`http://www.eecs.nwu.edu/perl/perl.html`	A Web site maintained by Jennifer Myers with a large collection of resource information and links
`http://www.perl.org`	The PERL Institute (which manages this site) is dedicated to making PERL more useful for everyone. They are a non-profit organization, established to support the community of people who use PERL and to support the development of PERL as a language.

The following books should be of value to you if you have an interest in PERL.

60 Minute Guide to CGI Programming with PERL 5

By: Robert Farrell
Publisher: IDG Books
ISBN: 1-56-884780-7

Developing CGI Applications with PERL

By: John Deep
Publisher: John Wiley & Sons
ISBN: 0-47-114158-5

PERL 5 Unleashed

By: Kamran Husain
Publisher: Macmillan Computer Publishing
ISBN: 0-67-230891-6

Teach Yourself CGI Programming in PERL 5, 2nd edition

By: Eric Hermann
Publisher: Macmillan Computer Publishing
ISBN: 1-57-521196-3

Programming PERL

By: Larry Wall
Publisher: O'Reilly & Associates
ISBN: 1-56-592149-6

PL/SQL

PL/SQL is Oracle's procedural language extension to SQL. The language has become extremely popular in the last few years. And, for good reason, PL/SQL allows programming constructs that are impossible with garden-variety SQL. And what's better, it comes built into the Oracle 8 Server. Although based on the venerable language Ada, its constructs are similar enough to BASIC, C, and PASCAL, that an experienced programmer can pick it up quickly.

Because PL/SQL is tightly coupled with the database engine, PL/SQL is highly efficient. Procedures and functions can be built and stored right in the database. This enhances performance even more because the code does not have to be compiled at each execution. PL/SQL encourages code reuse—thereby leveraging a project's development time. PL/SQL has a sophisticated error handling system that, if properly implemented, makes debugging an application a breeze.

But, the language's greatest strength can haunt you if your needs ever change. PL/SQL's close connection to the database can be devastating if you ever decide to migrate your application to another database—PL/SQL supports Oracle only. This may not be as much of a problem as it seems, though. As more and more companies choose Oracle, PL/SQL is gaining a stronghold in the developer community. Additionally, you can use PL/SQL to handle internal DBMS issues, and then use another development language to handle access to other DBMS products.

The following book is a great reference to learn the ins and outs of PL/SQL:

Oracle PL/SQL Programming

By:	Steven Feuerstein
Publisher:	O'Reilly
ISBN:	1-56-592142-9

Shell Scripts

Shell scripts are ASCII text files that contain Unix and shell commands. UNIX commands are essentially similar to DOS commands you'd enter at a command line. Shell commands are those commands that are interpreted directly by the shell you specify. Shell commands are commonly used for branching, looping, decision making, etc. They are similar to the commands in various programming languages, particularly C. Currently, the two most popular shells are the Bourne (sh) and C (csh) shells. Other less popular shells are the tcsh and ksh shells.

The following shell script example prints the content-type of the generated document and displays a message to the user that includes the value entered by a user in the lname field on the form:

```
#!/bin/sh
echo 'Content-type: text/html'
echo ''I was given the following last name by the user: $WWW_lname:
```

Shell scripts are very useful for repetitive coding situations. For instance, if you wanted to copy a series of files with separate file extensions from one directory to another, a script could be written that would save you a lot of typing. The commands you enter in a shell script are executed by typing the name of the script instead of each individual command. This causes Shell Scripts to serve the same purpose as EXECs in CMS, CMD files in OS/2, or BAT files in MS/DOS.

The bottom line on Shell Script is this. The biggest problem with Shell Script is that if you want to write code to access any type of database other than UNIX's internal database system, interfaces to these other RDBMSs are hard to find. This makes Shell Script a very poor choice for a Web database application when the demand is to access database data.

Useful Shell Script Language URLs

Table 3–4 presents a list of useful URLs if you are using Shell Script in the construction of your Web database applications.

The books listed following the table may be of value if you are interested in learning more about shell scripts.

Table 3–4   Shell Script URLs

URL	Description
`http://www.hyperion.com/~koreth/uncgi.html`	This is a site built and maintained by Steven Grimm that offers a popular package for using CGI in Shell Scripts.
`http://physics.ucsc.edu/tutor/shell.html`	This site presents a tutorial on using Shell Scripts.
`http://www.ccpo.odu.edu/ug/shell_help.html`	Another useful site describing how to write a shell script.
`http://theory.uwinnipeg.ca/UNIXhelp/scrpt/`	A site maintained by the University of Winnipeg and devoted to dissemination of information specific to Shell Scripts.

UNIX Shell Programming, 3rd edition

By: Lowell Jay Arthur
Publisher: John Wiley & Sons
ISBN: 0-47-159941-7

UNIX Shells by Example

By: Ellie Quigley
Publisher: Prentice Hall
ISBN: 0-13-460866-6

Visual Basic

Visual Basic (VB) is fast approaching being the preeminent language in which to develop Web database applications. Its native support for Microsoft Access 97 databases, coupled with its extensive support via ODBC of the most popular RDBMS packages makes this a worthy contender. Additionally, there is a very extensive selection of third-party products that complement and enhance the basic (pardon the pun) capabilities of the product.

If your plans call for building a CGI application for deployment on a Windows NT or 95 platform, this is a language worthy of consideration. Its language is concise, the syntax is familiar, the "visual" drag-and-drop programming interface is efficient, and applications developed in VB are easily maintained.

Perhaps the biggest drawback to using VB as a programming language is Microsoft Corporation's reluctance to recognize any other operating system besides Windows (and occasionally one of the Macintosh OS'). Applications written in VB will not run natively in a UNIX environment.

The bottom line on Visual Basic is this. It is hard to do wrong making a decision to use Visual Basic as your Web application development. It is equally hard to do right making a decision to use VB as your Web application development tool if your application would ever run on a non-Windows, non-32-bit operating system.

Useful Visual Basic Language URLs

Table 3–5 presents a list of useful URLs if you are using Visual Basic in the construction of your Web database applications.

The books listed below should be of value to you if you want to learn more about Visual Basic.

The Visual Basic Programmer's Guide to Java

By:	James W. Cooper, Ph.D.
Publisher:	Ventana
ISBN:	6-04-5274

Beginners Guide to Visual Basic

By:	Peter Wright
Publisher:	Wrox
ISBN:	1-87-441655-9

Table 3–5   Useful Visual Basic URLs

URL	Description
http://www.microsoft.com/vbasic/	This is Microsoft Corporation's Web page to its Visual Basic product.
http://www.vbonline.com/	This site is created and supported by VB Online magazine and contains a wide selection of tips, techniques, and free stuff.
http://www.apexsc.com/vb/	Carl & Gary's Home Page
http://www.vbxtras.com/	The ultimate tools catalog!
http://www.apexsc.com/vb/clbv-digest/	CLBV Digest—Archived Issues
http://coyote.csusm.edu/cwis/winworld/vbasic.html	California State's Archives of VBX's
http://www.windx.com	Visual Basic Programmer's Journal
http://www.ionet.net/~robinson/vb.shtml	Visual Basic Resource Index—Robins Company
http://www.inquiry.com/techtips/thevbpro/	Ask the VB Pro page
http://www.vmedia.com/commodity/onlinecompanions/	A site maintained by Ventana Communications Group with an abundant selection of resources and links.
http://www.jumbo.com/prog/win/vbasic/	Jumbo!—Programming: Windows: Windows Visual Basic Programming

Building Internet Applications with Visual Basic

By: Kate Gregory
Publisher: Macmillan Computer Publishing
ISBN: 0-78-970213-4

Building Windows 95 Applications with Visual Basic

By: Clayton Walnum
Publisher: Macmillan Computer Publishing
ISBN: 0-78-970209-6

Database Developers Guide with Visual Basic

By: Roger Jennings
Publisher: Macmillan Computer Publishing
ISBN: 0-67-230652-2

PowerBuilder

Sybase Corporation's PowerBuilder products is emerging as one of the leading Web database application development tools available. In the early to mid 1990s it established itself as a very powerful client server application development toolkit. When Sybase acquired Powersoft (the original developer of PowerBuilder) in 1994, they saw a movement in the industry to provide tools for Internet application development. Because Sybase is a major RDBMS product company, they combined the development components of PowerBuilder with their RDBMS products to provide a complete Web database application development environment. PowerBuilder remains a strong contender for non-Sybase systems too.

The Enterprise edition of PowerBuilder gives you the ability to extend the capabilities of a Web browser to use its DataWindow Viewer. The DataWindow Viewer is a GUI interface to a database. That database can be either a Sybase database, or any other vendors database that provides an ODBC interface. This includes Oracle, Microsoft Access 97, Informix, DB2, etc.

PowerBuilder uses a similar metaphor to CGI application development as Visual Basic. The content of a HTML form is retrieved through either the Win CGI specification or a proprietary vendor-supplied library. Then whatever database operations required are performed. PowerBuilder takes the output from the database operation, formats it in a manner you describe, and sends it to the browser in a manner that conforms to HTML standards.

A strength of PowerBuilder is that you can develop an application on a Windows 95 (or NT) machine, and deploy that application on either Windows 3.1, NT, Macintosh, 95, or Unix devices. Sybase is committed to ensuring cross-platform support for PowerBuilder which is good news for someone considering using PowerBuilder to build a Web database application.

The bottom line on PowerBuilder is this. It is a main contender as a tool to use to build a Web database application. InfoWorld has recently given PowerBuilder its "Enterprise Development Tool of the Year Award." Its native driver support for Sybase databases and ODBC support for Oracle, MS Access 97, DB2, Informix, etc. is well known and clean. The product offers a very clean GUI interface for developers and allows for a great deal of application control through its proprietary PowerScript programming language.

Useful PowerBuilder Language URLs

The following table presents a list of useful URLs if you are using PowerBuilder in the construction of your Web database applications.

The following book references should be of value to you if you want to learn more about PowerBuilder.

Developing PowerBuilder 5 Applications, 4th edition

By: Bill Hatfield
Publisher: Macmillan Computer Publishing
ISBN: 0-67-230916-5

PowerBuilder 5—A Developer's Guide

By: David McClanahan
Publisher: M&T Books
ISBN: 1-55-851473-2

Table 3–6   Useful PowerBuilder URLs

URL	Description
http:\\www.powersoft.com	The home page for Powersoft Corporation.
http://\\www.sybase.com	The home page for Sybase Corporation, the parent company of Powersoft Corporation.
http://computers.science.org/	A site published and maintained by Science.Org, a non-profit organization devoted to the application development community.
http://www.advisor.com/pa.htm	The home page for the PowerBuilder Advisor magazine.
http://www.powercerv.com	The home page for PowerCerv Corporation, one of Powersoft Corporations most successful partners and the provider of training, consulting, and add-on products.
http://www.sigsoft.com/	The home page for Signature Software, another of Powersoft Corporations most successful partners.
http://ntweb.sigsoft.com	Home of the on-line PowerBuilder and Java Developer journal.
http://world.std.com/~gorsline/kgfram.html	A site maintained by an avid user of PowerBuilder that provides links to other information sources.
http://www.vmedia.com/commodity/onlinecompanions/	A site maintained by Ventana Communications Group with an abundant selection of resources and links.

Professional PowerBuilder Programming

By: Paul Bukauskas
Publisher: Prentice Hall
ISBN: 0-13-508145-9

Teach Yourself PowerBuilder 5

By: David McClanahan
Publisher: MIS Press
ISBN: 1-55-828474-5

Visual Basic Script

Visual Basic Script (VBScript) is a subset of the Microsoft Visual Basic language. In its current implementation, it is a fast, portable, lightweight interpreter for use in World Wide Web browsers and other applications that use ActiveX Controls, OLE Automation servers, and Java applets.

VBScript, being a subset of Visual Basic, is ideally suited to accessing documents used in Microsoft Excel, Project, Access 97, and the Visual Basic development system. The product is designed to have a very small footprint and to be a lightweight interpreted language. Because of this, it does not use strict types (only Variants). Also, because VBScript is intended to be a safe subset of the language, it does not include file I/O or direct access to the underlying operating system. VBScript is Microsoft's attempt to compete in the JavaScript market.

When used in an enabled Web browser, VBScript is directly comparable to JavaScript (not Java). Like JavaScript,

> VBScript is a pure interpreter that processes source code embedded directly in the HTML.

> VBScript code does not produce stand-alone applets but is used to add intelligence and interactivity to HTML documents.

For the millions of programmers who already know Visual Basic, VBScript is a valuable alternative to JavaScript in activating web pages. Its comparability to Visual Basic syntax and structure will make learning VBScript a smooth proposition. In addition, you have the advantage of using existing Visual Basic applications and code.

VBScript is available or under development for Windows 95 and Windows NT (including native versions for Alpha, MIPS, and PowerPC architectures), 16-bit Windows, and Power Macintosh. Microsoft is working with third parties to provide UNIX versions for Sun, HP, Digital, and IBM platforms.

The bottom line on Visual Basic Script is this. It is a valuable language component to people writing Web database applications. Its conformity to Visual Basic syntax makes it a serious language to consider if you have Visual Basic skills. However, because this is a Microsoft product, you should be aware that Windows derivatives will always be the preferred Operating System for this product. If portability is of key importance to you and you don't have a huge investment in Visual Basic skills, and if you have the need to write some code in a scripting language, then you may want to continue looking toward JavaScript.

Useful VBScript Language URLs

The following table presents a list of useful URLs if you are using VBScript in the construction of your Web database applications.

The books listed below should be of value if you want to learn more about Visual Basic Script.

The Comprehensive Guide to VBScript

By: Richard Mansfield
Publisher: Ventana
ISBN: 1-56-604470-7

Creating Cool VBScript Web Pages

By: Bill Hatfield
Publisher: IDG Books
ISBN: 0-76-453031-3

Teach Yourself VBScript in 21 Days

By: Keith Brophy
Publisher: Macmillan Computer Publishing
ISBN: 1-57-521120-3

VBScript Web Page Interactivity

By: W. Orvis
Publisher: Prima Publishing/Random House
ISBN: 0-76-150684-5

Table 3–7   Useful VBScript URLs

URL	Description
http://www.microsoft.com/vbscript	Microsoft's VBScript site.
http://www.vbonline.com	Home page to Visual Basic Online magazine
http://www.netins.net/showcase/legend/vb/	A site maintained by Ryan Heldt as a valuable resource for VBScript techniques
http://www.vmedia.com/commodity/onlinecompanions/	A site maintained by Ventana Communications Group with an abundant selection of resources and links.
http://www.vbonline.com/	This site is created and supported by VB Online magazine and contains a wide selection of tips, techniques, and free stuff.

COBOL

COBOL is an acronym that stands for COmmon Business Oriented Language, although many people are trying to modify history and continue the life of COBOL as a development language by claiming that COBOL stands for Common Object Business Oriented Language.

COBOL is a language that just won't die. Much to the chagrin of the nay-sayers in the 1980s and early 1990s, the venerable COBOL is continuing to reinvent itself as a significant application development tool. That COBOL is a viable and valuable application "maintenance" tool is not to be underestimated. But the subject of this book is building Web database applications, and with that as a subject, COBOL is not ready for prime time.

Like Pro*C, Oracle offers a precompiler for COBOL called, aptly enough, Pro*COBOL. With this tool, SQL and PL/SQL can be tightly integrated into COBOL applications. The same efficiency gains that Pro*C offers are found in Pro*COBOL as well.

> COBOL is enjoying a resurgence as a development language. COBOL programmers are seeing their salaries increase faster than many other segments. Consulting companies and recruiters cannot locate enough COBOL programmers to meet demand. Why, then, has Micro Focus LTD. seen a flattening recently of its sales for its base COBOL development suite?

A number of company's are racing to develop products that allow COBOL to be used for either client or server side Web application development. IBM has its VisualAge product, Computer Associates has the CA-Realia product, and Micro Focus has its Object COBOL.

IBM's product (VisualAge) is touted as soon to include a full range of CGI specification support. This is likely to happen as IBM is committed to being a major Internet tools vendor. Micro Focus's product (Object COBOL) is also being positioned as its tool for Internet application development. Micro Focus has announced support for the use of this product to develop Internet applications, but it is not there yet.

Useful COBOL Language URLs

The following table presents a list of useful URLs if you are using COBOL in the construction of your Web database applications.

Table 3–8 Useful COBOL URLs

URL	Description
http://www.microfocus.com	MicroFocus LTD. home page
http://www.software.hosting.ibm.com/ad/cobol/	Home page for IBM's COBOL tools
http://www.cai.com	Computer Associates home page

The following books should be of value if you want to learn more about COBOL.

COBOL from Micro to Mainframe, 2nd edition

By: Robert Grauer
Publisher: Prentice Hall
ISBN: 0-13-310764-7

DB2 for the COBOL Programmer, Part 1

By: Steve Eckols
Publisher: Mike Murach Mike & Assoc, Inc.
ISBN: 0-91-162559-3

Object Oriented COBOL

By: Edmund Arranga
Publisher: Prentice Hall
ISBN: 0-13-261140-6

Structured COBOL Programming, 8th edition

By: Nancy Stern
Publisher: John Wiley & Sons
ISBN: 0-47-11388-6

Moving On

Because of the designed standardization benefits from the CGI specification, the choice of which programming language to use to develop a Web database application is not easy. Many languages support this specification. It is not a matter of "what" language is available to use to write a Web application, but more a matter of "which" of the many options is best suited for my needs?

Java is the universally accepted language for Web application development. As you've read in this chapter, that is no longer a "rubber stamp" decision. It will remain a venerable language, but other languages will continue to erode the position that Java has.

Next chapter will introduce you to Java and Java Script. I believe these two languages are significant enough as to warrant a chapter of their own in this book. You will learn about the strengths and weaknesses of each of these languages and how they are used to build Web database applications.

CHAPTER 4

Overview
of Java and
JavaScript

The release of Java from Sun Microsystems preceded slightly the release of JavaScript. Partly because of this, some people view these two languages as being an either/or decision. This is not the case. They do share similar syntax and use objects similarly, but the languages were developed to solve different sets of problems. The two languages are not very much related to each other and their intended use is quite a bit different, as you will learn in this chapter.

Introduction to Java

The hype over Java primarily cannot be overstated. *InfoWorld* magazine, "The Voice of Client/Server in the Enterprise" as it claims, is published weekly. This magazine has carried an article on some aspect of Java on at least one of the first three pages of every issue for at least the last 30 issues, which is when I stopped counting. In fact, as I write this chapter, I am looking at the February 24, 1997 issue, in which the following topic headings appear on the first three pages:

Java to revive aging PCs

IBM assumes Java mantle

Javasoft's JDK 1.1 Raises Microsoft's Ire

It is not only unfortunate but also unjustified that Java will probably never gain its full potential as a development language. Certainly the trend we see is for the developers of other products, such as Sybase with PowerBuilder and Microsoft with Visual Basic, to build enough functionality into their products that the momentum to Java may ebb.

Java is now the fastest growing language of all development languages. It is in a better position to "take over" as the most popular computer application development language. As you will see throughout this book, there are many languages and development suites currently available that provide the majority of the same benefits of Java, and sometimes more, but without the limitations. Other major software developers, as well as some very well funded startup companies, have had time to recognize and address the need for Internet/intranet development languages and facilities. Certainly the language will continue to improve. At the same time that Java will grow as a language, so too will features and improvements be made in the other languages and tools available. But the genie is out of the bottle now, and the entire computing industry is able to compare and contrast what exists in the Java language with what is needed in a corporate Web application development and database access tool. Java was the first robust Web application and database access tool, but it is certainly questionable whether it is the best.

Though Java still has relatively small market share, it is moving up quickly. Sun expects a 15% increase in programming market share this year, and 10% again next year. Weak implementations and slow compilations have hurt the acceptance of the language, but both are improving and C and C++ gurus are definitely worried that Java could swamp them. Also, although it took C and C++ years to get into the CS 101 course curriculum, Java already has a 10% share, and is growing fast.

Visual Basic, PowerBuilder, C, and C++ all have their limitations that will hold them back whereas Java can and still is adaptive. I think Java will surpass 50% market share by the year 2,000.

For those of you interested in reading what the developers of Java intended to accomplish with their new language, you can find the "White Paper" they developed at:

```
http://www.javasoft.com/nav/read/whitepapers.
```

For those of you who are highly interested in the underpinnings of the Java language specification, you can find this at:

```
http://www.javasoft.com/nav/read/index.html
```

Java as a programming language was conceived in 1991 and developed by Engineers at Sun Microsystems in 1995 to be a common Web application development language. A little known piece of trivia is that the engineers that developed Java did so out of frustration working with C++.

Java is the first programming language that provides a complete solution to Internet application development. Since the release of Java version 1.0, coupled with the Java-enabled versions of Web browsers currently available, new animated sites are appearing on the Web at a record pace. An example of this animation is seen in Figure 4–1 along with the HTML code that triggers the Java applet that accomplishes this animation. Although you cannot see it in this very static media of the printed page, what you'd see if you looked at this in a browser is a ticker tape symbol running across the page displaying a text message.

As seen from within a browser, Figure 4–2 is the actual HTML code that executes the Java applet in Figure 4–1. Traditionally, an applet was considered to be a small pro-

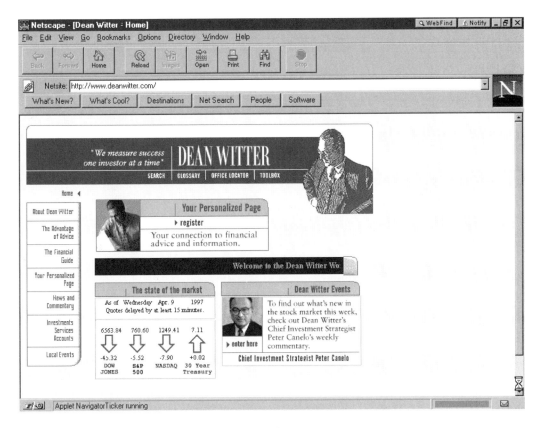

Figure 4–1 A Web site with a running Java program.

gram written in Java that is included in a Web page and downloaded on demand to be executed on a client machine. The current thought is that applets can also be written in JavaScript.

In Netscape Navigator, you'd be able to view HTML code by clicking on View|Document Source while any Web page that you wanted to see the HTML code for was displayed. As you can see in the figure, embedded in the HTML code is the text string that displays across the ticker-tape symbol on the Web page. Using this technique, the developer was thinking ahead! She or he he decided to write the Java program so that it would dynamically read and display a text string that could be changed at any time without causing the need to have to recompile the Java program.

Tip: Don't worry if you can't make sense of the HTML code seen in Figure 4–2. My intention here is to show you how uncomplicated a process it is to cause a Java program to execute from within HTML code. Chapter 6 of this book introduces you to HTML syntax and coding conventions.

```
Netscape - [Source of: http://www.deanwitter.com/]                    _ | 8 | x
        <TD ALIGN="RIGHT">
            <applet code="NavigatorTicker.class" codebase="/" width=392 height=26 >
            <H3>Welcome to the Dean Witter World Wide Web Site.</H3>
            <param name=count value=1 >

            <param name=msg0 value="Welcome to the Dean Witter World Wide Web site . . . Disc
   for retirement or for a child's education with The Financial Guide . . . Use the Toolbox to find

            <param name=speed value=5 >
            <param name=bgco value=0,0,0 >
            <param name=txtco value=107,204,20 >
            <param name=linkco value=107,204,20 >

            </applet >
        </TD>
```

Figure 4–2   The HTML code that triggers the Java applet for Fig. 4–1.

Since Java is a full fledged programming language, it can also be used to write serious, robust, data-aware business-to-business, business-to-employee, and business-to-customer applications. The most critical component to developing these applications is the need to have the ability to perform transaction processing from Java that accesses corporate data stores.

To many, Web applications are written in either Java or JavaScript, with no other possibilities. In a January 7, 1997 article written by Bill Catchings and published in *InfoWorld* magazine, he estimates that "There are over 200,000 Java developers, and before long every one of them will be writing code to access corporate information databases." If this is an accurate estimate, then it is a safe assumption that for every Java or JavaScript developer, there are at least three people using other languages and products to build Web applications.

As noted at the beginning of this chapter, Java and JavaScript share similar syntax conventions and object use, but they are used to solve different sets of problems. The decision to use Java or JavaScript is much like the decision to use C or C++ to solve a business problem.

That Web applications are always written in either Java or JavaScript is one of the common misconceptions we will look at in this chapter. We will investigate the use of Java and JavaScript as programming languages. We will describe how Java and JavaScript programs are used, along with their benefits and shortcomings.

Benefits of Java

The Java developer enjoys a number of significant benefits over the non-Java developer. These are:

Platform Independence

Java applications are executable without modification on many different operating systems and platforms. In fact, Java was the first programming language that could earnestly make this claim. Some of the operating systems that this support is provided for are: Windows 95, Windows NT, Unix, Macintosh, OS/2.

Object Oriented

Since its inception as a development concept in IBM labs in the mid 1960s, the popularity of tools that support Object Oriented (OO) development is rapidly rising. With the advent of Object Oriented Programming (OOP) languages such as C++, SmallTalk, and Java, it is hard to imagine a development team that is tasked with building a computer system that does not use tools that support OO concepts. Even the venerable COBOL language is conforming to OO. Micro Focus Ltd., the PC-based application tools development vendor in Palo Alto, California markets its OO COBOL product, with full OO support.

A section later in this chapter titled Java and Object-Orientation goes into detail to describe the features of Java specific to object-orientation.

Robust

Java was created to be a development tool for building corporate and enterprise applications. This encompasses Web applications, as well as non-Web applications. Java is well known for its reliance on the early detection and removal of problems before the code is placed "in production." Many people think of Java as a newer flavor of C++. Although it is true that Java relies on OO design and construction principals much the same as C++, Java uses a process of variable and array management (called a pointer model) that eliminates the possibility of overwriting memory and thereby corrupting data held in memory. Java gives you the comfort of knowing that you can never access a bad pointer within your program and thereby create memory allocation errors.

Distributed

Java has excellent networking capabilities. The Java language and the Java Developers Kit (JDK) both provide an extensive library of routines for coping with the various TCP/IP protocols like HTTP and FTP. With these routines that are easy to use, a Java programmer can access data files across the world over the Web via URLs with the same ease as a traditional programmer would access a data file on their local machine.

Definition: TCP/IP—Transmission Control Protocol/Internet Protocol is the common name for a collection of over 100 different protocols that are used to connect computers and networks. Telnet and FTP are two of the most popular of these protocols.

Definition: FTP—File Transfer Protocol is a common name for one of the TCP/IP protocols used to transfer files from one computer or network to the other.

Definition: Telnet—This is a TCP/IP protocol that allows you to establish a terminal session with another computer.

Definition: HTTP—HyperText Transfer Protocol is one of the TCP/IP protocols that facilitates the quick retrieval of information resources located at different remote sites. HTTP also provides support for advanced functions such as document searching, front-end update, and annotation.

Security

With all the hype surrounding firewalls and data security, it is sometimes overlooked that the Java language provides excellent security capabilities. It was designed to be a tool used to build networked and distributed applications. Whereby firewalls and the like provide additional layers of security from what is afforded within the Java language, the use of Java as a development language enables the developer to create applications that are fundamentally tamper-resistant and virus-free.

Architecturally Neutral

As shown in Figure 4–3, Java applications that are compiled are executable on many platforms, under many different operating systems, without modification. This was one of the main objectives of the original developers of the language. The Java compiler accomplishes this architectural neutrality by use of a Java runtime system. Each different operating system requires a Java runtime system which, when installed, provides full architectural neutrality. The magic behind this process is in the type of executable code created from the compile. The Java compiler creates bytecode instructions which have nothing at all to do with a particular operating system or architecture. Although the use of bytecodes does negatively affect performance to a degree, many people believe that the benefits of this architectural interoperability far outweigh the performance considerations.

Portability

Portability refers to the ability to move an application (and the data accessed by that application) from one computing environment to another without the need to make extensive changes. An example of this is a Web database application that is written for the UNIX operating system and is "ported," or moved, to the Windows NT environment. Such an event would occur if a company decides to shelve their UNIX computing environment and implement a Windows NT architecture.

With Java, binary data is stored in a fixed format. Strings are stored in a standard Unicode format. Consequently, writing code in Java represents little of the "implementa-

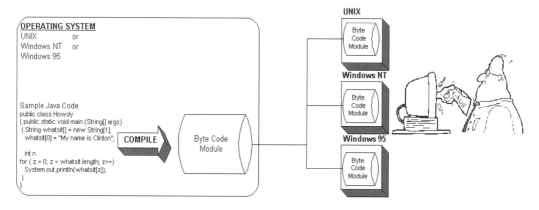

Figure 4–3   Java is architecturally neutral.

tion-dependent" issues addressed by C++ developers. For example, an int in Java is always a 32-bit integer value, while in C++ an int can be an integer of any size that the manufacturer of the compiler chooses. This portability is not without its problems. For example, Java programmers generally don't have the control over the look-and-feel of a screen as do non-Java programmers. However, when it comes to a Web application, portability is often much more of a critical component than how pretty the screen appears.

Interpreted

One of the most significant benefits of Java is that the Java interpreter can execute Java bytecodes directly on any machine that the interpreter is running on. Although compiled Java code executes much faster than bytecodes, and Java compilers are coming available, the development process of applications is frequently much more rapid than with other languages such as C++, VB, and Delphi.

Multithreading

Multithreading is the ability of one program to accomplish more than one task at any one time. It is the programming equivalent of cluster bombs: One program (or bomb) spawns multiple other programs (or clusters of bombs) that all perform processing (explode) at the same time. Multithreading is very easy to implement in Java. Additionally, Java threads can be written to easily take advantage of devices that use multiprocessors.

Dynamic

As a language, Java is seeing much more growth and development than any other programming language. Libraries of functions and classes are adding new methods to the language at a record pace.

Java and Object-Orientation

For most of the past 25 years, the dominant programming paradigm has been "structured" programming. This is where all the code in the application that is necessary to be processed together and as a unit is combined together in a common manner. OOP is changing this however.

Java is one of the purest OO languages in existence. In fact, it is impossible to write a Java program in a structured or procedural style. There are many compelling benefits of Java being a pure OO language:

- It is much easier to write bug-free code
- The code that is written is produced much quicker
- There is no need to manually allocate memory
- True arrays are allowable and printer arithmetic is eliminated
- Elimination of the possibility of confusing an argument with a test for equality in a conditional statement
- Elimination of multiple inheritance

The Java/Web Concept

Java programs actually come in a number of varieties. For example, they can be written and executed completely outside of the Web. With the advent of Java compilers and linkers, you can create a Java program that executes without relying on any Web-specific component such as HTTP or CGI. CGI, or Common Gateway Interface, defines how a Web server and an external program (also called a CGI program) communicate together.

This book is not concerned with this type of Java program. The type of program you write (as evidenced by the purchase of this book) is a Web-based program that accesses a database. A Web-based Java program is called an applet, regardless of whether that program accesses a database. Figure 4–4 shows the URL for a Web site that is a great source of applets. Take a look at some of the areas that can be accessed from this Web page—you may want to refer to this Web page often as you begin to acquire the tools and develop the techniques of Web database application development.

For people considering writing applets in their Web pages to access databases, the following advantages exist:

Figure 4–4   A great source of applets is www.gamelan.com.

Responsiveness

Responsiveness is the speed in which a program supplies the user with requested information. A program is said to be responsive if it processes a users request for information quickly. As Java is a programming language, it is simply a matter of supplying the correct syntax to make the applet responsive. Responsiveness is a very critical element to many Web applications, particularly those that access databases. This is due to the nature of the way in which that data coming from the databases is massaged and used by the person sitting at the computer.

GUI-Aware

Java is a modern programming language that offers Graphical User Interface (GUI) support for all OS' that support a GUI. Applets can include text boxes, command buttons, list boxes, drop down list boxes, etc. Additionally, applets can track the movement of a mouse and can track keystrokes.

If you want to see the action of tracking the movement of a mouse on a Web page, take a look at any "image map." An "image map" is a particular type of graphic appearing on a Web page that has special and powerful characteristics. Depending on where on the image map your mouse is located when you click, you will go to a different Web page—or URL. To understand this, think of an image of a globe appearing on a Web page. If you clicked on an area on that image of the United States, your browser could go to a Web page specific to the United States. If you clicked on an area on that image of Australia, your browser could go to a Web page specific to Australia. Move your cursor over the image map and watch the various URLs display at the bottom of your browser window. If you want to see an example of this, check out: `http://www.z100portland.com`. This is the image map used by a radio station in Portland, Oregon to help users navigate to various areas on its Web site.

Support for Fat-Client

An applet causes the processing contained within the applet to be offloaded to the user's system. This supports the Fat-Client model for client/server architectural design. Fat Client is a term used in client/server architecture to describe the amount of the application that processes on the client machine. The more components of an application that process on a client machine, or the more intensive the operations that execute on a client machine are, the fatter the client. As today's Web servers are often over-loaded with thousands of transactions occurring every minute, it makes good sense to isolate as much processing as possible on the users machine.

A common use for applets has traditionally been to display animated images. The applet shown in Figures 3–1 and 3–2 is an example of this. The applet displays a text string that is designed to appear as if it is a ticker tape. Use care in animated applets however as the GIF files used in these animations can become quite large. It will leave a frustrated user when they have to wait for a 1.5 megabyte GIF file to be transferred over a 28.8k modem.

HotJava

In 1995, Sun Microsystems spun off a subsidiary and named it Javasoft. This company is responsible for the development and support of both Java and the HotJava browser. The objective of HotJava was to build a Java-enabled browser that had the ability to dynamically adjust to new types of information coming to it. When a developer needs to send a new type of algorithm, file, etc. to the browser, a small content handler is developed that is shipped with the new data to instruct the browser how to process it.

Is It Java or Coffee?

There have been many misconceptions about Java, many of which still persist. The material in this section is here to dispel many of these and help you see Java for what it really is . . . and what it is not!

It Is NOT an Extension of HTML

HTML is a page-description language, not a programming language. Java is a programming language, not a page-description language. The only overlap between these two entities is that HTML provides facilities for placing Java applets on the Web page. Java programs can run independently of HTML pages, and HTML pages frequently contain no Java applets.

It Is an Easy Language to Learn

Java is an extremely powerful programming language. In many ways, it is more powerful than C++. Like C++ and unlike COBOL, Java is not an intuitive language to learn—that is it is not one that is particularly comfortable to learn. I know some people will take exception to the use of the word comfortable. In my case I can say with certainty, though, that Java was a very difficult language to learn.

Java Is an Easy Environment in Which to Program

Java is an incomplete programming environment. The Java that you download for free from a number of sources is a very incomplete application development environment. There is an increasingly large number of tools and products coming available that add to the robustness of the base Java compiler. These are tools such as the JDK from Javasoft, JBuilder from Borland, JavaBeans, and Café from Symantec. Barring the use of this type of tool and assuming you still want to use Java to write your code, you will need to acquire a number of additional components to complete your toolset. These include but are not limited to an editor, debugger, and design tools. These tools, when combined to form a complete development environment, suffer the same ease-of-use issues that you'd expect from any computer system where the components are thrown together—not built together.

Java Is a Universal Web Development Tool

This was the hype in 1995 and 1996, but I think few people that are students of the Web industry think this is still the case. There are many reasons for this, many of which we've already discussed. Perhaps the biggest reason is that Java was not and still is not a complete development environment. It is a language. Tools are built by vendors that are meant to be used with the language. Vendors are coming online with tools that are complete development environments without any Java compiler. These are perhaps the biggest impediment to Java being recognized as a universal web development tool.

Java Is Too Slow for Serious Applications

This may certainly have been an accurate statement until mid-1996. Until then, Java code was not compiled to machine code. It was converted to Java bytecodes. These bytecodes were then interpreted on the client machine by an interpreter that was appropriate for the operating system on that machine.

In 1996, however, Java compilers began appearing. What these compilers do is convert the Java bytecodes into native machine code. Although this machine code executes much quicker, the interoperability that was a hallmark of Java is compromised. It is not possible to take compiled machine code that is generated for a Unix machine and have it execute unmodified on a Windows NT machine. This, however, is possible with Java bytecodes. The negative consequence to Java bytecodes is performance.

Java Programs Require a Web Page to Run

As I've said, Java programs do not require a Web page to execute. Java applets do, however, require a Web page to run. This in fact is the definition of a Java applet—a Java program that is run from within a Web page. It is very possible and certainly probable that skilled Java programmers are currently called on to write an application for deployment in non-Web environments.

> It is questionable whether the developers of the original Java had in mind that it would be a language so heavily associated with the Web. What the developers perhaps did not see was the explosive growth of the Web and the search for a programming tool that could build applications (applets) that would function as desired across multiple environments. The use of Java to write applets eclipses the use of Java to write applications presently. As development suites become increasingly popular, the use of Java as a tool to write applets will subside. However, the use of Java as a tool to write standalone applications will continue to increase.

Java Eliminates CGI Scripting

As you will see in Chapters 7 (Overview of CGI) and 14 (Accessing Oracle Databases Using CGI Programs), CGI scripts handle the communication between a server and an applet. In fact, many argue that CGI is the most popular and easiest communication path between the server and client. This argument is frequently won. Java and CGI can co-exist.

Client Server Computing Is Dead

Although it is possible that the applications developed for and deployed on the Web may significantly modify what we think of when we consider what client/server computing is, Java will not be the demise of client/server. As you'll see in Chapter 8 (Web Application Design and Development), application components written in Java to be run in a Web database application is clearly an extension of (not a replacement for) client/server architectures and concepts. With the ability to connect to corporate databases through ODBC and JDBC, the use of Java as a programming tool to develop client/server applications over the Web is practical.

Java Allows Me to Use an Inexpensive Internet "Appliance"

Web "appliances" are chic. People like to talk about them and investors are placing some very large bets that these inexpensive devices will be big. Sun is exploring a micro kernel-based operating system that promises to add intelligence to a new generation of low-cost Internet terminals—a Web appliance.

For you who are reading this book with very little or no mainframe development experience, a Web appliance is very similar in capability to the old IBM 3270 mainframe terminal—what is appropriately called a "dumb terminal." Both the IBM 3270 terminal and the Web appliance share the following common denominators:

- No local data storage
- Attached keyboard
- Limited ability to attach external devices
- Limited power

Oracle Corporation is investing huge amounts of resources to develop and market Web appliances, and promoting these devices with a public relations and marketing onslaught that is huge. Take a look at Oracle's Web site at `http://www.oracle.com` to see the emphasis that they are putting on this technology.

An example of a current Web "appliance" is being sold by Motorola Corporation with the name—WebTV. Perhaps you've seen this advertised. WebTV is a keyboard that attaches to a small box that is plugged into a television set. The television set functions as the monitor for Web access and the keyboard is the input device. There is no local storage and all the memory required to use this setup is contained in the small box that the keyboard is plugged in to. There are a number of devices of all sizes, many specifically devoted to Internet access, but most with multiple functions under development. So far, no single product has taken off.

Who Owns Java?

As we have discussed, a team of engineers at Sun Microsystems wrote Java. In 1995, Sun started a subsidiary called Javasoft to continue the support and development of the language. In 1996, Bill Gates announced that although Microsoft had initially missed the Internet market, the company was going to invest huge amounts of capital to make sure that they were a dominant tools provider. To those familiar with how Bill Gates and Steve Ballmer approach a market opportunity, this does not mean that they will be content to simply be "in the game." They see the Internet and the tools and applications used by and deployed over the Internet as the next great computing opportunity.

Having learned the lessons of the fallen victims of early Microsoft pursuits, Sun is wary of the Microsoft competitor. To bolster its forces, Sun is teaming with companies like Apple, IBM, Oracle, and Netscape to form a coalition. The result of this is the more broad-based support Sun has for its language, and the greater likelihood that developers and third-party providers will support it.

Not to be outdone, Microsoft is tuning Java and the Java virtual machine support for its Internet Explorer browser for running on Windows 95 and Windows NT. Although Microsoft is committed to delivering a compatible implementation of the Java virtual machine in its browser technology, they have also developed some extensions to the native Java language. These extensions, called "proprietary lock-ins," have the effect of improving the performance of Java applications run in a Windows 95 or Windows NT environment. Unfortunately, many they won't run at all in a non-Windows environment.

This lack of portability is at the heart of Sun's initiative to insure and certify that the Java API becomes the API of the Internet. API, or Application Programming Interface, is a collection of predefined standard functions provided for programmer.

Sun understands, as does Microsoft, that the product or company that controls the API to a computing environment controls that environment. Sun's coalition with various other hardware and software vendors, nicknamed Sun's "100% Pure Java" initiative, is the tactical strategy used to confront Microsoft in the marketplace. This initiative calls for a process whereby any company's products that support or work with Java are certified to be 100% compatible with Java.

The problem, at least in the short-term, for developers and the Internet community as a whole, is that Microsoft is not a member in this coalition. Therefore, there will ultimately be either one initiative that wins, or at least some sort of compromise will be reached. Will it be Sun with its determination to keep Java platform and operating system independent, or will it be Microsoft with its determination to have Java be another Windows programming language? As of this writing, Sun is winning this battle. Microsoft is gaining ground however.

Oracle's View of Java

Oracle Corporation, like most software vendors, is afraid of being left behind by the Next Big Thing. Consequently, Oracle has embraced Java as a development platform. Oracle is serious enough about its commitment to the language that, in early 1997, it licensed Borland Corporation's Java tools. Oracle is currently integrating Java support in all of its development tools, including Oracle Power Objects, Developer/2000, Designer/2000, and its forthcoming Sedona.

But, Oracle's interest in Java doesn't come just from its database division. Larry Ellison, Oracle's CEO, spearheaded the company's plunge into the world of Network Computers (NC), those web-browsing terminals that have been so much in the news. Mr. Ellison and Scott McNealey of Sun, are hoping to flood both the business world and homes around the world with these relatively inexpensive devices. Since these NCs are really graphically-based terminals, with no hard drive and little computing power of their own, they depend on Java applets to provide a rich user environment.

The development in the NC world is already spilling over to the database side of Oracle. The jury is still out on how these NCs will fare in the marketplace. As long as Oracle is pouring money into the venture, however, Java development will hold a important role for Oracle.

Introduction to JavaScript

Unlike Java, which is an interpreted language, JavaScript is a scripting language. It was developed with the hope that it would be easier to learn than Java, and make HTML "documents" more flexible. JavaScript includes a suite of powerful tools that add interactivity to your Web pages with very little effort. Because JavaScript is a scripting language and is highly interactive with HTML, it is written directly in the HTML for the Web page it is associated with.

A scripting language like JavaScript offers fewer commands in a simpler syntax that is well-suited for implementing simple, small programs.

The syntax and command structure of JavaScript are very similar to Java. If you know Java, learning JavaScript is greatly simplified. In addition to the syntax and command structure, JavaScript also uses many of the same security components and flow constructs as Java.

Uses for JavaScript

Here are just some of the uses for JavaScript. If you understand the base structure of the language, you will uncover a plethora of uses for the language.

Dynamic Forms. With JavaScript, you can create dynamic forms with built-in error checking.

Frames. As seen in Figure 4–5, frames give the Web page a segregated and partitioned look. In this Figure you'll see one large frame plus two smaller frames. With frames, the screen is split into rectangular sections, with each section referencing a different URL. Each frame functions as its own mini-Web page within the larger Web page from which it is viewed. JavaScript includes excellent support for frames.

Spreadsheets. JavaScript has functions that allow for simplified creation of spreadsheet-like forms. For example, a real estate company would use JavaScript on their Web page to provide browsers with the capability of calculating a mortgage payment.

User Interaction. JavaScript provides excellent user interaction capabilities in the form of warning messages, confirmation messages, and interactive forms. Additionally, JavaScript is ideal for calculating or determining the value of one field based on the changes made to data on another field.

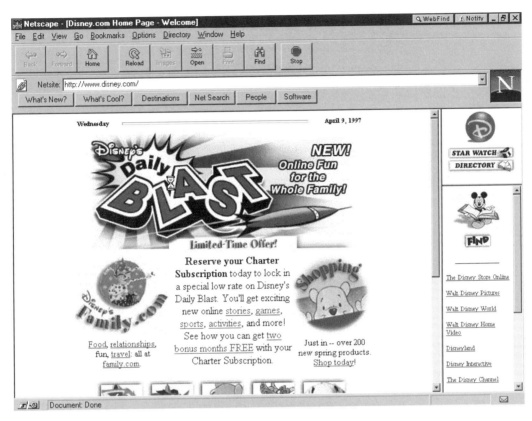

Figure 4–5   The Disney page uses frames.

Ease of Development.   JavaScript eases development and debugging because it is not compiled. Therefore, changes made to JavaScript can be tested interactively and immediately, without having to execute a compile.

Search Engines.   JavaScript is an ideal language to build database queries that are then sent to a remote database.

Java Mortar.   The term "Java Mortar" refers to the process of data created from one Java applet being massaged and passed to another Java applet via a JavaScript program. Because of the high degree of user interaction that is easily programmed into Web pages due to JavaScript, you will be able to transfer data easily between Java applets with JavaScript.

Dynamic URL Building.   JavaScript is well suited to build customized URLs based on user-specified selections on forms.

Replace CGI.   JavaScript is very useful for replacing much of the functionality that exists in CGI scripts used in client-side processing.

The following is a basic example of JavaScript that demonstrates how it could be used to add interactivity to a form.

```
var y_name=prompt("Enter your first name: ")
var f_name=prompt("Enter a friends first name: ")
alert("You, " + y_name + & " + f_name + " are friends.")
```

The JavaScript code above performs the following:

- The first line of code is a prompt to enter your first name.
- The second line of code is a prompt to enter your friends first name.
- The last line of code is a message box that displays a friendly message.

Figure 4–6 is the input box that displays as a result of the first line of sample JavaScript executing. Figure 4–7 is the input box that displays as a result of the second line of sample JavaScript executing. Finally, Figure 4–8 is the message box that displays a message to inform you that you and the person named in Figure 4–7 are friends.

Strengths and Weaknesses of JavaScript

Much the same as a seamstress determines which type of stitch to use to bind material together based on the fabric and how the fabric is worn, so too is it valuable to you to understand the strengths and weaknesses of JavaScript to better determine its suitability to a task. These are discussed in this section.

Strengths of JavaScript

Reduced Learning Curve. JavaScript is easy to learn. Although it borrows much of its syntax and nature from Java, much of the complexity and rules of Java are absent.

Portability. Because JavaScript is included in HTML pages, any Web browser that is capable of interpreting JavaScript will execute the code. Currently, this includes all the major Web browsers and the majority of the less well-known ones.

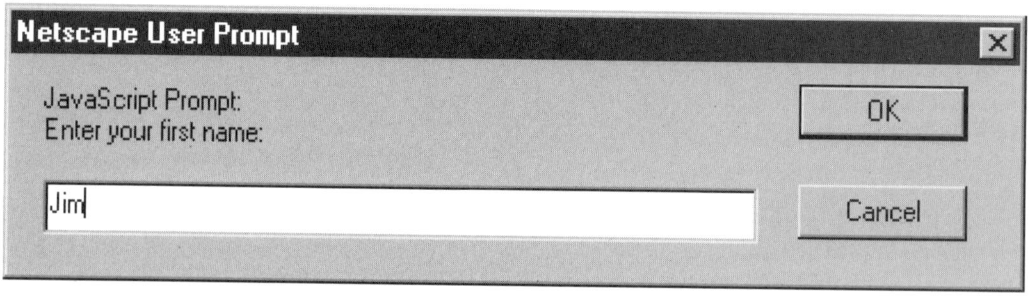

Figure 4–6 The first prompt statement in the JavaScript.

Netscape User Prompt
JavaScript Prompt:
Enter a friends first name:
Robin
OK
Cancel

Figure 4–7 The second prompt statement in the JavaScript.

Improved Productivity. JavaScript is a very productive language. The simple examples in Figure 4–6–4–8 were written using 3 lines of code. To accomplish the same processing in C++ or Java would have entailed much more code.

Small Overhead. JavaScript programs are quite a bit smaller than a Java or C++ object module. This reduces storage requirements to contain the code on the server as well as the download time to transfer the JavaScript program or Java/C++ program from the server to the client device.

Weaknesses of JavaScript

Code Is Viewable. Because JavaScript is written directly in the HTML code, and as most commercial browsers include a HTML viewing capability, the JavaScript code you write is viewable. This makes it possible for anyone to copy and thus steal it.

Limited Methods. Although the range of methods (methods are the functions that exist within classes, or types, of objects) supported in the most popular commercial browsers increases with each release, the full range of methods is not yet supported.

Limited Support Tools. As is the case with Java, there is limited availability of support tools to the JavaScript developer.

Netscape
JavaScript Alert:
You, Jim & Robin are friends.
OK

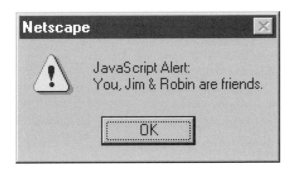

Figure 4–8 The alert statement in the JavaScript.

ODBC

Although the remaining chapters of this book include a great deal of information specific to ODBC and JDBC, the information here is meant as an introduction. ODBC, or Open DataBase Connectivity, is Microsoft's standard cross-platform SQL API that allows programmers to create a gateway connection between an application program and a database engine. JDBC, or Java Database Connectivity, is on the other hand, an API proposed by Sun Microsystems to connect a Java program directly to a database.

ODBC is a Microsoft initiative that has become a well accepted standard for attaching databases to application programs that access them. Most of the leading DBMS vendors have enabled their applications to support ODBC. To be competitive, a development tool must be ODBC-enabled as well. Most pundits believe that ODBC will continue to be the most commonly used API for heterogeneous RDBMS access for many more years.

The ODBC interface provides for:

- A library of ODBC function calls that allow an application to access a DBMS, execute SQL query statements, and retrieve the results.
- A standard representation of data types.
- A standard set of error codes.
- A standard way to connect to, access, and log off a DBMS.
- Support for DBMS native SQL syntax as well as syntax based on the X/Open and SQL Access Group (SAG) SQL CAE specification, first published in 1992. SQL, or Structured Query Language, is the set of commands used to query and transform the data contained in a database.

A diagram of an ODBC application is seen in Figure 4–9. As you can see in this diagram, the ODBC component resides between the application program and the database. Its only purpose is to handle the translation of a database request coming from a program to a format that the database understands, and then accomplish the translation of the result coming from the database to a format that is recognizable by the program.

JDBC

JDBC is a database connectivity API that provides the necessary means for a Web application to access a database directly, without having the overhead of ODBC. Because JDBC represents a more direct method of communication between a program and a database, it is frequently a quicker form of database access.

There are two fundamental ways to use JDBC. First, an applet making a call to a database. This configuration is seen in Figure 4–10. In this figure, the Java applet initiates a request for database access which is received and interpreted by the JDBC interface into a format that is recognizable by the RDBMS. The results of that database access are then reformatted by JDBC into something that the Java applet can process. In the second scenario, a standalone Java application has direct access to all available network components directly.

There are four primary interfaces described in the JDBC API. These are:

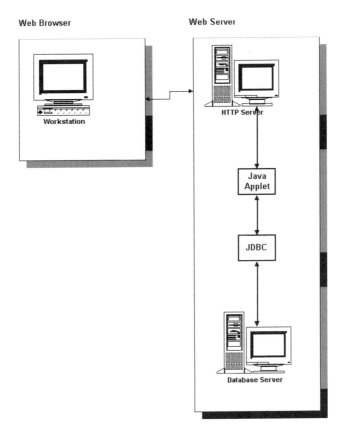

Figure 4–9   Web application with ODBC database access.

- *Environmental*—The environmental interface provides support for the creation of connections from a device to a database.
- *Connection*—The connection interface provides the connection to a particular database.
- *Statement*—The statement interface encapsulates the SQL statement coming from the program or applet and executes the statements.
- *Result Set*—The result set interface provides the facility to access the result set of the SQL statements executing against the database.

Moving On

Java was the first programming language that provided a complete solution to Internet application development. In the couple of short years since Java burst on the scene, it has gained in popularity at a pace equal to the popularity of the Web. JavaScript, a program-

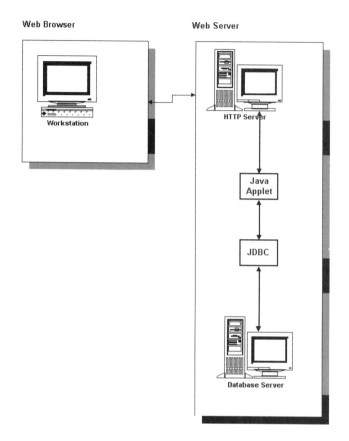

Figure 4-10   Web application with JDBC database access.

ming language that was released soon after Java, is also an increasingly popular language for Web application development.

There are a number of benefits in choosing to develop a Web application that needs databases access in languages such as Java, or JavaScript. Most of these are well publicized. These benefits must be evaluated carefully when deciding what language to use in which to develop an application. The choice is definitely no longer one of Java, JavaScript, or nothing.

In Chapter 5, you will be introduced to Web database application suites. And, you will look at several of the most popular development suites used to build Web database applications.

CHAPTER 5

Application Development Suites

I n the late 1980s, a British based company named Micro Focus Ltd. introduced a PC-based COBOL language compiler. Although a few customers were interested enough in the technology to purchase the product and fund R&D for Micro Focus, sales for the company's product did not begin to accelerate until they developed a testing tool called the Animator. Of course sales of the COBOL compiler with the Animator testing tool funded additional R&D, which caused Micro Focus Ltd. to develop an Editor, a File Translation tool, and a File Transfer tool. When Micro Focus Ltd. released version 2.4 of their Micro Focus COBOL Workbench, they had incrementally created a PC-based COBOL application development suite. An application development suite is a grouping of tools and utilities sold as a single entity that provides a comprehensive range of the toolset needed to build and maintain an application. Sales of the product sky rocketed and the company became a huge success in the COBOL applications market.

Application development suites are one of the quickest growing segments in the Web market. Companies, both customers and suppliers alike, learned in the early 1990s that a development tool used in isolation and detached from other tools often becomes a little used tool. Application suites remedy this problem by offering a selection of tools used to develop Web applications. For example, HAHTsite IDE (IDE stands for Integrated Development Environment, which is an acronym describing a collection of tools and utilities melded into a common interface and sold as a single product solution), the tool used in this book to create examples, is comprised of the following integrated components:

- WYSIWYG development interface
- An Image Map editor
- Ability to write HAHTtalk Basic or JavaScript scripts
- Basic compiler
- Debugger
- Web Publishing tool
- Application Server (An Application Server is a Web database application architectural component that resides between the Web server and a database that maintains an open connection to the database at all times.)
- 30-day evaluation copy of Quarterdeck WebStar Server

HAHT Software is including the 30-day evaluation copy of the Quarterdeck WebStar Server in its product so that purchasers have all the tools they need to develop and publish sophisticated Web pages on one CD-ROM. This is the essence of an application suite.

This chapter will present information on a number of application development suites. The major features of the products are described along with contact information. Only some of these products have been reviewed by me, so it would be unfair (and therefore I won't do it) to recommend one product over the other. Most vendors will supply you with evaluation copies of the their products, and in many cases, you can download these evaluation copies directly from the Web. Most of the products described here are included on the companion CD-ROM.

Disclaimer and Legal Notice: Companies, and products offered by those companies, are appearing (and disappearing) at an extremely rapid pace. In writing this book it is not humanly possible to objectively or thoroughly evaluate all of the products listed below. And, if it were possible, I doubt it would be of much use to you as the intended use of the products is distinct to your environment. Consequently, the information provided for each of the listed products is written, supplied, and owned by the vendor.

Amazon

Company Name:	Intelligent Environments
Address:	67 South Bedford Street
	Burlington, MA 01803
Phone:	(617) 272-9700
URL:	http://www.ieinc.com/

Amazon, the flagship product from Intelligent Environments, is self-billed as the first open Web development tool for quickly deploying scaleable, interactive Internet applications that leverage legacy systems investments. Scalable means the ability to expand a database or application to accommodate more users, more data, and more complexity. Amazon supports native connectivity to DB2, Oracle, Sybase, and SQL Server, and ODBC connectivity for Informix, Lotus Notes and other databases.

Using Amazon, developers can build applications that employ an organization's unique business logic using Amazon's Intelligent Rules Language while bridging the gap between legacy data sources and network computer users. Future Amazon cartridges (the vendors terminology for interfaces) will significantly improve the performance and response time for users running Amazon Web applications that require dynamic data access via Oracle's Web Server.

Amazon is browser independent and so Amazon applications can be accessed from browsers from Netscape, Microsoft, Sun, NCSA, Spry and SpyGlass. Amazon supports advanced features such as HTML 3.0, Netscape and Microsoft extensions to HTML, support for SSL (Secure Sockets Layer) secure links to Microsoft and Netscape browsers.

Amazon works with Java applets that can be downloaded and executed on any Java-enabled browser, such as Netscape Navigator and Microsoft's Explorer.

Browsers are available for all popular operating systems, including Windows, Mac, Motif, UNIX and OS/2. This means that Amazon applications can be accessed for any of these platforms making it possible to develop a single application that can be used by anyone with a browser on either your intranet or across the Internet.

Amazon works with any server that supports the CGI server interface. CGI is supported by all the major web servers. Amazon also supports high-performance direct API access to Netscape's servers using NSAPI and Microsoft Internet Information Server (IIS) using ISAPI. Direct API access is about ten times faster than CGI access.

ISAPI, which stands for Internet Server Application Programming Interface, is an Application Programming Interface (API) developed by Microsoft Corporation that provides interfaces for third-party software developers to write programs that interact with Web servers in a standard manner. On the other hand, NSAPI stands for Netscape Server Application Programming Interface. This is an Application Programming Interface (API) developed by Netscape Communications that provide interfaces for third-party software developers to write programs that interact with Web servers in a standard manner.

Autobahn

Company Name:	Speedware Toronto
Address:	150 John Street, 10th Floor
	Toronto, Ontario M5V 3E3
Phone:	Telephone: (416) 408–2880
URL:	http://www.speedware.com/

Speedware Autobahn lets you build applications that allow your Web server to support dynamic, on-the-fly web pages in your Internet applications. This allows your users to see what they want, not what you guess they want. Autobahn lets Web users run database applications residing on your WWW server. You can offer custom-tailored forms, live reports and batch jobs. Your old COBOL or C programs can be plugged in to the Autobahn server, so you'll leverage your development investment. You can mix both static and dynamic information to create interactive systems.

The package offers many features and benefits. It includes a complete high-level (albeit proprietary) programming language. It can run programs that handle forms, reports, jobs, batch updates, transactions and subroutine calls.

Autobahn is intended for MIS professionals who don't want to be bothered about networks and interprocess communications. You don't need Internet experts or C language gurus to set up your site. Autobahn lets you control users' access to your information as precisely as you want.

Autobahn applications can mix text, transactions and multimedia content. Your databases can hold images and sound files to enhance the interface. The Autobahn agent, the Open Application Server and the databases can all be on different machines, so large organizations can use their resources as they prefer. For example, if you have a dedicated Web server, you can put the application server on a production machine close to the data. In this way, you can build a firewall and spread the processing load.

Because Autobahn works via the Speedware Open Application Server (OAS), you can run programs on several computers simultaneously. Your Autobahn applications can run locally or across a network. Autobahn can work with Web servers from different vendors such as NCSA and CERN.

Speedware Autobahn works with the Netscape Commerce Server, which supports secure transactions that use credit card numbers or other confidential data. Applications created with Autobahn can run on any Speedware supported platform with almost no changes. The Speedware OAS can access 14 different DBMS and file systems.

Centura Web Data Publisher

Company Name:	Centura Software
Address:	1060 Marsh Rd.
	Menlo Park, CA 94025
Phone:	(415) 617–4782
URL:	`http://www.centurasoft.com/`

Centura Web Developer provides all of the programming facilities necessary for building transaction intensive, database connected, enterprise business applications for the Web. Centura Web developer helps you deliver business applications for the Web with tremendous efficiency, not only by quickly producing the first application, but by providing for object re-use in subsequent development, by scaling to deal with complex business rules and very large numbers of users, and by easing on-going application maintenance.

All aspects of Web Developer's integrated development environment are designed to enhance productivity. With Centura Web Developer you can navigate easily through application code, move between coding facilities, design WYSIWYG pages and debug with unparalleled ease.

The applications that you create with Web Developer can encapsulate the most complex business logic into objects that can be used over and over again. It's easy because of the strong object orientation of Web Developer's powerful fourth generation programming language, SAL. In addition, objects created in Java and ActiveX integrate seamlessly into Web Developer applications.

Web Developer applications serve up HTML pages that deliver corporate data and application logic to Internet or intranet clients—with full application security.

dbWeb

Company Name:	Microsoft Corporation
Address:	10500 NE 8th Street, Suite 1300
	Bellevue, WA 98004
Phone:	(800) 426-9400
URL:	`http://www.microsoft.com/intdev/dbweb/`

Microsoft Corporations dbWeb is a gateway between Microsoft Open Database Connectivity (ODBC) data sources and Microsoft IIS. You can use Microsoft dbWeb to publish data from an ODBC data source on the World Wide Web (WWW) or on your internal network without specialized client software.

With dbWeb, you create a schema that contains the specification for your data and the Web pages. Microsoft dbWeb then produces fully functional Web pages for retrieving and displaying your data. dbWeb supports real-time database queries based on a "client-pull" model, formulating dynamic Web pages as users query your data source over the Internet. Visitors to your Web site can use familiar hypertext-style navigation via standard Web browsers to find information with little or no training.

Using dbWeb, you can publish information from the following client/server and desktop databases: ORACLE, Microsoft SQL Server, Microsoft Access, Microsoft Visual FoxPro, and other databases that support 32-bit ODBC.

Delphi

Company Name:	Borland International Inc.
Address:	World Wide Headquarters
	100 Borland Way
	Scotts Valley, CA 95066
Phone:	(408) 431–1000
URL:	`http://www.borland.com/delphi/`

Delphi Desktop 3.0

Delphi Desktop 3.0 is the easiest way to create the fastest applications for Windows 95 and Windows NT. It combines the most intuitive, object-oriented development environment with over 90 customizable, reusable components for immediate productivity. Drag and drop database tools provide an innovative interface for building 32-bit applications.

Delphi Desktop 3.0 applications run up to 300–400% faster than 16-bit Delphi, and up to 15–50 times faster than those built with p-code interpreters. Delphi 3.0 leverages Windows' 32-bit architecture, adds an Object Repository, and supports the reuse of data modules once again raising the bar for application development tools. All Delphi 3.0 version include the 16-bit Delphi 1.0 for Windows 3.1.

Delphi Developer 2.0

Delphi Developer is the fastest way to build 32-bit professional multi-user applications for Windows 95 and NT. It is the next step for Delphi 1.0 owners. Since Delphi 1.0 and Delphi Developer 2.0 are code compatible, no matter where your Windows based applications reside today, Delphi provides a complete solution.

In addition to the features found in Delphi Desktop, Delphi Developer includes: a scaleable Data Dictionary, Multi-Object Grid, complete ODBC support, source code to over 100 native Delphi components, sample OCXs, an expanded Open Tools API, Report-Smith, Local InterBase Server and much more. It includes 16-bit Delphi 1.0 for free.

Delphi Developer is targeted to professional developers who want to develop high-performance desktop applications accessing local and LAN databases, including: dBASE, Paradox, Local InterBase and ODBC.

Delphi Developer 2.0 includes these additional features for the professional:

- Scaleable Data Dictionary
- Multi Object Grid
- Over 100 VCL components for rapid application development
- 32-bit ReportSmith, for high volume client/server reporting
- BDE low-level API support and Help Files
- ODBC Support
- Single User Local InterBase Server
- InstallShield Express for easy installation and deployment
- Winsight32 for monitoring windows messaging
- Expanded Open Tools API
- Team Development Interface (Requires Intersolv PVCS)
- Visual Component Library Source code and complete manual
- Full documentation of Delphi Desktop plus ReportSmith Creating Reports, Delphi Reference Library Guide, InterBase Server, Getting Started

Delphi Client/Server Suite 2.0

Delphi Client/Server Suite 2.0 contains everything you need to build and deliver high-performance client/server applications. Unmatched performance, data integrity, and code reuse are all contained in a robust object-oriented interface, that maximizes productivity across the enterprise. With a host of tools for optimized client/server development, Delphi Client/Server Suite 2.0 offers a complete solution.

The suite also includes a 2-developer copy of InterBase for Windows NT, a fast and efficient SQL database server; a complete set of database design and analysis tools; integrated team-development support; and native 32-bit SQL Links for royalty free deployment on Sybase, Oracle, InterBase, and SQL Server.

Delphi Client/Server Suite is targeted to corporate developers, departmental programmers, VARs, system integrators, consultants, and ISVs who want to develop high performance workgroup and client/server applications.

Delphi Client/Server Suite 2.0 includes these additional features for professional client/server developers:

- High performance 32-bit SQL links native drivers for unlimited deployment
- SQL Database Explorer to browse server meta data

- SQL Monitor for testing, debugging and performance tuning
- 2 user InterBase NT License
- Data Pump Expert for rapid upsizing and application scaling
- Integrated Intersolv PVCS Version Control
- ReportSmith SQL edition
- Visual Query Builder to easily create SQL queries
- Cached Updates
- Client/Server Documentation
- Includes 16-bit Delphi Client/Server 1.0 for Windows 3.1
- Full documentation of Delphi Developer plus Getting Started SQL Links, InterBase Language Reference, InterBase Data Definition Guide

DynaWeb

Company Name:	Inso Corporation
Address:	1 Richmond Square
	Providence, RI 02906
Phone:	(401) 421–9550
URL:	`http://dynabase.eps.inso.com`

The DynaBase Dynamic Web Publishing System combines sophisticated content management capabilities with a powerful, dynamic serving environment. Designed for use by distributed work groups in both commercial and corporate Web publishing environments, DynaBase brings control, extensibility, and automation to Web managers and their teams. DynaBase enables authors, developers, production personnel, and managers to collaborate directly on Web site projects over the Internet and corporate intranet. It is designed to handle all types of content and work with a variety of editors, enabling publishers to easily select and use the best tools for each task.

This product offers the user many benefits. It simplifies the management of Web content. It enables developers to achieve their interactive design goals more quickly. It reduces skill requirements for individuals in Web projects. It eliminates many repetitive tasks. And it allows managers to focus on interaction, design, quality, and consistency.

The DynaBase Web Management System consists of:

- DynaBase Server
- DynaBase Web Manager
- DynaBase Web Developer

The DynaBase Server is a version controlled multimedia repository for all files and scripts used in Web site publishing. The DynaBase Server organizes and manages the links between items in a web, dramatically reducing the Web administrator's maintenance tasks. Through version control, the DynaBase Server allows items in various stages of development to coexist in the system so that end-users who depend on continued access to specified versions remain unaffected. DynaBase's multiple editions capability provides configuration management over entire Web sites, making publishing large sets of interrelated content a snap. The DynaBase Server is designed to "plug into" either the Netscape or Microsoft Web Servers. DynaBase Server is the only version controlled repository for professional online publishing.

The DynaBaseWeb Manager is a "file manager" for Web sites. It provides access to, and control over the files and programs used in a Web site. Using an intuitive graphical user interface that resembles a file system browser, Web masters and contributing authors may edit, organize, test, and manage content with "drag-and-drop" ease. The Web Manager provides a launching pad for HTML, graphic and multimedia applications from vendors like Netscape, Adobe, and Macromedia. DynaBase Web Manager is the only open authoring environment for professional on-line publishers.

The DynaBaseWeb Developer is a full featured interactive development environment for Web Basic. Web Basic is a BASIC language which has been designed to be both compatible with Microsoft's Visual Basic syntax yet remain portable across platforms. Within the Developer, Web Basic can be used to develop both CGI scripts and HTML methods in industry standard BASIC syntax.

Edify Electronic Workforce

Company Name: Edify Corporation
Address: 2840 San Tomas Expressway
Santa Clara, CA 95051
Phone: (408) 982–2000
URL: http://www.edify.com/

The Electronic Workforce software bridges the gap between customers and traditional information systems. With this tool you can create and deliver complete interactive service applications through whatever medium is best: phone, fax, e-mail, PC clients or the World Wide Web. All of your back-office systems, Oracle included, whether host, client-server or PC based, are easily accessed from a single delivery platform— one that schedules and manages interactive applications and coordinates phone, host and network resources. With the award-winning Agent Trainer visual development environment, there's no need to write code. Now you can focus on developing new applications faster and more cost-effectively.

The Edify Electronic Workforce has three main components: Edify software agents, the Agent Trainer development environment, and the Agent Supervisor run-time environment. Together these components comprise the most comprehensive, fully integrated software platform available for interactive service solutions.

At the heart of the Electronic Workforce are the "agents" that provide interactive services on behalf of an organization. Edify software agents have the widest range of skills possible so they can perform tasks such as answering a phone, operating a host application or exchanging information through online PCs. By defining the sequence of tasks agents will perform, you can quickly create robust interactive service applications that span across various media and back-office systems.

Because software agents are so flexible and multi-skilled, you can concentrate on creative valuable services, without the hassles of hard-coded system integration.

Edify's Agent Trainer is a powerful, object-oriented visual development environment where you define and customize interactive service applications. Agent Trainer's unique point and click interface lets you quickly build interactive services that agents will provide. Because all of the agent skills are represented in Agent Trainer as visual objects, you can create sophisticated applications without writing a single line of code. And to make development even easier, there's an integrated set of graphical tools, giving you everything you need to create services unique to your organization.

The Agent Supervisor is a robust run-time environment that schedules software agents and assigns them to service applications built with Agent Trainer. Once agents and service applications are paired, Agent Supervisor manages all of the phone, fax, PC, host and network resources necessary for interactive service delivery. All of these resources are managed through an architecture that ensures reliability and security. With Agent Supervisor, you can deploy multiple interactive services, confident that they will be delivered through a secure run-time environment whose capacity scales to your needs.

HAHTsite IDE

Company Name:	HAHT Software, Inc.
Address:	4200 Six Forks Road
	Raleigh, NC 27609
Phone:	(888) Get–HAHT
URL:	`http://www.haht.com/`

The HAHTsite Integrated Internet Development System merges content creation, client- and server-side logic development, data access (ODBC or native API), automated distributed deployment to multiple sites, team development, and application lifecycle management into one seamlessly integrated software system.

Extending far beyond point products, such as an authoring tool or database utility, HAHTsite combines hundreds of features into an end-to-end solution designed specifically to address the unique technology and lifecycle requirements of complex Internet or intranet applications.

The HAHTsite system is made up of three components: The HAHTsite Integrated Development Environment (IDE), the HAHTSite Application Server, and the HAHTsite Software Developers Kit (SDK).

The HAHTsite IDE is the main interface to the HAHTsite System for all members of the Internet/intranet development team, allowing them to work in a single, drag-and-drop oriented environment for content creation, application logic development and data access, site deployment/publishing, and project lifecycle management and maintenance.

The IDE features a WYSIWYG, drag-and-drop interface that provides a visual workspace to accommodate both content creators and professional developers, and has been carefully designed to utilize familiar wizards, toolbars, metaphors and visual cues, while providing powerful, object-oriented capabilities and project management features, as well as full server-side application debugging.

TheHAHTsite Application Server is a secure, scalable multi-process, multi-threaded deployment engine used to run compiled HAHTsite applications in conjunction with any CGI 1.0 compliant web server software, and can also take advantage of NSAPI and ISAPI interfaces.

Server-side application logic developed in the IDE using HAHTtalk Basic (a VB syntax-compatible programming language) is compiled at publish time into machine independent P-Code which is executed by the HAHTsite Application Server. The Application server also manages "state" or session information, maintains database connections across multiple pages, and handles accessing any server-based service—any API, DLL, OLE/OCX/ActiveX, shared library, shell, DDE, etc.

The HAHTsite Software Developers Kit turns HAHTsite into a platform for internal and third party development, and exposes HAHTsite as an ActiveX amd OLE server.

As an add-in to the IDE, the SDK allows IS/IT professionals to extend the power of HAHTsite with custom, enterprise-wide Widgets (reusable encapsulated code objects) programmed in HAHTtalk Basic, a VB syntax-compatible programming language. Widgets can be used, for example, to control access to corporate resources and simplify complex tasks for other members of the team.

IQ/LiveWeb

Company Name:	IQ Software, Inc.
Address:	3295 River Exchange Drive
	Suite 550
	Norcross, GA 30092
Phone:	(770) 446–8880
URL:	`http://www.iqsc.com/`

IQ Software answers the challenge of providing corporate database content to intranets with IQ/LiveWeb, a complete Web-enabled decision support solution. IQ/LiveWeb can be implemented in a matter of days and provides everything a company needs to automatically disseminate database information on an intranet.

IQ/LiveWeb takes advantage of existing intranet infrastructure and standard Internet browsers to provide a complete solution for database reporting on an intranet. IQ/LiveWeb combines IQ/Objects, an award winning object-based reporting tool, and IQ/SmartServer for comprehensive server publishing capabilities for UNIX and Windows NT.

IQ/Objects and IQ/SmartServer, generally recognized as the leading technology for sophisticated client/server reporting, are real world tested, mission critical tools. Today, these tools are in use in thousands of companies worldwide and serve as the technological foundation for IQ/LiveWeb. Extending these tools with Internet features provides several unique capabilities that set IQ/LiveWeb apart:

- Powerful, object-oriented technology enables reuse of previously developed reports and report components which makes it easy to build reports from the simplest to the most sophisticated, all without any programming or scripting.

- Support for a wide variety of report types including multi-dimensional crosstabs, tables, charts and bitmaps.

- Server-based processing and robust scheduling and administrative facilities support automatic report publishing to an intranet.

- Users can request on-demand execution of reports, taking advantage of high performance, server-based processing to initiate a database query and generate a report containing up-to-the-minute information "on-the-fly."

IQ/LiveWeb supports server-based processing and report publishing for both UNIX and Windows NT environments.

IQ/LiveWeb's object-based reporting tool lets users create simple columnar reports, multidimensional cross tabulations and charts and even sophisticated reports that combine previously created reports and information from multiple databases into one report.

IQ/LiveWeb has a familiar Microsoft Office look and feel. It offers a customizable work environment with floating toolbars and palettes, and consistent tabbed dialogs. IQ/LiveWeb is available for Windows 3.1, Windows 95 and Windows NT.

Objects can be dragged and dropped into a visual report designer to create an unlimited variety of reports. Standard templates make it easy to create professional-looking reports. Business views give users access to database tables, columns and calculated objects. URLs also can be stored as objects in the Object Directory.

IQ/LiveWeb provides a selection of chart and graph styles as well as several styles for presenting cross-tab information.

IQ/LiveWeb provides comprehensive server-based processing capabilities that make it possible to completely automate and manage the process of publishing reports. Since IQ/LiveWeb supports server-based processing in both UNIX and Windows NT environments, using servers to access databases and perform all the processing required for publishing reports is a very efficient architecture. In addition, server-based processing allows IQ/LiveWeb to support on-demand server execution of reports by end-users with access to a standard Web browser.

You can control execution schedules and decide whether existing reports are overwritten each time a new report is generated, saved for future use, or kept for some specified period then purged. Once the schedule is established, reports will continue to execute automatically until the schedule is changed.

IQ/LiveWeb reports are published in an HTML format. All users need to view them is a standard Internet browser.

IQ/LiveWeb provides complete status information for every report scheduled to be published. Comprehensive task monitoring, tracking and error handling capabilities reduce support requirements.

IQ/LiveWeb supports multiple UNIX and NT application servers, allowing scalability from dozens to hundreds or even thousands of users.

To request and view IQ/LiveWeb reports, all users need is a standard Internet browser such as Netscape Navigator or Microsoft Internet Explorer. A simple point and click is all it takes to display the desired report. In addition, users who need up-to-the-minute data can run reports in real-time with just a point and a click . . . and see the results immediately.

Using a standard Internet browser, any user can:

- Select a specific report
- View a report

- Specify a report to be executed on-demand
- Pass specific parameters to customize an on-demand report
- Drill down to linked reports for additional detail

By taking advantage of the existing Internet backbone, IQ/LiveWeb makes it possible for companies to give their users the ability to access scheduled and on-demand database information when they need it from virtually anywhere in the world. IQ/LiveWeb is a total Web-enabled reporting solution that removes the barrier between corporate information sources and the Internet, providing flexibility and robust capabilities to meet the needs of users from novice to expert.

Krakatoa

Company Name:	CADIS, Incorporated
Address:	1909 26th Street
	Boulder, CO 80302
Phone:	(303) 440–4363
URL:	`http://www.cadis.com/`

Delivered in either SUN's Java programming language or HTML/JavaScript, Krakatoa allows Web users to search through structured content by interactively refining their search criteria with attributes of interest. At each mouse-click selection, the count of qualifying items is instantly updated, allowing the user to quickly locate the products or documents of interest. Once a desired product is identified, Krakatoa enables the user to request additional product or ordering information, or request a sales contact.

National Semiconductor Corporation is using Krakatoa to publish their extensive product line of over 30,000 component parts over the Web. National's Home Page implementation is the first site of its kind that enables online interactive access to a manufacturer's product information based on attributes of interest to the user. Other customers, including Hitachi, Philips Semiconductors, Burr-Brown, Perceptive Scientific Imaging, and the CMP Group will be using Krakatoa for similar applications.

Krakatoa is an object-oriented client-server system implemented for the Web. The server software consists of the Krakatoa knowledge base management system, schema authoring tool and an API (C++ and Perl). The Java-based client is a Java applet that is downloaded from the Web browser and will run natively on PC's using MS Windows 95, MACs and Motif client systems. The HTML client has been implemented using the latest in Netscape Frames/JavaScript technology.

LivePAGE WebMaster

Company Name:	Netscape Communications Corp
Address:	501 E. Middlefield Rd.
	Mountain View, CA 94043
Phone:	(415) 937–2555
URL:	`http://www.netscape.com/comprod/products/`
	`tools/`

Our product family, known as LivePAGE, is a system of open, non-proprietary text and information management software products that takes full advantage of SGML and SQL relational database technology. LivePAGE was developed based on commonly used and generally accepted standards. It stores SGML documents in an SQL relational database, on Microsoft Windows platform, using client/server architecture. The suite of products has been designed using component architecture so that there is a seamless integration with other commonly used software products.

When a LivePAGE document is published, all of the generated HTML files and extracted graphics are saved in one directory. You can save your non-HTML files, such as sound and video, in another directory. It is unlikely that you would store these files in your LivePAGE database. The URL reference in your document would be similar to: `<img src='video/vidfile.avi'>`. In this example, the "video" subdirectory must exist and contain the file vidfile.avi.

LiveWire and LiveWire Pro

Company Name:	Netscape Communications Corp
Address:	501 E. Middlefield Rd.
	Mountain View, CA 94043
Phone:	(415) 937–2555
URL:	`http://www.netscape.com/comprod/products/tools/`

Netscape LiveWire and LiveWire Pro provide an online development environment that enables novice users to create and manage Web content, Web sites, and live online Web applications for intranets and the Internet, while offering experienced application developers the power to manage highly complex Web sites and scalable client-server applications.

Netscape LiveWire consists of: Netscape Navigator Gold, LiveWire Site Manager, LiveWire JavaScript Compiler, and LiveWire Database Connectivity Library. LiveWire database connectivity allows direct SQL connectivity to Oracle, Sybase and Informix databases and ODBC connectivity to many others.

LiveWire is fully integrated in the Netscape Enterprise Server product from Netscape. Oracle7 Workgroup Server is also currently integrated in this product.

Experienced webmasters know the difficulties of maintaining a large Web site with many pages, images, media types, and links. A single page can contain dozens of links to other pages and files. The process of managing a Web site is a challenging one. Links between pages and content can be broken easily. Universal Resource Locators (URLs) can be changed without the webmaster's knowledge, often leading unwary users into "dead ends" and "cul-de-sacs" when they link to a page that no longer exists. To solve these problems and to simplify Web site management for novice and experienced webmasters, Netscape has developed LiveWire Site Manager, a visual site-management tool for creating and managing Web sites with drag-and-drop ease.

For rapid development of client- and server-side applications without requiring extensive programming experience, Netscape and Sun Microsystems developed JavaScript.

Today, JavaScript has been widely adopted as the standard scripting language for adding "intelligence" to Web pages. With LiveWire, Netscape brings JavaScript to Web servers.

Netscape's FastTrack and Enterprise Web Servers both include the capability to run compiled JavaScript applications. The LiveWire JavaScript Compiler enables application developers to quickly and easily convert JavaScript applications and HTML pages incorporating JavaScript code into platform-independent byte codes ready to run on any Netscape Server. A simplified version of the JavaScript Compiler is also built into the LiveWire Site Manager for one-button compiling.

Microsoft FrontPage 97

Company Name:	Microsoft Corporation
Address:	10500 NE 8th Street, Suite 1300
	Bellevue, WA 98004
Phone:	(800) 426–9400
URL:	`http://www.microsoft.com/frontpage/`

FrontPage 97 with Bonus Pack makes creating professional-quality Web sites effortless powerful new functionality, support for the latest Web technologies, and seamless integration with Microsoft Office.Microsoft FrontPage 97 with Bonus Pack is a good way to get professional-quality Internet or intranet sites up and running fast. It offers all the best new Web technologies, plus powerful tools for all your creation and management tasks.

Microsoft FrontPage 97 with Bonus Pack can quickly turn you into a Webmaster. Use more than 30 built-in templates and wizards to build entire Web sites and individual pages easily. And with the WYSIWYG FrontPage Editor, there's no need to know HTML! Insert hyperlinks and add information from Microsoft Office and other sources with drag-and-drop simplicity. And manage your Web sites easily with the graphical tools in the FrontPage Explorer.

The latest Web technologies are at your fingertips. Drop WebBot components onto your pages to add such advanced functionality as full-text searching and forms. Customize your Web sites with JavaScript and Microsoft Visual Basic® Scripting Edition, using an intuitive user interface. Or easily connect to databases or add ActiveX controls, Java applets, Netscape plug-ins for interactive, compelling Web pages.

FrontPage 97 with Bonus Pack gives you powerful tools to create rich content and manage your Web sites effectively. You can enliven your Web pages with images designed in Microsoft Image Composer, included in FrontPage 97 with Bonus Pack. You can edit HTML code directly in the FrontPage Editor and preview your Web pages in any browser—without leaving FrontPage and use advanced tools to remotely author and edit your Web sites.

Oracle's Tools

The first stop in the process of selecting your application development tools should be Oracle's own offerings. Oracle has created a host of development tools and web technologies that integrate well with the Oracle Relational Database Management System. The use of these tools is safe yet can be more expensive than some of the third party Web development tools discussed in this chapter. You will find additional functionality in some of the third party tools. Indeed, Oracle is working to support the development of third party tools. Nonetheless, Oracle's efforts through the release of the Web Developer Suite and in particular Oracle Web Application Server (part of that suite), Oracle's Intranet Solutions, and Oracle's developer platforms warrant close examination.

Oracle Web Developer Suite

For a beginning to end Web application development and deployment solution using Oracle, Oracle Corporation offers Oracle Web Developer Suite. Oracle Web Developer Suite (OWDS) is actually a collection of the relevant tools Oracle offers in the database/Web arena. OWDS offers the following:

- Oracle 7 Server
- Oracle Web Application Server
- Oracle Designer/2000
- NCA Web Cartridge Developer's Kit
- Oracle InterOffice
- Oracle Developer/2000
- One year in the Oracle Developer Programme

OWDS is available on the following platforms:

- NT
- Solaris
- AIX
- HP-UX
- Digital Alpha

As you might expect, this product isn't cheap. Although the Suite is currently 15% off the regular list price, it still runs $6,400 to $10,400 depending on the platform. In the upcoming sections we will introduce you to the Oracle Web Application Server, Oracle Designer/2000, Oracle Developer/2000 and a product not in OWDS, Oracle Power Objects.

Oracle Web Application Server

The cornerstone of the Oracle Web initiative is the Web Application Server product. Oracle Web Application Server (OWAS) is a transactional Web Server supporting Novell, Spyglass, Netscape and Microsoft HTTP servers. With OWAS, you can conduct secure real time transactions through persistent Internet sessions between the significant third party browsers, OWAS allows you to develop and deploy robust commerce, business, and just about any database applications you can think of, on the Web. OWAS was voted the best new product at Spring 1997 Internet World. OWAS is available in a standard edition and an Advanced Edition. The Advanced Edition offers transaction services and multi-vendor database connectivity.

OWAS is shipped on a number of partner platforms most notably with HP 9000 Enterprise Servers and with Novell's Intranet Ware, Web Server, and NDS software. OWAS is a part of Oracle's broader Network Computing Architecture platform which is their software development initiative for building Internet applications. NCA will allow any PC or other client device to access any database server, Web Server or application server on any network supporting NCA. NDS is fully supported.

Through Web Connect Pro, a bind cartridge that plugs into OWAS, users get a secure connection to legacy applications through a host of standard browsers. So OWAS works with any client, any server, and any datatype without changes to existing legacy systems.

OWAS also contains Open Vista, a development environment allowing drag-and-drop development of Java applets that can produce simple user screens, graphical browser front-ends, and data access, manipulated and retrieval functions with legacy applications. With all it has to offer, Web Application Server is a product you should definitely look to for your Web Server. Now let's look at the developer platforms Oracle has created.

The following information, unlike the other sections in this chapter, was NOT retrieved from the vendors Web sites. In the case of Oracle Corporation, there was not sufficient time to gain the necessary approvals. Consequently, the three sections listed below were written by the author of this book:

- Designer/2000
- Developer/2000
- Power Objects

Oracle Designer/2000

Company Name:	Oracle Corporation
Address:	500 Oracle Parkway
	Redwood Shores, California 94065
Phone:	(415) 506-7000
URL:	`http://www.oracle.com/products/tools/des2k/`

Oracle Corporation's Designer/2000 product is a tool designed specifically for developing and prototyping enterprise-wide Web and non-Web information systems. This is a second generation product that delivers on the promise of assisting software developers to design computer systems that meet the specific needs of both small and world-class organizations. Designer/2000 facilitates the modeling of complex business systems. Using a common repository of information, this tool allows for flexible modeling and methodology support in a unified client/server environment using an open architecture. Used in conjunction with Developer/2000, these two tools cover the entire life cycle of an application development project.

Using Business Process Re-engineering (BPR) techniques incorporated in the tool, Designer/2000 allows the systems professional to analyze and redesign fundamental as well as complex business processes, diagramming the processes in an easy-to-understand graphical format. This tool allows you to incorporate sound, images, animation, and full motion video to construct and represent business processes.

Oracle Developer/2000

Company Name:	Oracle Corporation
Address:	500 Oracle Parkway
	Redwood Shores, California 94065
Phone:	(415) 506-7000
URL:	`http://www.oracle.com/products/tools/dev2k/`

Used in conjunction with Designer/2000, this product has the ability to allow you to design, create, and deliver complete enterprise-wide information systems without having to write a single line of code. Although the more complex your application is the greater is the likelihood of having to write some code by hand, this product certainly expedites the process.

The product consists of a number of components which, when used together, provide for full life-cycle support. When used individually, the product components allow you to easily create the following application components:

- Form-based entry, access, deletion, and modification of data stored in Oracle databases
- Generation of reports that access data stored in Oracle databases
- Creation of charts using source data stored in Oracle databases

Developer/2000 gives you, the developer, the following advantages:

- *Easy-to-use environment*—Because of the heavy use of MS Windows controls, this product is easy to use and consequently quick to become productive using
- *Scalability*—Due to the inherent architecture of the product, Developer/2000 allows you to include functionality in your applications such as: array database cursors, bind variables, savepoints, sequences, and drag-and-drop partitioning of procedures.
- *Portability*—Using Developer/2000, you can create applications in either MS Windows, Apple Macintosh, or Motif environments and deploy that application in any of those environments, as well as in a character mode environment.

Oracle Power Objects

Company Name:	Oracle Corporation
Address:	500 Oracle Parkway
	Redwood Shores, California 94065
Phone:	(415) 506-7000
URL:	`http://www.oracle.com/products/tools/power_` `objects/`

Oracle Power Objects is a highly advanced, object-oriented, client server and web database application development environment. Oracle Corporation designed this tool so that it combines the agility of popular visual programming environments with robust datahandling capabilities that you'd expect to find in an enterprise-level application development tool. The syntax of the language used by the product, Oracle Basic, is syntactically very similar to Visual Basic, with intelligent extensions to support object oriented methodologies and concepts.

Rather than relying on wizards, gadgets, or gizmos, Power Objects relies on a concept known as drag-and-drop-everything. This aids the developer in becoming productive quicker using the tool, as well as staying more productive once it is learned. The product also allows you to create reusable application components that include true multilevel inheritance from within the product.

The product not only includes native interfaces to Oracle databases, but native drivers for Microsoft SQL Server, and Sybase System 11 databases. The product also supports ActiveX controls.

Oracle Intranet Solutions

So far we have focused on major products form the Oracle but there are a number of technologies that represent pieces of NCA that you can take advantage of in creating your Web site.

Oracle Video Server. Oracle Video Server is a component of Oracle Universal Server. It allows for scaleable streaming video over the Internet, intranets, and broadband networks using a variety of compression techniques. If you wish to include streaming video in your application, you should look into Oracle Video Server.

Creating Application Cartridges. Oracle offers its NCA Web Cartridge Developer's Kit as part of the OWDS package. Oracle stands firmly behind the development of Java-based application cartridges but cartridges can be developed in multiple programming languages. Oracle has licensed VisiBroker for Java to deploy distributed applications across the Web. VisiBroker conforms to both CORBA (Common Object Request Broker Architecture) and IIOP (Internet Inter-ORB Protocol) which are both fundamental to NCA.

Oracle Internet Commerce Server. If you're interested in selling in a secure environment over the Web and want a tool that will get you there quickly, look to Internet Commerce Server. Using templates, you can quickly set up a multimedia environment that can scale, that seemlessly integrates with back-end applications, and allows for customization and easy maintenance.

Oracle Security Server. Oracle Security Server is an Oracle-specific tool used for the purposes of authentication and authorization. It provides security management for Oracle and OWAS.

Oracle Revisited

Oracle offers a number of fine products to meet the needs of the typical Web developer. If these products seem like overkill or do not meet your specific needs, then the rest of this chapter discusses useful third party products. Most of these products work with multiple database products. You will find the products arranged alphabetically for convenient lookup.

Personal Web Site (PWS) Toolbox

Company Name:	W3.COM, Incorporated
Address:	444 Castro Street #431
	Mountain View, CA 94041
Phone:	(415) 969–6760
URL:	`http://www.w3.com/`

The W3 Toolbox is a collection of four software tools that greatly reduce the time it takes to create a monster Web site. The W3 Toolbox is bundled with the Personal Web Site but can be purchased independently!

WebSpin lets you generate HTML pages automatically, from any simple flat file database, using a number of intuitive templates. WebSpin is the ideal solution for online publishing involving massive collections of identically formatted record based documents. Update your site as often as you need without having to manually edit your HTML files or program macros.

WebScan is a Web site search engine that creates search functions for a Web site. Search for one specific field or any combination of fields on flat databases and WebScan will work in conjunction with WebSpin to return customized HTML pages of matched records. Your users will be able to handle the information displayed on your site more efficiently by focusing on what's important to them.

WebForm simplifies online form handling by generating custom responses to standard HTML fill-out forms without CGI scripting. WebForm automatically saves submitted input to a text file, sends customized email to any address based on the input, and returns an HTML response to the user.

WebSweep allows the quick updating of bodies of text, which are common to multiple HTML Web pages by simply replacing common data with macros.

PowerBuilder 5.0

Company Name:	Sybase, Inc.
Address:	6475 Christie Avenue
	Emeryville, CA 94608
Phone:	(510) 922-3500
URL:	`http://www.powersoft.com/products/`
	`devtools/pb50/`

Powersoft's new Internet Developer Toolkit is packed with the Internet components, libraries, and productivity tools you need to turn PowerBuilder into a powerful Internet development environment.

If you're puzzled by HTML, or struggling with CGI programming, the Internet Developer Toolkit offers a fast and thorough solution for quickly "Web-izing" your development capabilities. For developers already familiar with the basics, the Internet Developer Toolkit offers the high productivity of point-and-click wizards, HTML controls, sample

Plug-ins, and controls for ActiveX. Leverage your distributed PowerBuilder applications to the Web with standard extensions all in a highly affordable package.

The Internet Developer Toolkit includes everything you need to build a range of Internet and intranet applications, including: PowerBuilder web.pb, PowerBuilder Window Plug-in, DataWindow Plug-in and Control for ActiveX, Internet Class Library, Personal Web Server, and the web.pb Wizard.

Distributed PowerBuilder makes a powerful and sophisticated application server environment for the Web. Now, web.pb, serves as the glue to bind Distributed Power-Builder applications to Web servers. This means developers can build high-performance database applications on the Web and take advantage of the robustness and flexibility of PowerScript and the patented DataWindow technology to generate dynamic HTML. PowerBuilder supports a true "thin client" architecture—in fact, a Web browser is all you need to run a distributed PowerBuilder application. In addition, you can access Distributed PowerBuilder applications from Web and PowerBuilder clients simultaneously, eliminating the need for multiple coding of business logic.

The PowerBuilder Window Plug-in allows developers to run existing PowerBuilder applications in a Web browser. PowerBuilder 5.0 child windows may be embedded in HTML pages and sent to Plug-in-enabled browsers when the pages are referenced. This enables you to dynamically deliver applications as needed to your users, eliminating the costly cycle of upgrade and maintenance installations. Users will be amazed to work with sophisticated presentation objects—such as Windows 95 tab controls and tree lists—inside a Web browser.

The PowerBuilder DataWindow is Powersoft's patented technology for manipulating and presenting database information. As a Plug-in or ActiveX control used to extend your browser, the DataWindow adds richly formatted presentation of query results to an otherwise bland HTML document.

Now your Web applications will benefit from a class library designed to enable "state management"—the maintenance of session or state information across HTML pages—critical to application server development. The Internet Developer Toolkit also provides PowerBuilder objects that create advanced HTML forms, such as a form with a dropdown list box or radio set, from a DataWindow result set.

The Internet Developer Toolkit includes Web site™ 1.1 from O'Reilly and Associates, a 32-bit multithreaded World Wide Web server for Windows NT 3.5 (or higher) and Windows 95 platforms. WebSite 1.1 provides a tree-like display of all the documents and links on your server with an easy-to-use facility for locating and repairing broken links.

Using CGI, you can run a desktop application within a Web document on WebSite. Its also features access security to the different areas of your Web server. And because of its support for ODBC, you have full access to your Oracle databases.

A major productivity tool for connecting your distributed PowerBuilder applications to the Web, web.pb Wizard will automatically generate the HTML forms you need to make appropriate calls to your distributed applications. For example, this wizard helps locate the server, then helps you pick which non-visual user object (NVO) to use, which function within the NVO, and which arguments to pass to the NVO. Then, it creates the HTML form and code required to send the request.

The Internet Developer Toolkit also includes: Samples and examples for Plug-ins, libraries, web.pb, and ActiveX controls.

Sapphire/Web

Company Name:	Bluestone Software
Address:	1000 Briggs Road
	Mount Laurel, NJ 08054
Phone:	(609) 727-4600
URL:	`http://www.bluestone.com/`

For developers creating network computing applications, Sapphire/Web is the Web-and-Java-to-database development tool that makes it easy to create high-performance Internet/Intranet applications. Unlike other tools that deliver server-side only solutions and technology look-in, Sapphire/Web offers Interactive Java client and server-side business logic in an open approach giving you the choice of Java, ActiveX, and the security and scalability to meet the needs of Enterprise-Wide and World-Wide applications.

Sapphire/Web is designed to work in a manner similar to other application builders for Windows and Motif. And, via an ODBC interface, allows access to and support for your Oracle databases.

Sapphire/Web also provides for testing and loading of the application program in the specified http server.

SiteBase

Company Name:	Cykic Software
Address:	123 Camino De La Reina, Suite
	San Diego, CA 92108
Phone:	(619) 220-7970
URL:	`http://www.cykic.com/`

Hype-It 3000 is a Web server with built-in relational database and developers tools. It is a complete Web program development environment allowing you to create any full-blown database (including Oracle, Access, Sybase, and Informix) application accessible to Web clients through CGI (Common Gateway Interface). This is a developer's server and tool set. To make use of Hype-It 3000, xBase programming skills are necessary. If you or your clients require the full power of Hype-It 3000, you must provide the programming, or at your option, we can contract to provide custom programming, to your specifications.

The development environment of Hype-It 3000 is the MultiBase operating system/database language. This environment offer the following:

- Supports a multi-user, multi-tasking program development (dBASE-like dot prompt) environment.
- Allows the programmer to create CGI programs to function with HTML documents.
- Supports native xBASE language—a composite of FoxPro, dBASE, Clipper, and over 150 function extensions.

- Gives Hype-It a developer's environment for writing code to interface to the Web server.
- Supports relational databases for Web applications.
- Supports powerful search functions for text or data search requirements.
- Includes graphics library for image manipulation and graphic image database types.
- Includes fax functions to tie into the Web application (fax-back abilities)
- Supports programmers tools for debugging; cross-reference; text editing.
- Supports multiple workstations for program development across a LAN.
- Gives programmers TCP/IP functions for direct access to the Internet: ping a site, send e-mail, reverse name look-up, etc.

Tango

Company Name:	Everyware Development Corporation
Address:	6733 Mississauga Rd., 7th Floor
	Mississauga, Ontario Canada L5N 6J5
Phone:	(905) 819.1173
URL:	`http://www.everyware.com/products/tango/`

Tango allows developers to create dynamic Web applications that are integrated with databases. Tango allows you to integrate data from any ODBC database including Oracle, Sybase, Informix, SQL Server, FoxPro, and Microsoft Access. Tango's versatility lets you easily create Web applications on Windows NT, Windows 95 or Macintosh and deploy your solutions on your Web servers running on Windows NT, Macintosh, or Solaris.

WebHub

Company Name:	HREF Tools Corporation
Address:	316 Occidental Avenue South, Suite 406
	Seattle, WA 98104
Phone:	(206) 812–0177
URL:	`http://www.href.com/`

WebHub technology provides a complete object oriented framework for industrial strength web application development.

WebHub is Fast! The apps you build with WebHub components will compile to native Intel machine code. Screamin' fast. Typical non-db page requests take 15 to 50 milliseconds. With a strong database server, you can easily serve a million new surfers a day. With just a P90 and 32meg RAM on NT, you can serve three dynamic pages per second.

WebHub is proven technology. WebHub has been chosen by MCI, Lockheed-Martin, Conoco, the states of California, Utah, Georgia, and Massachusetts, SecureTax, and many other organizations that needed to write applications for the web.

WebHub is reliable. Compared to writing your own web interface for ISAPI or CGI, you'll find that it's much easier to use a fully tested, 60Kb, WebHub "runner" and stay focused on your real goal! WebHub has been tested by thousands of developers.

WebHub saves you development time. Re-use your existing code and skills. Web-Hub's architecture promotes re-use in every way—of HTML as well as program logic. By using the WebHub framework, you save weeks of work. A complete, extensible save-state mechanism is built-in to the system.

WebHub is flexible. No brick walls. No limits. WebHub is solid OOP technology for the Delphi and C++ application builder that needs to build an application with Oracle (and other ODBC compliant RDBMS products) access. It's designed to give you maximum development speed with plenty of room to be creative.

Webinator

Company Name:	Thunderstone Corporation
Address:	11115 Edgewater Drive
	Cleveland, OH 44102
Phone:	(216) 631–8544
URL:	`http://www.thunderstone.com/`

Webinator is a Web walking and indexing package that will allow a Website administrator to create and provide a high quality retrieval interface to collections of HTML documents, including those documents that support access to Oracle databases. Webinator serves as an example of the type of applications that can be built around Thunderstone's Texis RDBMS.

From the Administrator's perspective Webinator offers the following benefits:

- Indexes multiple sites into one common index.
- Provides detailed verification and logging of document linkages.
- Will index/update documents while database is in use.
- Allows multiple databases at a site.
- Provides an SQL query interface to the database for maintenance and reports.
- Allows remote sites to be copied to the local file system.
- Multiple index engines may run concurrently against a common database.
- Adobe Acrobat/PDF file support (commercial version option only)

From the User's perspective Webinator offers:

- Simple navigation.
- Included with the products is a powerful and easy to use capability to construct queries for:
- Natural language
- Set logic
- Special pattern matchers (regular expressions, quantities, fuzzy patterns)
- Relevance ranking
- Proximity controls
- Document similarity searches (Doc Surfing).

- Link reference reports.
- In Context result listings.

WebObjects

Company Name:	NeXT Software, Inc.
Address:	900 Chesapeake Drive
	Redwood City, CA 94063
Phone:	(415) 366-0900
URL:	`http://www.next.com/webobjects/`

WebObjects is an environment for developing and deploying World Wide Web applications. For development, it provides a scripting language and objects that you use to create Web applications. For deployment, it provides a system of interrelated components that connect your WebObjects applications to the Web.

WebObjects applications are portable across a wide variety of operating systems and hardware platforms. These include:

- Solaris
- Windows NT
- HP-UX

Industry-standard databases from Oracle, Sybase and Informix can be accessed from a WebObjects application without writing database specific code.

WebObjects gives you all the benefits of object technology. At the same time, it scales to accommodate the complexity of your programming tasks. You can create simple applications without having to compile anything—just implement the logic in scripts.

Scripted applications can even access your corporate database. For more complex tasks, you can easily combine WebObjects with your own compiled objects.

WebObjects is designed to help corporations create dynamic, server-based applications for the World Wide Web. These applications can be deployed on a company's internal network or externally to the general public.

WebObjects is especially suited to sophisticated applications that need to serve large numbers of clients. WebObjects is also designed to leverage a company's current investments in technology, data, and training.

Many companies are trying to build sophisticated Web applications in order to improve productivity, better respond to customer's needs and generate new business opportunities. Delivering on these goals has proven to be a difficult, if not impossible task. Robust web applications are often difficult to create because existing web development tools prevent companies from:

- Leveraging their investments in existing applications and data
- Integrating with complimentary technologies—Web-based and others
- Deploying robust Web solutions in a timely fashion

WebObjects is designed to preserve investments in existing computing resources. Using this technology, Web applications can be easily integrated with legacy technology and data.

Companies can leverage their existing investment in the following areas:

- Windows applications
- Mainframe applications
- Hardware
- Databases
- CORBA 2.0 objects

For example, a WebObjects application can be designed to extend an existing order management system to the World Wide Web. By extending the application in this fashion, the public can place orders directly via the World Wide Web.

The Web application can add value, coexist and share information with the existing order management system. In this case, WebObjects brings the company closer to its customers by allowing them to use the World Wide Web. It also minimizes the costs of doing so by seamlessly integrating the Web application with their existing order management system.

WebObjects supports all major Web standards with the flexibility to embrace new technologies as they evolve. WebObjects supports the creation of web applications implemented with Sun Microsystems' Java language. Within a WebObjects application, Java can execute as both client-side applets and server-side business engines. WebObjects offers browser and HTTP server independence.

WebObjects supports native HTTP server APIs. WebObjects provides a scripting framework for application creation, allowing developers to use the language of their choice such as Perl or JavaScript.

WebObjects provides the foundation for the development of robust Web applications. With WebObjects, developers need only focus on implementing relevant business logic. Developers are isolated from the complexities of combining their business logic with HTML and data access to form a complete web application. This segmentation accelerates the development of Web applications.

Moving On

The realm of Web database application development suites is rapidly evolving. If it is true that the vendors of PC software products have abandoned the yearly cycle of major product upgrades, it is particularly true that Web database tool vendors are on a more aggressive release schedule. By the time you read these words, there no doubt will be new versions of some of the products listed, as well as some new products that have not been listed at all.

The information in this chapter is as factual and timely as possible. If you see a product or range of products that interest you, take a look at their Web page. You will also find evaluation copies of the majority of the products evaluated on the CD-ROM accompanying this book.

Beginning with Chapter 6, we will lay the foundation for considerations in designing, building, and maintaining a Web database application. Chapter 6 specifically presents an overview of HTML and introduces you to the command syntax you would use to create your Web pages.

CHAPTER 6
Overview
of HTML

This chapter is an overview of the HyperText Markup Language (HTML). Hyper-Text Markup Language is a specific language (just as Java and C are other types of programming languages) used by Web browsers to display text, images, graphics, hyperlinks, and play audio or video files. If you are new to the Web, this chapter gives you a good introduction to what HTML is, how to read it, write it, and how to use it. If you are an experienced Web developer or user, you too will find useful information in this chapter on topics such as the structure of HTML, advanced HTML topics, good HTML coding practices, and the future of HTML.

Have you ever looked at an ASCII file of a word processed document? If so, then you probably noticed a lot of codes around what was just text in your document. These codes are understood by the word processor and help it format the text. HTML is analogous to the word processor codes, acting as a standard for Internet applications.

HTML describes how the data is to be displayed, *not* how it should be laid out. HTML lets you describe pieces of information such as headers, lists, and inline images. It does not let you describe a header as being 32-point Arial, or a bulleted list with a checkmark (✓) for a bullet. In the future, HTML will support such page layout and presentation functions, but the future is not here now.

HTML is a wonderful facility for defining how data appears on a Web page, but it is not very good at describing how it is to be laid out. For example, it is very easy to describe a text string as appearing in bold typeface, but it is very difficult to position that same text string 1.275" from the top border and 3.250" from the left border. HTML is not a desktop publisher—yet.

As you'll see later in this chapter, HTML specifications are evolving to include more page layout capabilities. This trend is certainly expected to continue. Much the same as

PC-based word processing tools are evolving so that the distinction between word processors and page layout packages are becoming blurred, so too will HTML specifications evolve to include more page layout control.

The information in this chapter is important to you to fully understand Chapter 13, which is HTML Forms and Database Access. Whereas HTML used by itself to display static information drawn from non-database sources has been its traditional use, tools and technologies recently developed and currently being developed extend its core functionality to that of database access and dynamic page presentation. With WYSIWYG editors and generators, these new tools have the effect of moving the user further and further away from writing hard HTML code. I do believe, though, that it will be a very long time before Web page designers and developers do not need to know and understand HTML.

Introduction to HTML

Creating a Web page using HTML is actually quite simple. As you'll see in this chapter, there are a limited number of commands (in HTML terminology these are called "tags'" and "tag pairs") that are easy to remember. Although a large selection of tools exist to facilitate and expedite HTML editing, if you have access to a text editor or word processor, you can do it.

HTML stands for HyperText Markup Language. "HyperText Markup" means the character strings that are embedded in a text file and are designed to cause text to display in a specified format in a Web browser. HTML uses tags and tag pairs to accomplish this formatting. HTML documents consist of the following:

- The data that is to be displayed on a Web page that is either included directly in the file that contains the HTML code, which is termed *static*, or is retrieved from an external source such as a database query, which is termed *dynamic*.

- The structure of the data, such as headings, paragraphs, and so on—these are the tags and tag pairs.

    HTML supports the following features:

- Structure of a document
- Text formatting
- Style of lists
- Format and layout of tables
- Inline graphics images and the placement of text around those images
- Hypertext anchors
- Image maps (An image map is a feature in HTML that allows a user to click in different portions of a graphic image to link to different HTML documents.)
- E-mail
- Forms to transmit user supplied data to the server

    The code snippet below is a sample of HTML code that formats data on a Web page. Figure 6–1 is a screen print of that page as seen in a browser.

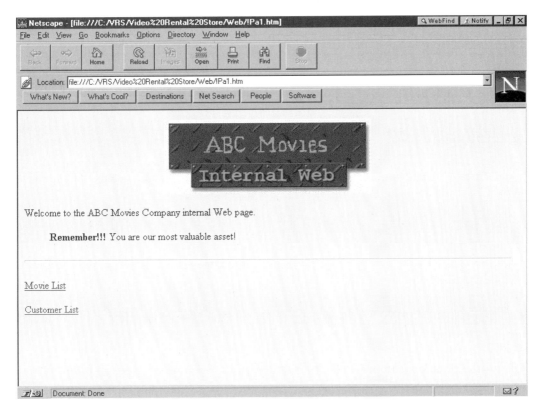

Figure 6–1 The WEB page of the HTML code in the above code.

```
<HTML>
<HEAD>
<TITLE>ABC MOVIES INTERNAL WEB SITE</TITLE>
<P ALIGN=CENTER><IMG SRC="SimpFold/Images/INT_WEB.jpg" WIDTH=322
HEIGHT=117></P>
<P>Welcome to the ABC Movies Company internal Web page. </P>
<BLOCKQUOTE><P><STRONG><FONT SIZE="+0">Remember!!!</FONT></STRONG> You are our
most valuable asset!</P></BLOCKQUOTE>
<P><HR></P>
<P><A HREF="Page2.html">Movie List</A></P>
<P><A HREF="CustList.htm">Customer List</A></P>
<P> </P>
</BODY>
</HTML>
```

Benefits of HTML

Although you really don't have much of a choice when deciding to build a Web database application (you *really should* use HTML), you should be aware of some of the benefits available by using HTML. These are:

- A rapid development environment, especially with the crop of HTML editors and Web application development suites coming available.

- Extensive cross-platform support that is so important when deploying an application over the Internet.

- Support for multiple types of media to be included in the page, such as audio, video, images, and text.

Limitations of HTML

Like everything else in the world of computing, HTML is not free from limitations. Although the standard is rapidly evolving to remove many of these limitations, the day will probably never come when this tool is free from limitations.

The limitations of HTML as a Web page development tool are:

- Limited user-input capabilities.

- Cannot specifically locate an object (for example, place a text box in row 12, column 25).

- Limited programmatic capabilities (for example, HTML relies on interfaces to modules developed in other languages to execute complex logic).

Tags

Tags are ASCII characters or an ASCII character string delimited by angle brackets (< >) that contain a HTML formatting command. HTML uses tags and tag pairs to instruct the browser how to format the document sent to it. Tags and tag pairs also instruct the browser what to do with audio clips, video files, and graphic image files. Additionally, tags and tag pairs are used to specify hypertext links, accept user input, and launch programs via the Common Gateway Interface (CGI). Hypertext is text in a HTML page that links one page to another. It is usually bound by a blue border. In graphics browsers, the mouse pointer may convert to a hand when passed over the hypergraphic. You'll learn more about tags and tag pairs later in this chapter.

HTML is termed a markup language in that the HTML codes, what are called tags in HTML terminology, are embedded in the text itself. For example, in the previous HTML code snippet is the following line:

```
<P>Movie List</P>
```

The HTML code in this example is everything to the left and right of the words: Movie List. You'll notice one of the basic constructs of the HTML language—HTML tags are keywords that are enclosed in the characters "<" and ">." These tags have specific meanings and cause text to format and display in a specific manner.

HTML tags that format a block of text always come in pairs. However, not all tag-pairs are formatting commands for text. There are a number of HTML tags that are independent of text and include no text. For example, the <HTML> and </HTML> tags identify the information contained between this tag pair as an HTML-formatted document.

HTML Conformance

Although the examples in the previous HTML code snippet and Figure 6–1 are a very simple rendition, it does give you an idea of the structure and syntax of HTML. You can see that the HTML snippet consists of special formatting tags included to describe the layout and presentation of the page. HTML documents are based on the Standard Generalized Markup Language (SGML), with generalized formatting tags used to present information on the screen in a wide range of domains. SGML is a document description language, of which HTML is a subset.

SGML is an internationally recognized standard of document exchange over the internet. HTML is a subset of this specification. HTML documents are SGML documents with an important distinction—HTML documents use generic semantics to form and present information. Together with URLs and HTTP, HTML forms the foundation of the World Wide Web.

There are five levels of specifications to the HTML language. The HTML code that you write should conform to a standard that is no higher than the standard supported by the HTML specification supported by the browsers the people accessing your application are using. For example, Netscape Navigator and Microsoft Internet Explorer browsers both support up through level 3.2, but do not support the level 4 specifications yet. They do support aspects of it and so are, in some respects, "ahead of the game." These five levels of specifications are:

- *Level 0*: This level describes HTML structure and comment elements, as well as headings. Also included in this level are header, list, and image specifications.
- *Level 1*: This level describes image-handling and character formatting and display specifications.
- *Level 2*: This level describes forms and character definition specifications.
- *Level 3.2*: This level describes tables, figures, and graphical backdrops (backdrops are synonymous with wallpaper in a Windows environment) specifications.
- *Level 4*: This level is not yet ratified but describes the formatting and use of mathematical specifications.

Now that you've been introduced to the basic concepts and features of HTML, the following section introduces you to the structure of HTML tags. You will see how easy it is to write the HTML tags and tag pairs to accomplish a wide variety of data display styles.

Structure of HTML

This chapter is not intended to be a thorough presentation on HTML. There are many volumes written that are devoted singularly to this topic. Rather, this chapter, and more specifically, this section, is written to give you an overview of HTML and get you to begin to think about how you could use HTML in the development of your Web database application.

At present, HTML specifications impose no restrictions on using upper or lower case characters when writing tags and tag pairs, and I know of no browser that cares about it. Most of the code examples in this book are written in upper case for readability purposes only.

Header and Document Tags

There is usually a pair of tags that officially mark the beginning and ending of the HTML document. These are <html> and </html>. Although most browsers do not require this tag pair to work, you should include it if for no other reason than it has been a part of every HTML standard published. Included within this tag-pair are two major components: the header and the body. As you'd expect, there is a tag-pair to identify the beginning and end of each of these sections.

The HTML code earlier shows the use of the html, head, and body tag-pairs. Specifically, these are:

```
<HTML>
   <HEAD>
   </HEAD>
   <BODY>
   </BODY>
</HTML>
```

> The indentation in the code above is for readability—HTML standards include no requirement to indent tags and tag pairs.

In addition to the document, header, and body tag-pairs, you'll notice one more tag-pair. This is the Document Title tag, which reads:

```
<TITLE>ABC MOVIES INTERNAL WEB SITE</TITLE>
```

The document title tag is used inside the <HEAD> tag pair to identify the content of the current HTML document. The text you supply inside the <TITLE> . . . </TITLE> tag pair appears centered on the title bar in a users browser. Although this is not a required tag, it is good practice to include it.

Tip: Many search engines use the text contained in the <Title> tag as a search index. Bear this in mind when creating your <Title> tag line.

Body Tags

Body tags are the formatting codes used within the <BODY> tag-pairs. These tags can be placed in the following groupings:

- Headings
- Block Elements
- Lists

- Text
- Anchors
- Images

This section describes many of the commands in these groups.

Headings.   HTML specifications provide for six levels of headings, although you will probably never use more than two or three. These six are shown in the snippet of HTML code below:

```
<HTML>
<HEAD>
<TITLE>Demo</TITLE>
</HEAD><BODY>
<H1>This is an example of Heading 1</H1>
<H2>This is an example of Heading 2</H2>
<H3>This is an example of Heading 3</H3>
```

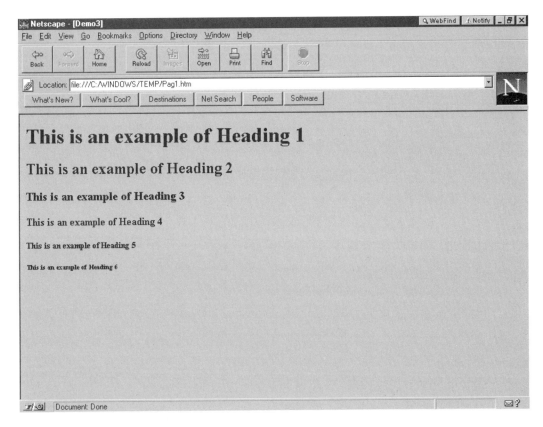

Figure 6–2   Generated HTML header levels as seen in a browser.

```
<H4>This is an example of Heading 4</H4>
<H5>This is an example of Heading 5</H5>
<H6>This is an example of Heading 6</H6>
</BODY>
</HTML>
```

Headings (`<H1></H1>` through `<H6></H6>`), as seen listed above, are not to be confused with a header tag pair (`<HEAD></HEAD>`). The information contained within the header tag pair does not display on a Web page and is intended to identify a section of the HTML document. Headings do display on the Web page.

Tip: Because Web browsers handle formatting differently, you should experiment with Headings to pick the one best suited for your page(s). There is no requirement that an `<H2>` tag follow an `<H1>` tag. To the contrary, think of each of the six heading levels as completely independent of each other—they are formatting styles.

Block Elements. Text information is formatted into paragraphs in HTML pages. The formatting of these paragraphs and the type of formatting between the paragraphs are block elements. The block elements described in this section are:

- Paragraph tags `<p>` and `</p>`
- Blockquote tags `<BLOCKQUOTE>` and `</BLOCKQUOTE>`
- Horizontal rule tags `<HR>`
- Address tags `<ADDRESS>` and `</ADDRESS>`

The code snippet below is the HTML example of the most used block elements, while Figure 6–3 is a screen print of these block elements.

```
<HTML>
<HEAD>
<TITLE>Miscellaneous Stuff</TITLE>
<BODY>
<P>This is a paragraph.</P>
<P>This is a second paragraph.</P>
<BLOCKQUOTE>This is a block quote that demonstrates the formatting and
display
characteristics of the &lt;blockquote&gt; and &lt;/blockquote&gt; tag
pair.
It should appear in a browser as an indented block of text.</BLOCKQUOTE>
<P><HR></P>
<P>This is an address:</P>
<ADDRESS>1122 SE 1st Avenue</ADDRESS>
<ADDRESS>Gresham, Oregon 97030</ADDRESS>
</BODY>
</HTML>
```

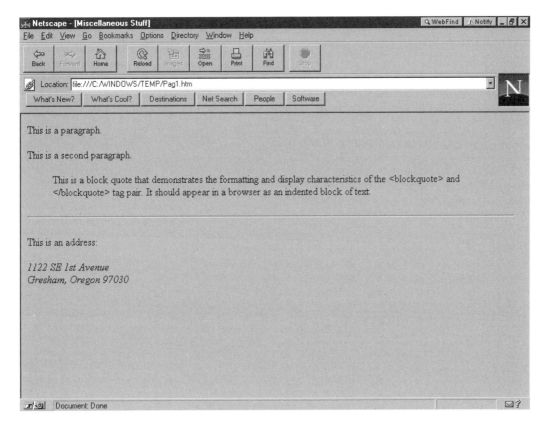

Figure 6–3   Generated HTML block elements as seen in a browser.

Paragraph tags (<p> and </p>) are used to format the text between the tag pair into a consistent looking paragraph, separated from other paragraphs and objects by a blank line.

Tip: To insert a blank line in a Web page, you could use the <P> tag without a closing </P>. If you use the <P><P> combination, this inserts two blank lines.

Blockquote tags (<BLOCKQUOTE> and </BLOCKQUOTE>) are used to indent text, as you'd expect in a cited quotation.

Horizontal rule tag (<HR>) is used to draw a straight line horizontally across the full width of the page. You'll notice that this tag does not have a matching </HR>. These types of tags are less frequent than tag pairs, but nonetheless present. The reason there is no accompanying end tag (</HR>) is that such a tag would be redundant—the <HR> tag extends the full width of the Web page.

Address tags (<ADDRESS> and </ADDRESS>) are used to contain address-type information in a formatted and indented manner on a Web page.

Tip: Since all document formatting is accomplished by tag pairs, blank lines, indentations, and white space that you might add in the HTML source is ignored by Web browsers. There are special tags that handle indentation and blank lines which are presented later.

Lists.   Lists are a common feature in most Web pages. HTML specifications provide for four types of lists. These are: Unordered list, Ordered list, Menu list, and Definition list. As seen in the code below, the HTML code to create these various lists is simple. Depending on the type of list you define, the output will vary, as seen in Figure 6–4.

```
<HTML>
<HEAD>
<TITLE>Demo</TITLE>
</HEAD>
<BODY>
<UL>
```

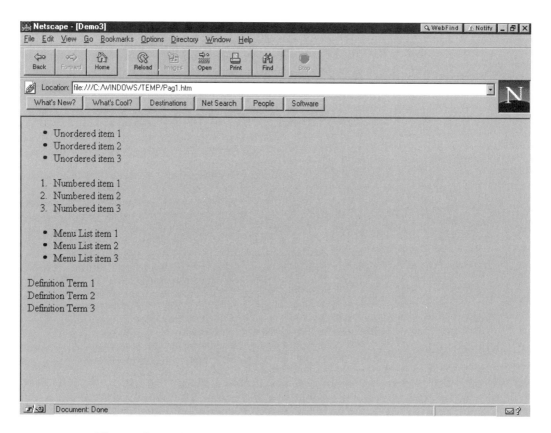

Figure 6–4   Generated HTML lists as seen in a browser.

```
<LI>Unordered item 1</LI>
<LI>Unordered item 2</LI>
<LI>Unordered item 3</LI>
</UL>
<OL>
<LI>Numbered item 1</LI>
<LI>Numbered item 2</LI>
<LI>Numbered item 3</LI>
</OL>
<MENU>
<LI>Menu List item 1</LI>
<LI>Menu List item 2</LI>
<LI>Menu List item 3</LI>
</MENU>
<DL>
<DT>Definition Term 1</DT>
<DT>Definition Term 2</DT>
<DT>Definition Term 3</DT>
</DL>
</BODY>
</HTML>
```

The first list, the unordered item list, is identified by the <UL>...</UL> tag pair and is used to identify list items that should be grouped together, but without a number preceding each item in the list.

The second list, the numbered item list, is identified by the <OL>...</OL> tag pair and is used to identify list items that should be grouped together and preceded by a number.

The third list, the menu item list, is identified by the <MENU>...</MENU> tag pair. It is used in much the same way as the unordered item list in that it identifies list items that should be grouped together without a preceding number. However, some browsers present the items in a menu list in a more compact format than unordered list items.

The fourth list, the definition list, is identified by the <DL>...</DL> tag pair. It is used occasionally to separate a word or word-string from its definition in a consistent manner. However, as seen in Figure 6–4 it can also be used to present a list of items without a preceding bullet or number.

Text. Text characters can be one of four styles, and these styles can be mixed in any configuration. The code snippet below shows the HTML code to define a number of different text styles, while Figure 6–5 shows what the HTML code looks like in a browser.

```
<HTML>
<HEAD>
<TITLE>Demo</TITLE>
</HEAD>
<BODY>
<P>Normal Text</P>
<P><STRONG>Bold (Strong) Text</STRONG></P>
<P><EM>Italicized Text</EM></P>
```

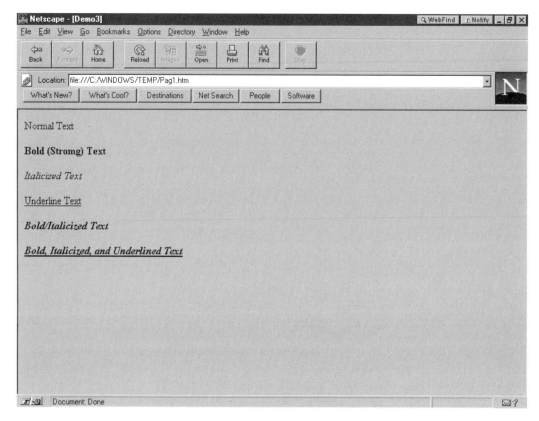

Figure 6–5   Generated HTML formatted text as seen in a browser.

```
<P><STRONG><EM><U>Bold, Italicized, and Underlined Text</U></EM></STRONG></P>
</BODY>
</HTML>
```

Tip: There is an additional tag called emphasis. Its tag pair is `<EM>` and `</EM>`. This was a tag developed primarily for text-only Web browsers and usually translates in GUI browsers to an italicized font. You should probably avoid the emphasis tag (`<EM>`) and use the italics tag (`<I>` and `</I>`) if you want your text to appear italicized.

You'll notice in the HTML code above that highlighted (bold) text is written using the `<STRONG>`...`</STRONG>` tag pair. Most people that write HTML code prefer to use the `<B>`...`</B>` tag pair. Also, where I have used the `<EM>`...`</EM>` tag pair, most people prefer to use the `<I>`...`</I>` tag pair. In a GUI-based Web browser, each of these are interchangeable with the other—it makes no difference. However, in a text based browser the `<B>`...`</B>` and `<I>`...`</I>` tag pairs do nothing to control the format of text. I've developed the habit of using the more universally consistent tag pairs to avoid problems in certain Web browsers.

You can combine tag pairs for some interesting effects. For example, you can write a line of HTML code as: `<EM><U><H1>Scruples—The Movie</H1></U></EM>`. This creates a Heading1 that is underlined and italicized.

Anchor Tags. Anchor tags are a mechanism in HTML to create links to other Web documents or sites. The syntax for anchor tags is `<A>...</A>`. Optional attributes that you can include inside the `<A>` anchor tag allow you to build a link from the current location in the Web page to one of the following:

- Another section in the same Web page
- Another Web page
- Images
- Audio files
- Application programs

When these attributes are used within an anchor tag, this is frequently referred to as a hyperlink, or hypertext link. The difference is that a hyperlink is a link to one of the above types of entities from a graphic element that the user clicks on while a hypertext link is a link to one of the above types of entities from a text string that the user clicks on.

Tip: The anchor tag is one of the few HTML tags that requires a parameter. In this case, it requires the URL for the linked Web document as well as a text string that is displayed in the Web browser.

```
<HTML>
<HEAD>
</HEAD>
<P ALIGN=CENTER><IMG SRC="SimpFold/Images/INT_WEB.jpg" WIDTH=322
HEIGHT=117></P>
<P>Welcome to the ABC Movies Company internal Web page. </P>
<BLOCKQUOTE><P><STRONG><FONT SIZE="+0">Remember!!!</FONT></STRONG> You are our
most valuable asset!</P></BLOCKQUOTE>
<P> <A HREF="Page2.html">Movie List</A></P>
<P> <A HREF="CustList.htm">Customer List</A> </P>
</BODY>
</HTML>
```

To use an anchor tag pair, you specify the attribute name, followed by an equal sign, followed by its "value"—the "value" being the linked reference. The following line appears in the above code sample:

```
<A HREF="Page2.html">Movie List</A>
```

In this line of code, a link is made to the Page2.html document when a user clicks on the line of text on the page that reads "Movie List." Figure 6–6 shows the correct formatting of the anchor pairs in a Web browser.

There are two basic types of images recognized by HTML. These are inline images and image maps. Inline images are graphic pictures (usually) that serve many purposes, such as:

- provide smaller (often referred to as "thumbnail") images that are hyperlinked to a larger version of the same image
- window selection buttons
- block off an area on the page (this is done with a clear image) so that text can flow around the graphic
- add color and enhancements to an otherwise dull and blah page

Image maps are graphic objects that allow the Web client to identify specific locations within an image that the user has clicked on.

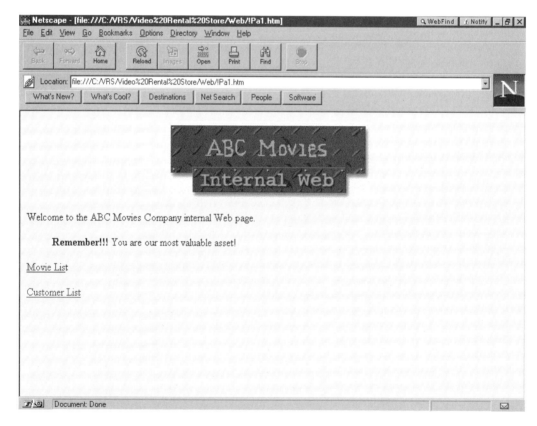

Figure 6–6   Generated HTML code for anchors as seen in a browser.

Tip: Image maps are a great resource for Web database applications. For example, an image map of the United States could be created so that as a user clicked on a region or state within the image map and a customized query would run against a database extracting statistical information specific to the selected region or state.

There are a number of formats for the graphic files used as inline images and image maps. Although the most common are GIF and JPEG, many others are supported by browsers. If possible though, you should use GIF and JPEG as these are the standard formats.

Multimedia and graphics are fast becoming the most popular component on Web pages. With the release of HTML specification 0—the very first one issued, these were supported. The tag for including images in a HTML page is `<img src="`*filename* `(specifications . . .)">`.

Referring back to the HTML code sample above, you see the following line of HTML code:

```
<IMG SRC="SimpFold/Images/INT_WEB.jpg" WIDTH=322 HEIGHT=117>
```

This line of HTML code instructs the browser to:

- Retrieve a graphics file named int_web.jpg from the SimpFold/Images subdirectory on the current machine.
- Display this image at the location on the Web page where this line of HTML code was encountered, where the image dimensions are 322 × 117 pixels.

The result of this line of HTML code is seen in the top-most graphic in Figure 6–6.

Tip: To learn more about image maps, you should visit the following site:

`http://hoohoo.ncsa.uiuc.edu/docs/tutorials/imagemapping.html`.

Because of the interest in extending the graphical aspects of Web pages and browsers, the format and syntax of the `<img src>` tag is changing rapidly. It is prudent to spend a little time to investigate the support provided by the tools in your development environment for the `<img src>` tag. Also, don't forget to consider the types and release levels of browsers that the people accessing your Web pages are using.

Netscape Communications has developed extensions to the IMG tag. Not to be outdone in the quest to make something that is magnificently scalable (like the Web), regrettably unscalable, Microsoft Corporation has released a powerful series of their own HTML extensions.

Comments and Special Characters. Comments are specified in HTML code by enclosing them in a special tag pair, which is: `<!— comment goes here —>`. Additionally, if you want to have a left arrow (<) or right arrow (>) display on a page, you have to format the source HTML code with special characters. Some of these are listed in Table 6–1.

Table 6–1   Special Characters in HTML

Character String	Character Displayed
&lt	<
&gt	>
&amp	&
&quot	"
&copy	©

Tip: Any ASCII character can be displayed on an HTML page by preceeding the ASCII code for the character by an ampersand (&).

The code sample below shows what the HTML code would look like for the above special characters, while Figure 6–7 shows what this code looks like in a Web browser.

```
<HTML>
<HEAD>
<TITLE>Demo</TITLE>
</HEAD>
<BODY>
<P>Less than sign: &lt;</P>
<P>Greater than sign: &gt;</P>
<P>Ampersand sign: &amp;</P>
<P>Double quote sign: &quot;</P>
<P>At sign: @</P>
<P>Copyright symbol: &copy;</P>
</BODY>
</HTML>
```

Tables.   The ability to define tables was added to HTML with the level 3 specifications. Consequently, some users may not be able to view the tables you include in your Web pages in the format that you've defined for them. This is because some browsers don't support HTML specification 3. Netscape Navigator and Microsoft Internet Explorer both do however.

There are a number of tag pairs that you can use to define the specification of a table. These are seen in the HTML code sample below and are also defined below:

`<TABLE> . . . </TABLE>`	Marks the beginning and end of a table definition.
`<TR> . . . </TR>`	Specifies the number of rows and the vertical/horizontal alignment of the data that appears in the rows.

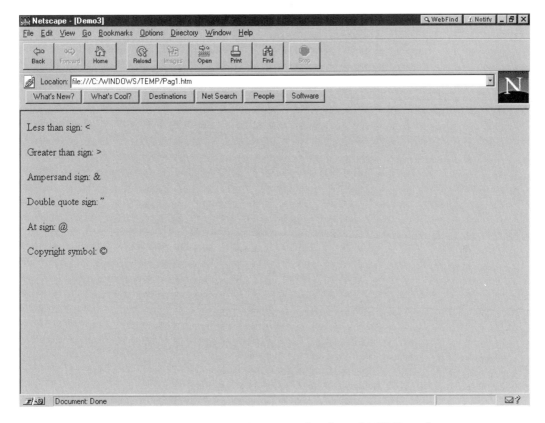

Figure 6–7 The Web browser display of HTML codes.

`<TD> . . . </TD>`	Defines a table cell that appears in a row as well as the alignment and other text attributes of the data that appears in the cells.
`<TH> . . . </TH>`	Defines the table header. Header cells are identical to data cells in all respects except header cells text appears in boldface and is centered in the cell.
`<CAPTION> . . . </CAPTION>`	Defines and describes the caption for a table, if one exists.

The code sample below shows what the HTML markups are to define a simple 4 row by 2 column table. Figure 6–8 shows what this table looks like in a browser.

```
<HTML>
<HEAD>
<TITLE>Demo</TITLE>
</HEAD>
<BODY>
```

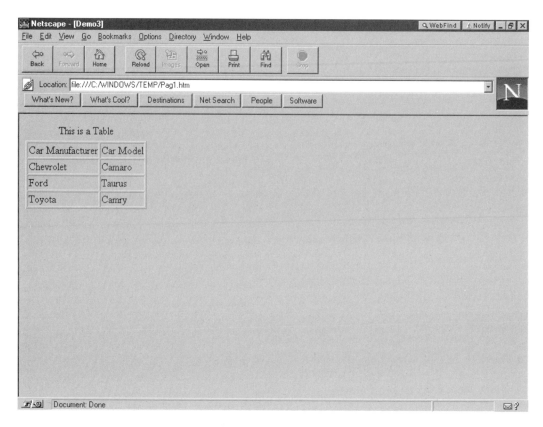

Figure 6–8 The Web browser display of a table.

```
<TABLE BORDER=1><CAPTION ALIGN=TOP>This is a Table</CAPTION>
<TR>
<TD><STRONG>Car Manufacturer</STRONG></TD>
<TD><STRONG>Car Model</STRONG></TD>
</TR>
<TR>
<TD>Chevrolet</TD>
<TD>Camaro</TD>
</TR>
<TR>
<TD>Ford</TD>
<TD>Taurus</TD>
</TR>
<TR>
<TD>Toyota</TD>
<TD>Camry</TD>
</TR>
```

```
</TABLE>
</BODY>
</HTML>
```

URLs

Uniform Resource Locators (URLs) are used by Servers to identify and locate documents. Although many people believe that each document or site must have its own unique URL, this is not the case. As the Web continues to burgeon, the instances of duplicated URLs increases.

The structure of an URL is fairly specific, and includes an identification of the type of resources, the address of the Server the resources are located on, and the location of the document. The syntax for an URL is:

```
resource://host.domain[:port]/path/filename [cgi parameters]
```

The following are valid URLs, going from the most simple to the most complex:

- `http://www.oracle.com`
- `file://c:\temp\demo.html`
- `http://teleport:80.mysimple/page1.html`
- `http://www.haht.com/cgi-bin/hsrun.hse/MultiThread/StateId/ AevayQAnv_QmLcvX-xGcLj6CLu/HAHTpage/ LinkMain?N=HS_ProdSide Nav&D= HS_Product`

Note: The second URL listed above (file://c:\temp\demo.html) points the browser to a file on a computer, not a Web site. This is acceptable!

Additional Resources

The following additional resources could be used if you want additional information on HTML specifications and coding.

HTML Publishing on the Internet for Macintosh

Author:	Brent Heslop
Publisher:	Ventana Communications
ISBN:	1-56-604228-3

HTML Publishing on the Internet for Windows

Author:	Brent Heslop, Larry Budnick
Publisher:	Ventana Communications
ISBN:	1-56-604229-1

The HTML Programmer's Reference

Author:	Robert Mullen
Publisher:	Ventana Communications
ISBN:	1-56-604597-5

Advanced HTML & CGI Writer's Companion

Author: K. Schengili-Roberts
Publisher: Academic Press Professional, Inc.
ISBN: 0-12-623540-6

HTML for Fun and Profit

Author: Mary Morris & John Simpson
Publisher: Prentice Hall
ISBN: 0-13-79678-2

Advanced HTML Topics

Now that you've learned some of the basics of formatting HTML code, it's time to peel back another layer and learn some of the advanced topics relevant to HTML.

Dynamic HTML

Dynamic HTML is HTML code that is generated on-the-fly. This means that the HTML code that produces the web documents seen in a browser is not created until that web document is prepared to be sent to the browser. This is an emerging sub-technology in the Web database application arena in that frequently the resulting sets of database queries need to be formatted and placed on a Web page at the same time that the Web page is created. In fact, the section titled CGI Generation of HTML, appearing in Chapter 7 of this book, includes material on how dynamic HTML is prepared and used in a Web database application.

Incorporating JavaScript into HTML

JavaScript scripts are incorporated directly into HTML code. One of the extensions to HTML specification 3.2 added by Netscape in its browsers allows this. The extension is the: `<SCRIPT> . . . </SCRIPT>` pair.

The <SCRIPT> . . . </SCRIPT> Tag Pair

To incorporate JavaScript into an HTML script is a very simple process of:

- Adding the `<SCRIPT>` tag to the place in the code that you want to begin adding JavaScript
- Write the JavaScript code
- End the JavaScript code by including the `</SCRIPT>` tag

The code sample below shows a very simple snippet of JavaScript code embedded in some HTML code that asks for the users first name in a message box. Once this is provided and the user presses ENTER, the code formats and displays a greeting line on the page displayed in the user's browser, as seen in Figure 6–9.

```
<HTML>
<HEAD>
<TITLE>Demo</TITLE>
</HEAD>
<BODY>
```

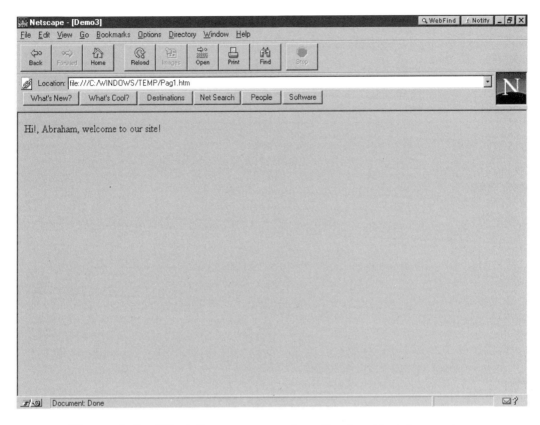

Figure 6–9 What the user sees when the JavaScript executes.

```
<P><FONT SIZE="+0"><SCRIPT LANGUAGE=JavaScript><!—
var fname=prompt("What is your first name: ","fname");
document.writeln("Hi!, " + fname + ", welcome to our site!");
//—></SCRIPT></FONT></P>
<P></P>
</BODY>
</HTML>
```

Tip: You can also reference a file containing JavaScript code (as discussed in Chapter 4) from your HTML code, thus separating the JavaScript code from the HTML code. Reusable code: What a concept!!! The tag pair to accomplish this is: `<SRC> . . . </SRC>`, and is an optional attribute of the `<SCRIPT>` tag.

You know that a comment in HTML code takes the format `<!— comments here —>`. A comment included in JavaScript code starts with a double-backslash (`//`). Also, you can use C-style multiline comments so long as the first line of comment begins with a slash-asterisk pair (`/*`) and the last line of comment ends with an asterisk/slash pair (`*/`).

Inline Images in HTML Files

There are a number of tag pairs used to define the source, layout, and presentation of GIF and JPEG format image files in HTML code.

Tip: There are a number of other formats for graphic files supported by HTML besides GIF and JPEG, but these are the most common.

Until HTML specifications provided support for inline images and browsers were developed to efficiently present these images, the World Wide Web was predominantly a text-based environment. The support for inline images is thought by many (including me) to be a substantial determining factor in the increasing popularity of the Web.

There are a number of parameters you use in conjunction with the <IMG> . . . </IMG> tag pair to help you define the layout and format of inline images. These are shown in Table 6–2.

IMG Tag Parameters. Most of these attributes, along with the <SRC> . . . </SRC> definitions are seen in the HTML code snippet below. The results of this definition is seen in Figure 6–10.

```
<P ALIGN=CENTER>
<A HREF="z100.map">
<IMG LOWSRC="t_open.gif" SRC="openpage.gif" HEIGHT=256 WIDTH=500 BORDER=0
 USEMAP="#mainmap" ISMAP ALT="Z100 Studio Image Map">
</A>
</P>
```

Things to Consider About Inline Images. There's no doubt about it—inline images add pizzazz to your Web pages. However, the overuse, or misuse, of inline images will render your pages and applications ineffective and problematic. Bear in mind that

---

Table 6–2   IMG Tag Parameters

Parameter	Description
SRC	The URL of the graphics file
ALIGN=	Describes how text flows around the image
ALT=	Specify a text message that displays in place of the image for users that have non-graphical browsers
ISMAP	Identifies the image as an image map
WIDTH=	Specifies the width of the image/image map in pixel units
HEIGHT=	Specifies the height of the image/image map in pixel units
BORDER=	Specifies the width of the line surrounding the image
HSPACE=	Specifies the amount of horizontal space between the image and any floating text
VSCAPE=	Specifies the amount of vertical space between the image and any floating text

Figure 6–10   The inline image map as seen through a browser.

many Web users access the Internet over a 14.4 mbps connection. That translates roughly to 1,800 characters per second. A single GIF image that is 75,000 bytes will take about 41 seconds to download to the users machine. That means that the user will wait 41 seconds before they see the image.

Now figure that your work-of-art contains 6 inline images, comprising a total of 450,000 bytes. These images would take over 4 minutes to transfer over that 14.4 mbps phone connection. When you design and build your Web database application, you should take into account several factors. For example, the number of graphics used on your web pages—the fewer the better while still making your page appealing to look at. Also, the size of the graphics files is a consideration—the smaller the better while still providing enough clarity and content to make the graphic meaningful. Finally, the speed of the connection that people will be using when accessing your page—the slower the connection, the longer it will take to transmit the graphics from your server to their browser.

Tip: Generally, a graphics file saved in JPEG format requires less disk space than if it were saved in GIF format. This means a quicker download for users. Even though there is a slight degradation in the quality of a JPEG image from a GIF image, this probably won't be a viable factor unless precision in the images viewed is vitally important.

Advanced Hypertext and Hypergraphics

A hypergraphic is a graphic image that links one document to another. It is usually bound by a blue border. In graphics browsers, the mouse pointer may convert to a hand when passed over the hypergraphic. As previously discussed, hypertext and hypergraphics are references in HTML code that cause the users browser to jump to another section in the same document, or another document altogether, when the user clicks on it. To create a hypertext or hypergraphic link, you use the tag pair: `<A> . . . </A>`.

The specific syntax for this tag pair is:

Hypertext link   `<A HREF=`*URL*`>text</A>`
Hypergraphic link   `<A HREF=`*URL*`><IMG SRC="Image URL"></A>`

where URL is the destination where the user will go when she or he clicks on the text (for a hypertext link) or image (for a hypergraphic link).

The code sample below provides an example of the HTML code used to accomplish both a hypertext and a hypergraphic link. Figure 6–11 shows what this HTML code would look like in a browser.

```
HTML>
<HEAD>
HEAD>
<P ALIGN=CENTER><IMG SRC="SimpFold/Images/INT_WEB.jpg" WIDTH=322
HEIGHT=117></P>
<P>Welcome to the ABC Movies Company internal Web page. </P>
<BLOCKQUOTE><P><STRONG><FONT SIZE="+0">Remember!!!</FONT></STRONG> You are our
most valuable asset!</P></BLOCKQUOTE>
<P> <A HREF="Page2.html">Movie List</A><A HREF="Page2.html"><IMG
SRC="MOV_LISTs.JPG" WIDTH=100 HEIGHT=45></A></P>
<P> <A HREF="CustList.htm">Customer List</A> <A HREF="CustList.htm"><IMG
SRC="CUSTLISTs.JPG" WIDTH=177 HEIGHT=65></A></P>
</BODY>
</HTML>
```

Now that you have the basics of HTML under your belt, here are some things to keep in mind when writing your own HTML. These are suggestions only as there are no defined standards of HTML authoring style. The information in the next section is what I and many other HTML authors that I've worked with consider to be good HTML practices.

Good HTML Practices

The Web has been, is, and will largely remain an unrestricted information collection and dissemination vehicle. Companies such as Sun Microsystems seek desperately to have the Web remain as open and unrestricted in terms of architecture as possible. Other companies such as Netscape and Microsoft claim to want to do this, but fall short of demonstrat-

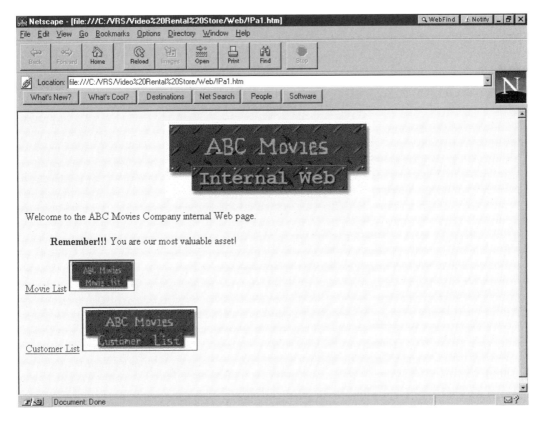

Figure 6–11 Example HTML display for hypertext and hypergraphics.

ing this intent by supplying extensions in their browsers to current HTML specifications. An extension supplied by Netscape and used by a developer will render a problematic HTML page to a user that views this page using a browser that does not support Netscape extensions.

There are a number of things that you could and should do that fall into the category of "Good HTML Practices." These are:

- Use standard HTML
- Make your pages printable
- Use hypertext and hypergraphic links
- Avoid unnecessary & meaningless links
- Carefully plan headings and organization
- Page size

Each of these is discussed in detail in the following sections.

Use Standard HTML

If you write your HTML code to the 2.0 specification, you can be pretty sure that *all* the browsers accessing your pages will see what you intend for them to see. Currently, not all browsers support HTML specifications beyond version 2.0, although the majority support HTML specification 3.2. Additionally, people using Netscape Navigator to view a page that was built using Microsoft extensions to HTML specifications may have problems.

You should have a knowledge of three critical elements when you write your HTML code. These are:

- What elements of HTML are specified in each version of the HTML specifications
- What browsers people accessing your pages will be using
- What HTML specifications are supported in the browsers used by your Web page readers

With knowledge of these three components, you can be comfortable that the HTML code you write that is non-standard will work as intended.

Signing and Time-Stamping Pages

"Authoritativeness" is a problem faced by anyone trying to find information on the Internet. Frequently people develop and publish a Web site or page with an intent to update it frequently, only to have it grow stale while other interests are pursued.

To do your share to fix this problem, you should get in the habit of signing and dating all documents on your site. This is done so that people viewing your pages will have some data they can use to determine how authoritative the information on the pages really is. For example:

```
<HR>
<!- Originally written: October 30, 1995 ->
<!- Last modified: March 27, 1997 ->
<ADDRESS>
<A HREF="http://www.teleport.com/~jhobuss/">Jim Hobuss</A><BR>
<A HREF="mailto:jhobuss@teleport.com">jhobuss@teleport.com</A>
</ADDRESS>
```

In the code sample above, notice the information contained on the second and third lines that are comments only—they will not appear in a users browser. This gives people that work on these pages in the future some documented history of the age and last modification date. You could even carry this one step forward by maintaining a "change log"—thereby recording the date and nature of every change made to a page.

Make Your Pages Printable

We have tried for years to become a paperless society. My eight-year-old son Andrew, complete with 10 green fingers (okay, 8 green fingers and 2 green thumbs), is very environmentally conscious (thus the green digits) and believes we are moving too slowly in that direction. I have to agree with his insight. As much as computers, the Web, and e-mail facilitate the electronic dissemination of information, we are still bound by paper.

As you design your Web page, you must recognize and provide for this. People have the ability to print what they see on your Web page. Help them out and format the information in a way that will print well, and therefore increase its likelihood that it actually *will be* read at a later time. As Andrew (my son) says, "If you're going to catch a fish and if you kill it, you have to eat it. If you cut down a tree in a forest to make boards and paper, you must make something with the boards and write something on the paper so people can read it." If you're going to create a Web page that you hope people will print for later reference, make sure you format the page in a way that people will actually want and be able to read it later. Way to go Andrew! — we can learn from eight-year-olds, if we stop to listen.

Hypertext and Hypergraphic Links

One of the advantages of reading information on a Web page over reading the same information in a book is the ability to drill down on any topics that interest you. This is done with hyperlinks. When Bill Gates' book *The Road Ahead* was published, the publisher included a CD-ROM that contained the complete text of the book. I tried reading the CD-ROM version of the book and found it to be a sterile activity. It was hard to feel nearly as comfortable reading sitting up in a chair at a desk staring at a computer screen than it was curled up on the couch with some good mood music playing and a fire roaring in the fireplace.

When I started to click on some of the hypertext links in the CD-ROM version of the book, things became much more interesting. When Gates was writing about his activities as a Harvard student, I was able to click on a hypertext link of the word Harvard and read some detail information about the University that included a hypergraphics link to a picture of the dorm that Gates stayed in. With a couple of clicks on the <Back> button, I was back to the main body of the book from where I left. This experience was much more tailored to my interests than any experience I could have reading the hard copy version of the book.

Avoid Unnecessary and Meaningless Links

If you are convinced that hypertext and hypergraphic links add depth to your Web pages, then you need to understand that these features can be overdone. It is distracting for someone to read 1,000 words of text in a Web page if every other word is a hypertext link. Just because you have the ability and information at your disposal to include a hypertext link on a page, only include it if it adds enough value to the reader to warrant their time to link to it.

You should also consider carefully the wording you use in the text of your link. For example, consider the following two examples:

Example 1: <u>[Figure 3.2: Click Here To Read About Dogs]</u>

Example 2: <u>[Figure 3.3: A Dog Demonstrating His Ability To Herd Sheep.]</u>

There are two problems with Example 1. The first problem is the phrase "Click Here." This is redundant and wastes the reader's time. In their browser, they will see that this is a hypertext link and know what to do, you don't have to tell them. The second problem is that there is nothing to entice the reader to click on the hypertext link. Example 2 resolves both of these problems nicely.

Headings and Organization

Remember I wrote earlier that it was possible to structure your headings so that a heading level H2 was used for a section heading that was actually a subsection of something that used the heading level H3? Although it is possible to do this, for maintenance reasons, you should avoid doing this. Structure your pages so they are hierarchical. Headings used on a page should be in sequence. This means that HTML specifications do not require that an H3 heading follow an H2 heading, and an H2 heading should follow an H1 heading, while an H3 heading never directly and immediately follows an H1 heading.

Organizing your Web pages so they flow smoothly requires forethought and planning. Laying out a series of Web pages before construction begins is much akin to the way cartoonists lay out a story on storyboards before they ever begin to draw the first frame of a cartoon.

On a site that has been available for a long time and seen frequent changes, this may mean a re-write of the pages to put them back into a logical and hierarchical sequence. Links between the pages in old, yet dynamic, Web sites become increasingly more difficult to maintain.

Page Size

A number of pages where the information on each of the pages is easily viewable without having to scroll is much more attractive than having the user scroll though a seemingly endless document. Recognizing that this is not always possible (for example if your Web page includes a fairly long Press Release), try to break your pages into smaller units to make them more aesthetically pleasing.

The Future of HTML

HTML will never go away. It will continue to be embellished and enhanced with new tags and tag pairs. You will be able to have more and more control over sophisticated page layouts. As this evolution continues, the language will become increasingly more complex. To handle this complexity and insulate you from it, HTML editors and Web application development suites will evolve to become more graphical. As was noted in the beginning of this chapter, though, your ability to read and write HTML is and will continue to be an important component in your toolset of Web database application development tools.

Another exciting evolutionary enhancement to HTML is VRML—Virtual Reality Markup Language. This language extension to HTML allows the user to explore scenes in 3 dimensions. For example, a perspective customer could select an automobile from a list of automobiles and take a virtual tour of the inside of the automobile, or even take the automobile for a virtual test drive through the scenery of their choice. Another application is to be able to see what landscaping looks like by (virtually) walking through the landscaped area. The current release of Netscape Navigator supports VRML, although the sites that provide this are limited. VRML is a separate support module to HTML specifications that allow the user to download and move through a virtual window from within their Web browser.

Tip: If you are using Netscape Navigator and want to see what VRML technology looks like, check out URL `http://www.kgw.com`. This is the site for a television station in Portland that distinguishes itself from the other stations by its extensive use of a helicopter. On this site you can take a virtual tour of the inside of this helicopter using VRML technology.

Moving On

This chapter is an introduction and overview of HTML. Most, but not all the HTML commands were covered in this chapter—this is not an HTML coding book. If you knew nothing about HTML when you started reading this chapter, you should know enough now to build useful HTML pages using most of the available HTML commands. If you knew a little about HTML before this chapter, you should have learned some things that you can apply immediately.

Chapter 7 is to CGI what this chapter is to HTML—an introduction and overview. You will learn what CGI is, how to incorporate it in your Web database application development project, how to read user data into a CGI program, and learn a few principles of good CGI programming.

CHAPTER 7

Common
Gateway
Interface
(CGI)

Whereas Chapter 6 is an introduction to HTML and its role in the Web database application, this chapter is an introduction to Common Gateway Interface, commonly referred to as CGI. CGI is a means by which Web servers interface to other application programs and thereby extend the services provided by the Web server. By way of CGI scripts, users gain program access to Web servers, and extend the capability of HTML.

In this chapter, you'll learn about the Common Gateway Interface and the role it has in Web database application development. Being one of the most important links that connect Web pages to databases, CGI plays a critical role in Web database design and use. You'll learn about the CGI standard as it applies to UNIX and Windows operating systems. Simple programs are used to communicate and demonstrate CGI capabilities.

CGI Introduction

CGI scripts are executable files—programs written, compiled, and linked in one of a number of different languages. The most common language for a CGI program is Perl, but other languages include C, C++, Java, JavaScript, Visual Basic, PowerBuilder, etc. Perl's dominance as a CGI development language has recently been challenged by not only many of these other languages but also by Web development tools. For example, with HAHTSite IDE, all of the capabilities traditionally provided by CGI programming languages are built in to the tool.

118

As you know, HTML has no facilities to directly query a database. Through CGI, this capability exists. By utilizing CGI scripts, a request can be sent from within HTML, and processed by the HTTP Server, to query the database for specific information, and then display the result set in dynamically built HTML code. With this capability, there is no need to have to manually change a Web page whenever data on that page changes. Simply place the data in a database, and build a CGI script to access the data and display it dynamically. Whenever a request is made to view the page that contains the CGI script, the Web server initiates a request to the database and formats the most-current data into a dynamic Web page.

CGI is one of the facilities that make the Web a true client/server environment. Without CGI, Java applets, and facilities like these, the Web would be what it was just a few short years ago—an architecture to collect and display static information in a very static format and style.

Although the CGI script is written on and received from a client-side device, it is executed on the server—thereby becoming a server-side process that functions as an interface to other application programs and databases. These programs can reside on the same device as the HTTP Server, or on a machine distant from the HTTP Server.

The CGI Expanded

CGI programs, CGI scripts, and gateway programs are synonymous. They are the programs and computer code that perform a very specific and crucial function in a Web application: to accept a request initiated by a browser that is interpreted by a server, accepts passed data from the server, and takes an action predefined and described by the programmer. This action can be any of the following individually or a combination of two or more:

- Accessing of data either locally or remotely
- Processing of data
- Accessing available resources that are either local or remotely attached
- Creating output

Because of CGI, the Web database application has the ability to extend its reach beyond the confines of the HTTP server. A user in Bangkok, Thailand could provide input on an HTML form that is transmitted from his or her HTTP browser to the company's HTTP server in New York, where that server processes the HTML code and the request to initiate an external program. That external program could access a regional database located in Charlotte, NC, receive the result set, and format that result set into an HTML form that is then transmitted back to the HTTP browser that initiated the request in Thailand.

CGI Architecture

To fully understand CGI you must understand its architecture and how it works. Once this is understood, you can use whatever language you are most comfortable with to write the actual CGI code. Without a grasp of the CGI architecture, you won't be able to fully utilize CGI.

CGI Process Flow

Figure 7–1 displays the normal CGI process flow.
      This process is described below.

Step 1.   A user, accessing an HTTP browser, sends a request to an HTTP server via HTML. This HTML includes a request to execute a CGI program, as well as any parameters the CGI program might need.

Step 2.   The HTTP server receives the request from the HTTP browser, processes the HTML, and encounters the request to execute a CGI program. The HTTP server initiates the CGI programs execution by calling it and passing it any parameters that were received from the HTTP browser.

Step 3.   The CGI program executes. In its execution, it may:

- Access no other resources
- Access databases either locally or remotely

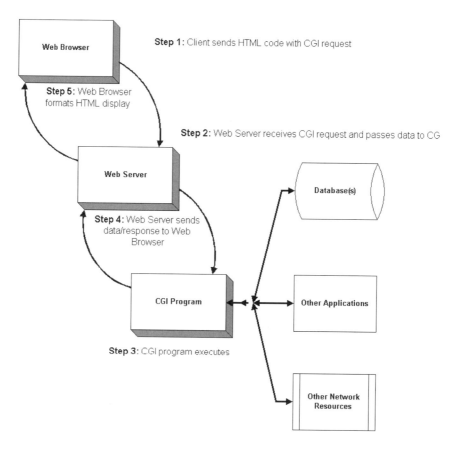

Figure 7–1   The CGI process flow.

- Access other applications or initiate the execution of other programs
- Access other network resources

Step 4. The HTTP server receives a result set from the CGI program if one is returned, and sends the data and/or response back to the HTTP browser via HTML.

Step 5. The HTTP browser receives the HTML sent to it from the HTTP server and formats and displays the data received.

HTTP Server and CGI Program Communication Methods

Step 2 in Figure 7–1 is the process of the HTTP server initiating the execution of the CGI program. Although a CGI program could execute with no parameter input, such an event would be an exception. Generally, the CGI program's execution path is determined by parameter data that it receives.

This parameter data is passed to the CGI program, and the CGI program subsequently passes information back to the HTTP server in one of four ways. These are:

Command Line. By far the most common method, command line input passes the data the program needs in the same command string that is used to initiate the execution of the CGI program. The following is an example of a command line query string:

```
http://www.jackaroo.com/cgi-bin/acctlist.exe?Sydney+Australia
```

Note: The string `Sydney+Australia` is passed to a CGI program named `acctlist.exe` that is in a directory named `cgi-bin` on a server named `www.jackaroo.com`.

Environmental Variables. CGI programs can read the values of environmental variables on the HTTP Server, act accordingly, and they can even set environmental variables on the HTTP Server.

Standard Input. This is the system's standard input file descriptor and can be a terminal device or the output from another CGI program.

Standard Output. This is the system's standard output file descriptor and can be a terminal device or the input to another CGI program.

CGI Input Data

CGI input data is data that is passed to the HTTP server from the HTTP browser, with the intent that the HTTP server will pass it to the CGI program. The CGI program uses this data to determine its logical execution path and to (potentially) format a query to a database.

Additionally, the HTTP server can format and pass information to the CGI program that describes the type of data that was passed. This is what happens when data is passed to a CGI program via standard input. By providing this type of information, the CGI program can determine how to process the data it receives.

CGI Output Data

There is one, and only one, way that CGI programs return output. That is by standard output. Even in situations when a CGI program returns no data it still formats and generates a response via standard output that indicates there was no data sent.

CGI standard output data is returned in one of two formats: *parsed header output* and *non-parsed header output*. With parsed header output, the data created by the CGI program is received and interpreted by the HTTP server and then sent to the HTTP browser. With non-parsed header output, the HTTP server has the responsibility (and overhead) of generating the header information and sending it, along with the rest of the response, to the HTTP browser.

CGI Environmental Variables

CGI scripts use environmental variables for a number of reasons—not the least of which is to pass data between the HTTP server and the CGI program. There are two types of CGI environmental variables: *request-specific* and *not request-specific* variables.

Request-specific variables are those environmental variables that are specific to the client request that the CGI program is fulfilling. Not request-specific variables are those environmental variables that are set during all client requests. Remember: A client request is any send of an HTML page from a browser to a server. Request-specific variables are those that are very specific to the type of request received from the HTTP browser while not request-specific are those that are very generic to any or all types of requests received from the HTTP browser.

CGI environmental variables, regardless of their type, are used by CGI programs to:

- Specify the type of processing and database request the CGI program must perform
- Indicate the type of browser the client is using
- Maintain and pass state information

Note: The Web is a *stateless* environment. This means that after an HTTP client formats and sends a request to an HTTP server, or after the HTTP server formats and sends a response to an HTTP client, all knowledge of the transaction is lost. This is because the connection between the HTTP server and HTTP client is dropped. It is sometimes advantageous to maintain state—that is to know what processing has occurred when a request for follow-up processing is received.

There exist CGI environmental variables that are assigned in a variety of means, each dependent on the operating system and type of HTTP server. Although most are request-specific, some are not request-specific. To achieve a sense of how these variables are used, a few are presented here.

CONTENT_LENGTH—The length in bytes of the buffer sent by the HTTP browser to the HTTP server to accommodate the data transferred between the two devices. An example is:

```
CONTENT_LENGTH=256
```

GATEWAY_INTERFACE—This specifies the version of the CGI specification that the HTTP server is expected to comply with. An example is:

```
GATEWAY_INTERFACE=CGI/1.1
```

QUERY_STRING—An URL-encoded string that is appended to an URL. This character string references a CGI program and is seen in the URL as the character string that follows a question mark (?). An example is:

```
http://microfocus.com/cgi-bin/prod-info?&pname=COBOL&version=4.0
```

REMOTE_ADDR—The IP address for the requesting HTTP browser. An example is:

```
REMOTE_ADDR=63.628.528.777
```

SERVER_NAME—The HTTP server name, Domain Name Server (DNS), or IP address of the HTTP server. An example is:

```
SERVER_NAME=haht.com
```

Definition: Domain Name Server (DNS) is software that converts host names to IP addresses. IP addresses are what is actually used to contact a computer. The DNS can be thought of as a telephone book where a number used to contact something is identified from a given name.

SERVER_SOFTWARE—The name and version of the HTTP server software that is responding to HTTP browser requests and initiating the execution of CGI programs. An example is:

```
SERVER_SOFTWARE=WebSTAR/2.1
```

Windows CGI Variables. The environmental variable examples listed in this section are in the format they would appear on a UNIX server. The format if the HTTP server were on a Windows machine is slightly different, although the way they are used is the same.

On a Windows NT/95 machine, these "environmental variables" are placed in a *.INI file, with each "environmental variable" being a variable. Windows provides two

UNIX CGI	Windows CGI
CONTENT_LENGTH	Content Length
GATEWAY_INTERFACE	CGI Version
QUERY_STRING	Query String
REMOTE_ADDR	Remote Address
SERVER_NAME	Server Name
SERVER_SOFTWARE	Server Software

APIs (*GetProfileString()* and *PutProfileString()*) to create and retrieve entries in INI files. The following table lists some of the UNIX CGI environmental variables and their Windows CGI counterparts.

Passing CGI Data Streams

There are several ways that an HTTP client can transmit data strings to a CGI program— three being the post popular. These are:

- GET
- ISINDEX
- POST

These are described in this section.

GET Method to Transmit CGI Data Streams.   You use the GET method when passing data provided by users via HTML forms to CGI programs. Because of the limitation on the amount of data that can be passed (usually 256 characters) to a CGI program using the GET method, it is the least desirable way (of the three listed) to transfer data to the CGI program. Its strength is in its ease-of-use when passing only a few data fields.

The GET method appends a query string to the action URL when the user presses the <Submit> button on a form. The complete string passed to the HTTP server may look like:

```
GET /cgi-bin/processform.pl?action=READ&screen=QUERY HTTP/1.1
```

ISINDEX Method to Transmit CGI Data Streams.   You use the ISINDEX method when the need exists to perform database queries. The latest HTML specifications allow for the addition of the <ISINDEX> tag to your HTML code. This tag allows the HREF URL to perform a query based on data input by a user. The syntax for this is:

```
<HEAD>
<ISINDEX HREF="URL-CGI Program">
</HEAD>
```

In this example, `URL-CGI Program` is the URL for the CGI program to execute. Therefore, assuming an URL for a CGI executable is: `http://teleport.com/cgi-bin/processit.exe`, and this includes passed parameters of: `?lastname+taxyear` the HTML code would like as follows:

```
<HEAD>
<ISINDEX HREF="http://teleport.com/cgi-bin/processit.exe?lastname+tax
year">
</HEAD>
```

Following this example, the HTTP browser would pass the following string to the HTTP server:

```
http://teleport.com/cgi-bin/processit.exe?lastname+taxyear
```

The HTTP server receives this string, and causes the `processit.exe` CGI program to begin execution with a passed command string of: `lastname taxyear`.

POST Method to Transmit CGI Data Streams.   The POST method is conceptually similar to the GET method, with much broader application. Whereas the GET method appends the user supplied data to the ACTION URL, the POST method is formatted and sent to the server in a stream of data of varying length which is passed to the CGI program.

A specific example of using the POST method to receive CGI data streams follows.

```
POST /cgi-bin/processit.exe HTTP/1.1
Accept: text/plain
Accept: text/html
Accept: */*
Content-type: application/x-www-form-urlencoded
Content-length: 42
state=OR&politics=Republican&Minimum=25000
```

When this data stream is received by the HTTP server, it passes it directly to the CGI program named: `processit.exe`. This CGI program would then read it as any other program would read input passed to it as a command string.

Tip: The Content_Length environmental variable is not required, but it is a very good idea to include it—and to be accurate when using it. The reason you should use it is that some servers do not send an end-of-file marker to CGI programs. Without the Content_Length variable, the CGI program may not receive the correct data. The reason it is important to establish the correct parameter to signify the passed string length is that you may end up truncating or sending extraneous data to the CGI program in the passed string.

Reading User Data into CGI Programs

You've seen in the previous section three ways to get user-supplied data streams to a CGI program. In this section, you'll see how to read and process that data in a CGI program.

As you know, CGI programs can be written in a number of different languages. You have your favorite one, which probably is not mine. Therefore, the basic steps to read user data into a CGI program are described below in *pseudo-code*:

```
IF the GET method was used to transmit data THEN
   Parse the QUERY_STRING environmental variable name-value pairs into
   their respective components
ELSEIF the ISINDEX method was used to transmit data THEN
   Parse the QUERY_STRING environmental variable into its component parts
ELSE
   Read the value of the passed string from the CONTENT_LENGTH environmen-
   tal variable and parse this number of characters from the string in the
   QUERY_STRING environmental variable.
END
```

Once the passed string is either separated into its component parts or parsed appropriately, it can be processed by the CGI program accordingly.

CGI Generation of HTML

One of the frequently used benefits of CGI programming is the ability to generate HTML code at run-time. This means that one set of HTML code could be generated based upon the results of data input supplied by a user while another set of HTML code would be generated for another user.

To use this feature which is so important if you are using CGI in your Web database application, you are advised to remember that output from CGI programs is always to the standard output device. For the HTTP server to know that the data coming out of a CGI program is HTML code, the following format is required:

```
Content-type: text/html
<HTML>
. . .
</HTML>
```

Given this structure, the following example, written in Bourne shell script (a CGI programming language), dynamically builds an HTML page based on the value of the environmental variable: REMOTE_USER.

```
#!/bin/progs
echo Content-type: text/html
echo "<HTML>"
echo "<HEAD><TITLE>CGI HTML CODE GENERATION</TITLE></HEAD>
echo "<BODY>"
echo "<H2>Main Menu</H2>"
echo "<HR>"
echo "<P>"
IF $REMOTE_USER = "AL" THEN
  echo Press <F1> For Help "<BR>"
  echo Press <F2> For Employee Listing "<BR>"
  echo Press <F3> For Department Listing "<BR>"
  echo Press <F4> For Vendor Listing "<BR>"
  echo Press <F5> For Parts Listing "<BR>"
ELSE
  echo Press <F1> For Help "<BR>"
  echo Press <F2> For Account Input "<BR>"
  echo Press <F3> For Account Inquiry "<BR>"
  echo Press <F4> For Status Update "<BR>"
  echo Press <F5> For Message Log "<BR>"
END IF
echo "</P>"
echo "<HR>"
echo "</BODY>"
echo "</HTML>"
```

The following is a brief description of what this bit of code does and how it is used in an application:

1. The user, after viewing a Web page, initiates a request to the server. This request uses the FORM POST method, and places a user-defined value in a variable named: REMOTE_USER.

2. The server initiates the execution of a CGI program whose purpose is to format the HTML code as seen earlier in this section.

3. The CGI program sends the HTML code to the standard output device, where it is picked up by the server, and sent back to the user's browser.

4. The user then sees a custom Web document that is specific to the request identified in step 1.

Assuming you are already a programmer, well schooled in sound programming techniques, there are a few issues unique to CGI programming you need to be aware of. These are described in the following section.

CGI Programming Principles

Although many HTTP servers allow you to control where you place CGI programs, it is common practice to place CGI programs in a directory named cgi-bin. Without security software, due to the way this library is used, its presence represents a security risk.

Thought: When I started developing Web pages and database applications, I relied on an Internet Service Provider (ISP) for my Web site. The ISP I chose would not allow me to place CGI programs into their cgi-bin directory as they had it secured and opening up to developers was not something they were willing to do. Guess how long it took me to find another ISP? (Hint: How long does it take to punch 7 numbers on a telephone?)

Definition: Internet Service Provider (ISP) is a company or organization that provides Internet connections and access to paying customers on an hourly, monthly, semi-annual, or annual basis.

Application Performance

Applications delivered over the Web are going to run slower than most applications delivered over the desktop. Be aware of the fact that users will already be waiting while graphics load or huge files transfer over a 14.4 bps modem and code your CGI programs as efficiently as possible.

Comments

All CGI programming languages include self-documentation syntax. Use these language comment facilities extensively. Because you, the developer, know what you meant by naming a function the way you did, will a programmer working on the CGI program 6 months from now recognize it as a function? Or, would they initially view it as a variable?

HTTP Protocol

Learn about HTTP protocol. The time invested will be more than returned if you plan on using CGI programming in your Web database application.

Language Choice

Because of the nature of the Web, choose a CGI programming language that is at least as portable as it needs to be based on the scope of the complete application. If your completed application is deployed over the Web for execution on all Operating Systems, you need to make sure that your CGI programming language provides at least this level of support.

Naming Conventions

When writing a CGI program, follow the naming conventions for that program. For example, Perl naming conventions are different than those for Visual Basic or C++. This will make maintenance much easier.

Separate Development Site

Use your test Web site as the initial execution environment for any new CGI program. CGI programs can sometimes produce erratic and unexpected results and you don't want your product HTTP Server brought down because of a buggy CGI program.

Standards

If your company has standards on what language to use for CGI programs—follow the standards. It will make maintenance easier and save your company money in consultant fees. If your company has no standards on CGI programming languages, use the language you are the most comfortable with, and stick with it.

Use Libraries

When possible, find code that has already been written for routine CGI-program tasks. Newsgroups and Web sites are excellent places to find already-written CGI programs that read data, format data into HTML, and perform database access.

CGI Program Architectures

Figure 7–2 displays the most typical form of CGI program architecture—sometimes referred to as straight CGI program.

The straight CGI Program architecture was the first, and remains the most popular, CGI architecture on the Web. This is the architecture that has been discussed throughout this chapter. In this architecture, an HTTP browser sends a request via an URL to an HTTP server. The HTTP server then recognizes that the URL contains a reference to a CGI program. It optionally retrieves user-supplied input data from either environmental variables or in the URL that it receives. The HTTP server then passes control to the CGI program that performs its processing—in the case of Figure 7–2, that processing is to perform a database access.

Figure 7–3 is a representation of the hybrid CGI program architecture.

In this architecture, two components (a "thin" CGI program and a much larger CGI partner program) produce much better performance than the straight CGI program. This

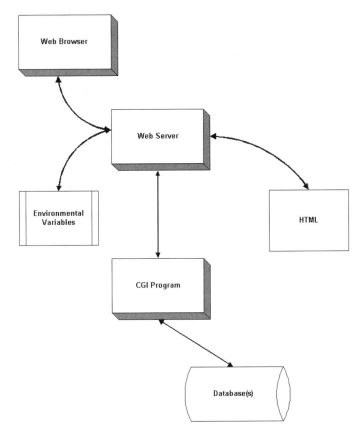

Figure 7–2   Straight CGI program architecture.

increased performance is attributable to the CGI partner program being loaded only once and always available for CGI requests sent to it from the "thin" CGI program.

Because the majority of the required functions from the CGI process are performed within the CGI partner program, the "thin" CGI program can be very small. This causes it to load more quickly and execute faster.

Additionally, because database processing is requested by the CGI partner program, and as the CGI partner program stays resident in memory, database connections (which are time-expensive to establish and terminate) stay active. This is another efficiency gain.

Note: The HAHTSite IDE that is used throughout this book for demonstration purposes uses this architecture.

Figure 7–4 displays the API extension architecture—what Microsoft and Netscape are trying to establish as Web standards. Microsoft is promoting its ISAPI standard while Netscape is pushing its own standard, called NSAPI.

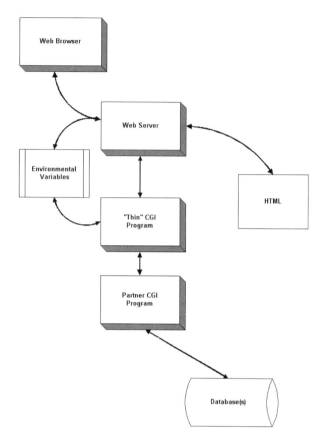

Figure 7–3   Hybrid CGI program architecture.

In these architectures, the server extension program is implemented as a DLL (for Windows NT/95) or a shared object (for Unix). These server extension programs replace the functions performed by CGI programs. Server extension programs extend the base functionality of HTTP servers via libraries of routines that perform predefined functions. These libraries extend the base functionality of HTTP servers by the functions in the libraries. Because this increased functionality is provided by libraries, these libraries can be added, altered, or deleted as demand describes.

As you have already learned, the main problem with both Microsoft's and Netscape's architectures is that they are competing, and therefore non-standard. Microsoft's ISAPI and Netscape's NSAPI can not co-exist.

The potential for this architecture is a very responsive environment that is truly dynamic. The capabilities of the network can be expanded by adding libraries without necessarily having to write program code.

Thought: As already discussed, CGI programs in a straight CGI program architecture represent a potential security risk. This risk is in the form of confidential user-supplied

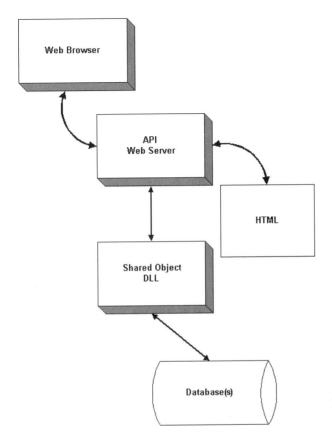

Figure 7-4 API application architecture.

data that is passed from the HTTP browser to the HTTP server being compromised. A web site with a substantial amount of information on this subject is available at:

```
http://www.cerf.net/~paulp/cgi_security/
```

Moving On

This chapter is an introduction and overview of CGI. You learned what CGI is, the various architectures comprising CGI, and how to incorporate CGI in your application on one of three different ways. If you knew nothing about CGI before reading this chapter you should have a good understanding of what it is by now. If you had a familiarity with CGI prior to starting this chapter, hopefully by now you are very comfortable with it.

Chapter 8 goes ever deeper into the process of Web database application development and design by presenting the architectural issues relevant to the actual design and development of the application. You will learn about the parallels that exist between Web database application development and client/server application development.

CHAPTER 8

Web
Application
Design and
Development

As I've already stated in earlier chapters, the analysis, design, development, and implementation of a Web database application is very much similar to the same functions of a client/server project. If you are familiar with client/server concepts, then you will find the application of those concepts to Web database application development a very easy migration.

Advantages of Deploying an Application on Your Chosen Platform

There are a number of advantages to a company building and deploying an application in a Web database application environment. The items listed below should be self-evident. If they are a bit fuzzy, everything will be made crystal clear as you read through this chapter.

- Enhanced data sharing
- Integrated services
- Sharing of resources
- Data interchangeability
- Masked physical data access
- Location independence of data and processing
- Maximization of workstation resources

Absent from this list, and probably the greatest single strength of building a Web database application, is its "reach." Reach, a marketing term, is defined as the number of entities that will be exposed to your message. By an order of magnitude that is so great it is almost incomprehensible, a Web database application has much greater reach than a similar application deployed in any other type of architecture.

Characteristics of a Web Database Application

All Web database applications share the following characteristics:

- *Service*—They provide a service via either display of information, acceptance of input, provision of a service, or processing of data.
- *Shared resources*—Web database applications share at least some of the resources that components execute on. Perhaps the most easily recognized shared component in a Web database application is the database.
- *Platform independence*—The pinnacle underlying strength of the Web is its platform and operating system independence.
- *Message-based interface*—The role of the server, as you will see later in this chapter, is to translate the messages received from Web browsers into something meaningful and actionable.
- *Server transparency*—The promise of Web applications is to be able to build and deliver an application where the users of the data belonging to that application don't know (nor care) where the physical data resides. Tell me, what is the name of the server that is physically attached to the URL `http://www.microsoft.com`? This is server transparency!
- *Scalability*—Web database applications are very scalable in that it is a very easy process to add more disk space to accommodate a larger database, add a few more modems to increase the number of concurrent users to your Web, etc.
- *Separate responsibilities*—In a Web database application, the functions of the application performed within a Web browser are separate and distinct from those executed on the http server, or on the database server.
- *Many-to-one relationship*—In a Web database application there are many more Web browsers accessing the application via the http server than there will be http servers.

Keys to Successfully Implementing a System

There are as many opinions about what the critical success factors are to building and installing a Web database application as there are people having those opinions. The following four items are consistent throughout all the literature.

- *Management commitment*—It has taken a few years, but corporate MIS management are now beginning to see the value in building and deploying Web database applications.
- *Tool integration*—As you saw in Chapter 3, the abilities of the tools required to build a Web database application are becoming increasingly recognized in the soft-

ware community. This is evidenced by the frequency in which new integrated tools are coming to market.

- *Environmental and architectural support*—Every application, regardless to whether it is a Web database application, a client/server application, or a 3270 application, should include serious consideration to the amount of support that application requires.

- *Training*—Many MIS executives underestimate the amount of training required before successfully building a client/server application. Training on the tools and architecture behind client/server is a key and very critical component to a development effort. This is certainly true for a Web database application development project.

The four items here are not a comprehensive list. However, if you get 100 people together to compare their lists of critical success factors to successfully developing and implementing a Web database application, you will find these four items on every list.

The Process

The following are steps for the development of a Web database application:

- Step *n*: Build new systems by taking advantage of what was learned and the information present from the previous systems

- Step *n + 1*: Reuse as much of existing applications as possible

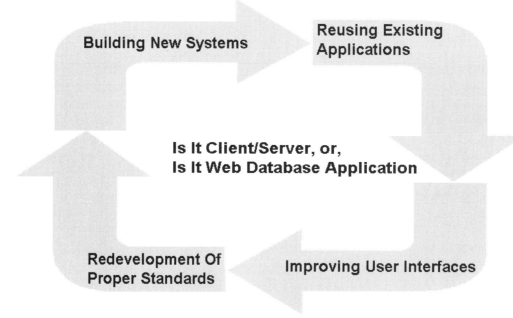

Figure 8–1   What development cycle is it?

- Step $n + 2$: Improve the user-interfaces in the newly designed systems
- Step $n + 3$: Redevelop the proper standards to support the development process

A Wish List for Development Tools

The list below was culled from a training manual that I was given in 1994 when I attended a client/server analysis and design course. Even though the list was targeted to a client/server project, the items are just as valid today for a Web database application.

- Operating system interoperability
- Supports team development
- Highly interactive debugger
- Good object orientation capabilities
- Easy to use documentation
- Supports portability
- Highly responsive and intuitive help system
- Vendor commitment for added features
- Supports popular GUIs
- Supports SQL specifications
- Supports class libraries
- Integrates with other tools when/where necessary
- Vendor financial stability

I think you can agree that the items listed above are significant to a Web database application. In the following section, you'll see a thorough description of the design process of a Web database application.

The Design Process Described

In this section we will take a look at some of the design issues specific to a Web database application development project. This lays the foundation to go deeper into the process in succeeding sections. This section is not meant to be "tell-all" by any means. Rather, its intention is to describe the people, events, and processes at a sufficiently high level so you can begin to ask the questions you need to ask to tailor this information to your unique environment.

The Process of Design

The design of a Web database application is a process that is as dynamic as the variety of companies building Web database applications. This process is flexible by necessity as the tools and standards are evolving so rapidly. It is adaptable and malleable to each requirement or environment in which it is used. As flexible as it is, though, there are still components that share commonality.

One of these similar components are the *participants*. Each Web database application development project requires one or more of a number of different skillsets. Often, one person will be responsible for more than one of the following sets of skills. This is acceptable for the smaller, less complex projects. As the application and the application interfaces becomes larger, it is generally more desirable to spread the required skillsets among more individuals. These roles are described below.

- *Project leader*—This person has the same responsibility as a project leader for any other type of computer application development project. The issues may be somewhat unique for a Web database application, but the responsibilities are very similar.

- *Webmaster*—Whereas a Webmaster's responsibilities used to be that of primary developer and maintainer of a Web site, the role is changing to be more of a system engineer. In many companies, the Webmaster is also the project leader.

- *End-users/audience*—The people that use the computer applications that people build are the ultimate authority on the validity of the computer system. Web database applications are no different. One of the lessons learned in the 1980s regarding computer application development is to involve the users of the system in the early stages of the project. This is particularly true for Web database applications. What many companies are doing to accomplish this is to use focused groups of users during each stage of the development process.

- *Web page developers*—In the early days (about 3 years ago!), the Webmaster was also the Web page developer. As the ways in which companies are using the Web to deploy applications become more sophisticated, there is an effectual split in these two roles. Web page developers have responsibility for the development of the more static components of a Web site. Consequently, these people are very skilled in either HTML or HTML authoring tools.

- *Programmers*—As the sophistication of Web database applications increases, the reliance on highly skilled programmers increases as well. It is the responsibility of programmers in a Web database application project to extend the range and capability of the server-side services as well as write code to implement client-side services.

- *Graphic artists*—Let's face it, the Web is a cornucopia of graphical wonder. Companies spend huge sums of money on bitmaps, image maps, and graphics displayed on Web pages in an effort to make them more attractive. Skilled graphic artists are as necessary to a medium-to-large-size Web database application project as they are to the development of marketing collateral material.

- *System administrator*—The system administrator is the technician responsible for the system hardware, initial troubleshooting of networking difficulties, system backup and security, and maintenance of system software. This person does not need to know a lot about Web database applications, but she or he should be very knowledgeable on the hardware/software/network components used to create and deliver the system.

- *Database administrator*—The DBA is the person responsible for setting up, maintaining, tuning, and supporting the RDBMS. Additionally, this person is responsible for the security of the data contained within the database.

- *Network engineers*—Network engineers are responsible for the setup, support, maintenance, and tuning of the communication components of the system. As is the case with system administrators, the network engineer needs to know very little about the Web database application to do his or her job in supporting the network that it is developed and/or delivered on.

Tip: The focus of this chapter is on Web database application design. By the nature of this there is little information dealing with Web "page" design standards or approaches. You may read and download one of the most definitive works on this subject. *The Web Manual of Style*, written by Patrick Lynch, can be found at:

`http://info.med.yale.edu/caim/StyleManual_Top.html`

The Design in Progress

There is no single approach to describe the process of designing a Web database application. The technology and standards are evolving too rapidly to do this.

A typical first step is for one of the team members to identify the business requirements for the system. The first step in the design of a Web database application might be to model the database. Still another first step might be to design the user interface. The point is that what works for one project probably will not be the correct approach for the next project, or next company for that matter.

If you understand the architecture of a Web database application, the roles of the participants, the business need precipitating the development of the Web database application, and the capabilities of the tools you are considering using in the construction of the application, then the approach that makes the most sense for your project will become clear.

Web Database Application Components

There are four major components in a Web database application environment. You need to understand what these components are and their function before you can develop either a front end user interface or an efficient back end database.

Tip: The terms "browser," "Web browser," and "HTTP client" are used synonymously throughout this book, and are generally recognized to mean the same thing.

This section of Chapter 8 discusses these five components to give you an understanding of their roles in the development process. These five components are:

- Server
- Application server
- Web client
- CGI program
- RDBMS

The Server

The server, also known as the Web server, is the software component that reacts to and interfaces with browsers. It has no ability to create or update Web pages or documents. Rather, it reads a request for information coming to it from a browser, usually in the form of an URL, locates the requested page, and sends the requested page back to the browser.

You are probably well aware of what an URL that accesses a HTML page looks like. The receipt of an URL and processing of that address to retrieve the request for a Web document, find the document, and then format/send it back to the user is an example of the most widely used feature of servers—*document mapping*.

If you've provided an incorrect URL, or if the server the requested file is on is not accessible by your server, the server issues an error message which tells you the URL you requested was not found (accessible) by your server. This is seen in Figure 8–2.

Additionally, a server can function as a gateway to external programs and processes when it receives a request for information via execution of an external program or script. This type of interaction between the server and an external program occurs through a

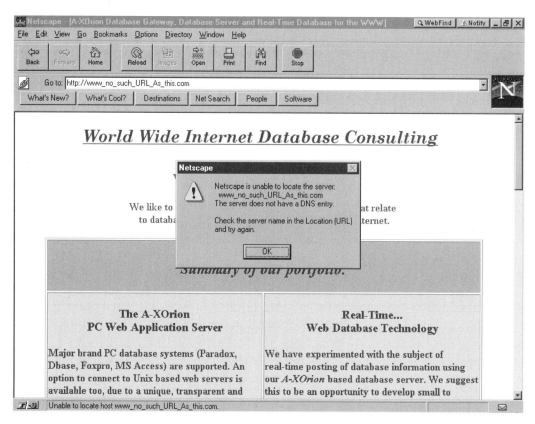

Figure 8–2   Server response when URL requested was not found.

Figure 8–3   An URL with a CGI execution string.

standard interface called Common Gateway Interface (CGI) and is commonly referred to as *CGI mapping.* An example of an URL with a CGI execution string is seen in Figure 8–3.

Another key function of a server is to redirect one URL (usually supplied by a user) to another URL. The target URL is usually on another server. This is called *redirect mapping.* Generally when this occurs the user is unaware that the redirection has occurred. Upon reflection, you probably have been the victim of this HTTP server function. Have you ever input an URL such as `http://www.worldinfo.com`, and when this page displays in the browser with a translated URL of something like `http://www2.worldinfo.com`? If so, then this was redirect mapping.

The final main function for a server is to perform *content mapping.* When content mapping occurs, a specific file extension (i.e., *.DOC, *.TXT, *.HTM) is associated with a content type. A content type is a form of document classification and is defined using Multipurpose Internet Mail Extensions (MIME) format. MIME is a standard for attaching non-text files to standard Internet mail messages. Non-text files include graphics, audio and video files, spreadsheets, word processed documents, etc. This is discussed in greater detail in Chapter 16.

Application Server

As seen in Figure 8–4, the role of the application server is to sit between the server and RDBMS and is responsible for maintaining an open connection between the server and the RDBMS at all times.

In this architecture, a CGI program or script that uses the HTTP server API communicates with the application server. The application server takes this request and actually processes the query against the database, retrieves the result, and passes the result set to the program requesting the information.

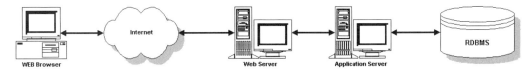

Figure 8–4   A browser, a server, an application server, and an RDBMS system.

With a Web architecture that relies on an application server, the design of the application is not constricted by the availability of the various components. Rather, the designer is allowed to concentrate on the application.

A variation of this architecture, as seen in Figure 8–5, is becoming increasingly popular. In this architecture, the server sends an applet to the browser. The browser, via the applet, establishes the connection with the RDBMS and retrieves the data needed directly. The main advantage to this architecture is that more of the processing is done on the browser, thus freeing cycles and resources on the server.

Web Client

The Web client is the software that runs on a client machine and performs necessary communication functions. The main functions performed by Web clients are:

- Establish and maintain communications with a server
- Pass user requests to the server
- Pass user data to the server
- Display information received from a server
- view files not originating from a server

The three most popular Web client packages are:

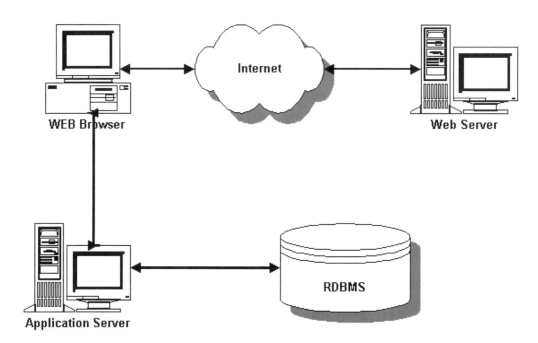

Figure 8–5   A browser, a server, an application server, and an RDBMS system with applets.

- Netscape Navigator (used in the preparaton of this book)
- Microsoft Internet Explorer
- Mosaic

A user does not require a server to make effective use of a Web client. You can use a Web client to view the contents of a range of file types, regardless of whether that file is on a server, a shared data server, or in a directory on your machine. Figure 8–6 is a screen print of such an event.

CGI Program

The CGI program, an optional component, is intended mainly to interact with the server by using one of a number of different standards. Its primary method of server interaction in a Web database application is to connect the server to external programs. CGI is discussed in detail in Chapter 7 and 14.

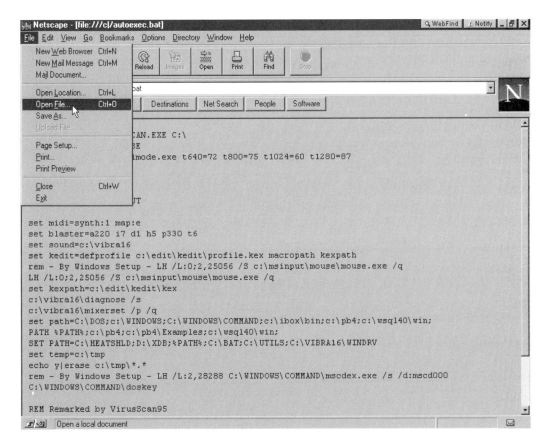

Figure 8–6   Using the Web client to view the contents of a text file.

A graphic (albeit simplistic) representation of how a CGI program fits into the mix of components is seen in Figure 8–7. Unlike a server or client, the CGI program remains resident on the server only as long as it takes to accomplish its intended task. Once it finishes this, it terminates.

> In a Web architecture where CGI programs are used, it is possible for a server to receive concurrent requests from separate clients to execute the same CGI program. Such occurrences are acceptable and allowed, especially in multitasking operating systems such as Windows NT and Windows 95. However, you should be aware of the possibility of this in the design of your application.

You can usually recognize the data that is passed to a CGI program from a client by looking at the URL. Figure 8–3 is an example of this. The person that develops the CGI program controls how data is to be received into it from the client in the form of the command string displayed in the URL. For example, programmer A could develop his CGI program to accept a parameter string that looks like "?StateCd=OR" while programmer B could develop her CGI program to accept the same parameter in a string that looks like "#State_Code=OR". For this reason, the person developing the CGI program needs to be in communication with the person developing the HTML pages.

RDBMS

The Web database application that you develop needs (obviously) a database to make it whole. These databases could be of the following types:

- Local, tab delimited text file
- Sophisticated RDBMS system such as Oracle 8 (your database of choice), MS Access 97, Sybase, Informix, DB/2, etc.
- Mainframe DB2, CICS, VSAM, IMS

The RDBMS system you choose is based on factors that are outside the scope of this book. But, obviously you (or your employer) have made that choice to get to the point

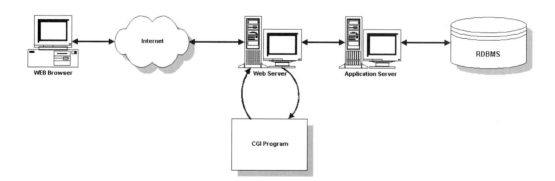

Figure 8–7   Web architecture with a CGI program.

that you are at now. The point is to recognize that the power and capability exists in most programming languages and tools to perform whatever type of data access and manipulation that is required in a Web database application.

With the previous sections as an introduction, the remaining sections in this chapter discuss the details specific to designing Web database applications. Let's begin this material with a discussion of some of the steps to designing a Web database application.

Web Application Design Primer

Designing your Web database application is an intricate activity. There is much to consider and many items to correlate, especially if you incorporate audio/video clips or applets. Consequently, it is best to view the design of your application in terms of four distinct components:

- Database
- Function
- User Interface
- Implementation

In this section, I'll guide you through the process of identifying the various issues of concern in each of these four areas.

Database

In this section, let's consider the four basic types of databases available to you. These are:

- Flat-file database
- Relational database
- Object-oriented database
- Hybrid database

Function

When you design a Web database application, you must begin to consider the functions desired in the application from a very high level. Gradually break the high-level functions (think of these in terms of *groups*) into more discrete and granular functions.

For example, consider a class registration system. Some of the high-level functions might be:

- Collect information
- Process registration
- Invoice-payment processing
- Certification

Once these groups are identified, you can then dissect them into smaller, more discrete chunks. Some of the tools you could use in the course of modeling the data used by your application would be useful when you isolate the application functions. Specifically, consider a CRUD diagram. CRUD stands for Create, Read, Update, and Delete. This is a device used by system and data architects to help collect and classify the relationships in a business system between the entities that exist in that system and the functions used by those entities.

If we look at a CRUD diagram that could be produced for one of the above groups, the Process Registration group, we could develop the CRUD diagram shown at the bottom of this page.

Once we have the CRUD to help us identify the required functions in the new system, we can begin to partition the application into meaningful pieces.

User Interface

The User Interface of a GUI-based application, such as the one you are going to deploy after reading this book, is often considered to be the most important component in a Web database application. For example, if your application has a single purpose (such as displaying an account balance on your credit card), then the appearance of the interface that you create is a significant component.

There are a number of books available that discuss effective GUI design techniques. Although the author in most of these had a Windows-based environment in mind when the book was written, the principles are the same regardless of platform. Most HTTP Browsers are based on the Microsoft Windows metaphor.

If you decide to use a CRUD to begin to dissect your application, you can use the CRUD to begin to consider how the user interface to your application should look. However, this process should *not* be completed until you have a firm handle on the data location and dependency issues (which we will discuss in detail later in this chapter!).

Entity —-> Function V	Web Master	Student	Training Manager	Training Devlpr	Sales	Shipping	Execs
Register/Take Course		C					
Sell/Record Learning Credits					CRUD	CRUD	
Ship Learning Credit Coupons					CRUD	CRUD	
Adjust Course List	CRUD		CRUD	CRU			
Produce/View Status		C	R	R	CR	CRU	R
Adjust Learning Credits			CRUD		CRUD	CRU	

C = Create   U = Update

R = Read   D = Delete

Note: The CRUD Diagram presented here has been simplified for the sake of brevity.

> The process of designing and developing a Web database application is an iterative-based work activity. *When done right*, you will proceed through multiple cycles of: analysis, design, construction, testing. The operative phrase is: "When done right." An effective MIS or business manager recognizes that the process of developing this type of an application is repetitious in nature and will resist the temptation to plunge the first iteration of the system into production.

Implementation

In this context, implementation does not mean slamming the programs, pages, etc. into production. Rather, implementation refers to the placement of functions, events, and processes in the application directly below the user interface layer. This is the level where you define the subroutines needed by your application, the number of programs, the need to access external libraries, and other specifications.

The techniques and processes that you use to implement a Web database application are very similar to the processes you would use in a mainframe application development project, or a client/server application development project. There are some important distinctions however. These are discussed below but listed here as:

- Open architecture
- Client program components
- Statelessness

Open Architecture.   The Web is a much more open architecture than what you would probably ever consider in a client/server environment. In a client/server environment you have a pretty good idea what is available on the server and on the client side. In a Web environment, you don't have this luxury. As a result, you need to plan for and accommodate this.

It is important that you maintain separate development and production environments. This is for reliability reasons, as well as for security reasons. Regarding reliability, the consequences of a CGI program failing when you move it into production are often more significant than when you move a client/server program into production. The nature of the Web is such that its reach far extends anything you would encounter in most client/server applications. Regarding security, the open architecture of the Web means that anyone can access your server. Whether they get past the server is a function of how much security you've implemented and how determined they are to gain entry. A separately created and supported (from the production environment) development environment addresses both of these considerations.

Client Program Components.   In a client/server application. the placement of program function (on the server or on the client) is largely based on where it makes the most sense. In a Web database application, your choice of where to place program function is a bit more complicated. If you are using CGI, there is very little program function that you can place on the client. The CGI program executes on the server. If you are using

JavaScript or one of a number of new tools, then your choice is made a bit easier. JavaScript and these other tools give you the ability to perform logical operations on the data *after* it is sent to the client from the server.

Statelessness. Another important consideration when designing and building Web database applications is the inherent stateless environment of the Web. Consider the following example, which is quite easy to implement in a non-Web application.

1. A user initiates a query of all the employees in a given department.
2. Seeing a row that is of interest, the user selects that employee and pulls up a screen of information specific to that employee.
3. After reviewing this screen, the user observes that one of the pieces of information on the screen is a field named Dependents. In this field is the number 3. The user clicks on this field to see a list of the names and birth dates of all the children for the selected employee.

In a Web database application, the above scenario presents some problems. Without maintaining the state of the application, when Step 2 is executed, the HTTP Server or program has lost its knowledge of what department was used for the query executed in Step 1. As if this were not enough, the stateless Web application would forget what the name of the employee was that the user selected in Step 2 to be able to display the names of the dependents in Step 3.

The good news is that statelessness is quickly becoming a thing of the past in terms of Web database applications. Most of the new development suites coming available, and a lot of the existing languages have facilities for maintaining state. If you are planning on using a development suite or programming language that has no facility to handle state (this includes Oracle 8), then consider doing what most people do—they include a hidden text field in the form that includes a transaction identification number. This is seen below:

```
<input type=hidden  name=state_cd  value=state_cd>
```

In this example, a CGI program can distinguish one form from another based on the hidden fields and perform required processing accordingly.

All right, you know a bit more now about the steps and processes of designing a Web application. So, let's peel back one more layer and look at some of the issues specific to designing a Web *database* application.

Web Database Application Design

In this section, you'll drill down another layer and learn more of the details surrounding the design of a Web database application. It is a process that becomes complicated due *only* to the immature state of the tools and evolving architectures. Regarding the immature state of tools, the process and activities described here are pertinent and relevant regardless to the state of the tools or even to a lesser degree which tools are used. Specific to the evolving architectures of the Web, it is also true that the processes and issues described here are relatively immune to the types of architectural changes occurring.

The Web Database Application Development Methodology

The Web database application development process is a nine-step process that is usually an iterative activity. In other words, as soon as step nine is complete, the process begins again on the same application with step one. Although some companies prefer to combine these nine steps into a three-step Rapid Application Development (RAD) approach, or a four-step prototyping approach, each of the listed activities still occurs. These nine steps are:

1. Systems planning
2. Project initiation
3. Architecture definition
4. Analysis
5. Design (optionally create, update, or reference a system encyclopedia)
6. Development
7. Facilities engineering
8. Implementation
9. Post implementation support

In the analysis phase, work flows are broken down into detailed Object, ERD, and CRUD matrices. These diagrams then become the basic deliverables into the next phase of the cycle: data modeling, user interface prototyping, and process modeling, collectively known as execution architecture. In this phase, the requirements of the application are matched against the current architecture and new tools and data/process distributions are identified.

Once the technology architecture is determined, the application release is designed via the network design, database design, and process design. When this design work is complete, actual component construction is conducted.

Remember, in a Web database application development project, each activity or phase should produce a formal deliverable that documents, for user signoff, the understanding gained at that stage. It is unfortunate, but the trend in Web database application development is to be sloppy during most of the phases of the project. If history is any predictor of the future, I don't think that this "sloppiness" will be allowed to continue much longer.

The Web Database Application Environment

The Web database application development environment is the mix of hardware, software, interfaces, standards, procedures, and training that are used by an enterprise to optimize its information systems professionals abilities to support business objectives. A Web database application development environment should include the following:

- Built-in navigation from one process and/or tool to another
- Standardized screen design
- Integrated and uniformly consistent help and hypertext facilities
- Integrated table maintenance in program modules

- Comprehensive security that permits easy navigation for the authorized and barriers to entry for the unauthorized
- Standard skeleton templates

I want to comment on several of the items listed above. The first being *standardized screen design* and the second being *standard skeleton templates*. Regarding standardized screen design, this is a process of combining good Graphical User Interface (GUI) design principles with the facilities available to accommodate these principles in HTML specifications. Chapter 6 of this book listed references for HTML style guides. Regarding standard skeleton templates, you will define your standard skeleton template based on the unique requirements of your site. The objective of this step in the environment is to construct a framework whereby all the visual components in an application have a consistent look and feel and the processing components take advantage of as much reusable code as possible.

The following section is an introduction to some of the issues specific to security in your Web database application. Although the entire Chapter 19 of this book is devoted to this subject, the material introduced here should help you to understand how security is accommodated in and supplied to a Web database application.

Web Database Application Security

Oracle 8, like other major RDBMS products, includes a number of features that are designed to safeguard access to data, and to the data itself. These features work the same in a Web database environment as they do in a non-Web database environment. If a user is granted access to a database, then as far as Oracle 8 is concerned, that permission is granted regardless to whether the user is accessing the data from the Web or from a non-Web application. In this section, we'll take a look at some of the issues specific to the security of a Web database that are *outside* of the features built in to the Oracle 8 product.

The perils of Web commerce have been discussed at length in the media. As a result of all the attention paid to the subject historically, the development and deployment of commercial Web sites is much less dangerous. There are four primary areas where you must ensure that proper security safeguards are in place to protect your data and resources. These four areas are:

- *Physical*—This is perhaps the easiest component area to ensure safety in that the physical security of computers and computing devices has been an issue of concern to MIS managers for a number of years.

> How many of you remember when you could walk into the mainframe computer operations room with a tape, mount it on the drive, and execute your program from the console? I do, and I don't think I'm that old. Conversely, I also remember the year I was told I could no longer have this type of direct access to the mainframe. It was 1978. That was almost 20 years ago (and I was 24 years old!!!), which means companies have been serious about physical security for at least that long.

- *Software*—Your software is much more vulnerable on a Web site than in almost any other type of delivery method. The Web is a very "open" environment. If you see a graphic on a Web page, or an applet that you'd like, it's easy (albeit illegal) to snag it. Because of this, you must be keenly aware of the security issues persistent as you design your application.

- *System hacker!*—The meaning of this word is clearly understood by even the most neophyte computer user. The consequence of a hacker breaching your system and causing damage of some sort could range in severity from annoyance to catastrophic. Even the variety of breach that is more annoying than anything else will cause you great embarrassment when your boss asks you how someone was able to break through the security layers and gain access to your system. Be warned, making your system too secure from hacker attack is something that is very hard to do, without making it cumbersome or difficult for the good people to access.

- *Data*—"Protect your data!" As much as "Protect yourself" was a moniker for the 1980s and 1990s, "Protect your data" will become an identifying phrase for the 1990s and beyond. An easy argument could be made for paying more attention to protecting the integrity and confidentiality of the data accessed by your Web database application than to the security of the system as a whole.

For additional information on security of your Web database application, check out the following Web sites:

```
http:///www.netscape.com/newsref/std/ssl.html
http://www.nortel.com/entrust/certificates/primer.html
http://www.w3.org/hypertext/www/security/overview.html
http://www.primus.com/staff/paulp/cgi-security
```

The following books are listed here as well as in Chapter 19 as references to you if you want to learn more about Web application security.

Title:	Internet Commerce
Author:	Andrew Dahl and Leslie Lesnick
Publisher:	Simon & Schuster
ISBN:	1-56-205496-1

Title:	Special Edition Using Microsoft Commercial Internet System
Author:	Peter Butler, Roy Cales, and Judy Petersen
Publisher:	Que Books
ISBN:	0-78-971016-1

Title:	Web Site Administrator's Survival Guide
Author:	Jerry Ablan
Publisher:	Sam's Net Publishing
ISBN:	1-57-521018-5

Title:	Special Edition Using CGI
Author:	Jeffry Dwight, Michael Erwin
Publisher:	Que Books
ISBN:	0-78-970740-3

Problem Management

In a Web database application environment, effective problem management is at least as critical as a company's internal applications. Effective problem management means that plans are in place and tools necessary to support the following three areas that are acquired or developed:

- Troubleshooting
- Debugging and problem tracking
- Vendor management

Troubleshooting problem management systems are a critical element to gain productivity and reliability in your applications. Fortunately, features specific to this area are appearing more frequently in Web database application development suites.

Debugging and problem tracking tools facilitate the identification and removal of problems and bugs in the Web application while it is being developed and after it is in production. It is amazing to me, even now, how ineffective most Web applications currently being written really are. In a random, non-scientific survey that I conducted in preparing to write this chapter, I developed the following statistics:

- Number of Web sites visited where I initiated a bogus problem report with a request for a verification contact . . . 46

- Number of Web sites where I reported (with a request for a verification contact) a bug via an e-mail interface to someone identified as SUPPORT@, or WEBMASTER @ . . . 45

- Number of Web sites that had a 1-800 number provided to call in problems . . . 1

- Number of calls received from the 45 companies where I initiated a bogus e-mail problem report on their Web site . . . 0

That's right . . . out of 45 e-mail messages that I sent out reporting a bogus problem with a company's Web site, no one got in touch with me, even though I specifically asked for a direct contact. OK, so you could argue that the person receiving the e-mail investigated the reported (bogus) problem and found nothing wrong and dismissed the whole thing. If you offered this argument, I'd respond that how do they know that the problem I reported either will not happen again or is a problem specific to my HTTP browser? Don't you think they should know this?

Six Principles of Function Placement

A Web database application is in some ways more complex than a client/server application development project. One of those ways is in determining where (what device) to place system functions. You no longer are limited to having to place all of an application's functions on the HTTP server or application server. In this section we'll look at what I call the Six Principles of Function Placement, which are:

- Frequency and Scope
- Application Concurrency
- Location of Data
- Code Reusability
- Processor Allocation
- Application Development Tool

Frequency and Scope. In this context, frequency refers to how often a particular function is needed while scope refers to the diverse ways in which a function is used. Frequency and scope are often at odds with each other in the design stages of a development project. This does not need to be the case. Intuition tells you that if a function is used frequently, it should be placed as close to the calling source as possible to eliminate network degradation. If that happens to be on the HTTP client, then you can do that through an applet.

Generally, the greater the number of calls to a function, the greater is that functions scope. A function that is called by many other functions is said to have "broad scope."

Application Concurrency. Applications deployed over the Web in the form of Web database applications have the opportunity to execute many functions at the same time—in parallel. A sound Web database application design will recognize this and support it.

There are a number of ways to accomplish application concurrency. First, the application can be deployed on a multi-tasking operating system such as Windows NT or Windows 95 so that multiple instances of the application can be running concurrently. Second, data that the application accesses can be partitioned across multiple database servers. In this way, access to the different servers can be controlled programmatically. Third, *cookies* can be placed on a client to keep track of the state of the application. A cookie is a small packet of information that a server stores on a client machine to keep track of certain application-specific information. The interaction between the cookie and the program accessing the cookie allows for application concurrency.

Location of Data. The location of data is often a more complex issue than what most people initially believe. There are choices. It no longer is required that all the data that an application accesses be located on the server. The following are some of the choices that should be considered for where to locate data accessed by the Web database application: Web servers, database servers, application server, client, file server(s).

Code Reusability. Code reusability allows you to more quickly deploy Web database applications that are more reliable than a like application built without taking advantage of code reusability. When building a Web database application, code reusability is certainly a component to be considered.

There are two ways to achieve code reusability. First, by use of Remote Procedure Calls (RPCs), and second, is by providing a linked library of subroutines. Remote Procedure Calls are programs that intercept calls to subroutines, convert those calls to messages, send the messages to the computer where the subroutine really is, and then invoke the subroutine on that computer. In a Microsoft Windows environment, this is via Dynamic Link Libraries (DLLs). Regardless of which method you use, and you could use both simultaneously, you should achieve a higher degree of productivity and reliability in your application the more you are able to take advantage of code reusability.

Processor Allocation.   If your Web application consists of two components only, that being the server and the client, and assuming the client does no more than display HTML pages, then you don't have much of an opportunity to allocate the workload of the application across multiple processors. If this is not the case in your environment, you need to consider processor allocation in the design and construction of your application.

For example, you may have an architectural environment where you have the following components; client, server, application server, and a database server.

Each of these components has a processor. Recognition of each of these processors in the design of your Web database application is important to effectively place functions. An example (albeit extremely simplistic) of this is a scenario where a client asks for a single record to be displayed on his or her machine from a database of 100,000 rows. Does it make more sense to scrub the database for the one record requested on the database server before sending it to the client or to transmit all the rows on the database server across the Web to the client, and then have the client scrub out the one row requested? It makes more sense and is definitely more time efficient to scrub the database for the one record requested and then send that one record to the client.

Application Development Tool.   The choice of tools you make to develop the Web database application has an effect on where application functions are placed. For example, a program written in C++ handles concurrent requests much more efficiently than SmallTalk, or COBOL.

Be careful, though! As seen in Figure 8–8, there is a balance that should be achieved between designing the application within the bounds of the tool set used to construct it and retooling to meet the needs of a new application.

On the one hand, a development environment that continually retools to develop each new application is inefficient and not nearly as productive as it could and should be. On the other hand a development environment that spends excessive resources designing an application to arbitrarily fit the constraints of an existing toolset may be better off investing in a new set of tools and saving the time to try to get the new system to "fit." A development environment that is balanced most efficiently utilizes all of its available resources.

Application Partitioning

Many application partition models exist today. They range from a seven-layer model that tends to be overly complex for Web database applications to a three-layer model. The three-layer model is the simplest, the most widely recognized, and the one that I prefer. This model is comprised of the following layers:

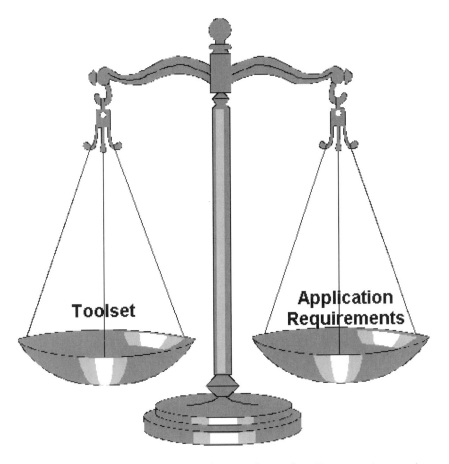

Figure 8–8   Balance the toolset with application requirements.

- Presentation
- Function
- Data management

Using the three-layer model, there are five different ways in which you can partition the tiers on the different platforms that comprise the Web database application. Each of the following are examined in detail on the subsequent pages.

- Distributed presentation
- Remote presentation
- Distributed function
- Remote data management
- Distributed database

Distributed Presentation

Figure 8–9 displays a little used but still valid partition type called distributed presentation. In the distributed presentation architecture, the presentation components of the application are split between two or more different platforms. For example, a customer inquiry application may have certain components that display on the HTTP client machine while other components display on the machine located on the desk of the accounting supervisor. In this model, the *Function* and *Data Management* components reside on the same device as the *Presentation* services.

Remote Presentation

As seen in Figure 8–10, in the remote presentation architecture, the *presentation* components of the application reside on one device type while the other two application tiers reside on another device type. For example, an inventory application for an automobile dealership would provide *presentation* services on the devices of the people accessing the Web application while all application *Function* and *Data Management* services are handled by a server device in a separate location.

Distributed Function

In the distributed function architecture, the *Presentation* and *Function* components of the application reside on the HTTP client device while other portions of the *Function* components of the application and the *Data Management* components reside on another device. For example, a customer service application for a bank may have the *Presentation* and some of the *Function* components of an account inquiry application on the HTTP client device while the other *Function* components and *Data Management* services were provided on an HTTP server and database server.

Remote Data Management

In the remote data management architecture, the *Presentation* and *Function* components of the application reside on the HTTP client while the *Data Management* components reside on another device, either the HTTP server or the database server. For example, a medical

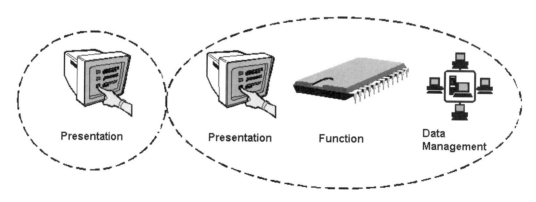

Figure 8–9 Distributed presentation partition type.

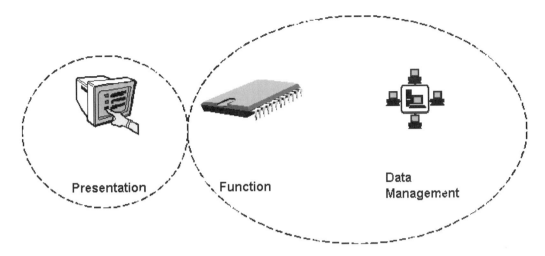

Figure 8–10   Remote presentation partition type.

records application would have the *Presentation* and *Functions* components of the application processing on a Web browser while the *Data Management* components reside exclusively on a separate device type.

Distributed Database

In the Distributed Database architecture, the *Presentation*, *Function*, and some of the *Data Management* components of the application reside on the HTTP client device while other features of the *Data Management* component reside on either the HTTP server or the database server. For example, consider a remote order entry system. This system may have the *Presentation*, *Function*, and some of the *Data Management* components of an application

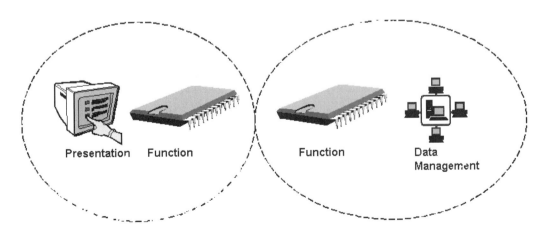

Figure 8–11   Distributed function partition type.

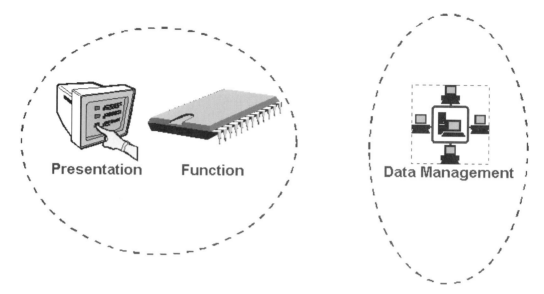

Figure 8–12   Remote data management partition type.

residing on the HTTP client devices. At the same time, at a remote sales office other aspects of the *Data Management* component, such as historical data storage, reside on the HTTP server or database server.

In the research I did prior to writing this book, I found a number of books available that described the process of building Web database applications. By my count, and as of the time I'm writing these words, there are seven. In all cases, the authors presented one application partition strategy—Remote Presentation!

This presentation not only is overly simplistic, but it does not recognize the other strategies you could use to develop and deploy an application to take advantage of the unique combination of the architecture of the Web and the architecture of your company. When you begin to think of the Web, from an application architecture perspective, as little more than an extension of a client/server architecture, then you will subsequently begin to grasp the full potential of this environment for deployment of database applications.

Application Partitioning Summary

There are many issues that determine the method used to partition the application. As the number of Web database applications installed by a company increases, and as organizations implement strategic, mission-critical applications, companies are continuing to look more closely at how they allocate the application components that comprise the three tiers. In the early days of client/server (initially) and Web database applications (secondarily), the Server was used for data management services while presentation and function services were allocated to the client. As technology evolves, a shift of some of the application functions from one device to the other will occur.

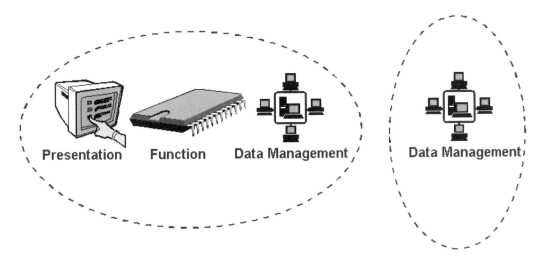

Figure 8–13 Distributed database partition type.

If you want to learn more about application partitioning, I suggest the following sources:

Title:	Application Prototyping
Author:	Bernard H. Boar
Publisher:	John Wiley & Sons
ISBN:	0-47-18931-7

Title:	Implementing Application Solutions in a Client/Server Environment
Author:	Robert L. Koelmel
Publisher:	Wiley-QED
ISBN:	0-47-106068-2

Moving On

In Chapter 9, we peel back one more layer and look at the features in Oracle 8 that are specific to creating database objects such as databases, tables, indexes, queries. You will learn about table relationships, and how to establish and modify them. We also investigate ODBC in greater depth.

CHAPTER 9

Introduction
to Oracle

I n earlier chapters we discussed some of the peripheral issues related to the development of Web database applications, such as:

- An evaluation of Java and JavaScript
- A survey of the most popular development languages
- A review of the most popular development suites
- The design of a Web database application

Beginning with this chapter and continuing into Chapters 10, 11, and 12 you are introduced to the Oracle RDBMS. This chapter shows the process for installing the Oracle server. In addition, it provides an overview of Oracle Enterprise Manager, the software that Oracle provides to administer its databases. Also, new features in Oracle 8 are discussed.

Chapters 10 and 11 cover beginning, intermediate, and advanced queries using Oracle. Chapter 12 delves into Oracle's stored code and new object-oriented features. Then, in later chapters and after covering other necessary material related to Web database application development, we will tie together the issues of Web database application development using Oracle.

What Is Oracle?

I could describe for you what Oracle is, but perhaps it would be more meaningful if I show you what Oracle Corporation has to say about its database products. The following quotation was taken off Oracle Corporation's Web site: `http://www.oracle.com/corporate/press/html/PR061097.102527.html`.

> Oracle 8 is designed to address the needs of today's largest and most complex mission-critical database applications. For demanding online Transaction Processing (OLTP) and high-end data warehouse environments, Oracle 8 provides greater scalability, availability, reliability and manageability than any previous Oracle Server release. At the same time, Oracle 8 brings proven object-relational capabilities and enhanced complex data support to a mainstream commercial relational database.

While this may seem like just promotional hype, Oracle 8 really is a great database system. With all its power comes complexity. As you know, this book introduces you to the process of designing and building Web applications that use Oracle databases. The intent of the book is not to teach you how to use all (or even most) of the features of Oracle. In subsequent chapters you will learn how to build the application components that allow you to access an Oracle database in a Web application. If you want to learn how to use Oracle to build non-Web database applications, I'd recommend the following books:

Title:	Oracle Developer's Guide
Author:	David McClanahan
Publisher:	Osborne-McGraw Hill
ISBN:	0-07-882087-1

Title:	High Performance Oracle Database Automation: Creating Oracle 8 Applications with SQL and PL/SQL
Author:	Jonathan Ingram
Publisher:	Coriolis Group
ISBN:	1-57-610152-5

In the next few sections, you'll learn how to use Oracle Enterprise Manager to connect to a database, to create a user that we'll use for examples in this book, and to create tables, the building blocks of an RDBMS.

What Are the Flavors of Oracle?

So far in this book, we've discussed the Oracle database as if it's a single entity. In actuality, Oracle offers many versions of its product on anything from your humble laptop to a Cray supercomputer. Currently, Oracle is ported to over 80 platforms. If you have a computer, it's a good bet that Oracle has a database that will run on it.

Like any software decision, your choice of which Oracle database to use depends on what you want to do with it. And, which hardware platform to use. Keeping an address list of your garden club certainly doesn't require a full-fledged Oracle Enterprise Server. Nor should you attempt to shoehorn your Fortune 500 order tracking system into a PC-based database. Either could be disastrous, both for your success and for your pocketbook.

Oracle offers its database software in four categories: Oracle Personal Lite, Personal Oracle, Oracle Workgroup Server, and Oracle Enterprise Server.

One of Oracle's strongest selling points is that all of its database products are based on the same database technology. An SQL statement written for Personal Oracle will run just fine in a Workgroup or Enterprise Server. In this way, Oracle's broad range of products allows for easy scalability. An application prototype can be created in Personal Oracle. Once accepted by management, it can be ported to a multi-user robust Workgroup Server environment. When the application runs so well and triples your business size in a year, you can move the database to an Enterprise Server. This will involve a conversion effort no doubt, but the database paradigm remains the same.

In addition, all of the various database types share a networking protocol, called SQL*Net. This allows any database to connect to any other database, regardless of type.

Here's a look at each product.

Personal Oracle Lite

Oracle Personal Lite, is Oracle's small footprint, with fewer megabytes than your average database. Oracle positions this product in three ways:

- As a prototyping database for use with its rapid application development tools, such as Power Objects
- As a stand-alone database for small database projects
- As an adjunct database to be used for mobile applications with a more powerful Oracle server

To fit Oracle Personal Lite into so little RAM and hard drive space, Oracle was forced to pare down its feature set. But don't worry, Personal Oracle Lite has your normal tables and views as well as SQL*Net and ODBC networking. In addition, to support mobile databases it has extensive replication functionality.

Personal Oracle

Want a database to run on your PC, but need more than Oracle Personal Lite can deliver? Then Personal Oracle is for you.

Oracle has positioned Personal Oracle to compete with such PC-based databases as Access 97, Paradox, and Approach. But, because its architecture is based on Oracle's Enterprise Server, Personal Oracle has many powerful features that you won't find in its competitors: a multithreaded architecture, a shared database buffer, and row-level locking, to name a few.

Both Personal Oracle and Personal Oracle Lite are shipped with Oracle Navigator, a GUI-based administration tool perfect for a PC-based database.

Oracle Workgroup Server

Next on the Oracle database ladder is its workgroup server, its workhouse platform—it doesn't get a lot of fanfare, but fills an important niche, running on Windows NT servers and low-to-medium end UNIX machines.

Oracle gave this product the name Workgroup Server to position itself in the small-business or workgroup database market. Oracle Workgroup Server shares a great deal of the functionality of its big brother, the Enterprise Server, but its price (starting at about $2,500) and ease-of-use make it a smart choice for a company just starting in the Oracle world. When the number of database users numbers less than two dozen, Workgroup Server makes sense.

In addition, Oracle smartly integrates its WebServer product with the Workgroup Server. With this product, you can create intranet solutions without the hassle of complicated setup or maintenance. Moreover, the Web components of the Workgroup Server are easily configurable through HTML forms.

Oracle Enterprise Server

Have you bought an airline ticket lately? Ordered a copy of your transcript? Paid your credit card bill? Chances are that somewhere in the process the information you see passed through an Oracle Enterprise Server. Oracle leads the industry in this category. Even traditionally mainframe data processing shops will probably have at least one Oracle database churning away. Oracle Enterprise Servers are used for online transaction processing systems, decision support systems, and data warehouses.

As the name suggests, the Enterprise Server is built to withstand the pressures of the enterprise environment. With the proper hardware, it can support hundreds, even thousands, of simultaneous users. The Enterprise Server is tuned to take advantage of the high-end platforms (such as UNIX) that it runs on. It supports parallel querying for multiprocessor systems. Enterprise Server has built-in fault tolerance, with support for clustering. If you require impeccable reliability and performance, the Enterprise Server is your product.

Be forewarned, a piece of software as complicated as the Enterprise Server doesn't manage itself. While the other versions of Oracle don't require a lot of attention once set up, an Enterprise Server requires the services of at least one full-time database administrator (DBA). As the growing, ever-changing behemoth that it is, the Enterprise Server requires constant attention to keep it running and finely tuned.

Enterprise Manager, a powerful GUI database administration tool, is included with the Workgroup Server and the Enterprise Server. From a single PC, databases around the world can be monitored and maintained with the ease of a point-and-click environment. The table on the next page shows Oracle's spectrum of database offerings.

This information is correct at time of publication, but is subject to change. Consult Oracle's web site (www.oracle.com) for the latest product requirements and availability.

Oracle is a great tool to develop Web accessible and non-Web accessible databases. These databases can be accessed from a wide range of languages and application development tools. Its developer tools are very convenient and easy to use for building applications accessing Web databases and non-Web databases.

Useful Oracle URLs

The table on page 171 presents a list of useful URLs if you are using Oracle to build your databases to be accessible over the Web.

	Personal Oracle Lite	**Personal Oracle**	**Oracle Workgroup Server**	**Oracle Enterprise Server**
Platforms	Windows 3.1 Windows 95 Windows NT Mac OS	Windows 3.1 Windows 95 Windows NT IBM OS/2 Mac OS	Digital Unix HP-UX IBM OS/2 IBM AIX Windows NT Netware SCO OpenServer SCO UnixWare Sun Solaris	over 80 platforms, 40+ UNIX, VMS, MVS, VM, HP MPE/XL, Siemens, ICL, Novell Netware, OS/2, Windows, Windows NT, and Macintosh
Database Components	Personal Oracle Lite	Personal Oracle	Oracle Workgroup Server	Oracle Server Distributed Database Option TM * Parallel Query Option TM * Parallel Server TM Option* Advanced Replication Option* WebServer ConText Option* Spatial Data Option* Video Server*
Connectivity	Net (SQL*Net) ODBC drivers	Net (SQL*Net) ODBC drivers	Net (SQL*Net) ODBC drivers Oracle Objects for OLE	Net (SQL*Net) Oracle Advanced Networking Option* ODBC drivers Oracle Objects for OLE
Programming			PL/SQL Oracle Call Interface	PL/SQL Oracle Call Interface Pro*C/C++ Pro*Cobol Pro*Fortran SQL*Module ® (C, ADA)
Management	Navigator	Navigator	Enterprise Manager	Enterprise Manager Enterprise Manager Power Pack TM Option*
Memory Requirements	1MB	16 MB (24MB for NT)	32MB	large, depends on platform
Hard Drive Requirements	5MB	50 MB	65 MB except for UNIX 200MB	large, depends on platform
General Price Range	a couple hundred	a few hundred	thousands	tens of thousands to millions

* indicates an option

Table 3–1   Useful Oracle URLs

URL	Description
http://www.oramag.com	Oracle's print publication *Oracle Magazine* hosts this timely and informative site. Here you can read the latest news from Oracle, search the magazine's archives, get helpful SQL tips, and get a free subscription to the magazine.
http://www.oreview.com	A companion to the independent monthly *Oreview*, this site offers access to recent articles, links to Oracle sites and user groups, and a free subscription offer.
http://www.jcc.com/oracle.html	This site sponsors a search engine for the USENET Oracle newsgroup and listservers.
http://www.olab.com	Oracle's Internet Server Products division offers up-to-the-minute news on Oracle's Web-related products and trial versions of software for your download.
http://www.orafans.com	This is the site for, you guessed it, Oracle fans. This site links to Oracle sites worldwide and provides forums to discuss the gamut of Oracle offerings.

newsgroups:
  comp.databases.oracle.server
  comp.databases.oracle.tools
  comp.databases.oracle.misc
  comp.databases.oracle.market
	These four USENET news groups are a great place to pose questions to fellow users, to catch up on the latest Oracle scuttlebut, and to find that lucrative position as an Oracle developer.

In addition to the above URLs, you may find the following books of value.

Oracle: The Complete Reference, 3rd Edition

By: George Koch and Kevin Loney
Publisher: Osborne/McGraw Hill
ISBN: 0-07-882097-9

High Performance Oracle Database Applications

By: Donald Burleson
Publisher: Coriolis Group
ISBN: 1-57-610100-2

Interactive Web Publishing with Microsoft Tools

By: Evangelos Petroutsos
Publisher: Ventana
ISBN: 1-56-604462-6

Oracle DBA Handbook

By: Kevin Loney
Publisher: Osborne McGraw Hill
ISBN: 0-07-881182-1

The languages listed below are all front-end application development languages. By that I mean that they all can be used to write applications that access Oracle databases.

Setting Up Oracle

The first thing that you need to build a Web database is, well, a database. This section will show you the process for installing Oracle software and creating a database, specifically for an Oracle 8 Server on a Windows NT 4.0 machine. The installation process varies depending on the hardware platform and operating system. If you're using a different machine, refer to the platform-specific installation documentation that came with your Oracle Server software. At any rate, this section is useful to learn the general procedures for Oracle installation.

> If you're working in a corporate environment where you have an Oracle database administrator (DBA), ask him or her for an environment where you are able to experiment without the fear of breaking anything critical. Most shops have a machine or at least one database instance that can be used as a "sandbox" for such investigation. Explain what you're doing here. Just ask nicely and bring chocolate-chip cookies!

The installation process including three steps: installing the Oracle executable software on the server, creating a database, and setting up client software and networking.

Installing Oracle

Insert the Oracle 8 Server CD in your CD-ROM drive. If you have *autoboot* enabled, you're asked if you'd like to install Oracle as seen in Figure 9–1.

Otherwise, run the Setup executable from the Run selection of your Start Menu, where X: is your CD-ROM drive specificiation.

First, you're asked what language you'd like to run your Oracle products under. Oracle now supports over 20 languages. If the language of your choice is not supported by an Oracle product you're using, English is chosen as a default. Here we'll choose English.

Notice the Help button in the bottom left of the box. If you get confused at any time during the Installation, just click on the button for context-sensitive help. Here for in-

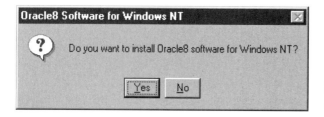

Figure 9–1   The CD autoboot dialog box.

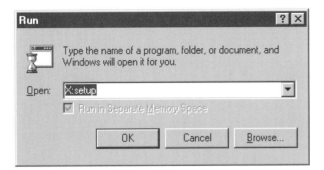

Figure 9–2 Starting the Oracle installation manually.

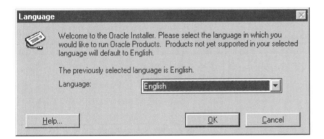

Figure 9–3 Choosing a language for Oracle.

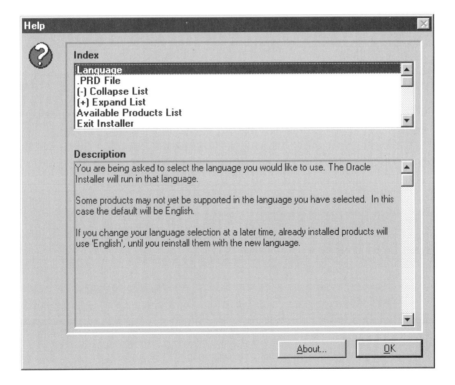

Figure 9–4 Getting help for choosing a language.

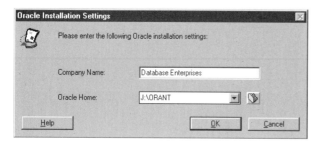

Figure 9–5 Supplying installation settings.

stance, you can get more information about choosing a language. Most Oracle Windows-based applications support this kind of help mechanism.

Next, Oracle asks you for your company name and Oracle Home. Oracle Home is the top-level directory where all Oracle executable and related files are stored. The default directory name on a Windows NT machine is \ORANT. Make sure that you have sufficient room on the drive to which you're installing—Oracle 8 for Windows NT requires approximately 200MB of disk space. If Oracle finds that there's insufficient room, it will ask you for another drive.

Once you've clicked on the OK button, you're next asked for the type of installation you want to perform. Since we're setting up an Oracle 8 Server in this case, leave the default "Oracle 8 Server Products" radio button selected. If you're creating a client machine that will not have its own Oracle Server, you can click on "Oracle 8 Client Products." If you'd like to install specific products, you can choose "Programmer/2000" or "Custom Installation."

After you've chosen to install the Server products, the Installer will process for a few seconds and then ask you if you want to create a sample database. In this case, we do. Choose the Replication database option, instead of the default Standard database, since you'll probably want to use replication in your Web database.

You can always create other database instances later, but it's nice to have Oracle create one for you automatically as you're getting the hang of the system.

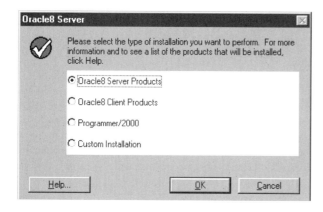

Figure 9–6 Choosing the installation type.

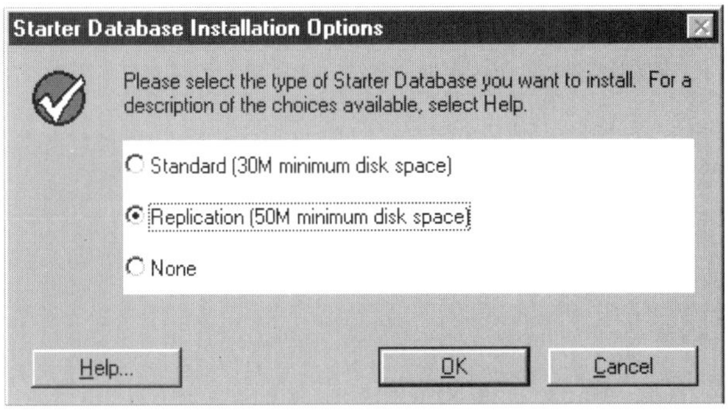

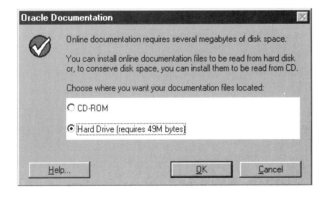

Figure 9–7 Requesting a sample database.

Next, you're asked if you want to install the Oracle Server documentation on your hard drive. If you've got the disk space, it's advisable to install the documentation onto your hard drive. Since Oracle no longer supplies a complete set of paper documentation with its Server purchase in most cases, it's important to keep the documentation easily accessible. Oracle has implemented its documentation using HTML and Java, so you can easily browse the contents using your favorite Web browser. If you don't have space, you can mount your Oracle 8 Server CD-ROM when you need it.

The CD-ROM will whirl for awhile while Oracle analyzes the dependencies among the various software components and then begins installing the Oracle software. This process can take 15 minutes to an hour depending on the speed of your machine. Fortunately, Oracle has provided a status bar to keep you apprised of its installation progress.

So, what exactly is Oracle installing anyway, you might ask. Oracle installs the Oracle 8 Server software, including all of its components, various database utilities (such as import, export, and loader), the SQL*Plus application, as well as the Oracle Enterprise Manager database administration suite. (No wonder it takes so much hard drive space!) And, since we requested it, a sample database, with replication features, is installed and started up.

Once you see the alert box as shown in Figure 9–10, you've successfully installed Oracle.

Figure 9–8 Asking for documentation installation.

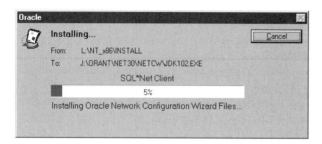

Figure 9–9 Installation status bar.

Once the installation is completed, you'll find that the installer has added two new program groups: Oracle for Windows NT and Oracle Enterprise Manager for easy access to your database programs. The two most common reasons an Oracle installation fails is a lack of disk space or another application is run during execution. Don't run any other application while the installer is running and be sure you have sufficient disk space. If the installation fails for some reason, delete the Oracle Home directory (by default \ORANT) and restart the installation.

The installation procedure creates NT services to automatically start up the sample database when you boot the machine. You can see the services by clicking on the Services icon in your Control Panel. All Oracle services are prefixed with "Oracle."

The installation process sets these services to start up the database and network when you boot the NT machine. If you'd like to start these services manually, you can make the change here.

The installation creates the default administration users: SYS (with a password of change_on_install) and SYSTEM (with a password of manager), as well as some sample demo users.

Oracle Enterprise Manager

For years, Oracle produced its database servers with the most rudimentary software for its administration. Third-party database administration tools proliferated and Oracle realized that it had missed its mark. In 1995, Oracle released Oracle Enterprise Manager,

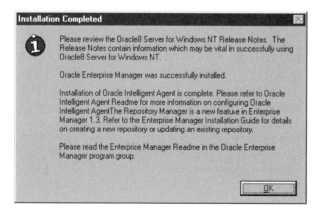

Figure 9–10 Message indicating that Oracle installation is successful.

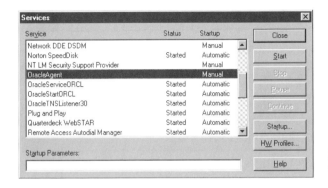

Figure 9–11   Oracle NT services.

as a tool included with the license of its Workgroup Server and Enterprise Server products.

Oracle Enterprise Manager (OEM) is Oracle's database administrator tool suite. Think of it as your command module from which you control your database. OEM comes standard with seven modules:

- *Enterprise Manager*—console serves as a central console for all OEM components; offers job scheduling, event management and proactive database monitoring
- *Security Manager*—controls user, role, and privilege creation and maintenance
- *Schema Manager*—provides a facility for creating, editing, and viewing database objects
- *Storage Manager*—manages the database's physical structure including tablespaces, datafiles, and rollback segments
- *Instance Manager*—allows starting up and shutting down of a database, changing of database configuration parameters, and managing connected users
- *Data Manager*—provides a graphical interface to Oracle's import and export utilities
- *Software Manager*—administers software distribution in a client/server environment

For an additional licensing fee, Oracle offers the Performance Pack, a set of utilities used to monitor how the database is functioning. By using these tools, you can diagnose a poorly-performing database or circumvent many performance problems before they occur. Components include:

- *Expert*—assists in the tuning of a database using well-tested performance techniques
- *Lock Manager*—monitors database object resource contention between sessions
- *TopSessions*—displays, in realtime, those database sessions that are using the most system resources

- *Tablespace Manager*—shows fragmentation and storage characteristics of tablespaces
- *Trace*—allows tracing of database and networking, helpful in determining the source of performance problems

---

Tip: It's no wonder that Oracle's code name for OEM was Battlestar! At the product's introduction at the International Oracle Users' Week in 1995, t-shirts and posters replete with starships and lasers covered the Philadelphia Convention Center.

If you're working in a corporate development environment, you'll need to ask your DBA for access to OEM and the proper grants to run. For the explanations in the rest of this chapter, we'll assume that you have an instance all to yourself with the password to the SYSTEM account. If you don't have such access and have to share a database with other users, ask your DBA for an account with these privileges:

CONNECT

UNLIMITED TABLESPACE privilege

SELECT_CATALOG_ROLE role

To get started, select the "Enterprise Manager" program item from the "Oracle Enterprise Manager" PROGRAM group. You are greeted with a dialog box "Repository Login Information." Here login as SYSTEM and supply SYSTEM's default password MANAGER. If, when you installed Oracle 8, you allowed the installer to create a default database for you, you don't need to supply a service name. Leave the Connect As: box set to "Normal."

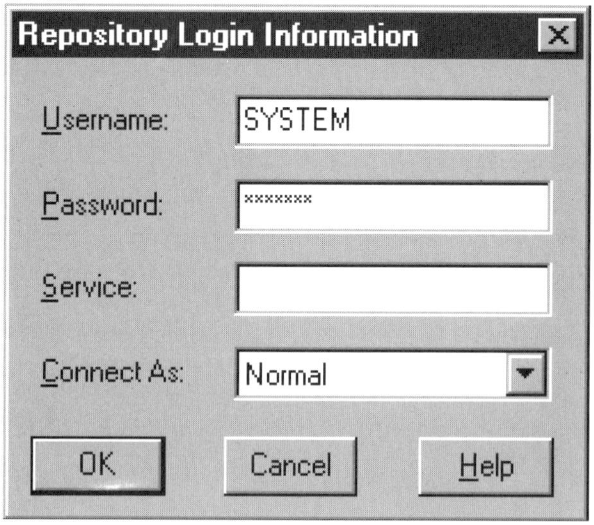

Figure 9–12 Repository Login Information dialog.

> If you're in a networked environment, you'll need to find out your database name from your DBA or network administrator. Specifying a database name allows OEM to use SQL*Net, Oracle's networking protocol, to connect to your database no matter where it is located on your network. If your situation requires a database name for connection, supply it in any of the login examples you see in this and the next three chapters.

Oracle attempts to connect to your database repository. Since this is a new instance, you'll be asked if you'd like to create one. Click on OK to create the repository. While you can create one repository to serve many database instances, for this exercise, the repository will be stored in your current instance. The repository stores information used as Oracle Enterprise Manager goes about its business.

Once connected to the repository, you are greeted with OEM's main console, which is made up of four windows, clockwise from the top left: Navigator, Map, Event Management, and Job Scheduling. The Navigator provides an object browser to show you your network and its various nodes. The Map offers a visual representation of your database network and the relationships among them. In Event Management, you can specify certain database events to be monitored on a periodic basis (such as whether the instances are up and running) and to be notified if something is amiss. Job Scheduling allows you to automate repetitive tasks.

The OEM console is designed to be a highly sophisticated administration tool for a complex network of databases across an enterprise or around the world. Unless you aspire to become a full-fledged Oracle DBA, you won't need to deal much with its details. For now, we'll use the console merely as a launching pad for the various Manager tools.

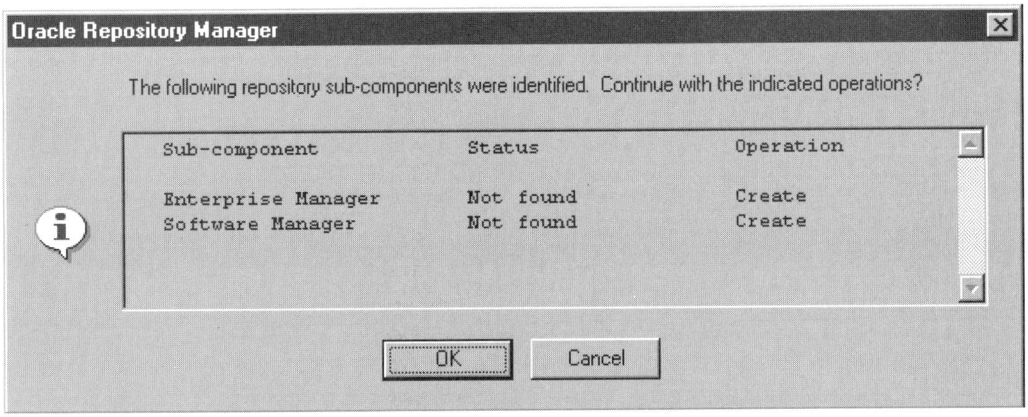

Figure 9–13   Creating an OEM repository.

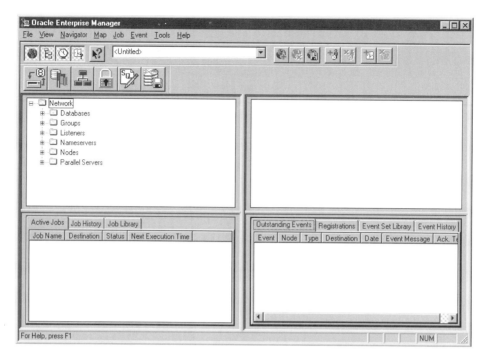

Figure 9–14   Oracle Enterprise Manager main console.

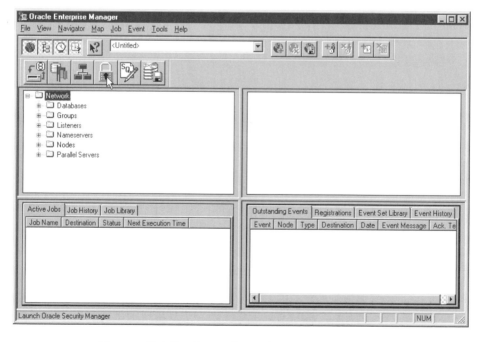

Figure 9–15   Launching Security Manager.

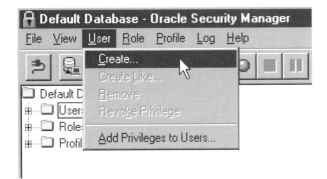

Figure 9–16 Choosing the Create User menu item.

Creating a User

We'll use OEM first to create a user. Since we're creating a web database, we'll create a user called *webdevel* with a password of *www* that will be used in examples through this, and the next three chapters. We'll use the Security Manager component to add the user. To start Security Manager, click on the Padlock icon in the tool bar.

Since we've only logged into the repository, it is necessary to log into the instance again. Log into your database as SYSTEM as shown in Figure 9–12.

To create *webdevel* user, select the User | Create menu item.

In the Create User dialog box, enter *webdevel* as the username. Enter the *www* in the password field (and again to confirm you've spelled it correctly in the next field). Using

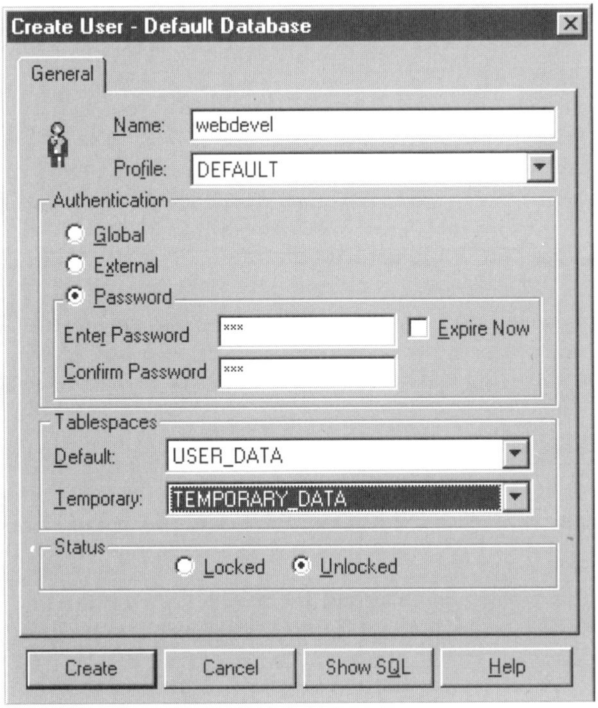

Figure 9–17 Creating the *webdevel* user.

the drop-down menu items, choose the USER_DATA tablespace as the default tablespace and TEMPORARY_DATA tablespace as the temporary tablespace. Leave all other fields as they are. Note that the username and password are not case-sensitive.

What's a tablespace? A tablespace is a logical storage area, made up of one or more physical files, where database objects such as tables and indexes are stored in an Oracle database. Whenever you create a table or index and you don't specify a particular tablespace, it will be created in your default tablespace. Sorting and other behind-the-scenes work that requires disk space is done in the temporary tablespace.

This dialog box, as well as many others in OEM, has a Show SQL button. If you click on it, OEM shows you the SQL (the language the database speaks) that will be run when you click on the Create button.

Not only is this helpful for checking your entries, but it is also a great way to learn SQL needed to administer a database. As you become more adept at using Oracle, you may find using SQL scripts instead of OEM more efficient. In the meantime, whenever you see the Show SQL button, click on it and study the SQL!

Click on the Create button to create the *webdevel* user. We can now use the Hierarchy in the left window of Security Manager to confirm that the *webdevel* user has been created. Double click on the Users node and then highlight the WEBDEVEL node. Information about the *webdevel* user can be seen in the right window.

If you wanted to make changes to *webdevel*, you can make changes in the right window, click on the Apply button, and the changes will take affect.

If you want to delete a user, click on the user's name and press the DELETE key. You'll be warned that you're about to delete the user.

Since we really want to keep the *webdevel* user, click on the No button.

Throughout our examples, we'll want the *webdevel* user to have full database access. We'll therefore grant the system *DBA* authority. This will allow *webdevel* to perform any action in the database. Normally you would never grant DBA access to a regular user, but we'll do it in this example to preclude any permissions problems. (Chapter 19 will describe privilege and other security topics in greater detail.)

To grant unlimited tablespace to *webdevel*, choose the User | Add Privileges to Users... menu item. In the Add Privileges to Users dialog box,

- Click on the *WEBDEVEL* user in the upper box
- Choose Roles from the Privilege Type: drop-down box

Figure 9–18 Displaying the SQL for Creating the *webdevel* User.

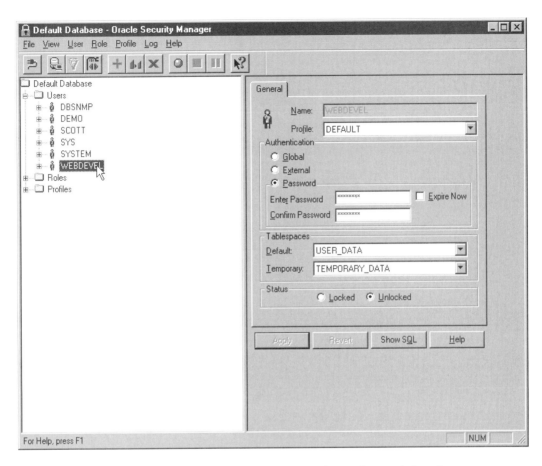

Figure 9–19   Displaying information about the *webdevel* user.

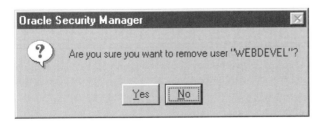

Figure 9–20   Deleting the *webdevel* user.

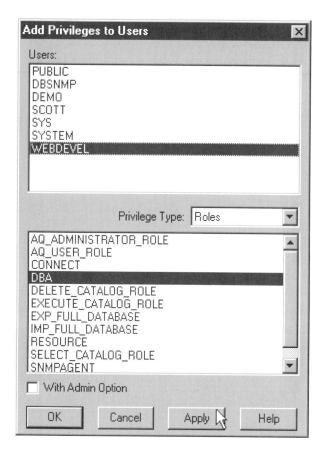

Figure 9–21   Granting the
DBA role to webdevel.

- Scroll down and highlight *DBA* in the lower box
- Click on the Apply button
- Close the dialog box by clicking on the Cancel button

You can see the privilege you granted by navigating down from the Webdevel node to Roles granted node.

Here you see the DBA role as well as the Connect role, which is granted when the user is originally created. The Connect role allows the user to gain access to the database. You can take away the Connect role from a user if you'd like to deactivate the user without deleting the user from the database.

This is all we'll do for now with the Security Manager. Close Security Manager from the menu item File | Exit to Console.

Creating a Table

Tables are the building blocks of any RDBMS, including Oracle. Tables are made up of columns that store specific information about each row of data. For the example below, we'll create two tables.

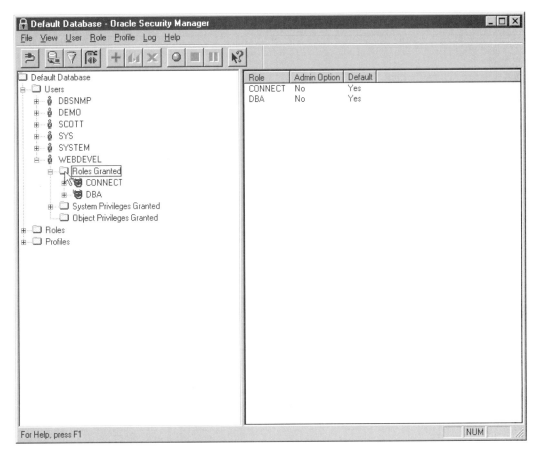

Figure 9–22   Viewing the roles granted to webdevel.

The first table is used to hold a list of sales representatives and the sales regions they serve. The table name is *sales_rep*. The columns and the type of data they hold are as follows:

- rep_id—a unique number (up to 5 digits) to identify a particular sales rep
- rep_last_name—a character string up to 20 characters holding the last name of the sales rep
- rep_first_name—a character string up to 15 characters holding the first name of the sales rep
- active_flag—a one character flag (Y or N) indicating if the sales rep is currently active
- region_code—a 5 character code representing the region the sales rep is responsible for

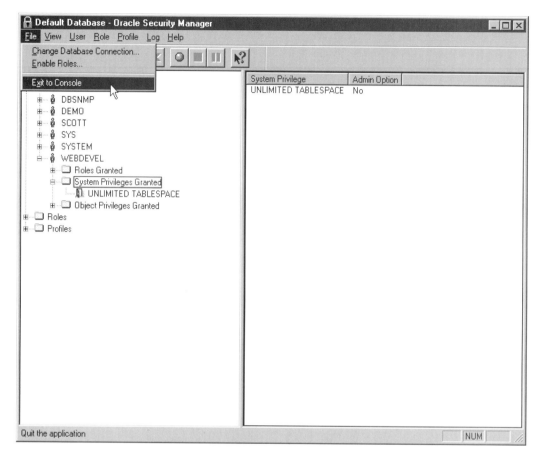

Figure 9–23   Exiting Security Manager.

The second table, *region*, holds a list of region codes and their descriptions:

- region_code—a 5 character code representing a sales region
- region_desc—a text description of the sales region

The Schema Manager is used to create tables in OEM. From the console, click on the Schema Manager icon.

Log into Schema Manager as *webdevel*, using the password you assigned, *www*.

Schema Manager looks very much like Security Manager. The left window has a hierarchy where you can navigate through the various database objects. The right window is used to display details about the object selected in the left window.

A "Schema" in the Oracle world is a user and objects owned by that user. You'll often hear of an object's owner referred to as the schema. In our example, *webdevel* is the schema. The tables *sales_rep* and *region* exist within *webdevel*'s schema.

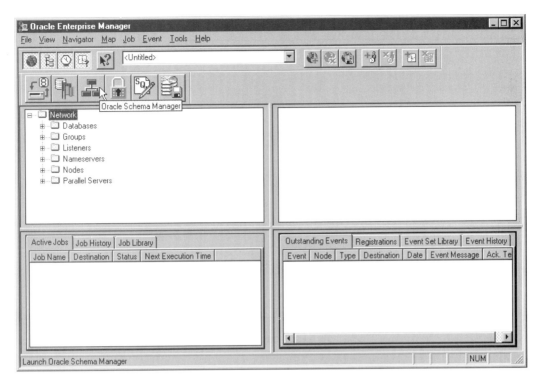

Figure 9–24   Launching Schema Manager.

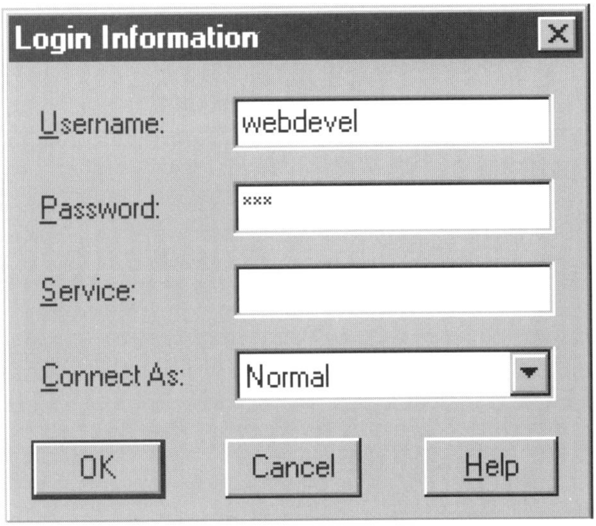

Figure 9–25   Logging into
Schema Manager as webdevel.

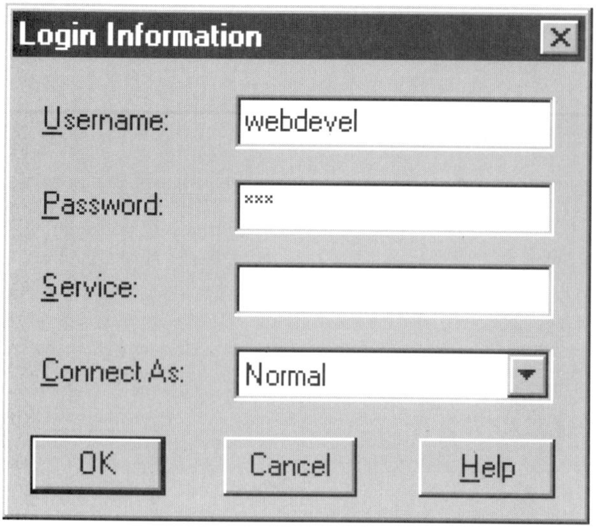

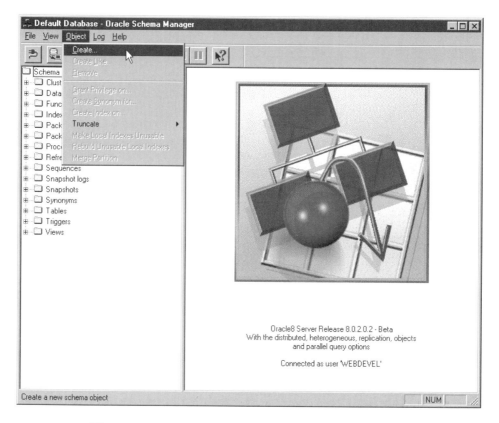

Figure 9–26   The opening Schema Manager screen.

Figure 9–27   Starting the table creation process.

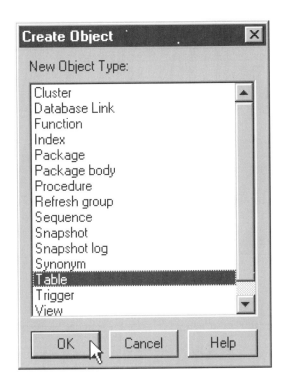

Figure 9–28   Selecting Table to create.

The Schema Manager allows you to create, delete, and change objects in your database. We'll use it now to create the *sales_rep* table.

To create a table, select the Object | Select menu item and choose table from the scroll list.

There are two ways to create a table: by using a table wizard or manually. We'll use the table wizard for this example.

Type in the table name in the first field. Leave the schema and tablespace as they are. Click on the `<Next>` button to go to the next screen.

Now we define the first column, using the following steps:

- Type `rep_id` in the Column Name field.

- Choose the Number datatype in the Column field.

Figure 9–29   Choosing to use the Table Wizard.

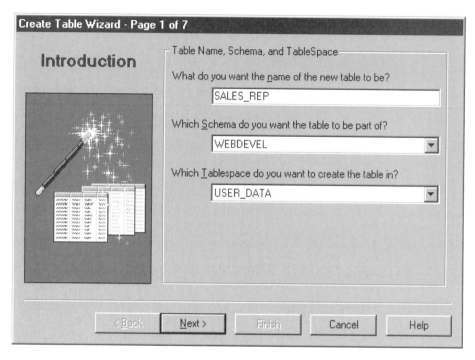

Figure 9–30 Specifying the Table Name.

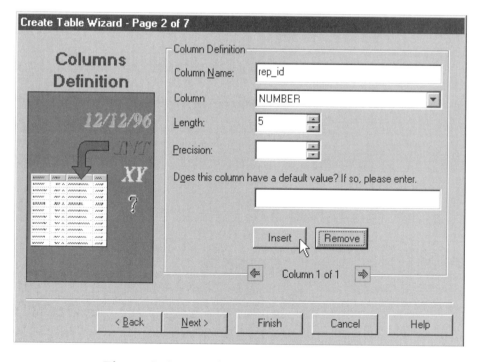

Figure 9–31 Defining the rep_id column.

- Enter the number 5 for the column width.
- Leave the other fields blank and click on the Insert button to continue to the second column.

Follow the same procedure for the rep_last_name column, but define the datatype as varchar2 (which stands for variable character string) and length as 20.

Repeat the procedure for the rep_first_name column with a datatype as varchar2 and length as 15.

Now create the active_flag column as a varchar2 with a length of 1. Enter the value Y in the default value field. This will set the column to Y if a value is not specified when the row is created.

Finally, create the region_code column as a varchar2 with a length of 5. Instead of clicking on Insert, click on the Next> button to go to the next dialog box.

You are asked if you would like to create a primary key for the table. A primary key is a column (or columns) that uniquely identifies a row in your table. In this case, the sales rep ID (rep_id) is the table's primary key. When a primary key is defined, a unique index is created on the primary key columns, which ensures that the primary key values are not duplicated and speeds access to the table data.

To create a primary key for the sales_rep table, follow these steps:

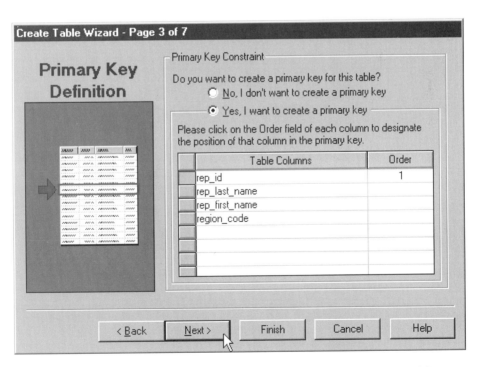

Figure 9–32   Specifying a Primary Key for the sales_rep table.

- Click on the Yes radio button
- Click on the column, rep_id. A 1 shows up in the order column to show what position in the primary key the column is. Since we're only defining a primary key with one column, we're done. Click on Next> to go to the next dialog.

Now you're asked whether each column can be null (that is, contains no value) and if it must be unique. We want to ensure that a value is entered in the active_flag column. Navigate to the active_flag column using the right arrow.

Click on the "No, it cannot be null" radio button to create a Not Null constraint for this column.

When you define a column as not allowing nulls or requiring uniqueness, a constraint is created for this column. A constraint validates data before it is saved into the database. If you try to insert or update data that violate these constraints, an error occurs and the operation fails. Because validation is performed at the database level, it need not be coded in your application.

Click on the <Next> button to continue.

The next page asks you to define foreign key relationships with other tables. A foreign key defines a relationship between a column (or columns) in one table to the primary

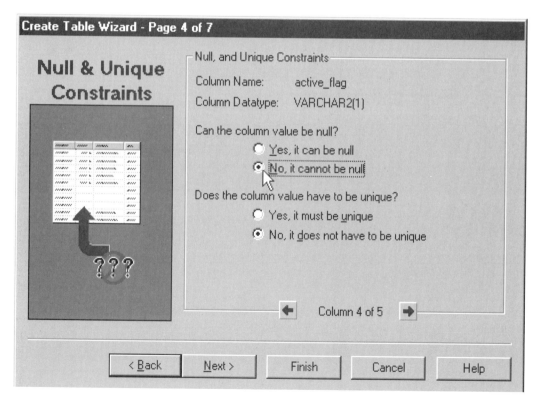

Figure 9–33   Defining Not Null and Unique Constraints.

key in another table. The database ensures that the column(s) defined as a foreign key exist as the primary key in the related table. Since we've not defined any other tables yet, this is not applicable. We'll be defining a foreign-key relationship in the next example.

Click on the <Next> button to continue.

Hang on, we're almost there. On the next page, you're asked if you want to define check conditions for any of the columns. A check condition is a constraint that ensures that a column value is in a certain range of values. The active_flag column should only allow a *Y* or an *N.*

Create a check condition by doing the following:

Using the right arrow, bring up the active_flag column.

Click on the "Yes, the column has a check condition" radio button.

Enter the following text in the check condition field: `active_flag` in ('Y','N')

Finally, we're at the last dialog box. Here you can look at your column definitions. Scroll right and left using the scroll bar. If you find that you didn't set something up correctly, use the <Back button to return to the appropriate page.

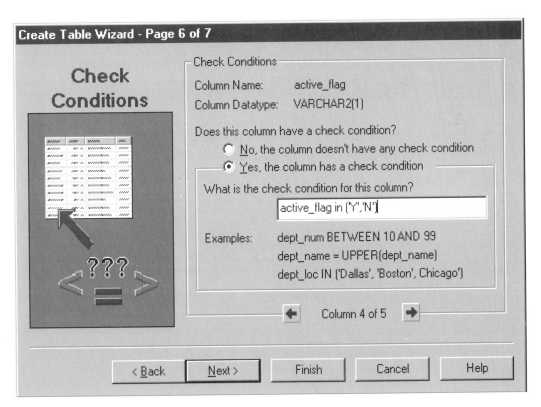

Figure 9–34   Entering a Check Condition for the active_flag Column.

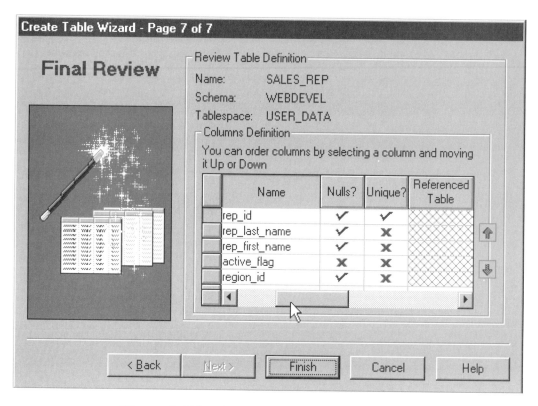

Figure 9–35   Reviewing the Table Definition.

You can reorder your columns at this point by highlighting a column name and then clicking on the up or down arrow until the column is where you'd like it. Let's leave the columns where they are. Go ahead and create the table by clicking on the Finish button.

Congratulations! You've created your first table. You can see the results of your handiwork using the object hierarchy that Schema Manager provides. To see the table definition:

- Double-click on the Tables node
- Double-click on the Webdevel schema node
- Double-click on the Sales_rep table node

You'll see the table definition in the right window. To see more attributes about each column, use the horizontal scroll bar.

Now that we've used the Table Wizard to create the *Sales_rep* table, let's create the region table manually.

Creating a Table Manually

Start the table creation process as you did earlier, as shown in Figures 9–27 and 9–28. But, when asked how you want to create the table, choose the "Create Table Manually" radio button and click the OK button.

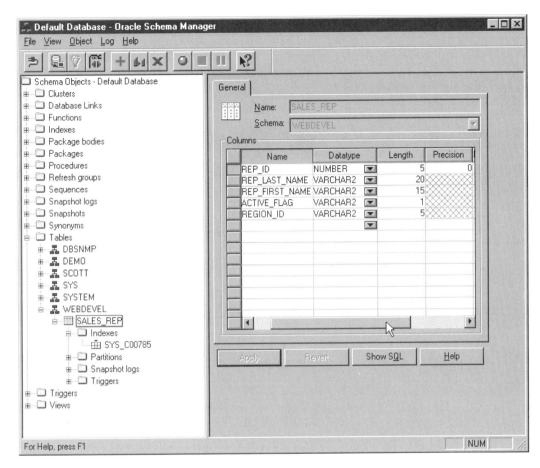

Figure 9–36 Viewing the *Sales_rep* table definition.

Figure 9–37 Choosing to create a table manually.

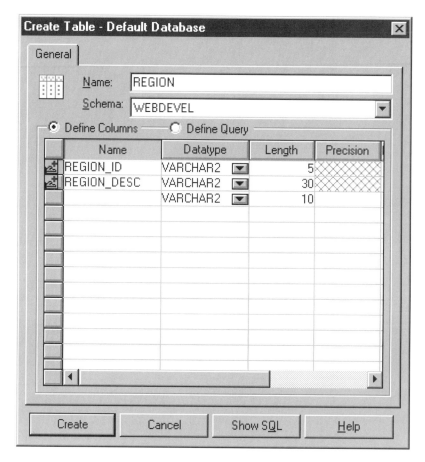

Figure 9–38   Defining the table *region.*

Enter the table name, region, and the two columns as shown in Figure 9–38.

To define the columns as not allowing nulls, slide the scroll bar to the right, click on the blue check marks until they change to red X's. An X means that nulls are not allowed.

The Show SQL button is available here. Click on it to see the SQL that will create the table.

Click on the Create button to create the table.

Now we'll add a primary key to the table. Here's how to do it:

- Highlight the Region table in the object hierarchy.

- Click on the Advanced Mode button (the fourth from the left) to enable advanced property sheets for the table. (A set of tabs will appear in the right window behind the General page.)

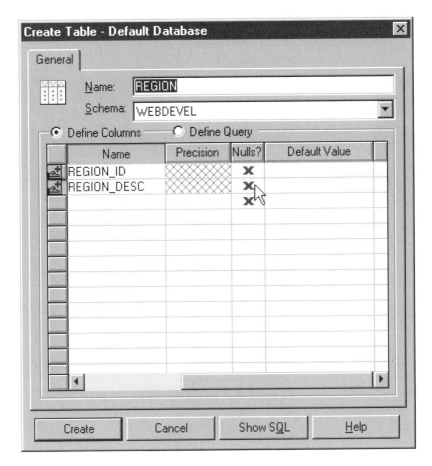

Figure 9–39   Setting *region*'s columns to Not Null.

- Click on the Constraints tab. You'll see that two check constraints (the Not Nulls that you defined earlier) appear in the upper-right region labeled Constraints on the Table. Under the check constraints, choose Primary from the drop-down list in the Primary column. Allow the constraint name to be system assigned.
- In the Constraint Definition region below, choose the Region_ID column.
- Click on the Apply Button to create the primary key.

Figure 9–40   Showing the SQL for table creation.

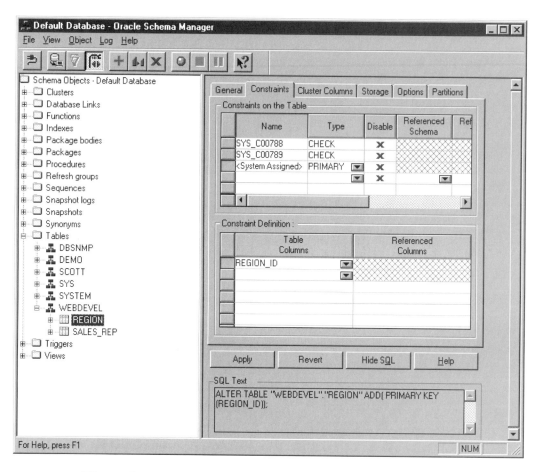

Figure 9–41   Creating a primary key on the Region table.

Now we'll define a foreign key relationship between the region_id column in the sales_rep table and the primary key of the Region table. This will ensure that no invalid region IDs are entered into the sales_rep table. To define a foreign key:

- Highlight the Sales_rep table in the object hierarchy.
- On the Constraints page in the right window, add a constraint of type foreign, with a referenced schema of Webdevel, and a referenced table of Region. You may need to use the scroll bar to see the referenced table column.
- In the Constraint Definition window below, select the region_id column from the drop-down list for both the Table Columns and Referenced Columns. This defines the foreign-key relationship between the region_id column in the Sales_rep table and the region_id primary key in the Region table.

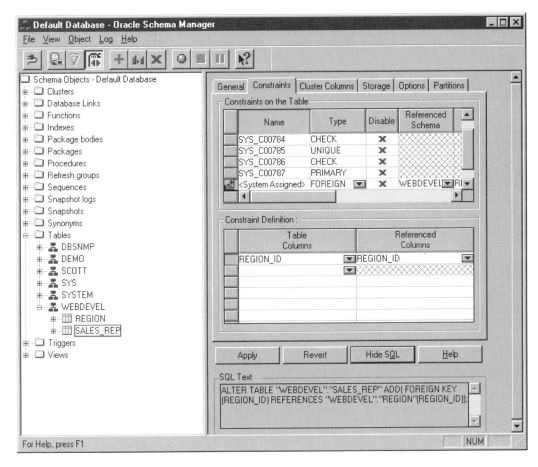

Figure 9–42   Defining a Foreign Key on the Sales_rep Table.

- Click on Show SQL to be sure that it matches what is shown in Figure 9–42 and click on the Apply button to create the Foreign Key constraint.

Creating an Index

When a primary key is created, a unique index is created automatically. An *index* is a database structure that speeds querying from a table. If you tend to make comparisons against a column in your queries, that column is a good candidate for an index. Instead of having to go through the index table to find a particular value, an index allows the desired row to be selected immediately. An index can be created on one column or a combination of columns.

When you create a primary key, a unique index is created on the column(s) that comprise(s) the primary key. This not only makes sure that primary key values are not duplicated, but also speeds access to the table via the primary key.

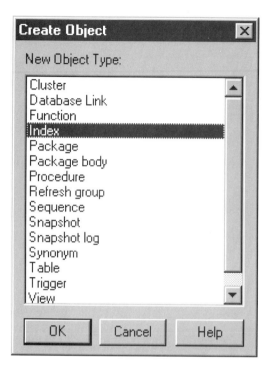

Figure 9–43 Selecting Index from the Object List.

An index is not automatically created when you define a foreign key. A foreign key is often joined to the primary key in queries, so it is a good idea to create a non-unique index to increase performance.

Let's create an index on the region_id column in the *Sales_rep* table.

Select the Object | Create menu item.

- Highlight Index on the Scroll List and click on the OK button.
- Enter an Index name such as IND_REGION_ID in the Name field.
- In the Table drop-down list, choose Sales_rep.
- Click in the Order column of the Region_ID column so that a 1 shows. This number indicates the Region_ID is the first column in the index.
- Leave the other options as is and click on the Create button to create the index.

This has been a good introduction to Oracle tables and to Enterprise Manager. As you become more familiar with Oracle, you'll probably start writing your table definition in SQL scripts. Once you're adept with the SQL language, this process is usually faster. And, because the table definitions are in script files, you can save them for future use.

Figure 9–45 shows what the SQL scripts would look like for the tables we created in the previous sections. In the next chapter, you'll learn how to use SQL*Plus, where you can run SQL scripts like this one.

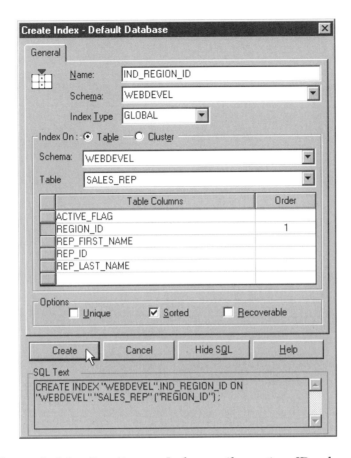

Figure 9–44   Creating an Index on the region_ID column in the Sales_rep table.

Learning More

The Oracle Enterprise Manager's User's Guide and the Oracle Server Adminstrator's Guide are good places to learn more about creating databases and database objects. The following books are also useful in learning more about administering an Oracle database:

Title:	Oracle DBA Handbook
Author:	Kevin Loney
Publisher:	Osborne-McGraw Hill
ISBN:	0-07-882289–0

Title:	The Oracle Cookbook: For Design, Administration, and Implementation
Author:	Harry D. Liebschutz
Publisher:	M & T Books
ISBN:	1-55-851454-6

```
create table sales_rep
(rep_id          number(5)    not null
                              primary key,
 rep_last_name   varchar2(20),
 rep_first_name  varchar2(15),
 active_flag     varchar2(1)  default "Y'
                              not null
          check (active_flag in ('Y','N')),
 region_id       varchar2(5));

create table region
(region_id       varchar2(5)  not null
                              primary key,
 region_desc     varchar2(30));

alter table sales_rep
add (foreign key (region_id)
references region
(region_id));

create index ind_region_id on
sales_rep
(region_id);
```

Figure 9–45   Table Creation SQL Script.

What's New in Oracle 8?

As described in Chapter 1, Oracle has been constantly enhancing its database products since the first public release of Oracle v. 2 in 1979. Nearly two decades later, Oracle 8 represents the state-of-the-art in the RDBMS world. If you ask an Informix developer, a Sybase user, or DB/2 fan, you might hear grumblings about what Oracle really offers in its products. But, with nearly half of the enterprise database installations, Oracle has shown its mettle in the marketplace.

In addition to the normal tweaks that occur with a new release, including fixes and performance enhancements, Oracle 8 brings to the table several important new features.

Objects

The most anticipated (and perhaps overhyped) enhancement in Oracle 8 is the ability to create database objects.

Let's suppose that you're building a database application to track your company's vendors. For starters, you like to record all vendors, their current mailing location, and their business type. To accomplish this in a relational model, you'd require at least three tables, with foreign key relationships among them. In an object model, the data is stored in just one table, through the use of types. For your application you might define three types.

First, you create a type that stores address information:

```
create type address_type AS object
(street_address_1  varchar2(30),
 street_address_2  varchar2(30),
 city              varchar2(20),
 state             varchar2(2),
 zip_code          varchar2(10));
```

Next, you make a type that records business data:

```
create type business_type AS object
(business_category  varchar2(20),
 annual_revenue     number(12),
 fortune_1000_rank  number(4));
```

Finally, you define a vendor type that incorporates the address and business types as well as member functions, or methods, that operate upon the data:

```
create type vendor_type AS object
(vendor_name       varchar2(30),
 address           address_type,
 business          business_type,
 record_created    date,
 last_updated      date,
 member function get_mailing_address return  varchar2,
 member function calculate_credit    return  number,
 member function update_revenue      return  number);
```

With these types defined, creating a vendor table is as easy as typing:

```
create table vendor of type vendor_type;
```

You can then insert data into your tables using these objects:

```
insert into vendor
 values
 ('Flanton Wafermania',
  address_type('550 Cornell Drive',
       NULL,
       'Beaverton',
       'OR',
       '97005-1932'),
  business_type('wafer fabricator',
       524000000,
       454),
  SYSDATE,
  SYSDATE);
```

One of the nice features of these new object-oriented features is that you can still access the data in a relational manner. The object framework, for better or worse, is superimposed on top of Oracle's well-tuned relational database model. As you become more familiar with objects, you can ease them into your projects, without breaking the relationally based databases you've invested so much time and money in.

Database Integrity Improvements

A database is only useful if its data is pristine and readily available. Database must be protected from both internal and external threats. From the inside, a database must be robust and easily recovered in case of a crash. From the outside, security must be available to keep both hapless and malicious users from damaging the data. Oracle has added several new features to keep your database safe.

Oracle 8 now includes a Recovery Manager that manages the process of creating database backups and restoring them. This is a great leap forward for a database that for years relied on the scripting prowess of DBAs to ensure a dependable backup.

Password management has been enhanced in Oracle 8. Passwords can now expire at regular intervals, requiring the users to change their passwords. Passwords can now be maintained in a password file external to the database, where the security features of the operating system can be used for extra protection.

Data Warehouse Enhancements

If you read the computer trade press, it seems like every company in the world is creating a data warehouse. Data warehouses are large-scale, often on the order of many terabytes (a trillion bytes!). As you may imagine, accessing data from mammoth tables, even with proper indexing, can take a long time. To ease this problem, Oracle now allows you to create a database object in several partitions.

Suppose you had a table that contained 50,000,000 phone book entries. You study the data and divide the table into 5 approximately even chunks. The chunks can be defined by the first letter of the listing's last name:

- A-E
- F-L
- M-P
- Q-S
- T-Z

When you create the table, you can tell Oracle to store each of the chunks in separate partitions. Then, when you request name from the table, the database engine knows which partition that the listing is stored in. Instead of having to scan 50,000,000 records, you need only look through 10,000,000, thereby potentially reducing your query time 80%.

New Datatypes

The world of databases isn't just text and numbers any more, especially in the domain of the Web. Oracle now supports several complex datatypes that can easily store image and sound data. The new Large Object (LOB) datatypes can store data up to four gigabytes in size. A Binary Large Object (BLOB) stores non-textual data, while a Character Large Object (CLOB) stores massive quantities of alphanumeric data. If four gigabytes isn't enough or if you want to keep your large objects outside the database, a BFILE datatype can be used, which stores a pointer to a remote object.

You could for instance create a table to store your favorite CD collection, with a table like this:

```
CREATE TABLE ALBUM
(id          number(10)  not null primary key,
 name        varchar2(100),
 artist      varchar2(100),
 lyrics      CLOB,
 soundtrack BLOB,
 cover_art   BFILE);
```

The table would hold the album name and artist conventionally, the lyrics in a character large object, the soundtrack in a binary large object, and a pointer to a file where the cover art is stored.

Moving On

This chapter introduced you to the Oracle 8 Server. You learned how to install the server and create a sample database. You learned how to create a user and grant privileges in Security Manager. Using Schema Manager, you've learned to create a table with the Table Wizard and manually. You've learned how to define a primary key, column constraints, an index, and a foreign key. Although there are many aspects of defining databases and tables that are outside the scope of this book, you learned enough to create a database and the tables contained within a database. Finally, you were introduced to important new features in Oracle 8.

In Chapter 10, you will learn how to use SQL*Plus, Oracle's command-line interface to the database. In Chapter 11, you will learn how to write your own queries and how to change data. In Chapter 12, you will learn more advanced Oracle topics.

CHAPTER 10

Using
SQL*Plus

In Chapter 9 you learned about the new features offered in Oracle 8. You also learned how to create and modify databases and tables, as well as define indexes and foreign key relationships with other tables. In this chapter you will learn the basics of SQL*Plus.

In this chapter you see the facilities in SQL*Plus that help you to build and execute scripts containing SQL statements. With this as an introduction, you will learn how queries are formatted and submitted in Web database applications via Common Gateway Interface (CGI) programs in Chapter 14 of this book.

What Is SQL*Plus?

SQL*Plus is an application that Oracle provides with its database products that allows a user to interface with the database server in a text-based, command-driven mode. It is a valuable tool when building a Web database application because of its ability to allow you to define, populate, and maintain Oracle 8 database objects. Think of SQL*Plus as an intermediary in a conversation between you and the database server. You make a request and SQL*Plus sends the command to the database. The database interprets your request and SQL*Plus returns the database output formatted for you.

Not only does SQL*Plus allow you to query the database, but it also provides functionality to make your interaction with Oracle easier. You can edit, store, retrieve, and run SQL statements and PL/SQL blocks. SQL*Plus provides report formatting commands where you can perform calculations and store column totals. You can list the column definitions for any table or view. You can access and copy data between databases. Finally, you can send messages to and accept responses from a user.

In the age of point-and-click, drag-and-drop GUI interfaces, why bother with a command-line driven program like SQL*Plus? SQL*Plus is no dinosaur—with Oracle 8 reinforcing its commitment to this product by releasing version 4.0. There are several reasons to use SQL*Plus:

- As you become more experienced with SQL, creating the SQL statements in SQL*Plus and running them directly is much faster than building the statements with a GUI tool.
- SQL*Plus's built-in output formatting allows for surprisingly complex reporting.
- SQL*Plus's command-line interface is perfect for a Web application environment. It is easy to execute an SQL*Plus script from a CGI program, save the output to a file, and then display it on a Web page.
- SQL*Plus is a true cross-platform product, offered for every machine that supports Oracle.
- SQL*Plus offers native connectivity to Oracle, thereby eliminating the overhead of ODBC and JDBC drivers.

This is not to say that Oracle has stopped enhancing the functionality of SQL*Plus. Oracle Corporation reinforced its commitment to this product by releasing version 4.0 of SQL*Plus along with Oracle 8.

The following sections introduce you to SQL*Plus and show you how to create and execute queries. Although this example demonstrates SQL*Plus version 4.0 for Windows 95/NT, these examples will work on any platform.

This chapter presents the parts of SQL*Plus that you need to know for Web database development.

Getting Started

On a Windows machine, there are two versions of SQL*Plus: a text version and a GUI version. Don't get the idea that the GUI version has capabilities to view database objects graphically. It is merely a Windows shell built around the command-line version. It does offer extra functionality, but it interacts with the database in the same way.

Starting Command-line SQL*Plus

To start the command-line interface, choose Run from the Start Menu. Then type sqlplus in the Open: field and choose OK. You don't need to specify a directory, because the SQL*Plus installation automatically adds the Oracle executable directory to your path.

Now let's login as the "webdevel" user that we created in the last chapter. Don't forget the password is "www."

If you enter an invalid user or id, you'll receive an error message like the following:

```
ERROR: ORA-01017: invalid username/password; logon denied
```

If that happens, just reenter the username and password. After three unsuccessful login attempts, SQL*Plus will quit. Note that the error message does not indicate whether the username or the password is invalid. For security reasons, Oracle tells you only that

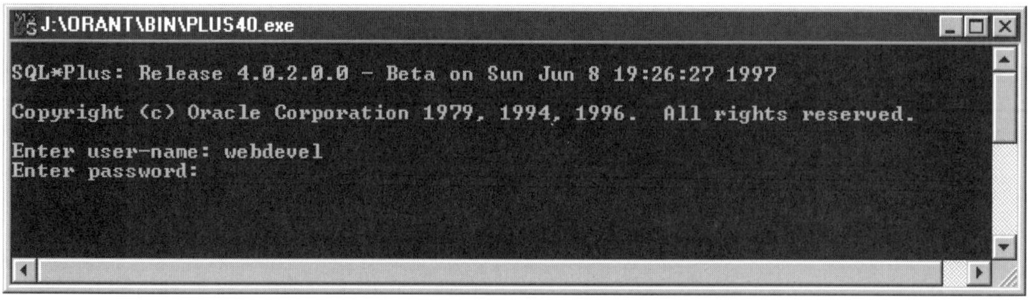

Figure 10–1   Command-line SQL*Plus login.

the login attempt failed. Otherwise, a hacker could attempt to login with various user-names. If Oracle returned a different message when the username exists but the password is incorrect, the hacker would have half the information needed to login to your database!

Otherwise, once you've provided a valid user and password combination, SQL*Plus returns information about the SQL*Plus version, time and date of connection, Oracle database version, and database options installed.

Starting the GUI SQL*Plus

Starting the GUI SQL*Plus is just as easy. From the Start Menu, choose the SQL*Plus program selection from the Oracle for Windows program group. Alternatively, you can choose Run from the Start Menu, enter plus40w in the Open: field, and click on OK.

You are greeted with the SQL*Plus connection dialog box, where you can enter your username and password.

Once connected, you see the same SQL*Plus and Oracle version information as are displayed in the command-line version.

Some Startup Options

Both versions of SQL*Plus allow the user to supply command-line parameters as the application is being started. These parameters are particularly useful if you set up scripts to run as a part of another script, because it allows sqlplus to start without any user intervention. The syntax is as follows:

```
sqlplus -s /nolog username/password @script
```

where:

-s runs sqlplus in silent mode, that is, only output from SQL statements is shown to the screen. The version information provided at connection as well as prompts are not displayed to the screen.

/nolog starts sqlplus without logging into the database. This parameter assumes that a CONNECT command is found inside the script to be run. If you have a script that connects to the database as different users, this can be helpful.

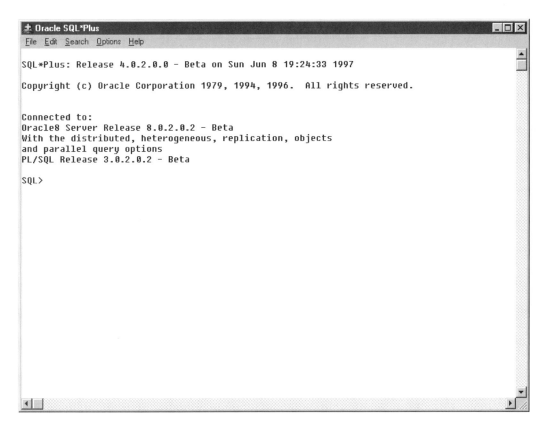

Figure 10–2   SQL*Plus' welcome screen.

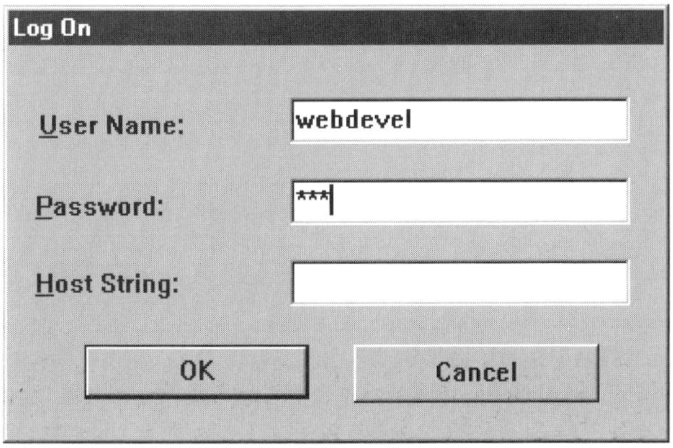

Figure 10–3   GUI SQL*Plus Login.

`username/password` allows you to supply the username and password without responding to the prompts or dialog box within SQL*Plus. This may seem like a useful feature, but some operating systems, namely UNIX, display the entire command line in its process listing. If you supply the username and password on the command line, anyone who happens to be checking the system's currently running processes can see your password. So, in general, it's best to embed the username and password within a CONNECT command inside your script. (Obviously, you cannot supply both the /nolog and the username/password parameters on the same command line.)

@script tells SQL*Plus to start a SQL script as soon as it begins running. This again is useful for unattended operations.

Changing Your Connection

If you decide that you want to change what user you are connected as, there's no need to log out of SQL*Plus. Just type at the SQL> prompt:

```
CONNECT USERNAME/PASSWORD
```

You will be connected to the database as a new user. One note of warning: if you provide an invalid username/password combination, Oracle will not maintain your previous connection to the database. Instead you are left in SQL*Plus unconnected to the database. Fortunately, in this event, SQL*Plus warns you:

```
ERROR: ORA-01017: invalid username/password; logon denied
Warning: You are no longer connected to ORACLE.
```

If this happens, merely use the CONNECT command to reconnect with a valid username and password.

Interacting with SQL*Plus

SQL*Plus, whether in its text-based or GUI modes, has a very simple interface. SQL*Plus waits for a command from the user. The user enters one command and SQL*Plus processes it. SQL*Plus can only do one thing at a time—it waits for one command to finish before starting the next one.

SQL*Plus indicates that it's ready for a command by displaying a prompt. By default, this prompt is:

```
SQL>
```

Here you can type in an SQL*Plus or an SQL command. If you type in a SQL*Plus command, SQL*Plus will process it and take the appropriate action.

So what's the difference between an SQL*Plus and an SQL command? SQL*Plus is an application that provides native connection to the Oracle database. An SQL*Plus command is one that defines the SQL*Plus environment in some way. Examples of SQL*Plus commands are SET and SHOW. An SQL command, however, interacts directly with the database, either querying data, changing data, or defining the database structure in some way. Examples of SQL commands are SELECT, CREATE TABLE, and COMMIT. An SQL command can be run from any application that accesses the database. An SQL*Plus command can be used only in SQL*Plus.

Configuring the SQL*Plus Environment

Once connected in SQL*Plus, you'll probably want to set up the environment to your liking.

Over 50 aspects of the SQL*Plus environment are configurable. You won't need all of them to use SQL*Plus. This section covers the most commonly used.

A SET command consists of the following:

```
SET system_variable parameter_value
```

So to set ECHO on, you'd type:

```
set echo on
```

> This is a good time to note that SQL*Plus like SQL and PL/SQL themselves is case-insensitive. The examples you see here are shown in lower-case, but that's a stylistic choice.

SET commands may either be entered interactively or within a script.

In the descriptions below, brackets indicate optional parts of each parameter name. For instance, the following are equivalent:

```
set autocommit on
set auto on
set autocom on
```

SET commands can be strung together on line. This is perfectly valid:

```
set pagesize 0 echo off feedback off
```

As long as the system variables are coupled with the appropriate parameter values, you'll have no trouble at all.

Following the parameter name is a list of permissible parameter values. The default parameter value is shown in bold. Italicized values should be replaced with an appropriate value.

Here's a list of the most commonly used SET parameters:

- AUTO[COMMIT] **OFF** ON
  tells Oracle whether to commit after each SQL statement or PL/SQL block automatically. If set to OFF, all commits must be done explicitly.
- ECHO **OFF** ON
  determines whether an SQL statement is shown on the screen before it is executed.

- FEED[BACK] **6** *num* OFF ON

  determines whether the count of records returned is displayed after a query. If set to OFF, the number is not displayed. If it is set to a number, the count is returned if at least the one record is returned. ON is the same as 1. This parameter is normally left to the default value for interactive querying and set to OFF in scripts.

- HEA[DING] OFF **ON**

  controls the display of column headings in a query

- LIN[ESIZE] **80** *num*

  sets the number of characters that SQL*Plus displays before starting a new line. The maximum value of num is operating-system specific

- NULL *text*

  instructs what SQL*Plus displays when a column is NULL. Normally a blank is shown for a NULL column. This is useful for clarifying what columns are NULL and which are not.

- NUM[WIDTH] **10** *num*

  sets the default width for displaying numbers

- PAGES[IZE] **14** *num*

  sets the number of lines for each page of output. Setting this parameter to 0 suppresses all headings, page breaks, titles, and initial blank lines. This is often used when the output file is later read by another process that expects no formatting.

- PAU[SE] **OFF** ON *text*

  controls the scrolling during queries. After each page, you must press [ENTER] to continue. If text is specified, the prompt is set to the text value. Don't use this command in any automated scripts or SQL*Plus will wait forever for a response!

- SERVEROUT[PUT] **OFF** ON SIZE *n*

  determines whether output of stored procedures is displayed. Note that if this is set to ON, you may also specify a number of bytes that can be buffered by Oracle; n must be 2000 to 1000000. An example: set serveroutput on size 100000

- SQLP[ROMPT] **SQL>** *text*

  allows you to set the SQL*Plus command prompt.

- TERM[OUT] OFF **ON**

  determines whether SQL*Plus displays query results to the screen when queries are run from a script. Because displaying data to the screen takes a lot of system resources, you can speed the execution of a script that saves output to a file by setting this to OFF.

- VER[IFY] OFF **ON**

  controls whether SQL*Plus lists the text of a command before and after substitution variables are replaced with values.

- WRA[P] OFF **ON**

  tells SQL*Plus whether to truncate the display of data if it is too wide for the currently set line width. OFF truncates the data item while ON wraps the data item to the next line.

The SET command, as we've seen, allows you to modify SQL*Plus' system variables.

The SHOW Command

The SHOW command allows you to view the variables' values. The show command's syntax is quite simple:

```
SHOW system_variable
```

SQL*Plus then responds back with the system variable name and current value. For example:

```
SQL> show pagesize
pagesize 24
```

Like the SET command, you can string several variable names together, like this:

```
pagesize 24
SQL> show echo feedback sqlprompt
echo OFF
feedback ON for 6 or more rows
sqlprompt "SQL> "
```

If you're really adventurous and would like to see all of the system variables and their current value, type:

```
SHOW ALL
```

This is also a useful command if you can't remember the parameter name that you're trying to set.

SHOW can display system variables that you can't define with the SET command. The most useful are:

- SHOW RELEASE
  displays the current release of ORACLE
- SHOW USER
  displays the user currently connected to ORACLE (highly useful if you forget how you've connected, have multiple personalities, or are having an identity crisis).
- SHOW SPOOL
  indicates whether output is currently being spooled to a file. (Spooling will be covered in a later section.)

Settings in the GUI SQL*Plus

Although the SET and SHOW commands work in both the text and GUI versions of SQL*Plus, the GUI version also allows you to view and to set SQL*Plus settings using a dialog box. To bring up the settings dialog box, choose the Options | Environment menu item.

Figure 10–4   Activating the Environment dialog box.

The dialog box has three panes: a scrollable list of options, the current value of the option currently highlighted, and screen buffer settings. To view current settings for a particular environment variable, highlight its name in the left pane.

The value pane tells us that pagesize is currently set to 24. We also know that pagesize is not set to its default value, because the Current radio button is chosen. If a variable is set to its default value, the Default radio button is chosen and the current settings are displayed below. The default value is displayed below, but is grayed out to indicate that it cannot be changed.

Here we see that the termout parameter is set to On, its default value.

If the highlighted environment variable takes a On/Off parameter, the On and Off radio button group is made active, instead of the value pane.

To change a variable's value,

- Highlight the variable's name in the scrollable list.
- If the variable's value is set to Default, click on the Current radio button.
- If the variable requires an On/Off parameter, click on the appropriate radio button. Otherwise, type the new value in the value field.

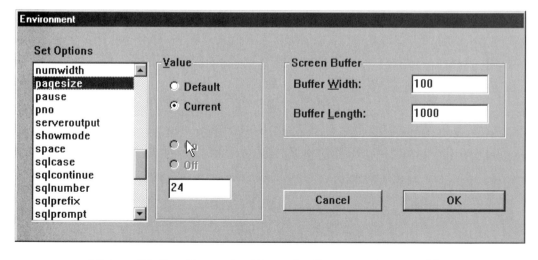

Figure 10–5   Current settings for the *pagesize* variable.

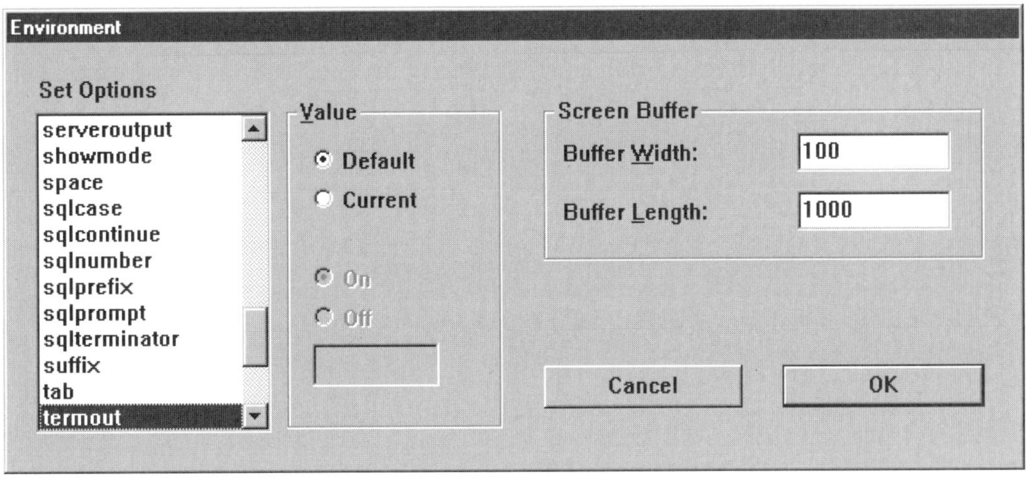

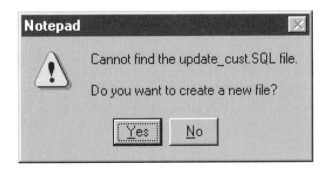

Figure 10–6   Displaying a variable with a default setting.

- Click on the OK button to save the changes. (Or click on Cancel to leave the variable's parameter set as is.)

You can change several variable settings without closing the dialog box. Just make all of your changes as described above, and click on the OK to save all of your settings.

Editing a File

SQL*Plus is often used interactively to query or update the database. But in a Web database environment, its ability to run scripts is where it truly shines. Scripting is particularly useful if you have routine tasks that need to be run repetitively or unattended.

A file run in SQL*Plus is usually referred to as an SQL script. You can create SQL scripts in any text or word processor that allows you to save to a pure ASCII text file, but you can also edit your SQL scripts from within SQL*Plus.

To edit a file from with SQL*Plus, type at the SQL> prompt:

Figure 10–7   Changing a variable's parameter.

```
edit script_name
```

where `script_name` is the file you want to edit. If you don't specify a path name for the file, it will be saved in your current directory.

SQL*Plus opens Notepad. If the script already exists, it is opened automatically ready for you to edit. If the file does not exist, Notepad will ask you if you want to create it.

Click on the OK button to create the file.

Note that if you didn't specify a file extension, SQL*Plus automatically appends ".SQL" to your script name. The default file extension is controlled by the environment variable SUFFIX and can be changed to meet your needs.

> In GUI SQL*Plus, you can also start the editor by choosing `File | Open` from the menu and responding to the File Selection dialog box. You must supply the .SQL extension in this case, because the File Selection dialog does not have access to SQL*Plus' default file extension.

Once you've edited your file to your liking, save the file by choosing `File | Save` from the Notepad menu and then choose `File | Exit` to return to SQL*Plus.

> If you start Notepad from within SQL*Plus using the technique described above, you cannot use SQL*Plus while you've got the file open in Notepad. SQL*Plus runs the Notepad application and waits for Notepad to finish before it is able to accept any other commands. If you find this a nuisance, you can start Notepad on your own and leave it running while you use SQL*Plus. If you're making a quick change to a script, using SQL*Plus' edit command to invoke an editor is useful. Otherwise, it's better to start an editor like Notepad on your own.

Like nearly everything in SQL*Plus, the default editor can be changed as well. If you'd prefer not to use Notepad, use the DEFINE _EDITOR command to change it. Let's

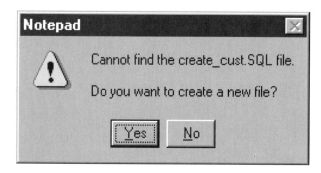

Figure 10–8 Notepad warning if the script does not exist.

say you prefer to use the MS-DOS editor (edit) instead of Notepad. Type the following at a SQL> prompt:

```
SQL> define _editor="edit"
```

Now when you type edit in SQL*Plus, the MS-DOS editor will be started rather than SQL*Plus. You can use this same technique to choose, say, WordPad or Microsoft Word as your SQL editor.

You can determine what your editor currently is set to by using the define command without the equal sign (=) and editor name:

```
SQL> define _editor
```

SQL*Plus responds:

```
DEFINE _EDITOR    = "edit" (CHAR)
```

If you don't specify the editor's directory, it must exist in your current path.

Creating Your First SQL Script

When learning a new computer language, most people write a program that displays "Hello, world!" on the screen. This is not a trivial exercise. Just learning how to use the tools to get the program to run is often half the battle.

So let's try writing our own "Hello, world!" program using SQL*Plus. Don't worry if the SQL statements don't make sense to you yet. In the next chapter, you'll learn about SQL, which allows you to query or change data in your database. But for now, let's make sure that you're comfortable using SQL*Plus.

First, log into SQL*Plus using your webdevel user as described earlier.

We want to create a file called hello.sql. So, as shown in the last section, type

```
SQL> edit hello
```

Since you probably don't have a file called hello.sql in your default directory, Notepad asks if you want to create the file. Click on the OK button to create hello.sql.

Type in exactly what you see in Figure 10–9, save the file, and exit back to SQL*Plus.

This script sets off column headings and other extraneous feedback and displays the literal text "Hello, World" to the screen. Note that the punctuation marks around Hello,

Figure 10–9 The "Hello, World" SQL script.

World are single quotation marks ('). If you're familiar with most programming languages, you would expect to see double quotation marks (") to indicate a literal string value. Double quotation marks mean something else to Oracle, so get used to always using the single quotes around any character literal in a SQL statement.

Executing an SQL Script

Now that you've created and saved your script, it's time to run it. Fortunately, it's quite easy. From the <SQL> prompt, type an "at" sign (@) and the script name, hello, and press Enter.

```
SQL> @hello
```

The script runs and produces the following output:

```
Hello, World!
```

If you see Oracle errors instead, you've probably mistyped part of the script. Restart Notepad and make sure that you've typed it in exactly as shown above.

Or, if you see the following error:

```
unable to open file "HELLO.SQL"
```

SQL*Plus cannot find the script in the current directory. Either specify the full path name of the script, for example:

```
@C:\orant\scripts\hello
```

or, in the GUI version of SQL*Plus, change the current directory by selecting the File | Open menu option and moving to the script of your choice using the file navigator dialog box.

Otherwise, you've successfully run your first SQL script!

What if you want to add more to the hello.sql script? It's easy—just add the SQL*Plus or SQL command and run it again.

Let's add another SQL command to the file. Open hello.sql and make it look like Figure 10–10.

Notice in particular that SQL*Plus commands (the SET commands here) are delimited by just a <Return>. The SQL commands must be ended by a semicolon (;) and a <Return> for the statement to be run.

Note as well that the two quotes in the added Select statement are both single quotes. The two successive single quotes tell Oracle that we want to include a single quote in the literal text. Since the single quote normally denotes the beginning or end of a literal character value, only using one single quote in the middle would confuse Oracle. For example:

```
SQL> select 'I'm confused'
  from dual;
ORA-01756: quoted string not properly terminated
```

So, run hello now:

```
SQL> @hello
```

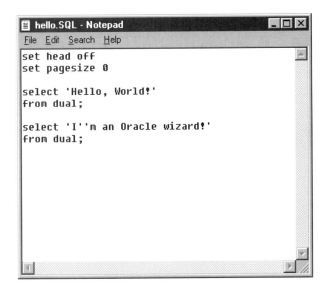

Figure 10–10   A modified
hello.sql Script.

```
Hello, World!

I'm an Oracle wizard!
```

Calling an SQL Script from Another SQL Script

It would be nice to add a line that indicated the date the script was run. As practitioners of modular code, we should create this as a separate script. Create a rundate.sql script that looks like Figure 10–11. Now, we just need to add a call to the rundate.sql script from our hello.sql script. Edit hello.sql as shown in Figure 10–12. Now the "Hello, World" script automatically calls the rundate script.

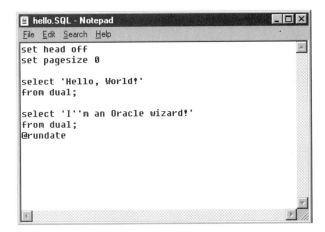

Figure 10–11   Creating run-
date.sql file.

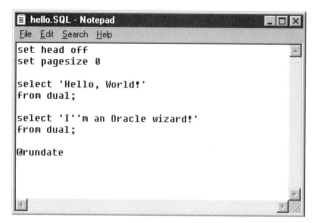

```
set head off
set pagesize 0

select 'Hello, World!'
from dual;

select 'I''m an Oracle wizard!'
from dual;

@rundate
```

Figure 10–12   hello.sql script with call to rundate.

```
SQL> @hello
Hello, World!

I'm an Oracle wizard!

Run on: 08-FEB-98
```

You can nest SQL script calls as deeply as your needs warrant. Using this technique, you can create a library of generic scripts that you can use for many purposes.

Saving Output

You've learned how to create and run scripts in SQL*Plus. Now you'll learn how to save the output of your SQL script to a file. The SQL*Plus command spool saves all SQL*Plus output, including prompts and error messages, to a file specified by the filename parameter:

```
SQL> spool filename
```

If you do not specify a file extension, SQL*Plus automatically appends '.lst' to your filename. Beware that if the file already exists, SQL*Plus overwrites the file without a warning.

When you want to stop saving to a file, type:

```
SQL> spool off
```

Let's add spooling capability to our hello.sql script. Change the file contents as shown in Figure 10–13.

Now run the script:

```
SQL> @hello
```

You can use Notepad to view the output file. Remember that SQL*Plus automatically adds a .lst suffix:

```
SQL> edit output.lst
```

Now you can see the script's output as shown in Figure 10–14.

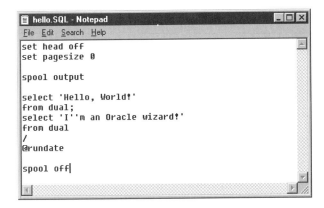

Figure 10-13 hello.sql with spooling command added.

SQL*Plus's spool command can be used in several ways:

- to save results of an object creation script for later debugging
- to create a report that is created by an automatically executed SQL*Plus script
- to hold the output of one script, which creates another SQL script, which can then be run from SQL*Plus

If you've set your script to run unattended or don't want to watch the results fly by on the screen, the termout variable can disable screen output. Often, the mere task of displaying output to the screen takes more time than it actually does to retrieve data from the database. By turning off screen output, you can often speed your script execution substantially. Before you start spooling, use the following statement:

```
set termout off
```

As the script runs, the output is not displayed on the screen while it is saved into the specified spool file.

Formatting Output

As you write more and more SQL*Plus scripts, you'll find that SQL*Plus doesn't always format query output the way you want it. SQL*Plus offers the COLUMN command to help with this problem. The COLUMN command has the following syntax:

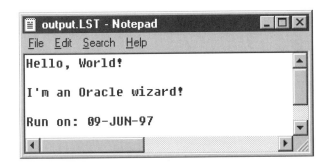

Figure 10-14 Spooled results of the hello.sql script.

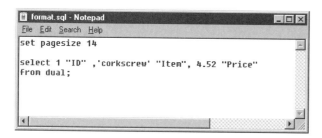

Figure 10–15   SQL script format.sql.

```
COLUMN column_name FORMAT format_model
```

To demonstrate this command, create the file format.sql with the contents as shown in Figure 10–15.

The pagesize command sets the page size back to the default value. We had previously set pagesize to 0 which suppresses the display of column headings. We want column headings to show for this example. The text shown in double quotation marks (") are column aliases that will show in the column headings. Again we're using a very simple example to focus attention on SQL*Plus rather than on SQL.

Now run the script:

```
SQL> @format
```

and you get the following output:

```
ID              Item        Price
----------      ---------   ----------
         1 corkscrew         4.52
```

Notice that the numeric columns (ID and price) are automatically right justified, with a default width of 10 characters. The text column (item) is left-justified.

We can use column commands to change the formatting. Add the column statements to the format.sql script.

Now, run the format script, and the output is displayed in a more friendly format:

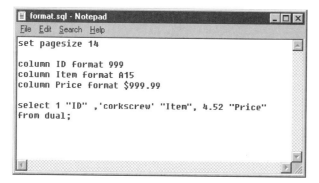

Figure 10–16   Format.sql with column formatting.

```
ID               Item      Price
----------    ---------  ----------
         1 corkscrew      4.52
```

The ID is now defined as three numbers. The item name is defined as fifteen characters. And the price column is displayed in dollars and cents.

In Oracle, an alphanumeric column, like *item*, is called a varchar, shorthand for "variable character." Oracle also supports fixed-length alphanumeric columns, called *char*, but you you'll rarely see them. You shouldn't use them, because varchars are stored more efficiently in the database.

The format model for a varchar or char is quite simple: the letter A (for alphanumeric) and the number of characters wide the column should display. The display width for a varchar or char defaults to the column width. Here's a sample format statement for a varchar column:

```
column street_address format a30
```

If the display width you define is less than the width of the column's contents, SQL*Plus's behavior depends on the value of the WRAP environment variable. If WRAP is set to ON, SQL*Plus will display the column wrapped to the next line. Otherwise, the column is truncated to the number of characters specified in the format model.

The format model for a numeric column is a bit more involved. This table displays the most common elements used in a numeric format model.

Format Element	Example	Use
9	999	Indicates the number of digits that should be displayed. Leading zeros are not displayed.
0	09999 990	Displays leading zeros. A null number is displayed as zero rather than blank.
$	$99999	Displays a dollar sign before a number.
B	B99	Displays a zero value as blank.
MI	999MI	Displays a minus sign (–) after a negative number.
PR	9999PR	Displays a negative number inside angled brackets. (<>)
comma (,)	9,999,999	Displays a comma in the specified position.
period (.)	99.99	Displays the number with the specified number of decimal places.

Here are some example numeric format statements:

```
column total_price format $9999.99
column ledger_value format 999999.99MI
column population format 999,999,990
column variance format 0.9999999
```

The default width for numeric columns is determined by the numwidth environment variable. If a number doesn't fit with a specified format, SQL*Plus replaces the number with asterisks to indicate an overflow error.

Exiting SQL*Plus

Exiting either version of SQL*Plus is quite simple. Just type exit at an SQL> prompt:

```
SQL> exit
```

SQL*Plus will commit any changes you have made to the database and then the SQL*Plus application will shut down.

Alternatively, you can end your SQL*Plus session using the application's menu.

For the text version, choose Close from the MS-DOS window menu.

For the GUI version, click on File | Exit from the menu.

Configuring SQL*Plus

Earlier you learned how to view and to change SQL*Plus's variable settings. But all these changes are temporary. If you close the SQL*Plus application again and log in again, all of the variables are set back to their default settings.

Fortunately, SQL*Plus allows you to set up your own configuration script. This script, called login.sql is executed automatically as the application starts.

Let's suppose that you'd like the SQL*Plus prompt to be "Yes? > " and you prefer not to have column headings returned for your queries. To set these up to be default settings, create a file, as described above, called login.sql, with the following contents.

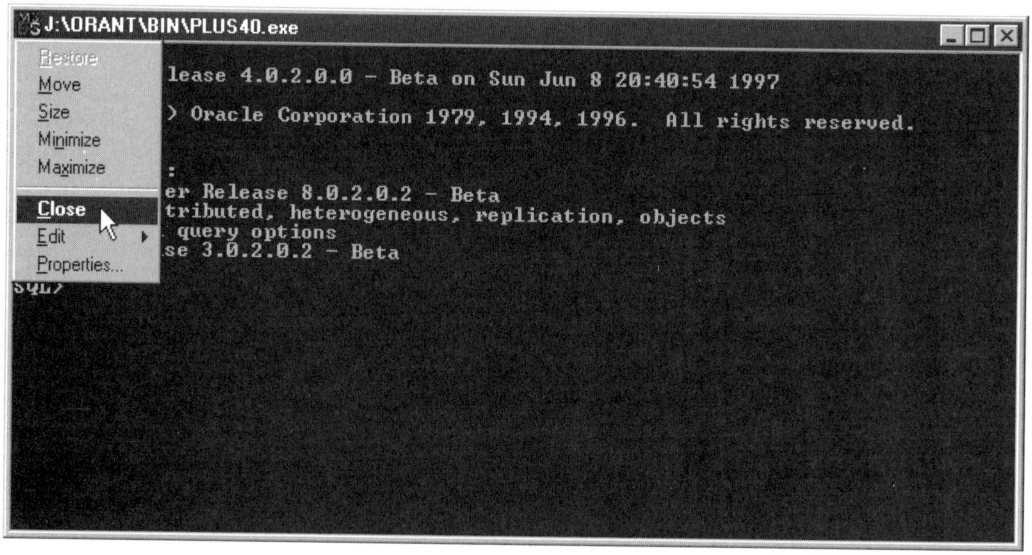

Figure 10–17   Ending the text-based SQL*Plus.

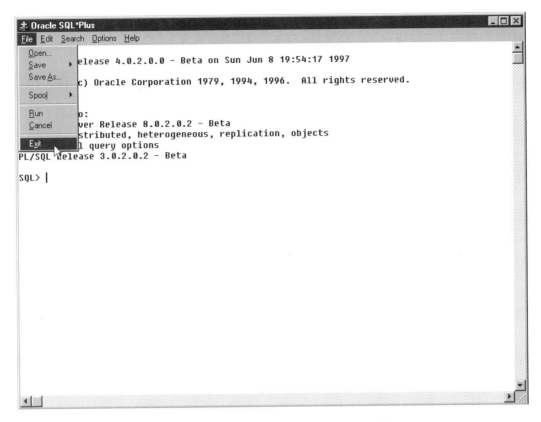

Figure 10–18   Ending the GUI SQL*Plus.

The login.sql file must be in your path, so it is best to save it in SQL*Plus' default directory. To activate your new default settings, log out of SQL*Plus, as shown in the last section, and start SQL*Plus again. Your new prompt and heading settings are now automatically set at startup.

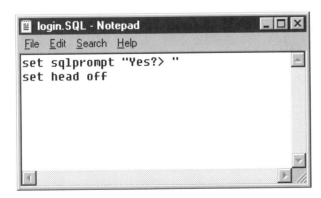

Figure 10–19   A sample login.sql script.

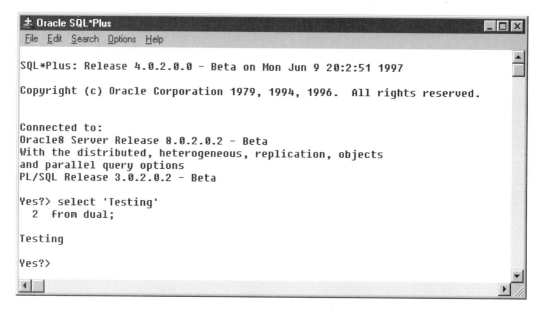

Figure 10–20   SQL*Plus with new login.sql settings.

You can always override any variable parameter values you've set in your login.sql script by entering SET commands at the SQL*Plus prompt or within your SQL scripts.

Getting More Information

This chapter has shown that, despite its appearances, SQL*Plus allows for sophisticated script creation and execution. It has other features that are beyond the scope of this book, including:

- detailed report formatting capabilities
- facility for copying tables from one instance to another
- complex error handling

    Refer to *SQL*Plus User's Guide and Reference* for more information on these topics.

Moving On

In this chapter, you have learned the ins and outs of Oracle's database-access tool SQL*Plus. You learned how to connect to your database and how to set the SQL*Plus environment to your liking. You learned how to create, save, and execute SQL scripts. In addition, you learned how to automatically set the SQL*Plus environment using a login.sql script. In the next chapter, you will learn to write SQL statements that allow you to query and change data in your database.

CHAPTER 11

Designing Oracle SQL Statements

I n Chapter 10 you learned how to use SQL*Plus to interact with Oracle. You were introduced to the various components in that interface. You also learned how to create an SQL script in which to store your SQL statements.

With this as an introduction, in this chapter you will go deeper into the facilities in Oracle to create advanced queries. This includes using multiple aggregate functions, applying criteria in the query, parameter queries, nested queries, and optimizing performance of queries. The information discussed in this chapter is valuable to any developer using Oracle as his or her back-end RDBMS, regardless of what front-end design and HTML tool is being used.

This chapter and the next are geared to the new database user. Their purpose is not to teach you all the intricacies of Oracle's SQL, but rather to familiarize you with the topic. If you've had a lot of experience writing SQL statements in Oracle, you may skip to Chapter 13, where we explore using CGI programs to access web databases. If you're familiar with another database's version of SQL (e.g., Access, Sybase, Informix, DB/2), you'll want to read these chapter to learn about Oracle's particular SQL implementation. If you'd like more detailed information about SQL coding, consult the Learning More section at the end of this chapter.

SQL's Advantage

If you're familiar with many computer languages (such as BASIC, COBOL, Pascal, or C), you have gotten used to procedural programming. In such languages, you tell the computer *how* to go about performing whatever task you want completed. You provide step-by-step instructions, which are executed by the computer one statement at a time. SQL, however, is a non-procedural language. You write SQL that tells Oracle *what* you want to retrieve. Oracle determines the best way to retrieve that information for you.

So why bother even learning a new language such as SQL? The answer is quite simple—most modern computing languages make data access quite difficult. SQL is built to handle one thing, interacting with a relational database, such as Oracle. Fortunately, it does that job very well.

Let's examine the differences between SQL and procedural languages. SQL's vast advantage for data access becomes quite clear. For the purposes of this discussion, imagine that you are an owner of a very small company that offers three products: the widget, the gizmo, and the thingie. You'd like to write a program to display your offerings. In a procedural language, such as C, you'd have to write something like this:

```
main()
{
/* Initialize variables:
   product: array of 3 elements, 10 characters long
   count: integer */
char  product[3][10];
int   count;

/* Assign array elements */
strcpy(product[0],"Widget");
strcpy(product[1],"Gizmo");
strcpy(product[2],"Thingie");

/* Print header */
     printf("\nItem  Name");
     printf("\n====  ==========");

/* Display products */
for (count=0; count < 3; count++)
  { printf("\n%d      %s",count,product[count]); }
}
```

When you executed the code, you'd get the following output:

```
Item  Name
====  ==========
0     Widget
1     Gizmo
2     Thingie
```

In order to get the list, you must guide the C compiler at each step, by initializing the variables, entering values into the array, displaying the header, and looping through the array. Although you could certainly modularize the code to allow certain functions to be reused, it is inconvenient to specify each operation just to print such a simple report.

SQL is a whiz at handling such a task. In this case, you'd create a table with two columns, item and name, to hold the data. Then extracting the data becomes a simple statement:

```
SELECT   item, name
FROM    product
ORDER BY item;
```

Oracle returns the following:

```
ITEM  NAME
=====  ===========
  0   Widget
  1   Gizmo
  2   Thingie
```

Note how simple it was to create this output. You didn't need to know where each data item was stored. You just had to tell Oracle what items you wanted and how to order them. SQL also allows you to change your request easily. If you later decided to sort your report by item name, you need only change the Order By clause to Order By Name. In C, you'd have to write a sort function to get the same functionality.

Procedural languages certainly are useful—fortunately, many languages allow SQL to be embedded into them, either using Oracle's precompilers or via ODBC calls. In this way, you can use all the features of your favorite language while leveraging SQL for its superior ability to handle database requests.

A Simple Example

Let's take a look at a more complicated Select statement, the way it is executed, and the contribution each part of the statement plays in producing the desired output. Like any SQL statement, any application that is connected to an Oracle database can issue a Select statement. Since in Chapter 10, you learned how to use SQL*Plus to interact with Oracle, we'll use that interface in this example. In SQL*Plus, you can enter a Select statement when you see the SQL> prompt. Keep the following pointers in mind about Select statements:

- Each Select statement begins with the keyword SELECT and ends with either a semicolon (;) or slash (/).
- Oracle doesn't care about returns or spaces—use them judiciously to create easy-to-read code.
- Keywords, such as SELECT, are case-insensitive. It's helpful, however, to use consistent capitalization to make them stand out from data elements.
- A Select statement is made up of two or more parts, called clauses. Each clause begins with a key word or words: Select, From, Where, Group by, Having, or Order by. The only two clauses that are mandatory are the Select and the From clauses.

As your company grew beyond three products, so did your Oracle database. You later decide to write SQL that displays gross sales for all products that grossed more than $100,000 in 1999. At the SQL> prompt, you type each clause. After you hit return for each line, SQL*Plus starts the next line with a new line number. Once you enter a semicolon (;) at the end of a line or a slash (/) on its own line, SQL*Plus sends your Select statement to Oracle for processing:

```
SQL> SELECT    item, SUM(gross_sales)
2    FROM      sales
3    WHERE     date between
4              ('01-JAN-99' AND '31-DEC-99')
5    GROUP BY  item
6    HAVING    SUM(gross_sales) > 100000
7    ORDER BY  SUM(gross_sales) DESC;
```

Oracle then parses your statement and looks for any syntax errors. If a problem is found, an error message is returned to you so that you can correct any misspellings or syntax errors. If no errors are found, Oracle determines the most efficient manner to gather the information you've requested. The desired data is then retrieved from the database. Next, any desired sorting or grouping of the data is performed. The data is then returned to the screen formatted, like this:

```
ITEM      SALES
=======   =======
Widget    543,129
Stuff     163,391
Thingie   101,921
```

Now let's look at each clause in more detail. Line 1, the Select clause, indicates what data should be output. In this case, we want to know the item name and the gross sales for that item. Each item in the Select clause must be a valid expression. Multiple expressions are separated by commas. Each expression consists of a single column, columns concatenated together, a literal value or columns manipulated by a function. Using more complex expressions is described later in this chapter.

Line 2, the From clause, tells Oracle what data sources are retrieved from. The data source can be either a table or view and may reside locally in the database or can exist in a remote database. In our example, we need only the table *sales* to retreive our desired output. If more than one data source is listed, they are separated by commas.

Lines 3 and 4 constitute the Where clause. The Where clause limits what data is returned from the database. In this case, we want only sales figures from 1999. A Where clause can have more than one condition. Parentheses and Boolean operators (AND, OR, and NOT) are used to combine multiple Where clause conditions. Such logic is described later in this chapter.

Line 5, the Group By clause, describes how retreived data should be combined to provide summary output. Here we group by item, so we can get total yearly gross sales for each product. Commas separate multiple Group By expressions. A Group By expression may, but need not, be an expression found in the Select clause.

The Having clause, shown on Line 6, is only used in conjunction with a Group By clause. We use it here to limit the returned data to those products whose summed sales is greater than $100,000. If more than one Having clause is necessary, Boolean operators like those used in the Where clause are employed.

Finally, line 7 shows an Order By clause, which sorts the output in a specified manner. In our example, we display the data in order of greatest gross sales to least. If you wish to order by more than one expression, separate them with commas and place them in the order of precedence you want the output sorted.

As you can see, each clause in a Select statement has a specific purpose. In the next section, we'll go into each of the clauses in more depth. With this knowledge, you will better understand how to form your own Select statements.

SELECT Statement Clauses

The SELECT clause is the basic SQL statement in not only Oracle but all RDBMS products. With it you have tremendous power and flexibility in not only querying data, but creating and deleting it. The control you exercise over what the SELECT statement does is available to you in the use of the various clauses available in the SELECT statement. The code seen below is an example of a SELECT clause that uses some clauses that comprise a SELECT statement.

```
SELECT
Rentals.Customer_ID,
Rentals.Rental_Date,
Rentals.Due_Date,
Customers.Customer_LName,
Customers.Customer_FName,
Sum(Rentals.Total_Amount_This_Rental)
"Sum Of Total_Amount_This_Rental",
Avg(Rentals.Total_Amount_This_Rental)
"Avg Of Total_Amount_This_Rental",
Min(Rentals.Total_Amount_This_Rental)
"Min Of Total_Amount_This_Rental",
Max(Rentals.Total_Amount_This_Rental)
"Max Of Total_Amount_This_Rental"
Count(*) "Count Of Rentals"
FROM    Customers,
        Rentals
WHERE   Customers.Customer_ID =
        Rentals.Customer_ID
GROUP BY Rentals.Customer_ID,
Rentals.Rental_Date,
Rentals.Due_Date,
Customers.Customer_LName,
Customers.Customer_FName
ORDER BY Rentals.Customer_ID DESC;
```

The clauses in the SELECT statement must appear in a certain sequence, otherwise, you'll probably receive a syntax error. You can use various front-ends to create SQL automatically, but to tap the full power of the RDBMS, you need to know how to formulate a SELECT statement on your own.

The table below is a schema of the various clauses in the SELECT statement. All the clauses are not mandatory. In fact, the only clause that is mandatory in a SELECT state-

Clause	Description
SELECT	Lists the column(s), data function(s), or aggregate function(s) to include in the result set. Listing 11–1 gives a good example of all of these.
FROM	Identifies the table(s) or queries used as the source to execute this query against. A query identified in the FROM clause of a SELECT statement is an example of a *subquery*.
WHERE	This clause is used a number of different ways: • To qualify the result set to specified criteria • To join tables listed in the FROM clause • To specify a criteria for an UPDATE or DELETE process
GROUP BY	Combines rows with matching values into groups using one or many functions. This clause is almost always used with aggregate functions.
ORDER BY	Sorts the result set of the query into a specified sequence. The default sequence is ascending.
HAVING	This is a corollary clause to the GROUP BY clause and limits the amount of data returned to the result set by the aggregate function.

ment is: `SELECT column-list FROM table-name`. The complete syntax for the SELECT statement is:

```
SELECT tablename(s).column(s)
   FROM     tablename(s)
   WHERE        condition(s)
   GROUP BY     tablename(s).column(s)
   ORDER BY     tablename(s).column(s)
   HAVING       condition(s);
```

Note: If two or more tables are joined in a SELECT statement, the query must include a WHERE clause specifying the relationship between these tables. Failing to do so will create a Cartesian Product result set, and you will not be invited to the annual Christmas party thrown by the company's DBA.

The From Clause

The one and only purpose of the From clause is to inform the SQL processor what tables in the database the query is to be executed against. It is not only possible (and frequently required) that you identify more than one table in the From clause, but these tables do not need to be in the same database as the other tables.

For example, consider an application where you want to compare information that resides in a table in the current database against archived information for the same table in a backup database. As seen below, this is possible:

SELECT accounts.acct_nbr, hist_accts.*

From accounts, hist_accts@MyCompany.MDB

Where accounts.acct_nbr = Hist_Accts.acct_nbr;

In this case MyCompany.MDB is a database link defined in the local database to tell Oracle where the remote table is located. (Database links are covered in more detail in Chapter 18.)

Another common use for the From clause is to assign aliases to Table names. An alias is frequently used to condense the amount of code that is written to create the SQL statement. Using the example above, it could be re-written using aliases as seen below:

SELECT   a.acct_nbr, b.*

FROM   Accounts "A",

      Hist_Accts@MyCompany.MDB "B"

WHERE   A.acct_nbr = B.acct_nbr;

The Where Clause

The Where clause has a dual purpose in an SQL statement:

- Constrain and reduce the size of the result set of a query
- Join two or more tables together

The format of the Where clause in an SQL statement is as follows:

WHERE tablename.columnname or expression [OPERATOR] [comparison value]

An example of a simple Where clause is:

WHERE MOVIES.RATING = "PG13"

An example of a Where clause using an expression as its operand is:

WHERE (to_char(RENTALS.DATE_RENTED,'yymmdd')) > 970401

The [OPERATOR] can be an Oracle mathematical operator or one of the operators described in the table on page 234. The sense of the operator can be negated by adding a "NOT" in the proper place, as indicated.

Oracle attempts to determine the type of Join operation required to satisfy the query based on the implications specified in the content of the query. There are four types of Join operations available.

Inner Join. A join is the most common type of join, the inner join is the result of linking two tables together on a matching, common column. The following is an example of an inner join.

Operator	Description
AND	Used to join two or more conditions together
OR	Used to identify two or more conditions that will return a result set if any of the specified conditions are found true
[NOT] IN	Used to compare the values in a column against a series of possible values
[NOT] BETWEEN	Used to compare the values in a column as being in a range of values identified by a lower and an upper boundary
IS [NOT] NULL	Used to extract all rows where the values for a specified column are NULL
[NOT] LIKE	Used to extract rows where a column that is defined as text contains a specified string pattern

```
SELECT   ACCOUNTS.ACCOUNT_NBR,
     HISTORY.*
FROM     ACCOUNTS, HIST
WHERE    ACCOUNTS.ACCOUNT_NBR =
     HISTORY.ACCOUNT_NBR;
```

In this example, the ACCOUNTS and HISTORY tables will be joined together on a column named ACCOUNT_NBR.

Note: Inner joins only select rows from the listed tables where the joined columns are equal.

Self Join.   A self join is a type of join where one table is joined to itself, producing a result set that is the sum of the table—duplicated. This is the least frequently used type of join and is only used in rare circumstances. The following is an example of a self join.

```
SELECT   A1.Acct_Desc "Account_Desc",
     A1.Acct_Bal,
     COUNT(A1.Acct_Owner) "Acct_Rank"
FROM     Account_Stats A1,
     Account_Stats A2
WHERE    A1.Acct_Bal < A2.Acct_Bal
GROUP BY A1.Account_Desc, A1.Acct_Bal
ORDER BY COUNT(A1.Acct_Owner);
```

This query produces a result set as seen below:

```
Account_Desc          Acct_Bal        Acct_Rank
============          ========        =========
Deposits             $1,120.05            1
Withdrawal            $912.00             2
Service Charge         $21.18             3
Reversals              $18.11             4
```

Left Outer Join.   A left outer join is a join in which all the columns in the left-most table (the first table listed in the FROM clause) are included in the result set, whether or not there is a matching value in the right column (the second table listed in the FROM clause).

Consider the following example that will be used to explain the left outer join and right outer join.

Name	Code	Code	Location
Accounting	10	10	Portland
Sales	20	20	Seattle
Sales	20	60	Vancouver
H/R	40		
R/D	50		

A left outer join would be written as follows:

```
SELECT   dept.*, location.*
FROM     dept, location
WHERE    dept.code = location.code (+);
```

The (+) indicates that the code value may be missing in the location table. This statement would produce the following result set:

Name	Code	Code	Location
Accounting	10	10	Portland
Sales	20	20	Seattle
Sales	20	20	Seattle
H/R	40	<Null>	<Null>
R/D	50	<Null>	<Null>

Right Outer Join.   A right outer join is the opposite of a left outer join. In a right outer join, all the columns in the right-most table (the last table listed in the FROM clause) are included in the result set, whether or not there is a matching value in the left columns (the first table listed in the FROM clause).

A right outer join on our tables looks like this:

```
SELECT   dept.*, location.*
FROM     dept, location
WHERE    dept.code (+) = location.code;
```

Here the (+) moves to the dept.code side of the equality. A right outer join on these tables would produce the following result set:

Name	Code	Code	Location
Accounting	10	10	Portland
Sales	20	20	Seattle
Sales	20	20	Seattle
<Null>	<Null>	60	Vancouver

The placement of the (+) may be a bit confusing. For a left join, the (+) goes on the right side of the equation. For a right join, it goes on the left. The rule of thumb is that the (+) goes on the side of the joined columns where the row may be missing. Note as well that there cannot be a (+) on both sides of the join; Oracle does not support a full outer join.

The IN Operator.   If you want to compare a column value against a list of specified values, the IN operator is for you. Let's suppose that you wanted to query all customers in the New England States. You could define the query using a list of states, but this makes for an unwieldly statement:

```
select customer_id
from    cust_address
where   state = "MA"
or      state = "RI"
or      state = "CT"
or      state = "VT"
or      state = "NH"
or      state = "ME";
```

The IN operator allows you to do this in a compact, more readable format:

```
select customer_id
from   cust_address
where state in ("MA","RI","CT",
"VT," "NH," "ME");
```

The IN operator's syntax is simple:

```
IN (value1, value2, value3, ... valuen)
```

Note that the values you're comparing are varchars, you need to enclose each value with single quotation marks.

The meaning of an In operator can be negated using NOT. This statement would find all customers who aren't on the West Coast of the United States:

```
select customer_id
from   cust_address
where  state not in ('CA','OR','WA');
```

The LIKE Operator. When constraining a query's results, it's not always possible to know the exact value that you want to match. The LIKE operator allows you to employ pattern matching in the WHERE clause. LIKE uses two wildcard values:

% means zero or more characters

_ means one character

Here are a few examples:

Fragment	Matches
column like 'BALTI%'	All rows where column starts with *BALTI*
column like '%MORE'	All rows where column ends with *MORE*
column like '%NEW%'	All rows where columns contains *NEW*
column like 'e_gplant'	All rows where column starts with *e*, is followed by one character and *gplant*
column like '1__5%'	All rows where column starts with *1*, is followed by two characters, *5* and zero or more characters
column not like 'Void%'	All rows where column does not start with *Void*

Note that LIKE, like the other equality operators in SQL is case-sensitive.

Watching out for NULL. A NULL to Oracle is different from a value of 0 or a string with zero length. It means that the value is not known or is indeterminate. Comparisons against a column with a potentially NULL value are tricky in Oracle.

Suppose Joan is in charge of your company's inventory system. She has this nifty table that stores all of the inventory item's retail prices and discounts offered to your retailers:

```
SQL> desc prices
Name                      Null?      Type
-----------------------   --------   ----
 ITEM_ID                  NOT NULL   NUMBER(10)
 RETAIL_PRICE                        NUMBER(8,2)
 DISCOUNT                            NUMBER(2,2)
```

Joan's boss asks her to check for any items that don't currently have a discount set. She remembers that there's a SQL*Plus SET parameter that can be used to replace a NULL value in a Select clause with a particular string. So, she types:

```
SQL> set null "<null>"
```

and diligently queries her table:

```
SQL> select * from items;
ITEM_ID RETAIL_PRICE DISCOUNT
--------- ------------ ---------
     1001    120.95          .1
     1002         134 <null>
     1003      29.99         .25
     1004          45          .2
     1005           5           0
```

Since Joan's company is still pretty small, it's easy for her to scan for the NULL value. But, she decides to write a statement that will pull up just the items with a missing discount:

```
SQL> select * from prices
2 where discount = ";
no rows selected
```

She scratches her head and tries again:

```
SQL> select * from prices where
2 discount = 0;
ITEM_ID  RETAIL_PRICE  DISCOUNT
--------- ------------ --------
   1005             5         0
```

Joan has fallen victim to a common confusion about NULL values in Oracle. A NULL to Oracle is different from a value of 0 or a string with zero length. It means that the value is not known or is indeterminate. Comparisons against a column with a potentially NULL value are tricky in Oracle.

To find her missing discount value, Joan needs to query as follows:

```
SQL> select * from prices
2 where discount is NULL;
ITEM_ID  RETAIL_PRICE DISCOUNT
--------- ------------ --------
1002            134 <null>
```

Here's another note about NULLs. NULLs can never be equivalent to anything. Thus, the = operator should never be used with NULL, rather the IS NULL must be used instead. This query will always return no rows:

```
SQL> select * from prices
2 where discount = null;
no rows selected
```

If you remember the behavior of NULLs, you'll have no problem as your queries become more complicated. Here's one more query example to drive home the point:

```
SELECT address_code
FROM  addresses
WHERE (valid_start_date < SYSDATE
OR valid_start_date IS NULL)
```

```
AND (value_end_date >= SYSDATE
valid_end_date IS NULL);
```

This Select statement will retrieve all rows where today (SYSDATE) falls between valid_start_date and valid_end_date. Since valid_start_date and valid_end_date can potentially be NULL, the extra logic is necessary here to get the correct rows.

The Order By Clause

Order By allows you to specify the sequence in which output rows are returned to you in a query. You can order by any column found in the table(s) in your Select statement. Let's use a simple Select for an example:

```
select    position_id, position_desc
from      position
where     position_desc like '%baseman'
order by position_id;
```

Produces the following output:

```
1B     first baseman
2B     second baseman
3B     third baseman
```

You can also refer to column in positional notation. Instead of listing the column name in the order by clause, use the number of the column in the SELECT clause:

```
select    position_id, position_desc
from      position
where     position_desc like '%fielder'
order by 1;
```

would produce the same results. Although positional notation is concise and easy-to-use, use it with caution. If you later add or delete a column in your select clause, you must also change the order by column numbers.

You can also order your data in reverse order by adding DESC after the column to be ordered. Changing the order by clause to:

```
order by 1 desc
```

returns:

```
3B     third baseman
2B     second baseman
1B     first baseman
```

You do not necessarily have to order your query by a column found in the select clause, nor does it have to be a plain column value. This query is perfectly valid:

```
select    position_id
from      position
where     position_desc like '%baseman'
order by substr(position_desc,2);
```

The substr built-in function is discussed in a later section, but trust that you'll get the position IDs ordered by the second letter of the position description:

```
2B
3B
1B
```

Using Group By

Group By is used to combine matching rows of data and to return the summarized result set. Group By functions are normally used in combination with aggregate functions—but this is not a requirement. Group By can also be used to group individual columns. This is an example of a query using the Group By clause:

```
select league_code, division_code, count(*)
from team
group by league_code, division_code;
```

In this example, you see that the query will group the output by the columns league_code and division_code, and it will use the count function to count the number of entries (rows) for each league and division combination. This is precisely what we'd want to see in a query that was designed to show how many teams are in each league and division.

```
L D COUNT(*)
- - --------
A C        5
A E        5
A W        4
N C        5
N E        5
N W        4
```

This query quickly shows that the western divisions of each league have one fewer team than the other divisions.

Let's delve in a bit deeper to see how the Group By works. Note that in the example that there was one aggregate function (here COUNT). In order to get the proper counts, we had to group by the remaining two columns. This is the rule of thumb in grouping. Any columns that you're not using aggregate functions on must be listed in the Group By clause.

Aggregate Functions

Using aggregate functions in a Select statement allows you to perform mathematical functions on a specific group or groups of data. The table below lists the available aggregate functions and the datatypes that the function is valid against. Oracle offers several aggregate functions which are shown in the table below.

Function	Returns	Datatypes
SUM	The total of all values in a column	NUMBER
AVG	Averages all the values in a column	NUMBER
MIN	The minimum value in a column	NUMBER, VARCHAR2, DATE
MAX	The maximum value in a column	NUMBER, VARCHAR2, DATE
COUNT	The number of non-null rows in a column	All
STDDEV	Standard deviation for a sample of all the values in a specified column	NUMBER
VARIANCE	Variance for a sample of all the values in a specified column	NUMBER

The Having Clause

Like the Group By clause, the Having clause is used in conjunction with aggregate functions. It limits the size of the result set returned from the query in a way similar to the Where clause. What is dissimilar is that the Having clause can limit the data returned in the result set based on an aggregate function. Using a Having clause is what is sometimes referred to as post criteria aggregation.

Let's suppose we want to know which divisions have a particular number of teams. We can use the Having clause to accomplish this:

```
select league_code, division_code, count(*)
from team
group by league_code, division_code
having count(*) = 4;
```

The Having clause looks at the results once the Group By aggregation has been completed. Here, we want only those divisions with four teams:

```
L D COUNT(*)
- - ---------
A W         4
N W         4
```

Single-Row SQL Functions

Earlier we looked at aggregate functions that returned a single value from a set of rows. Oracle provides a wealth of built-in functions that operate on a single row and return a particular result. You can use these to manipulate data directly within your SQL statements, thereby leveraging the power of the Oracle database engine to do your work for you. The tables that follow contain lists of those you're likely to use.

Numeric Functions

Syntax	Returns	Example	Result
ABS(x)	the absolute value of x	abs(−4)	4
CEIL(x)	the smallest integer greater than or equal to x	ceil(3.4) ceil(−2.6)	−2
FLOOR(x)	the largest integer equal to or less than x	floor(3.4) floor(−2.6)	3 −3
MOD(x,y)	the remainder of x divided by y	mod(14,3)	2
POWER(x,y)	x raised to the yth power	power(4,5) power(9,.5) power(−10,.5)	1024 3 error
ROUND(x,[y])	x rounded to y places (y defaults to 0; y can be negative to round to the left of the decimal point)	round(9525.66) round(9525.64,1) round(9525.64) round(9525.64,−2)	9525.7 9525.6 9526 9500
SIGN(x)	−1 if x is negative, 0 if x is 0, and 1 if x is positive	sign(54) sign(0) sign(−6.4)	1 0 −1
SQRT(x)	the square root of x	sqrt(64) qrt(−10)	8 error
TRUNC(x,[y])	x truncated to y decimal places (y defaults to 0; y can be negative to truncate to the left of the decimal point)	trunc(343.17,1) trunc(343.17) trunc(343.17,−1)	343.1 343 340

Functions Returning Character Values

Syntax	Returns	Example	Result
CHR(x)	the ASCII character whose numeric value is x	chr(87)	W
CONCAT(str1, str2)	*str1* concatenated with *str2*	concat('hello ',' world)	hello, world
INITCAP(str1)	*str1* with the first letter of each word capitalized; all other characters are in lower case	initcap('MR. JIMINY CRICKET') initcap('Joe McDonald')	Mr. Jiminy Cricket Joe Mcdonald
LOWER(str1)	str1 with all letters in lower case	lower('123 Sesame Street')	123 sesame street

Syntax	Returns	Example	Result
LPAD(str1, x, [str2])	*str1*, left-padded to a length of *x* with characters specified in str2; *str2* defaults to a blank space; if the length of *str1* is greater than *x*, *str1* is truncated to *x* characters	lpad('Chapter 11', 15,'*') lpad('This is a very long title', 10)	*****Chapter 11 This is a
LTRIM(str1, [set])	*str1*, with initial characters removed up to the first character not in *set*; *set* defaults to a blank space	ltrim(' right-justified text') ltrim('ABCDEFG', 'BACX')	right-justified text DEFG
REPLACE(str1, search, [replace])	replaces each occurrence of *search* with *replace*; if replace is omitted, *search* is deleted	replace('Portland, Oregon','land','smouth') replace('The Declaration of Indepedence',' ') replace('The Theory of Lathes','The')	Portsmouth, Oregon' TheDeclarationofIndepedence ory of Lathes
RPAD(str1, x, [str2])	*str1*, right-padded to a length of *x* which characters specified in *str2*; if the length of *str1* is greater than *x*, *str1* is truncated to x characters	rpad('Chapter 1', '20','.') rpad('hailstorm',5)	Chapter 1... hails
RTRIM(str1, [set])	*str1*, with trailing characters removed up to the first character not in *set*; *set* defaults to a blank space	rtrim('Lincoln, Abraham ') rtrim('1234567890', '1890')	Lincoln, Abraham 1234567
SOUNDEX(str1)	a character string containing the phonetic representation of *str1*	soundex('Johnston') soundex('Johnson')	J523 J525
SUBSTR (str1, x, y)	part of str1, beginning at character position x, y characters long; if x is positive, Oracle starts at the beginning of str1; if x is negative, Oracle starts from the end of str1; if y is omitted, all characters to the end of str1 are returned	substr('(503) 555-1532',2,3) substr ('Dickens, Charles', 10) substr('1234567 89',−5,3)	503 Charles 567
TRANSLATE (str1, from, to)	*str1*, which each character in from replaced with the corresponding character in to; if from has more characters than to, any characters without a corresponding value in to are deleted from *str1*	translate('1600 Pennsylvania Avenue', '0123456789','XX XXXXXXX') translate('Vowels are bad.','aeiou','——-')	XXXX Pennsylvania Avenue V-w-ls -r- b-d.
UPPER(str1)	*str1* with all letters in upper case	upper('Attention')	ATTENTION

Character Functions Returning Numbers

Syntax	Returns	Example	Result
ASCII(str1)	the ASCII value for the first byte of *str1*	ascii('A') ascii('Apple')	65
INSTR(str1, search, [x], [y])	the first character position in *str1* where search is found in the *y*th occurence; both *x* and *y* default to 1; if *x* is negative, Oracle searches from the end of str1; if search is not found, 0 is returned	instr('Earhart, Amelia',',') instr('She sells sea shells by the sea shore','ll',1,2) instr('Hip Hip Horray!','Hip',2) instr('Kansas City, Kansas','Kansas',–1)	8 18 5 14
LENGTH(str1)	number of characters in *str1*	length('shoes')	5

Note: brackets indicate that a parameter is optional.

Built-in functions can be nested to provide even more functionality. Let's look at a few examples of how these functions can be used.

Often, strings of text that will be indexed are often put in upper-case and spaces removed in order to eliminate unnecessary mismatches.

The examples given here use a special table in Oracle called DUAL.This table has but one column, called DUMMY, and one row. It is used when you need to exploit some SQL functionality, but don't actually need to retrieve any data from the database. So, if you type something like this into SQL*Plus:

```
select 'Hello, world'
from dual;
```

SQL*Plus responds quite dutifully,

```
Hello, world
```

Because we can depend on DUAL to have one row, we can use it to display literals using only SQL. SQL*Plus and PL/SQL both have facilities for displaying literal values, but it's nice to know that DUAL exists, particularly when you're testing the behavior of Oracle's built-in functions.

Often, strings of text that will be indexed are converted to upper-case and spaces removed in order to eliminate unnecessary mismatches. Here's a good example:

```
select upper(replace('For Whom the Bell Tolls',' '))
from dual;
```

```
FORWHOMTHEBELLTOLLS
```

Or suppose you want to center some text on a 30-character line:

```
select rpad(lpad('My proposal',
(30+length('My proposal'))/2,'-'),30,'-')
from dual;
---------My proposal---------
```

You may wonder why the string had to be repeated twice in this Select statement. We're using the string in two ways: one as a parameter to *lpad* and one as a parameter to *length*. In SQL*Plus or PL/SQL, the value "My proposal" would be stored in a local variable, which makes such repetitions less clumsy.

You can use the string-handling functions for parsing. Here's some SQL that will extract the last name from a name in the format "Last name, first name":

```
select substr
('Smith, Joe',1,instr('Smith, Joe',',')-1)
from dual;
Smith
```

As you can see, these functions can be quite powerful. It's worth spending some time trying out your own combinations to become comfortable with the built-in functions.

Using Substitution Variables

Once you've become adept at creating a query to pull data from your Oracle database, you can extend the functionality of your queries by allowing certain key values to be supplied at the time that the statement is being executed.

Imagine that Janet is a coordinator for a large-city animal hospital. Her boss asks her to create a list of Jack Russell Terriers that are currently admitted to the hospital. She comes up with the following query:

```
select pet.name, registration.admit_date
from pet, registration
where pet.pet_id = registration.pet_id
and   pet.breed_code = 'JRUSS'
and   registration.discharge_date is null
order by name;
```

And, lickity split, she gets her list. The query works so well that Janet finds herself often editing the pet_type_code and breed_code values to get lists for different sets of animal patients. SQL*Plus offers substitution variables to handle this very situation. A substitution variable is indicated in a SQL*Plus script by an ampersand (&) followed by the variable name. So, Janet can replace the hard-coded JRUSS with a substitution variable:

```
select pet.name, registration.admit_date
from pet, registration
where pet.pet_id = registration.pet_id
and   pet.breed_code = '&BREED_TYPE'
and   registration.discharge_date is null
order by name;
```

> As long as the SQL*Plus parameter SCAN is set to ON (which it is by default), SQL*Plus will prompt the user for a value for a variable. If SCAN is set to off, SQL*Plus treats the substitution variable name (including &) literally and won't ask the user for any input.

When the query is executed, SQL*Plus stops and requests the value to substitute for the variable:

```
Enter value for breed_type:
```

Once Janet enters the breed type and presses ENTER, the substitution value is replaced by whatever Janet types into SQL*Plus and off the query goes.

If Janet then wanted to run the query again and supply another breed type, she just needs to execute the query again (by rerunning the script or by typing / to run the query currently being held in the buffer). You can even use substitution variables to supply parameters for SQL*Plus commands, such as SET.

The following statement in a SQL*Plus script would request the value for the feedback parameter.

```
SET FEEDBACK &FEEDBACK_VALUE
```

It's important to note that SQL*Plus does no error checking when substituting a value for a variable. If you reply to the prompt with an invalid number, Oracle replaces the variable without questioning it. In this case, the set command responds with an error:

```
Enter value for feedback_value: No, Way!
feedback option not a valid number
```

Using Double Ampersands

Sometimes it is desirable to make several select statements in a SQL*Plus script, using the same variable. Using a double ampersand (&&) tells Oracle to remember the substitution value of the variable and will not prompt for the user on subsequent references.

Janet created another small report to gather some information about a particular pet by that pet's ID number. She created the following script:

```
spool pet_info.out
select name, breed_description
from   pet, breed
where  pet.breed_code = breed.breed_code
and    pet_id = '&&pet_id'
/

select admit_date, discharge_date
from   registration
where  pet_id = '&&pet_id'
/

spool off
undefine pet_id
```

The first time SQL*Plus comes to the pet_id variable, Janet is prompted for the pet ID, but since she used double ampersands, the same pet ID is used in the second query as well.

The undefine statement at the end of the script tells SQL*Plus to forget the value that Janet supplied for the pet_id. Otherwise, if Janet ran this script successively in the same SQL*Plus session, the script would substitute &&pet_id with the value she first entered. She'd get the same query output every time!

Syntax of Query Parameters

So you ask, how is this going to help me with my Web application, where the query is passed from the front end to the Oracle database to be executed? Conveniently, substitution variables can be passed as a SQL*Plus script is being invoked. If you're calling a script on the command line, use the following syntax:

```
sqlplus username/password @script_name variable1 variable2 ... variablen
```

From within sqlplus, you can call the script as follows:

```
@script_name variable1 variable2 ... variablen
Each variable is then referenced inside the script by an ampersand followed by
the variable number: &1, &2, &3, etc.
```

Janet's query by pet_id script above could easily be converted to using command-line substitution variables:

```
spool pet_info.out
select name, breed_description
from   pet, breed
where  pet.breed_code = breed.breed_code
and    pet_id = '&1'
/

select admit_date, discharge_date
from   registration
where  pet_id = '&1'
/

spool off
```

Assuming that Janet called her script get_pet_info.sql, she could run it from within SQL*Plus:

```
@get_pet_info 4566
```

or at the operating-system prompt

```
sqlplus janet/doggie @get_pet_info 4566
```

Note that in the script, only single ampersands are used, even though the parameter is referenced twice. When command-line parameters are employed, SQL*Plus assumes that the statement is being run non-interactively. The SQL processor replaces each occurrence of the numbered variables and undefines them automatically when the script is complete.

Using Subqueries

Oracle allows you to nest one query within another query: the nested query is referred to as the subquery. There are a number of reasons why you would want to design a subquery. These are:

- Accelerate query design by query reuse
- Subqueries are often more manageable
- Offload as much of the processor requirements onto the server machine
- Propagate changes made in queries by changing base queries

If you are not familiar with subqueries, the best way that I've found to conceptualize them is to think of a query running and producing a result set. That result set is then used automatically (and without you having to do anything special) as the source data for a second query. The result set for the second query is what is returned. Although it is possible to have many levels of nested queries, the truth is that they rarely exceed two levels, and almost never exceed three levels.

The process of creating and using subqueries is described in the next section.

Creating a Subquery

In most cases, the inner most Select in a nested query is a join of some sort on two or more tables. The columns in the result set of this inner query are frequently the product of the tables being joined. The outer queries then summarize or manipulate the result set from the inner query.

As an auto enthusiast, Tim maintains an Oracle database with information about cars. He decides to print a list of all cars produced by American car manufacturers, so he writes the following Select statement:

```
select make, model
from   vehicle
where manufacturer_name in
(select name
from   company
where country = 'USA');
```

Oracle obtains the results in two steps. First, the subquery returns a list of all companies located in the United States. The outer query then finds all rows where the manufacturer_name is found in the subquery's result set.

The subquery can even reference the same table as the main query. Consider this example:

```
select city_name
from location
where state_name =
(select state_name
from location
where city_name = 'Pittsburgh');
```

This query will return all cities in the same state as Pittsburgh. You can get the answer without even knowing what state Pittsburgh's in! The subquery gets the state name which is then used in the main query .

If the location had happened to have more than one Pittsburgh, the following error would have resulted:

```
ORA-1427: single-row subquery returns more than one row
```

Any subquery must be carefully examined. If it can return more than one row, the IN operator should be used. If one and only one row can be returned, the = operator is appropriate.

Sometimes, you don't care what value your subquery returns. You just want to know if anything was returned at all. The *exists* operator fills the bill here. It works much like the IN operator, but it doesn't check for particular column values.

Suppose you have a table that holds student's schedules. You want to list all rows for any student who's taking more than 4 classes.

```
select student_name, class_name
from class_list outer
where exists
(select 'x'
from  class_list
where outer.student_name = student_name
group by student_name
having count(*) > 4);
```

The outer in the above statement is referred to as a table alias. It's used here because we refer to the class_list table twice. The outer alias allows us to refer to class_list in the main query and within the subquery. The select clause uses just a literal "x," because all we're concerned about is where anything is returned in the subquery for a particular student. The NOT operand can be inserted before exist to reverse its meaning. This query would return the same results as the last query:

```
select student_name, class_name
from class_list outer
where not exists
(select 'x'
from  class_list
where outer.student_name = student_name
group by student_name
having count(*) <= 4);
```

Subqueries can often seem unnatural when first learning SQL. But, as long as you remember that the results of the subquery are passed back to the main query, it's easy to see what's going on.

DML Statements

SQL that creates, updates, or deletes rows of data are called Data Manipulation Language (DML) statements. DML statements fall into one of three categories:

- Insert
- Update
- Delete

Oracle gives you the ability to write and execute all three of the above DML statements.

Insert Statement

The Insert statement is used to add data to a pre-existing table. One or more tables of data are used for source data to add to the table that is to be appended. The main benefit of using an Insert query is that it saves the user time by not having to re-key data.

Prior to issuing an Insert statement, you must identify the table(s) to be appended, as well as the source table, and any selection criteria you want to apply. To create an Insert statement, follow the steps described here.

The Insert statement comes in two forms: one where the values to be inserted are explicitly listed. The other uses a query to insert the values into the table.

Let's suppose that you have a table that stores your video store's main movie collection. The table, movie, has the following structure:

```
id               number(9)    NOT NULL
title            varchar2(60)  NOT NULL
rating_code      varchar2(5)
category_code varchar2(10)
```

Let's suppose that you want to add a new movie to the table.

```
insert into movie
(id,
title,
rating_code,
category_code)
values
(10006,
'Miss Ima"s Revenge',
'PG-13',
'HORROR');
```

Upon executing this statement, as long as your values are legal for the columns, Oracle responds with:

```
1 row created.
```

The Insert statement takes the following form:

```
insert into table_name
(column1,
column2,
  ...
columnn)
values
(value1,
```

```
value2,
  ...
valuen)
```

Rows can also be inserted into a table using a query. Let's suppose that you maintain a separate table for movies that have not yet been released. The table, movie_prelease has the following definition:

```
id               number(9)     NOT NULL
title            varchar2(60)  NOT NULL
rating_code      varchar2(5)
category_code    varchar2(10)
release_date     date
```

You can periodically copy the releases to your regular movie table, with another type of Insert statement. Here's an example:

```
insert into movie
(id,
title,
rating_code,
category_code)
as select
id,
title,
rating_code,
category_code
from movie_prelease
where release_date <= SYSDATE;
```

This statement will copy any movies whose release date is today or earlier. (We're assuming that this select does not result in any rows that would violate the movie table's primary key. We'll show a statement to delete the rows from the movie_prelease table in the next section.)

In this form of insert statement, each column in the query is saved in the corresponding column in the movie table. There must be the same number of columns in the inserted table as the table being selected from, or an Oracle error will result.

Update Statement

The Update statement is a powerful tool used to change data that already exists in a table. Depending on the criteria you specify, you can update a specific row, a selection of rows, or all the rows in a table.

There's an easy way to think of an Update Statement. Take a simple Select statement, replace the Select and From clauses with Update and Set clauses, and voilà, you have an Update Statement! The Where clause, which in a Select state determines which rows your query returns, specifies which rows you'll change in an Update Statement. Here's how to write an Update Statement, using the movies table for an example.

Write a Select query that returns the rows you want to update. Let's say that you want to change the rating_code to "R" for all movies with the category code "HORROR." First write a Select statement with this criterion.

```
SELECT id, title
FROM   movies
WHERE category_code = 'HORROR';
```

Run this query and make sure that it returns the rows you're expecting. If so, remove the Select and From clauses and replace them with Update and Set clauses. The Set clause indicates which column(s) you want to update and the value(s) to set them to.

```
UPDATE movies
SET   rating_code = 'R'
WHERE category_code = 'HORROR';
```

You can update all rows in a table by leaving off the Where clause:

```
UPDATE moves
SET   category_code = 'UNKNOWN';
```

This statement would change the category code for all rows to the value "UNKNOWN." Such a blanket update is not normally done, except in extraordinary circumstances. So, if you see an Update statement without a Where clause, be sure to give it a second look.

Delete Statement

A Delete statement is used to remove one or more rows from a table. It simplifies the process of deleting a group or collection of rows, especially if those rows are identifiable by applying a selection criterion.

A Delete statement is very simple to create. Like an Update statement, it is a normal Select query with the exception of one additional step. The process of defining a Delete statement is described here.

Write a normal Select query as you've already seen. Apply whatever selection criteria you want to identify the rows that you want to delete. Let's use the movie_prelease again for an example.

Warning: As you may expect, this process can be dangerous and should only be done if: You are experienced with Oracle, you have backed up the data to be deleted, you run a SELECT against the table that is going to have data deleted from it, verifying that your DELETE identifies the correct rows. In the next chapter, you'll learn about the ROLLBACK statement that will help you get out of a jam if you perform the wrong delete.

```
select id,
title,
rating_code,
category_code
from  movie_prelease
where release_date <= SYSDATE;
```

Run the Select query and scrutinize the results closely. If you are satisfied with the results, merely remove the Select clause (including all of the column references) and replace it with the word DELETE:

```
delete
from  movie_prelease
where release_date <= SYSDATE;
```

This statement will delete the rows that the previous Select statement returned.

If you want to delete all the rows from a table, issue a Delete statement with no Where clause:

```
delete
from    movie_prelease;
```

CREATE TABLE AS SELECT

Although a CREATE TABLE AS SELECT statement is really a data-definition language (DDL) statement, it logically goes with the UPDATE, INSERT, and DELETE statements. It's a statement with a special twist. It takes the results of a Select statement and creates a table automatically with the columns as defined in the Select clause and inserts the rows returned from the Select statement into the newly created table.

In a Web database application development project, this is an important capability. For example, you may want to provide a subset of a master table that contains confidential information, stripping out the confidential information and only making available in the table (presumably outside the firewall) the non-confidential data.

Suppose you wanted to create a table of children's movies from your movie collection. Instead of reentering all of your table data, you can use the following statement:

```
CREATE TABLE movies_for_children AS
SELECT id, title, category_code, release_date
FROM movies
WHERE rating_code = 'G';
```

If you describe your new table, you'll see that the data types for the columns were inherited from the original table:

```
id             number(9)    NOT NULL
title          varchar2(60) NOT NULL
category_code  varchar2(10)
release_date   date
```

The column names in the new table don't have to retain the same names as the original table(s). Using a syntax similar to the Insert statement, merely list the preferred column names inside parentheses and separated by commas after the table name. For instance,

```
CREATE TABLE movies_for_children
( movie_id,
movie_title,
movie_category_code,
```

```
movie_release_date)
AS
...
```

Learning More

This chapter packed a lot of information getting you going on creating your own Oracle SQL statements. There are many more features of SQL that you can explore. Like any skill, SQL programming takes practice. The best way to become an SQL expert is to look at other's SQL and to write your own. *The Oracle Server SQL Language Reference Manual* is a good place to start. Every component of the language is listed, but there are unfortunately few examples. Although, not specifically geared to Oracle, these books will help you enhance your SQL prowess:

Title:	LAN Times Guide To SQL
Publisher:	Osborne McGraw Hill
Author:	James R. Groff, Paul N. Greinberg
ISBN:	0-07-882026-X
Title:	SQL For Dummies, 2nd revised edition
Publisher:	IDG
Author:	Allen G. Taylor
ISBN:	0-76-450105-4
Title:	Joe Celko's SQL for Smarties
Publisher:	Morgan Kaufman
Author:	Joe Celko
ISBN:	1-55-860323-9

Moving On

This chapter focused on presenting some of the more advanced components and features in Oracle for building queries. You were introduced to SQL's superior data-handling capabilities. You learned how to create a Select statement, how to apply aggregate and single-row functions and how to apply criteria to queries. You learned how to use SQL*Plus's parameter feature to make your SQL statements more extendable. You were introduced to Oracle's DML statements, so that you can change the contents of tables. Also, you learned how to create a table as a selection from another table.

The information discussed in this chapter is valuable to any developer using Oracle as their back-end RDBMS, regardless of the front-end design and HTML tool being used. Chapter 12 further extends your understanding of the Oracle database. It examines query tuning, views, dates, transactions, locking, stored procedures, and some features new in Oracle 8.

CHAPTER 12

Learning More About Oracle

T he information discussed in this chapter is valuable to any developer using Oracle as their back-end RDBMS, regardless of the front-end design and HTML tool being used. Two additional SQL topics, dates and views, are discussed. PL/SQL, Oracle's procedural language is described, as well as the ability to store code within the database. Oracle transactional logic and locking are explained. Finally, performance and tuning of SQL statements is covered.

With this and the previous three chapters as a foundation to the Oracle RDBMS product, the next few chapters present material specific to front-end Web application design and construction. Specifically, Chapter 12 describes how to use HTML markups and extensions to access corporate databases.

Dates in Oracle

It is hard to find a database application that does not store dates. Dates in Oracle are seemingly simple. If you query the database for the current date, for instance:

```
SQL> select sysdate from dual;
```

You'll get a response that looks like this:

```
15-OCT-98
```

Sysdate is a built-in Oracle function that returns the current date and time. This date format (date, month, year) is the default for Oracle. Even though the datatype that stores such a value is called date, a date column can hold time information down to the second.

To increase the flexibility of the date datatype, two built-in SQL functions must be employed: To_char and To_date.

TO_CHAR converts a date into a character string in virtually any format you'd like. The syntax of the function is:

```
TO_CHAR(date,'date_format')
```

A date can be converted from a character string to a date variable using the TO_DATE function, whose syntax is:

```
TO_CHAR('string','date_format')
```

The date format is made up of elements that are listed below. Any other text or punctuation in the date_format is returned as entered. (See the table on the facing page.)

Let's examine two examples:

```
SQL> select to_char(to_date('15-APR-99',
  'DD-MON-YY'),'DD Month YYYY')
  from dual;

15 April   1999
```

Here the date is returned, with a spelled-out month and a full four-digit year. The Month format element returns the month padded with blanks. They could be removed with the rpad function, if desired. Notice that in order to pass the date to the to_char function, the date had to be first converted from a character string.

```
SQL> select to_char(sysdate,
  'DD-MON-YYYY HH24:MI:SS')
  from dual;

14-JUN-1998 18:53:48
```

Here the date format is used to show the current system date and time, down to the second. Just selecting sysdate without the to_char function would show the default date format, which doesn't list the time element.

Oracle also provides several other built-in functions that makes dealing with dates easier.

Oracle will never have a year 2000 problem, because of the way dates are stored in the database. If the application that interfaces with Oracle does not handle 4-digit dates correctly, you may have problems. Make sure that you use the entire year when designing your database application.

Creating Views

When you create a complex database, there are times you would like to simplify access to your data. A view is a query that is stored in the database. It can be described and selected the same as a database table. You can provide a view to end-users to query upon, freeing them from the complexity of the underlying query.

Date Format Elements

Element	Description	Values
SS	seconds	0–59
MI	minutes	0–59
HH24	hours (using a 24-hour clock)	0–23
HH or HH12	hours (using a 12-hour clock)	1–12
AM or A.M.	before noon (with or without periods)	AM / A.M.
PM or P.M.	after noon (with or without periods)	PM / P.M.
DY	name of day (abbreviated to 3 letters)	SUN–SAT
DAY	name of day (right-padded to 9 letters)	SUNDAY–SATURDAY
D	day of week	1–7
DD	day of month	1–31
DDD	day of year	1–366
W	week of month	1–5
WW	week of year	1–53
MON	name of month (abbreviated to 3 letters)	JAN–DEC
MONTH	name of month (right-padded to 9 letters)	JANUARY–DECEMBER
RM	number of month (in Roman numerals)	I–XII
MM	number of month	01–12
Q	quarter of year	1–4
BC or B.C.	before Christian era	BC / B.C.
AD or A.D.	Christian era	AD / A.D.
RR	last two digits of a year	00–99
YEAR	year (in words)	
YYYY or YYY or YY or Y	year (with a corresponding number of digits returned)	
CC	century	
LAST_DAY(date)	the last day of the month in *date*	

Note: If the returned value is alphabetic, it will be returned in the case of the format element, whether it be upper-case, lower-case, or mixed case.

Let's look at a scenario to see how views may enhance your database environment. Martin is in charge of a database that stores customer information for his company's chain of electronics stores. He found himself constantly producing address labels to send out sales flyers. Instead of rewriting the select statement every time you want to create an address label query, he created a view, like this:

```
SQL> create view address_label as
        (name,
         address,
         city,
         state,
         zip)
as select name.first_name || ' ' ||
         name.last_name,
         address.street,
         address.city,
         address.state,
```

Built-in Date Functions

Syntax	Returns	Example	Result
ADD_MONTHS (date, x)	*date* plus *x* months; *x* must be an integer; if the resulting month has fewer days than date, the last day of the resulting month is returned; otherwise, the same day as date in the resulting month is returned	add_months('10-MAY-98',3) add_months('31-JAN-99',1) add_months('15-SEP-97',-4)	10-AUG-98 28-FEB-98 15-MAY-97
LAST_DAY(date)	the last day of the month in *date*	last_day('15-FEB-96')	29-FEB-96
MONTHS_BETWEEN (date1, date2)	the number of months between date1 and date2; if date1 is earlier than date2, the result is negative; if date1 is later than date2, the result is positive; if date1 and date2 do not have the same day of the month, Oracle computes the fractional number of months based on a 31-day month	months_between ('15-APR-97','10-FEB-97') months_between ('1-JUN-98','1-AUG-98')	2.1612903 −2
NEXT_DAY(date, str1)	the date of the first weekday indicated by str1 after date	next_day('15-MAY-98',' FRIDAY')	22-MAY-98
SYSDATE	the current system date and time on the machine where your Oracle database resides	sysdate	14-JUN-99

```
                address_zip
from            customer_name name,
                customer_address address
where           name.customer_id =
                address.customer_id;
```

Note that the create statement has four parts:

- CREATE VIEW view_name
- A list of column names for the view
- The word "AS"
- A SELECT statement

Now, Martin can select from his address_label view, instead of joining the customer name and address tables. With the view, he's hidden the complexity of the original table join.

There are a few things about views that you should know:

- The view column's database inherits whatever columns are being selected from the table.
- The query cannot have an Order By clause. Any ordering necessary is done on the view itself.
- Part 2 of the statement (the view column names) is not required. If omitted, the view column names are the same as the columns in the select line of the query.

When creating a view, you'll get an error if an object already exists with your view name:

```
ORA-00955: name is already used by an existing object
```

You can either drop the object if it's not needed and create the view again or you can add "OR REPLACE" to the create line:

```
CREATE OR REPLACE VIEW view_name ...
```

This is particularly useful if you have permission-grants defined for the object, because any grants stay in place when you use CREATE OR REPLACE VIEW.

Another use of views is to provide value-level security. A view can be defined to return a subset of a table's rows. Access to the view can then be granted to particular users.

Martin has a table that stores his company's employee salaries. He didn't want all users to be able to access this table, for obvious reasons. But, he did want to be able to grant access to a particular department's salary data to, say, a department head.

Suppose Tanya is supervisor for department 100 in Martin's company. The following view would allow Tanya to see only her employee's salaries:

```
create view salary_100 as
select * from salary
where dept_code = 100;
```

Notice that you can use an asterisk (*) to select all columns from the salary table. The new view, salary_100, therefore has the same column names as the base salary table.

While views are highly useful, a caveat about their use and database performance is in order. As we've shown, views are often used to create simple access to a complex, multi-tabled query. But, this hidden complexity can be a problem if a user then joins the view to another table. If the view is joined to a table that makes up the view, Oracle may perform an unnecessary self-join. With each new version of Oracle, the cost-based optimizer (described later in this chapter) is getting better at detecting these circumstances, but it's best to know what a view's definition is if you plan to join it to other tables or views.

PL/SQL and Stored Code

In the last chapter, you learned how to compose queries and to use DML statements. In this chapter you have learned how to create views to simplify access to your database. It is possible to never go beyond this level of database access, but you'd be missing a great deal if you didn't investigate PL/SQL and Oracle's stored code functionality.

As you may have surmised, there is a limit to what you can do with SQL as your sole database access language. SQL is by definition non-procedural. There are many times when a procedural language, one that performs an operation one step at a time, is necessary. Oracle realized this and with Oracle v. 6, introduced PL/SQL (for Procedural Language/SQL). Based on Ada, a language heavily used in the government and well-known for its error-handling capabilities, PL/SQL provided Oracle users for the first time with a procedural language closely tied to SQL. Originally envisioned for simple routines called from products such as SQL*Forms or Report*Writer, the language's flexibility and usefulness quickly put PL/SQL to the forefront of the Oracle development community. Soon programmers began building entire programs in PL/SQL. Oracle has continued enhancing to PL/SQL over the years to the current version 3.0, released with Oracle 8.

Let's look at a typical PL/SQL program. Linda works for a credit union that uses Oracle to track depositor's accounts. She wrote a PL/SQL program to go through active accounts and generate records that will cause letters to go out to customers. In this example, accounts with a negative balance get an "Overdraft" letter, accounts with a zero balance get a "Zero balance letter" and are automatically closed, and accounts with a balance of more than $10,000 get a letter of thanks from the bank. Once all accounts have been processed, the total balance for all active accounts is displayed.

```
SQL> declare
  total_balance number(12,2) := 0;
  cursor active_accounts is
    select acct_number, current_balance
        from account
        where close_date is null;
begin
  for currec in active_accounts
  loop
  if currec.current_balance = 0
    then
```

```
  begin
    insert into letter values
    (currec.acct_number,
    'ZERO BALANCE',SYSDATE);
    update account
      set close_date = SYSDATE
      where acct_number =
      currec.acct_number;
  end;
elsif currec.current_balance < 0
  then
    insert into letter values
    (currec.acct_number,
    'OVERDRAWN',SYSDATE);
elsif currec.current_balance > 10000
  then
    insert into letter values
    (currec.acct_number,
    'VALUED CUSTOMER',SYSDATE);
end if;
  total_balance := total_balance + currec.current_balance;
end loop;
  dbms_output.put_line('Total balance of active accounts: ' ||
total_balance);
end;
```

Note in particular that the SQL code is tightly integrated with the PL/SQL. The cursor defines a query (here the active accounts) from the database, whose results are fetched from the database one row at a time, by the For statement. There is no need to manually open the cursor and assign the cursor's variables to local variables. PL/SQL handles all of this work.

While PL/SQL programs like the one above can be written and run directly in SQL*Plus, usually the code is stored in the database itself. Not only does this make the code easier to find later, but it also is kept compiled, ready to be executed at any time. In addition, parameters can be defined that allow the user to pass data to and from the stored code. Additionally one program can call another program, thereby increasing the code reuse even more. Code stored in an Oracle database comes in three forms: functions, procedures, and packages.

Procedures

A procedure in Oracle is much like a function in C or a subroutine in Visual Basic. It is a set of a code that performs a particular function. Multiple parameters can be specified for a procedure, either as values being passed to the procedure, returned from the procedure, or both.

To understand better how a procedure works, let's look at how they may be used in everyday life. Mary has been tasked with creating a database application to track her trade organization's membership roster. She decides to use Oracle's stored code functionality to implement her application. She makes a list of the type of operations she needs to perform on her membership list on a frequent basis. The first she comes up with is a need to terminate a member from the roster.

Here's an example of a procedure Mary writes to handle this job:

```
SQL> create procedure terminate_member
   (i_membership_id IN number,
    i_termination_date IN date default SYSDATE)
  IS
    v_current_status   membership.status%TYPE;
BEGIN
  select status
  into   v_current_status
  from   membership
  where id = i_membership_id;

  if  (v_current_status = 'term')
  then
      raise_application_error(-20102,'Member already terminated');
  end if;

  update membership
  set     status = 'term',
          end_date = i_termination_date
  where   id = i_membership_id;

EXCEPTION
    WHEN NO_DATA_FOUND THEN
        raise_application_error(-20101,'Membership ID not found');
END;
/
```

This procedure takes two parameters, the membership ID and termination date. If the termination date is not specified, it is automatically set to the current date. The procedure first checks the record for the ID number passed to it. If no record is found or if the member is already terminated an error is returned. Otherwise, the member's status is changed to 'term' and the termination date is recorded.

Procedures can be called from another stored program or within a PL/SQL block. In this example, Mary uses SQL*Plus to update her membership roster.

```
SQL> select id, status, join_date, end_date
from membership
order by 1;

ID          STATUS JOIN_DATE END_DATE
---------- ------ --------- ---------
      1001 active 15-MAR-96
      1002 term   16-APR-96 13-JUN-97
      1003 term   10-FEB-97
```

```
SQL> begin
        terminate_member(1001,'15-OCT-97');
     end;
/

PL/SQL procedure successfully completed.
SQL> begin
        terminate_member(1002);
     end;
/

begin
*
ERROR at line 1:
ORA-20102: Member already terminated
ORA-06512: at "USER.TERMINATE_MEMBER", line 15
ORA-06512: at line 2

SQL> select id, status, join_date, end_date
from membership
order by 1;

ID         STATUS JOIN_DATE END_DATE
---------- ------ --------- ---------
      1001 term   15-MAR-96 15-OCT-97
      1002 term   16-APR-96 13-JUN-97
      1003 active 10-FEB-97
```

Member number 1001's record is terminated on October 15, 1997. The second call failed because member 1002 was already terminated.

Functions

Functions are identical to procedures, with one exception: They return a single value that can be assigned to a variable in the calling PL/SQL code. A function's definition looks like a procedure except for the Return value.

Mary finds herself constantly looking up the status of a member, so she decides to write a function to handle this task:

```
SQL> create function get_membership_status
  ( i_membership_id IN number)
  RETURN VARCHAR IS

v_membership_status    membership.status%TYPE;

BEGIN

SELECT status
INTO   v_membership_status
FROM   membership
WHERE id = i_membership_id;
```

```
RETURN v_membership_status;
EXCEPTION
  WHEN NO_DATA_FOUND THEN
     raise_application_error(-20101,'Membership ID not found') ;
END;
/
```

The function requires an ID and returns the member's status. If the ID is not found, an error is returned.

Like procedures, functions can have OUT parameters and can update, insert, or delete rows. This is not normally considered good programming form, however. Functions should, in general, pass one value back (through the Return PL/SQL statement).

Again, functions are called from within other stored code or in a PL/SQL block. Here Mary checks the current membership status of member 1001:

```
SQL> declare
  v_status   varchar2(6);
begin
  dbms_output.enable(10000);
v_status := get_membership_status(1001);
  dbms_output.put_line('The status is: ' || v_status);
  end;
/
```

The status is: active

PL/SQL procedure successfully completed.

Packages

After developing a set of functions and procedures, it is often advantageous to combine them into another type of stored code, a package. Using packages yields many advantages. Because the package is stored as a unit, all procedures and functions within the package are loaded into memory at the same time. Variables global to the entire procedure can be defined, thereby simplifying code creation. Packages allow you to select which functions and procedures are available outside the package and which can be used only within the package itself. You can therefore hide complexity and grant public access to only those subprograms you want.

A package consists of two parts: the body and the specification. The body is where the actual code goes while the specification provides the interface to the package. Only those procedures and functions defined in the specification can be called externally. You can define a procedure or function that's only called within the package by leaving it out of the specification.

Here's an example of a package definition for Mary's function and procedure described above:

```
SQL> create package package_membership
  IS
Function get_membership_status
  ( i_membership_id IN number)
  RETURN VARCHAR;
```

```
Procedure terminate_member
   (i_membership_id IN number,
    i_termination_date IN date default SYSDATE);
END;

SQL> create package body package_membership
IS
Function get_membership_status
  ( i_membership_id IN number)
 RETURN VARCHAR IS

. . .
```
function definition goes here
```
. . .
END;
Procedure terminate_member
   (i_membership_id IN number,
    i_termination_date IN date default SYSDATE)
   IS

. . .
```
procedure definition goes here
```
. . .
END;
/
```

To call procedures and functions within a package, the package name must be prefixed before the call. For example:

```
package_membership.terminate_member(1003);
member_id := package_membership.get_membership_status(1002);
```

This section just begins to show the vast power of PL/SQL and stored code within Oracle. Fortunately, there has recently been an explosion of interest in PL/SQL. Consequently, several good books have recently come out on the language. The following are the best:

Title:	Building Intelligent Databases with Oracle PL/SQL, Triggers, and Stored Procedures
Author:	Kevin T. Owens
Publisher:	Prentice Hall
ISBN:	0-13-443631-8
Title:	Oracle PL/SQL Programming
Author:	Steven Feuerstein
Publisher:	O'Reilly
ISBN:	1-56-592142-9
Title:	Advanced Oracle PL/SQL Programming with Packages
Author:	Steven Feuerstein
Publisher:	O'Reilly
ISBN:	1-56-592238-7

Title: Oracle PL/SQL Programming
Author: Scott Urman
Publisher: Osborne-McGraw Hill
ISBN: 0-07-882176-2

Transactions in Oracle

Have you ever really screwed something up and wished that you could just roll it all
back? Well, if you're using Oracle, you can do just that.

As you make changes to data, using Update, Insert, and Delete statements, Oracle
keeps track of these changes in an area called a rollback segment. Although they haven't
been written to the database itself yet, you'd see changes you've made if you queried the
changed tables. If at any point, you want to undo the changes you've made, just type

```
SQL> ROLLBACK;
```

All changes you've made are removed from the rollback segment, taking the database back to its state when you started. Once you decide that the changes should be written to the database, type

```
SQL> COMMIT;
```

The changes are then incorporated into the database and removed from the rollback
segment. If you then made more changes and rolled back these changes, you'd be returned to the database state after this Commit.

Let's create a simple table to demonstrate the behavior of Commit and Rollback:

```
SQL> create table flower
   name varchar2(30));
```

Let's insert a couple rows.

```
SQL> insert into flower values ('parsley');

1 row created.

SQL> insert into flower values ('rutabaga');

1 row created.
```

These values are noted in the rollback segment. If we query the table, we'll see both
rows:

```
SQL> select * from flower;

parsley
rutabaga

2 rows selected.
```

But, then we realize that our floral expertise isn't quite up to snuff and we had better
undo our inserts.

```
SQL> rollback;

Rollback complete.
```

And, now, happily the non-flowers are gone from the table:

```
SQL> select * from flower;

0 rows selected.
```

Let's add a few real flowers into our table:

```
SQL> insert into flower values ('rose');

1 row created.

SQL> insert into flower values ('carnation');

1 row created.
```

Now we're sure we've got the correct entries, so we commit the inserts:

```
SQL> commit;

Committed.
```

Let's update one of the rows:

```
SQL> update flower set name = 'eggplant' where name = 'rose';

1 row updated.
```

And, now we have:

```
SQL> select * from flower;

eggplant
carnation

2 rows selected.
```

Wait, that's not what we want. A rollback is definitely in order:

```
SQL> rollback;

Rollback complete.
```

We're taken back to our original two values.

```
SQL> select * from flower;

eggplant
carnation

2 rows selected.
```

Notice that the Rollback statement takes the database state back to the last the Commit, and no farther. If your rollback needs are a bit more complicated, Oracle provides Savepoints, multiple points to which you can roll back. Consider this SQL*Plus session:

```
SQL> insert into flower values ('dahlia');

1 row created.

SQL> savepoint a;

Savepoint created.

SQL> insert into flower values ('poppy');

1 row created.

SQL> savepoint b;

Savepoint created.

SQL> insert into flower values ('gardenia');

1 row created.

SQL> select * from flower;

rose
carnation
dahlia
poppy
gardenia

5 rows selected.

SQL> rollback to a;

Rollback complete.

SQL> select * from flower;

rose
carnation
dahlia

3 rows selected.
```

As is evident above, the savepoint allows us to rollback to a particular point in our inserts. A Commit or a plain Rollback (without a savepoint) removes all current savepoints. At this point, we still have one pending insert (the "dahlia" row), that can either be committed to the database or rolled back.

You may have noticed if you scrutinized SQL*Plus' Set commands closely enough, that "SET AUTOCOMMIT ON" is a valid command. This automatically commits changes to database after the update, insert, or delete statement is executed. In general this is not behavior that you'd desire, because it precludes any use of the Rollback statement.

In normal interaction with the database, an explicitly executed Commit statement is used to write changes to the database. Be aware that Oracle performs an implicit Commit in these circumstances:

- You gracefully end the database session. In the case of SQL*Plus, this occurs when you type EXIT. (This is important to remember. If you do something catastrophic in SQL*Plus, don't panic and log out. This will commit your changes and you won't be able to roll back.)
- You change the current user with the CONNECT command.
- After each Update, Insert, or Select statement if SQL*Plus' Autocommit variable is set to On.
- A DDL statement, such as CREATE TABLE or DROP VIEW, is executed.

Likewise, Oracle implicitly rolls back changes in certain situations:

- SQL*Plus, or another application that is connected to the database, abruptly halts.
- The physical database server or the database itself crashes.

Transactions

Oracle's Commit and Rollback logic is handy when making ad-hoc updates to the database. It's true utility, when creating robust database applications, is to support the concept of a transaction. A transaction is a set of database actions (updates, inserts, and/or deletes) that together make up a logical unit of work. If something stops the transaction from completing, all changes made during the transaction need to be rolled back.

When designing your Web database, it is important to define your transactions and place Commit and Rollback statements appropriately in your scripts or code.

Here's an example of what might happen if transactions are not appropriately defined. Suppose your bank uses Oracle to process teller transactions. You walk into your branch and fill out a slip indicating a deposit of a $500 check and a $40 cash withdrawal.

At night, the teller slip is read by an optical scanner. The deposit is processed and committed to the database. Then, for whatever reason, the withdrawal cannot be saved to the database. The operator receives an error message and reprocesses your slip. This time both transactions are processed. Because the deposit was committed the first time, you are incorrectly credited $920 instead of $460. That's nice for you but will put your bank out of business quickly!

Since the transaction slip must be processed as a whole, the commit should only happen after all of the deposits and withdrawals are recorded. If any errors occur, the entire transaction must be rolled back.

Concurrency

Not only is Oracle's Rollback and Commit facility helpful in case of errors and provides transactional integrity, but it is also vital in maintaining database concurrency. In the database world, concurrency refers to the ability for a database user to see a consistent view of the data while a query is processing.

Let's say your company has a table that stores orders. At 8 PM each evening, a process is run that inserts all of the orders received for the day into the order table. The inserts take about 10 minutes and if successful are followed by a Commit statement. Your supervisor, being impatient, queries the table at 8:05 PM to get a count of the number of orders.

Time	Without Concurrency	With Concurrency
8pm	There are 5,200 records in the orders table; a process is started to add the day's orders, totaling 500 orders, which will take 10 minutes to complete	
8:05pm	Supervisor queries number of total number of orders; while query is running, more records are inserted making the *resulting count unknown.*	Supervisor queries total number of orders, query returns 5,200
8:10pm	Insert process finishes and is committed to database	
8:11pm	Supervisor queries total number of orders; query returns 5,700	Supervisor queries total number of orders; query returns 5,700

Without concurrency, during the Insert process, the query results can never be predicted. But, with concurrency, because the 500 updates were considered one transaction and committed to the database together, the query results are predictable. Until the commit, the count is 5,200. At the moment the commit completes, the count is 5,700.

Locking

Oracle maintains civility among the various database connections using row-level locking. When a user updates a row, a lock is placed on this row. Any other session can still view the contents of the row, but no one can make a change to the row until the original session commits or rolls back the change. Unlike some databases, Oracle locks as little as possible in order to maintain integrity between sessions. Only those rows being updated maintain a lock.

Let's try an experiment using the flower table discussed above. We'll log into SQL*Plus twice, both times as webdevel. Even though we're using the same userid, Oracle treats each connection as a separate session. All database locks are created at the session level. To differentiate these sessions in the listing, we'll use the Set Sqlprompt command to make the prompts different. In the first session, type:

```
SQL> set sqlprompt "SQL1> "
```

In the second session, type:

```
SQL> set sqlprompt "SQL2> "
```

Let's add an extra column to record the flowers' light needs:

```
SQL1> alter table flower
      add (light_need varchar2(10));

Table altered.
```

Now let's set rose's light needs:

```
SQL1> update flower
     set light_need = 'full sun'
     where name = 'rose';

1 row updated.
```

In the second session, query the flower table:

```
SQL2> select * from flower;

NAME                           LIGHT_NEED
------------------------------ ----------
rose
carnation
```

We have no problem querying the table because Select statements are never blocked. Because the first session has not committed the change, we still see the table's pre-update contents.

What if we try to change rose's light needs from the second session? Let's try it:

```
SQL2> update flower
     set light_need = 'shade'
     where name = 'rose';
```

Nothing happens. Oracle just hangs, because there is a row-level lock on the *rose* row.

If we go back to the first session and commit the change:

```
SQL1> commit;
```

immediately, the row-level lock is lifted and the second update is processed, this time placing a lock on the rose row from the second session. Because an update will hang if there's a row-level lock, you should write your application; however, to keep a change pending (that is, neither committed nor rolled back) write only as long as necessary. Otherwise, in a rapidly updated database, you'll end up with users waiting on one another to release locks on particular rows of data.

The take home message about locks is that you don't need to worry about them most of the time—Oracle handles locking behind the scenes. Also remember that locking never affects querying: a Select statement never creates a lock and a Select statement is never blocked by a lock. If you start to see locking in your application, review your code and consult your DBA who can help you determine where your locks are occurring.

Tuning

Tuning an Oracle database for optimum performance is performed on two levels: the database level and the application level. From a database level, many settings can be tuned: memory allocated to Oracle, database block size, and number of database writers are just a few examples. These settings must be set to a level. This is really the task of a DBA. If you're on your own in setting up your database instance, there are several good references that can help you tune your system at the database level. *The Oracle Server Administrator's Guide* and *Oracle Server Tuning* manuals are good places to start. The following books are also helpful for tuning at both a global database level and an SQL statement level:

Title:	Tuning Oracle
Author:	Michael Corey, Michael Abbey, & Daniel J. Dechichio, Jr.
Publisher:	Osborne-McGraw Hill
ISBN:	0-07-881181-3

Title:	Oracle Performance Tuning, 2nd ed.
Author:	Peter Corrigan & Mary Gurry
Publisher:	O'Reilly
ISBN:	1-56-592237-9

As long as the Oracle Server-level parameters are set to reasonable levels and the hardware can support the load, most performance problems you'll come up against occur on the individual SQL statement level. In this section, we'll focus on how Oracle decides how to execute a query. We'll also take a look at the tools that allow you to see how the queries are being executed.

The Optimizer

One of the attributes of SQL that's different from computer languages that you might be familiar with is that it is not procedural. When you write a Select statement, you tell Oracle *what* you want to know, not *how* to find it. This is a benefit for the most part—you need not worry about the physical structures of the data, just the logical relationships among your tables.

So if you don't tell Oracle how to get the data, how does it decide how to retrieve data? The optimizer determines the most efficient method for accessing the data. Oracle uses two optimization methods: rule-based and cost-based. The rule-based optimizer (RBO), the only choice until Oracle v. 6, uses a simple set of precedence rules to determine how to access the data. With Oracle 7, the cost-based optimizer (CBO) came into play. Instead of relying on hard and fast rules, it examines the nature of the data (number of rows, size of table, data distribution) to determine the most efficient manner for producing the query results. The CBO assigns a cost, a somewhat arbitrary number that indicates the amount of processing power and disk accesses that a particular Select statement requires. The lower the cost, the faster the query runs.

The CBO relies on statistics on each table and index to make its decisions. These statistics are not computed automatically by Oracle. You must periodically gather statistics on each database table and index so that the optimizer can make valid judgments. The SQL statement used is ANALYZE. It takes the following format:

```
ANALYZE object_type object_name analyze_type STATISTICS;
```

The *object_type* is either Table or Index. *Object_name* is the table's or index's name. *Analyze_type* is either Compute or Estimate. If you choose Estimate, Oracle samples 1,064 rows of the table. Otherwise, all rows in the table are analyzed. When the analysis is complete, the statistics are stored in the data dictionary. The CBO then uses these statistics to make its data access path decisions.

The decision of how often to analyze your tables and indexes depends on how volatile your data is. If it changes quite frequently, a nightly analysis may be in order. If the table is relatively static, analysis can be performed weekly or less often. If the table is relatively small, using the Compute Statistics often makes sense. Otherwise, allowing Oracle to examine a subset of rows, using the Estimate Statistics clause, gives a statistically valid sample of all the table's rows.

If at least one table in a query has been analyzed, Oracle uses the CBO. Without statistics, however, the RBO is used instead.

Since the release of the CBO in Oracle 7, Oracle has constantly been improving its performance. With the release of Oracle 8, it has really come into its own. With the RBO, tricks were often employed to improve query performance, such as changing the order of tables in the Where clause. The idea behind the CBO, however, is to come up with the best query performance without a lot of thought of how the query is put together. Unfortunately, the CBO is not perfect. Sometimes, whether for a lack of information, or a strange distribution to the data, it comes up with a bad decision.

If queries are running quickly, you don't know, and don't care, how Oracle is going about getting the data from the database. But, when you start to have performance problems, Oracle provides a tool that allows you to see how the Optimizer is going about its business.

Optimizing Queries

Simple queries against tables with few rows and limited row lengths do not require much thought from the developer to determine the most efficient way to write the query. As the complexity of the query increases, or as the number of rows in the table(s) increase, or as the length of the rows in the tables increase, the developer must become increasingly concerned about optimizing the query for performance.

Oracle's cost-based optimizer is good about optimizing the query for you. It does not, nor will any RDBMS product ever be able to, overcome sloppy database design or query coding techniques. There are a number of things that you can do to optimize the performance of your queries.

- *Place indexes on the fields that are joined:* This decreases the time required by Oracle to access the correct rows because it searched the indexes of the table, avoiding having to scan the file directly.

- *Limit fields in a query:* Obviously the more data Oracle has to format and include in a result set, the more time it will take to create that result set and transmit it across data lines to your machine or browser.

- *Avoid restrictive query criteria:* Restrictive query criteria applied on calculated and non-indexed columns increases the amount of time it takes Oracle to execute the query.

- *Avoid calculated fields in nested queries:* If calculated fields are a requirement in a nested query, attempt to structure the query so the calculated field is formed by the outermost query.

- *Index sorted columns:* When possible, it is best to place an index on a column that is sorted in a query. This will increase the efficiency of the sort algorithm and return the result set to you quicker.

- *Limit the use of Group By columns:* Using a Group By on a column that does not require grouping slows the efficiency of Oracle supplying you with a result set.

- *Use nested queries over total queries with joins:* It is generally advantageous to split a total query that has a join into a nested query. The innermost query performs the joins on the table(s) while the outermost query calculates the totals.

- *Use EXPLAIN PLAN:* EXPLAIN PLAN is a tool by Oracle as an aid to determine where and why queries might run into performance problems.

Analyzing Query Performance with *EXPLAIN PLAN*

Oracle provides a tool that you can use to analyze your query's performance called Explain Plan. Because queries are the one component of a RDBMS system, and your Web database application, that will probably be the slowest, it is a wise idea to run the query performance analyzer against your queries before releasing them to production status.

Every time Oracle performs a query, it has to decide what the most efficient method is for doing so. Like a diligent worker, Oracle prepares a plan for executing the query. Normally, as Oracle moves on to its next query, it forgets about the last execution plan. The EXPLAIN PLAN statement, though, records Oracle's plan so that you can access it later.

In order to use the EXPLAIN PLAN tool, a PLAN_TABLE must exist for the current user. If it does not exist, you can create it by running utlxplan.sql. On a Windows NT machine, you can find this file in /ORANT/RDBMS80/ADMIN. If you have trouble finding the location of the file on your system, consult your Oracle installation guide or friendly DBA.

```
SQL> @/orant/rdbms80/admin/utlxplan
Table created.
```

If you get an Oracle error message, be sure that the current user has permission to create a table in its default tablespace. PLAN_TABLE looks like this:

```
STATEMENT_ID         VARCHAR2(30)
TIMESTAMP            DATE
REMARKS             VARCHAR2(80)
OPERATION           VARCHAR2(30)
OPTIONS             VARCHAR2(30)
OBJECT_NODE         VARCHAR2(128)
OBJECT_OWNER        VARCHAR2(30)
OBJECT_NAME         VARCHAR2(30)
OBJECT_INSTANCE     NUMBER(38)
```

```
OBJECT_TYPE            VARCHAR2(30)
OPTIMIZER              VARCHAR2(255)
SEARCH_COLUMNS         NUMBER
ID                     NUMBER(38)
PARENT_ID              NUMBER(38)
POSITION               NUMBER(38)
COST                   NUMBER(38)
CARDINALITY            NUMBER(38)
BYTES                  NUMBER(38)
OTHER_TAG              VARCHAR2(255)
PARTITION_START        VARCHAR2(255)
PARTITION_STOP         VARCHAR2(255)
PARTITION_ID           NUMBER(38)
OTHER                  LONG
```

If you're using Oracle 7, you may not see all of these columns. A few columns have been added to trace performance of partitioned tables in Oracle 8. This is an advanced tuning topic that we won't have to worry about here.

Running an EXPLAIN PLAN is quite simple. Here's the syntax:

```
EXPLAIN PLAN
SET STATEMENT_ID = 'statement_description_string'
FOR
SQL_statement;
```

Let's suppose Jack was trying to figure out why one of his queries was taking so long. His statement gets all of the player's names in the American League. So he used an explain plan on his statement.

```
explain plan
set statement_id = 'Player tune 1'
for
select last_name, first_name
from player, team
where player.team_code = team.team_code
and league_code = 'A';
```

Oracle responds tersely:

```
Explained.
```

When creating an explain plan, Oracle doesn't actually run the query. Instead, it determines how it would go about doing so and places its execution plan in the EXPLAIN_PLAN table you created.

You'd think that at this point, there'd be a built-in tool for viewing the saved plan. But, there's not. Fortunately, you can get readable output of the execution plan with a short SQL statement.

Here's a query that will show you the explain plan for a particular query:

```
SQL> select lpad(' ', 2 * (level-1)) ||
        operation || ' ' ||
        options || ' ' ||
        object_name || ' ' ||
        decode (id, 0, 'Cost: ' || position)
        "plan"
from    plan_table
start with id = 0
and statement_id = '&&statement_id'
connect by prior id = parent_id
and statement_id = '&&statement_id';
```

When you run this statement, respond to the prompt:

```
Enter value for statement_id:
```

with the name of the statement and the statement_id you set in the Explain Plan statement. You'll get output that looks something like this:

```
SELECT STATEMENT  Cost: 4
  NESTED LOOPS
    TABLE ACCESS FULL PLAYER
    TABLE ACCESS BY INDEX ROWID TEAM
      INDEX UNIQUE SCAN PK_TEAM
```

   This explain plan tells us that each row of the Player table was accessed and that it was joined to the Team table using the Team table's primary key. The cost is 4, which is relatively small, compared to a cost of 10, which is higher. This query, therefore, probably doesn't need tuning. If it had needed tuning, you would change the Select statement and rerun the Explain Plan and Explain Plan query, repetitively until you get the performance that you're looking for.
   Learning how to interpret Explain Plan's results takes some time. The ability to diagnose SQL performance problems, however, is highly valuable for keeping a database running at peak level. Refer to the books listed at the beginning of this section for more guidance.

Moving On

In this chapter, we delved deeper into the many features that the Oracle Server provides. You learned about dates and views, two important components of an Oracle database. You learned about PL/SQL and stored code and how they can be used to improve your database application. In addition, you learned how Oracle handles transactions, rollbacks and commits, and locking. Finally, you learned about tools that can help you improve the performance of your SQL statements. This chapter, along with the last three chapters, gives you a strong foundation in using Oracle to build your Web-based database application. In the next chapter, you will be shown how to use HTML markups and extensions to access corporate databases.

Section III: Interfacing with the Internet User

CHAPTER 13

HTML Forms and Database Access

This chapter continues with what was introduced in Chapter 6, "Overview of HTML." Specifically, Chapter 13 shows you how to build a well designed HTML form to accept user input and display the results of database queries.

An HTML form can appear anywhere in an HTML document and is designed to accept user input for subsequent processing. This could include:

- Posting of the information to a database
- Use of the information to query a database
- Generation of custom HTML pages based on user-supplied input

There are seven basic objects on an HTML form that you have available to receive input from users. These are:

- *Checkbox*—Allows the user to select one or more items from a selection of choices.
- *Command Buttons*—Allows the user to cause an action to occur to the form. The most common choices are: Submit (in Figure 13–1, this is labeled <Press To Send>), and Reset.
- *List Box*—Allows the user to select one of a list of choices that display when a control, usually a down arrow (V), is clicked.
- *Password*—Allows the user to input a character string while the echo of that string is asterisks (*), thus masking the input data stream.

- *Radio Button*—Allows the user to select one, and only one, of a group of choices displayed.
- *Text*—Allows the user to input a character string.
- *Text Box*—Allows the user to input a series of text lines.

Figure 13–1 is a screen print of what each of these input controls looks like on a finished HTML page.

Once a user inputs information into the form, nothing happens by pressing ENTER or typing in another URL. When the user clicks on the SUBMIT or PRESS TO SEND buttons, it is then that the HTML markup formats a CGI send request as discussed in Chapter 7. Once this request is received by the server, it initiates the processing of a CGI program that interprets and processes the input provided by the user. It is the responsibility of the CGI program to format and transmit back to the browser (the user) a response. This response could be a simple confirmation of receipt or it could be a display of a result set from a database query.

This chapter gives you a thorough introduction into the markups (controls) available to construct and transmit an HTML form. These markups, and the actions and attrib-

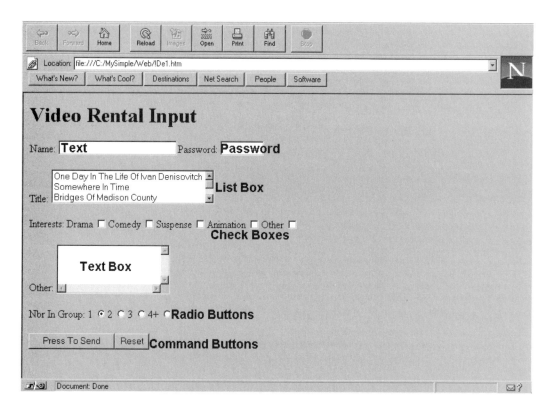

Figure 13–1   The various types of HTML form input objects.

utes you code to the controls on the form, are the input mechanism into your Web database application.

> The screen images you see in this chapter are not glitzy or even very aesthetically appealing. They are functional, however, and that is their purpose. Excessive graphics would detract from what I want you to see on these forms. This chapter is meant to introduce you to the various controls and facilities available to you when using HTML forms for database query and updates—it is not meant to be a GUI design chapter. A solid presentation of GUI design principles would take a book of its own.

Syntax of HTML Markups

The code snippet below gives the HTML markup syntax for the form seen in Figure 13–1 This section describes the syntax for these and a few other types of HTML markups.

```
<HTML>
<HEAD>
<TITLE>Demo2</TITLE>
<META NAME="GENERATOR" CONTENT="HAHTsite 2.0"></HEAD>
<BODY>
<FORM NAME=Form1 ACTION="Demo2.htm">
<H1>Video Rental Input</H1>
<P>Name: <INPUT TYPE=TEXT NAME=Renter_name SIZE=25 MAXLENGTH=40> Password:
<INPUT TYPE=PASSWORD NAME=Password SIZE=8 MAXLENGTH=8></P>
<P>Title: <SELECT MULTIPLE NAME=Movie_Titles SIZE=3>
<OPTION VALUE="One Day In The Life Of Ivan Denisovitch">One Day In The Life Of
Ivan Denisovitch</OPTION>
<OPTION VALUE="Somewhere In Time">Somewhere In Time</OPTION>
<OPTION VALUE="Bridges Of Madison County">Bridges Of Madison County</OPTION>
<OPTION VALUE="Beverly Hills Cop">Beverly Hills Cop</OPTION>
<OPTION VALUE="Beverly Hills Cop II">Beverly Hills Cop II</OPTION>
</SELECT></P>
<P>Interests: Drama <INPUT TYPE=CHECKBOX NAME=I_Drama> Comedy <INPUT
TYPE=CHECKBOX NAME=I_Comedy> Suspense <INPUT TYPE=CHECKBOX NAME=I_Suspense> An-
imation <INPUT TYPE=CHECKBOX NAME=I_Animation> Other <INPUT TYPE=CHECKBOX
NAME=I_Other></P>
<P>Other: <TEXTAREA NAME=Other_Interest_Text COLS=20 ROWS=3></TEXTAREA></P>
<P>Nbr In Group: 1 <INPUT TYPE=RADIO NAME=RadioGroup1 HAHTNAME=Group_1 CHECKED>
2 <INPUT TYPE=RADIO NAME=RadioGroup1 HAHTNAME=Group_2> 3 <INPUT TYPE=RADIO
NAME=RadioGroup1 HAHTNAME=Group_3> 4+ <INPUT TYPE=RADIO NAME=RadioGroup1 HAHT-
NAME=Group_4></P>
<P><INPUT NAME=Send_Button TYPE=SUBMIT VALUE="Press To Send"><INPUT
NAME=Reset_Button TYPE=RESET VALUE=Reset></P>
</FORM>
</BODY>
</HTML>
```

The information in the following sections elaborates on and explains many of the HTML components seen in the code sample above.

Form Specification

The `<FORM>` . . . `</FORM>` HTML tag pair is used to define the entire form. There are three parameters available when using this tag, these are METHOD, ACTION, and ENCTYPE.

`<FORM METHOD="GET|POST">`. As you learned in Chapter 7, there are two methods of sending information to a CGI script—GET and POST. When using the GET method, character strings and field names are supplied by the user on the form. They are intended to be sent to the CGI program and placed in environmental variables that the CGI program then retrieves for processing. When using the POST method, as seen here, the character string is sent to the CGI program directly with the URL that is sent back to the Server.

> Forms designed to transmit a single user input are well suited to use the GET method. Forms accepting several user inputs should be written to use the POST method because the amount of data that can be passed using the GET method is limited.

`<FORM ACTION="specified URL or CGI script")>`. The ACTION method is used to initiate a specific CGI program or trigger an identified URL. Such is the case in the following example:

```
<FORM ACTION="http://teleport.com/cgi-bin/acct_inq.exe">
```

The ACTION attribute is the way to trigger the execution of a CGI program on a Server. In the code sample above, the program named acct_inq.exe that resides in the cgi-bin directory on the teleport.com server is targeted as the program that is to be executed.

`<FORM ENCTYPE="application/x-www-form-urlencoded">`. The ENCTYPE attribute specifies the encoding method used for the content of the HTML form. This is specified to ensure complete and accurate transmittal of all user-supplied data. This attribute is infrequently used as the default encoding (as seen above) and is usually acceptable.

Input Specification

Let's take a look now at some of the ways you can supply users with the capability of inputting information to you via a HTML form. There are a number of HTML markup specifications available to define user input. These are:

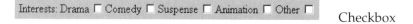 Checkbox

Figure 13–2   A checkbox as seen in a browser.

Command Buttons

Figure 13–3 Command buttons as seen in a browser.

List Box

Figure 13–4 A list box as seen in a browser.

Password

Figure 13–5 A password as seen in a browser.

Radio Button

Figure 13–6 Radio buttons as seen in a browser.

Text

Figure 13–7 Text area as seen in a browser.

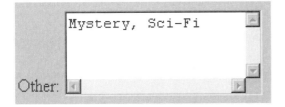

Text Box

Figure 13–8 Text box as seen in a browser.

Each of these is discussed in detail in this section.

Checkbox.   Checkboxes are used to allow a user to select between 0 and *n*, where *n* is the total number of checkboxes in the group, of non-exclusive choices. A checkbox is termed a two-state input field. That is, it can be in either on (checked) or off (unchecked). The code below shows the actual HTML code used to create the checkboxes as seen in Figure 13–2.

```
<P>Interests: Drama <INPUT TYPE=CHECKBOX NAME=I_Drama>
Comedy <INPUT TYPE=CHECKBOX NAME=I_Comedy> Suspense <INPUT TYPE=CHECKBOX
NAME=I_Suspense> Animation <INPUT TYPE=CHECKBOX NAME=I_Animation>
Other <INPUT TYPE=CHECKBOX NAME=I_Other></P>
```

The specific format for the checkbox syntax used in the examples above is:

```
<INPUT TYPE=CHECKBOX NAME=name>
```

In this example, the character string identified by `name` is the name part of the name/value pair that is sent to the CGI program. The `value` part of the name/value pair is determined by whether the control is checked or not. If it is checked, then the value is `yes`. If it is not checked, then neither the name, or the value is sent to the CGI program.

In this example, the checkboxes are placed horizontally across the page. You could combine HTML codes and place them vertically down a page in an ordered or unordered list. If a checkbox is checked when the user presses the `<Submit>` button, then a name/value pair will be sent to the server. In the case of the code above and Figure 13–2, if the user checks the Comedy and Suspense checkboxes, then the following named/ value pairs will be sent to the Server:

```
I_Comedy=yes&I_Suspense=yes
```

Command Buttons.   When the user has completed the form and is ready to send it off to the Server, they can press the `<Submit>` button. This causes the browser to format the CGI request using one of the 3 methods already discussed, and pass the request to the Server which interprets the URL and identifies the need to execute a CGI program.

There are two basic types of command buttons—`<Submit>` and `<Reset>`. Each of these has different methods. The `<Submit>` button performs the action just described while the `<Reset>` button causes the form to be cleared of all input values.

Here is the actual HTML code used to format the `<Submit>` and `<Reset>` buttons.

```
<P><INPUT NAME=Send_Button TYPE=SUBMIT VALUE="Press To Send"><INPUT
NAME=Reset_Button TYPE=RESET VALUE=Reset></P>
```

This code sample is standard HTML syntax and is the only way to describe a command button, short of using other types of development suites that customize how they handle command buttons from standard HTML syntax. As seen in the above code, the VALUE attribute allows the developer to specify the label on the button. In this case, I have chosen the label of `<Press To Send>`.

It is possible to have multiple command buttons on a HTML form, each sending a different name/value pair to the server. In such a case, a value must be supplied for each NAME attribute so the server can identify what command button initiated the action. You'll notice that in the code above, (reproduced in Figure 13–3) only one command button is shown that formats a name/value pair for transmission to a Server. The <RESET> button simply clears the form—it doesn't transmit anything to the Server. The following name/value pair would format HTML code for transmission to the Server if a user clicked on the PRESS TO SEND button:

```
UserRequest=Press+To+Send
```

List Box. List boxes allow a user to make an exclusive or non-exclusive selection from a list of choices. This list could be hard coded (as seen below), or could be retrieved from a database. If the values are retrieved from a database, it requires the use of a development tool suite that supplies necessary extensions to standard HTML syntax. It is these extensions that actually populate the list box with values retrieved from a database table. Because the purpose of this book is not to teach you how to use a development tool that would provide this functionality, the main point here is to recognize that this capability exists and where to go to acquire it.

As seen in the listing below, list boxes are accommodated in HTML code using the <SELECT> . . . </SELECT> tag pair. The results of this HTML code are seen in Figure 13–4.

```
<P>Title: <SELECT MULTIPLE NAME=Movie_Titles SIZE=3>
<OPTION VALUE="One Day in the Life of Ivan Denisovitch">One Day in the Life of
Ivan Denisovitch</OPTION>
<OPTION VALUE="Somewhere in Time">Somewhere in Time</OPTION>
<OPTION VALUE="Bridges of Madison County">Bridges of Madison County</
OPTION>
<OPTION VALUE="Beverly Hills Cop">Beverly Hills Cop</OPTION>
<OPTION VALUE="Beverly Hills Cop II">Beverly Hills Cop II</OPTION>
</SELECT></P>
```

To make a list box accept multiple user selection, include the keyword MULTIPLE in the <SELECT> tag as seen in the code listing above. To force the list box to allow only one selection, exclude the MULTIPLE keyword from the <SELECT> tag as seen below:

```
<SELECT NAME=Movie_Titles SIZE=3>
```

When a user selects one or more items from the list box, the browser formats a name/value pair for each item selected. For example, if the user had selected "Somewhere in Time" and "Bridges of Madison County" as multiple selections, the browser would format and transmit the following name/value pairs to the server for the CGI program:

```
Movie_Titles=Somewhere+in+Time&Movie_Titles=Bridges+of+Madison+County
```

Password. Password markups are an extension of Text markups in that what the user types in the input area is replaced with asterisks (*) in the form. This is most often used to control access to a site or a database.

> What the user actually types in a password field is what is transmitted to the Server—not the asterisks that are seen in the browser. This should be an area of concern if you are worried about hackers in that a clever hacker would be able to intercept the password that is sent to the server. The exception to this is if the Browser and Server both explicitly support data encryption. Data encryption is a more secure way to transmit data between browsers and servers and is discussed in Chapter 19 of this book.

There is one basic way to write the HTML code for a password control, as seen below. The SIZE=8 and MAXLENGTH=8 parameters can be increased to 255 characters each, but most passwords are 8 characters in length. The results of the HTML code below are seen in Figure 13–5.

```
<INPUT TYPE=PASSWORD NAME=Password SIZE=8 MAXLENGTH=8>
```

When a user completes a form that has a password control on it and presses `<Submit>`, a name/value pair is created and sent to the server. That name/value pair is then interpreted on the server by a CGI program. If found to be incorrect, the common procedure is to give the user 2 more tries before preventing them from making any further attempts. In the example seen above and displayed in a browser as seen in Figure 13–5, and assuming a password of SD12107 was entered, the following name/value pair would be sent to the server:

```
Password=SD12107
```

Radio Button. Radio buttons allow a user to make an exclusive selection from a list of possible alternatives. When one button is selected, the other buttons in the group are deselected, and there is no way to deselect ALL the radio buttons in a group. If such a need exists, that is to not select any of the available alternatives, you should consider using checkboxes without the MULTIPLE attribute.

The code snippet below displays the HTML code necessary to format and display the radio buttons seen in Figure 13–6.

```
1  <INPUT TYPE=RADIO NAME=RadioGroup1 HAHTNAME=Group_1 CHECKED>
2  <INPUT TYPE=RADIO NAME=RadioGroup1 HAHTNAME=Group_2>
3  <INPUT TYPE=RADIO NAME=RadioGroup1 HAHTNAME=Group_3>
4+ <INPUT TYPE=RADIO NAME=RadioGroup1 HAHTNAME=Group_4>
```

The specific syntax for a radio button is:

```
<INPUT TYPE=RADIO NAME=group_name HAHTNAME=haht_group (CHECKED)>
```

Note the following about the above HTML code:

- `INPUT TYPE=RADIO`–Identifies this form control as being a radio button
- `NAME=`*group_name*—Is a name given to a group of radio buttons. It is by giving a collection of radio buttons the same group_name that gives the control the ability to have only one radio button selected at a time
- `HAHTNAME=`*haht_group*–Is an extension to standard HTML code made by HAHT-site IDE
- `(CHECKED)`—Indicates that the radio button that carries this optional parameter is seen initially in a browser as being in an ON status

When using radio buttons, it is wise to identify all the buttons that belong together in a group. In the code above, the group name for the radio buttons is: `RadioGroup1`. This allows the browser to select/deselect the appropriate radio buttons when a selection is made.

After a radio button is selected and the user clicks on the `<Submit>` button, the browser formats a name/value pair for transmission to the server and ultimately to the CGI program. In the example shown above and seen through a browser in Figure 13–6, this name/value pair would be:

```
RadioGroup1=Group_2
```

It is by interpreting this name/value pair that the CGI program determines which radio button was selected (clicked) by the user. It is then that it can take whatever action is appropriate based on the user input. In the context of the figure and example in this section, the CGI program would determine that the second radio button in the group of four was selected, meaning that the user indicated that there are 2 people in the group.

Text. Text areas are used when short text strings are expected from a user. Longer text strings are provided for in text boxes, which are discussed in the next section. Text areas can be defined to a pre-specified maximum length (a good thing when you are using the GET method).

The results of this code are seen in Figure 13–7.

```
<INPUT TYPE=TEXT NAME=Renter_name SIZE=25 MAXLENGTH=40>
```

The specific syntax for the text control is:

```
<INPUT TYPE=TEXT NAME=control_name SIZE=control_size
MAXLENGTH=maximum_length>
```

where:

`INPUT TYPE=`*TEXT*—Indicates that this HTML statement specifies a text control

`NAME=`*control_name*—Is a name given to the form control to uniquely identify the control

`SIZE=`*control_size*—Specifies the number of characters, with a maximum of 255, that are viewable in a browser

MAXLENGTH=*maximum_length*–Specifies the maximum number of characters, up to a limit of 255, that the control length could be. If the MAXLENGTH value is greater than the SIZE value, the user will be able to scroll left or right inside the control to view all the input characters.

The Text area defined in the above code allows a user to input a text string of up to 40 characters. As defined, the first 25 characters will display in the window and the user can scroll horizontally to view up to the 40th character. Any text input beyond 40 characters is truncated.

When a user inputs a text string in the Text control and presses the `<Submit>` button, a name/value pair is formatted and transmitted by the browser to the server. The example above, as viewed in a browser, is seen in Figure 13–7.

`Renter_name=Peter+Rabbit`

The above name/value pair indicates that the user supplied the character string `"Peter Rabbit"` in the text control named Renter_name. The browser translates the space between the words Peter and Rabbit and makes the character string, or the value portion of the name/value pair, be `"Peter+Rabbit."` This name/value pair would be transmitted to the CGI program which would interpret it and take whatever action is provided and described in the program code.

Text Box. A Text Box is identified in HTML code with the `<TEXTAREA>` . . . `</TEXTAREA>` tag pair and is used to accept character input that might be too long to fit inside a Text area. The code snippet below shows the HTML code necessary to create a Text Box and Figure 13–8 shows the result of the HTML code in an HTML browser.

`<TEXTAREA NAME=Other_Interest_Text COLS=20 ROWS=3></TEXTAREA>`

Text boxes are defined within the `<TEXTAREA>` . . . `</TEXTAREA>` tag pair by a column (COLS) and rows (ROWS) attribute. These define the horizontal and vertical size of the text box. An attribute can be input that defines the word wrapping capabilities of the Text box. This attribute is `WRAP` and its values can be either `off`, `virtual`, or `physical`. `Off` means that all text entered will appear as a single line until an ENTER key is pressed. `Virtual` means that individual lines will word-wrap on the screen and when they are sent to the server. `Physical` means that individual lines will word-wrap on the screen but not when sent to the server—thus causing each individual line to be transmitted individually. If these are supplied, they can appear anywhere between the left bracket `"<"` and the right bracket `">"` that define the boundaries of the TEXTAREA control.

When a user inputs values in the Text box the browser formats a name/value pair that is transmitted to the server. In the code sample above and seen graphically in Figure 13–8, this name/value pair would be:

`Other_Interest_Text=Mystery,+Sci-Fi`

Assuming this name/value pair were sent to the CGI program from the users browser, the CGI program would determine that the user had input the character string "Mystery, Sci-Fi," and that the blank character that was input between the words "Mystery," and "Sci-Fi" was translated to a plus sign "+" for transmission. Once this is determined by the CGI program, the program will take whatever processes are needed and specified by the programmer.

Overcoming Limitations of Placing Objects on HTML Forms

Now that you've seen the syntax for controls that can appear on a form, this section presents information on some of the limitations that you will encounter when placing objects on HTML forms. Included in this discussion are suggestions you could implement to overcome these implementations.

You have limited control over where you place objects, controls, and text on an HTML form. For example, you have only three choices as to where on an HTML page or form you can place controls: on the left margin, in the center, and on the right margin. Also, there are no tab stops when you format text and objects, and you can not include more than one blank character to place white space between objects on a page.

In this section you'll learn about four ways to control the layout and placement of objects on an HTML page and form. These are:

- Using Tables
- Using Null Graphics
- Using <PRE> . . . </PRE> Tag Pair
- Server-Side Includes

Use Tables

One of the ways to exercise what limited control you do have is by using *Tables*. You can define a borderless table with deliberately empty cells to accommodate the placement of objects in a way you like. Figure 13–9 demonstrates how to place two types of list boxes on an HTML page using tables—in this case a borderless table.

The code snippet below is the actual HTML code used to create these two list boxes within a borderless table.

```
<HTML>
<HEAD>
<TITLE>Demo4</TITLE>
<META NAME="GENERATOR" CONTENT="HAHTsite 2.0"></HEAD>
<BODY>
<P ALIGN=CENTER><FONT SIZE="+2">
<STRONG>Selection Lists On Forms</STRONG></FONT></P>
<P><HR></P>
<FORM NAME=Form1 ACTION=SELF>
<TABLE>
<TR>
<TD><P><STRONG><EM>Multiple Selection Scrolled List</EM></STRONG></P>
<SELECT MULTIPLE NAME=List1 SIZE=6>
<OPTION VALUE=Chev>General Motors Corp</OPTION>
<OPTION VALUE=Ford>Ford Motor Corp</OPTION>
<OPTION VALUE=Nissan>Nissan Motor Corp</OPTION>
<OPTION VALUE=Toyota>Toyota Motor Corp</OPTION>
```

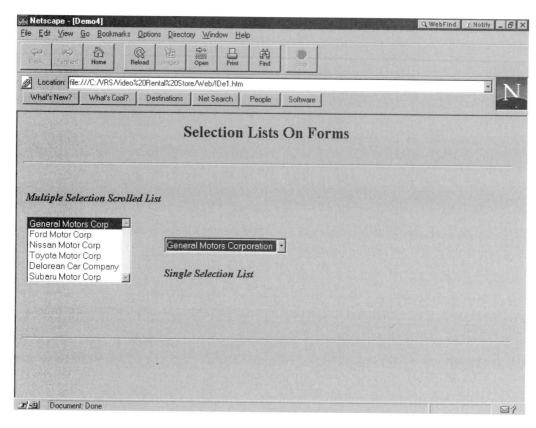

Figure 13–9   Two types of selection lists placed on a page.

```
<OPTION VALUE=Delorean>Delorean Car Company</OPTION>
<OPTION VALUE=Subaru>Subaru Motor Corp</OPTION>
</SELECT></TD>
<TD><P> </P><P> </P><P><SELECT NAME=Combo1 SIZE=1>
<OPTION VALUE=Delorean>Delorean Motor Corp</OPTION>
<OPTION VALUE=Ford>Ford Motor Corporation</OPTION>
<OPTION VALUE=Chevy>General Motors Corporation</OPTION>
<OPTION VALUE=Nissan>Nissan Motor Corp</OPTION>
<OPTION VALUE=Subaru>Subaru Motor Corp</OPTION>
<OPTION VALUE=Toyota>Toyota Motor Corp</OPTION>
</SELECT></P><P><STRONG><EM>Single Selection List</EM></STRONG></P></TD>
</TR>
</TABLE>
</FORM>
<P> </P>
<P><HR></P>
</BODY>
</HTML>
```

One of the things you should notice about the definitions of the items in the table is the use of the `Value=` attribute. This is seen here:

```
<OPTION VALUE=Chev>General Motors Corp</OPTION>
<OPTION VALUE=Ford>Ford Motor Corp</OPTION>
<OPTION VALUE=Nissan>Nissan Motor Corp</OPTION>
```

It is a good idea to use the `VALUE=` attributes in selection lists to provide a better level of control when coding CGI scripts, as well as limiting the number of characters needed to be entered or transmitted.

Using NULL Graphics

Another way in which you have control over the placement of controls and objects on a HTML page is by using NULL graphics as spacers. NULL graphics are graphic objects that are transparent, thereby taking up space on a HTML page without rendering an image. Dependent on the size of the NULL graphic, you have control over the placement of visible objects. For example, if you want a TEXT box to appear on a form 10 spaces from the left margin, you already know that you can not include 10 spaces in the HTML page. But, if you define a NULL graphic whose width is the equivalent of 10 characters, you can do this by placing the NULL graphic that is the equivalent of 10 spaces on the left margin, and then place the TEXT box directly to the right of it.

Figure 13–10 and the code sample below are the actual image and HTML code used to demonstrate this, respectively.

```
<HTML>
<HEAD>
<TITLE>Demo4</TITLE>
</HEAD>
<BODY>
<P ALIGN=CENTER>Radio Buttons And Check Boxes</P>
<FORM NAME=Form1 ACTION=SELF>
<P><STRONG><EM>What is your favorite car?</EM></STRONG></P>
<P><FONT SIZE=-1><INPUT TYPE=RADIO NAME=RadioGroup1
HAHTNAME=Radio1></FONT><FONT SIZE=-1>Chevrolet</FONT></P>
<P><FONT SIZE=-1><IMG SRC="SimpFold/Images/Spacer.GIF" WIDTH=70 HEIGHT=7
NOAUTO-RESIZE VSPACE=1></FONT><FONT SIZE=-1><INPUT TYPE=RADIO NAME=
RadioGroup1 HAHTNAME=Radio2></FONT><FONT SIZE=-1>Ford</FONT></P>
<P><FONT SIZE=-1><IMG SRC="SimpFold/Images/Spacer.GIF" WIDTH=140 HEIGHT=7
NOAUTO-RESIZE VSPACE=1></FONT><FONT SIZE=-1><INPUT TYPE=RADIO NAME=
RadioGroup1 HAHTNAME=Radio7></FONT><FONT SIZE=-1>Mercedes Benz</FONT></P>
<P><FONT SIZE=-1><IMG SRC="SimpFold/Images/Spacer.GIF" WIDTH=210 HEIGHT=7
NOAUTO-RESIZE VSPACE=1></FONT><FONT SIZE=-1><INPUT TYPE=RADIO NAME=
RadioGroup1 HAHTNAME=Radio4></FONT><FONT SIZE=-1>Jaguar</FONT></P>
<P><FONT SIZE=-1><IMG SRC="SimpFold/Images/Spacer.GIF" WIDTH=140 HEIGHT=7
NOAUTO-RESIZE VSPACE=1></FONT><FONT SIZE=-1><INPUT TYPE=RADIO NAME=
RadioGroup1 HAHTNAME=Radio5></FONT><FONT SIZE=-1>Volvo</FONT></P>
<P><FONT SIZE=-1><IMG SRC="SimpFold/Images/Spacer.GIF" WIDTH=70 HEIGHT=7
NOAUTO-RESIZE VSPACE=1></FONT><FONT SIZE=-1><INPUT TYPE=RADIO NAME=
RadioGroup1 HAHTNAME=Radio8>Subaru</FONT></P>
```

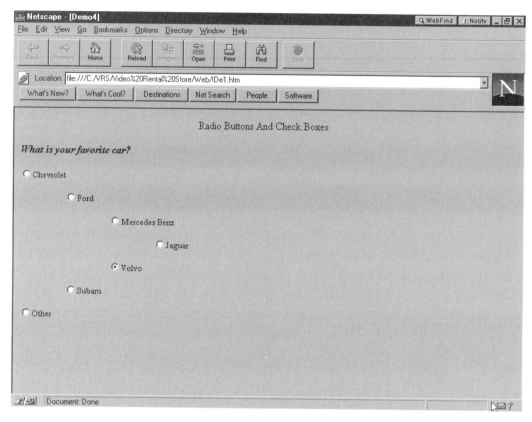

Figure 13–10 Browser view of null graphics and radio buttons.

```
<P><FONT SIZE=-1><INPUT TYPE=RADIO NAME=RadioGroup1
HAHTNAME=Radio6></FONT><FONT SIZE=-1>Other</FONT></P>
</FORM>
</BODY>
</HTML>
```

The actual code to position the graphic, and to give it a height and width dimension is seen in the example below:

```
<IMG SRC="SimpFold/Images/Spacer.GIF" WIDTH=70 HEIGHT=7 NOAUTO-RESIZE
VSPACE=1>
```

Using <PRE> . . . </PRE> Tag Pair

The preformatted tag pair is used to generate HTML documents that will appear exactly the same in a browser as they appear when created. All blank spaces, carriage returns, and blank lines enclosed within the <PRE> . . . </PRE> tag pair are retained when viewed by a browser.

Figure 13–11 displays what the use of this tag pair looks like when viewed in a browser. The code listing below is the HTML code that was written to create the page seen in Figure 13–11.

```
<HTML>
<HEAD>
<TITLE>Demo4</TITLE>
</HEAD>
<BODY>
<FORM NAME=Form1 ACTION=SELF>
<P ALIGN=CENTER><STRONG>Text Input And The PRE Tag</STRONG></P>
<P>A pre-filled, 3 row x 24 column TEXTAREA input control:</P>
<P><TEXTAREA NAME=MLText1 COLS=24 ROWS=3>Peter Piper picked a peck of
pickled peppers. If Peter Piper picked a peck of pickled peppers, how
many pickled peppers did Peter Piper pick?</TEXTAREA></P>
<P>Password: <INPUT TYPE=PASSWORD NAME=Text1 SIZE=8 MAXLENGTH=8
VALUE=Password></P>
```

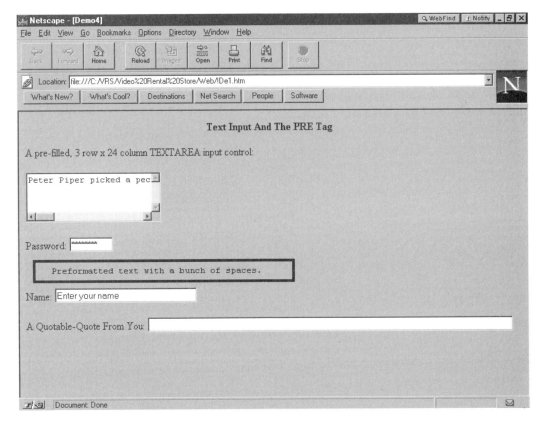

Figure 13–11   Browser view of <PRE> . . . </PRE> tag pair.

```
<PRE>    Preformatted text with a bunch of spaces.</PRE>
<P>Name: <INPUT TYPE=TEXT NAME=Text2 SIZE=30 MAXLENGTH=40 VALUE="Enter your
name"></P>
<P>A Quotable-Quote From You:
<INPUT TYPE=TEXT NAME=Text3 SIZE=80 MAXLENGTH=256></P>
</FORM>
</BODY>
</HTML>
```

The actual code using the `<PRE> . . . </PRE>` tag pair is seen in the example below:

```
<PRE>    Preformatted text with a bunch of spaces.</PRE>
```

The biggest issue that the use of this tag pair overcomes is the inclusion of more than one blank character before the control or text. In the example above, there are five blank spaces between the left margin and the first word of text.

Using the `<PRE> . . . </PRE>` tag pair with a string of blank characters to the left of a control or graphic is another way to control the placement of these objects on the HTML page or form. For example, if you want a graphic to appear 25 characters from the left margin, you could use the `<PRE> . . . </PRE>` tag pair with 25 spaces between the tag pair, and then follow it immediately with the graphic.

Server-Side Includes

If your site includes a number of objects, controls, or text that are consistent among HTML pages, you should consider using virtual includes—or what is sometimes referred to as *server-side includes*. By using server-side includes, you can embed a reference to a file of pre-written (and hopefully pre-tested) HTML code that resides on the server. By doing this, the HTML page (which incorporates the copied code from the server) is formatted in preparation to be sent to the browser.

Using server-side includes is much the same in concept as including header files in C programs, PBLs in PowerBuilder programs, or copybooks in COBOL programs. They overcome the limitation of having to write code for every action in every HTML page (or program) by giving you the capability of re-using code that is tested and verified.

Consider the following code:

```
<FORM METHOD="POST" ACTION="http://teleport.com/cgi-bin/mergeit"
<!--#include virtual="/common/html/headings.shtml" -->
<!--#include virtual="/common/html/banners.shtml" -->
… HTML code for the body of the page …
<!--#include virtual="/common/html/buttons.shtml" -->
</FORM>
```

In this example, the server would begin to interpret this HTML code and come to the first include statement:

```
<!--#include virtual="/common/html/headings.shtml" -->
```

At this point, it would retrieve the contents of the `headings.shtml` file from its `/common/html/` directory.

> The file extension does not *need* to be *.shtml. In the example here, this file actually contains HTML code, and could just as well have the file extension of *.SHTML, *.HTM or *.HTML. It is a commonly recognized convention to use a file extension of SHTML to represent server-side includes.

The contents of the `headings.shtml` file could be:

```
<H1>ABC Corporation</H1>
<H2>Our World-Wide Web Internet Site</H2>
```

Once this file is retrieved and placed in the HTML code, the server reads and interprets the next line of HTML code that requests a server-side include:

```
<!—#include virtual="/common/html/banners.shtml" —>
```

As expected, the `banners.shtml` file is retrieved from the `/common/html/` directory and merged into the body of the HTML form. The remainder of the HTML code is read and interpreted by the server until the last include is read:

```
<!—#include virtual="/common/html/buttons.shtml" —>
```

When this line is read, the `buttons.shtml` file is retrieved from the `/common/html/` directory and merged into the body of the HTML form. Once all the server-side include files have been read and merged into the HTML document, it is then that it is transmitted to the browser.

Database Queries and HTML

Now that you've seen how to overcome some of the limitations that exist in HTML to place objects on a HTML page where you want them, let's look into how to accommodate database queries in HTML. Much the same as there is very little capability in HTML specifications to control the placement of objects on a Web page, so too are there very limited specifications to allow you to connect to and access a database from HTML. You will see in this section how to overcome this situation.

HTML specifications provide no direct method for querying a database, and you cannot directly access a database from within a Web page or HTML form. There are a number of different methods you can use to build database connectivity into your HTML form without relying on the current HTML specification—which is a good thing as the current HTML specification provides no support for directly connecting to a database. These are:

Code-less Interfaces. These are software tool sets that work in tandem with developer defined template files. The purpose of the templates is to define various views into the database and describe how data is to be displayed once it is retrieved. When these forms are incorporated into an HTML page and sent to the server for processing, they are processed by CGI programs that perform the actual querying and formatting of the data.

Custom CGI Program.   These are "gateway" programs that are specifically written to accept and process SQL queries. These programs receive the users request for DBMS data, parse the user inputs and create a query to accommodate the user request, and dynamically create a HTML document that transmits the result set back to the user.

HTML Embedded SQL Extensions.   These are special HTML extensions supplied by some development and RDBMS tool vendors (Oracle Corporation included) that provide a mechanism to embed SQL statements directly into the body of the HTML file that is passed from the user to the HTTP server. When received at the server, this HTML file is parsed to pull out the SQL statements that are subsequently passed to a CGI program.

You'll note from the above three ways to accomplish database access that they all rely in one form or another on the use of a CGI program. Recalling from Chapter 7 that the execution of a CGI program on a server is triggered from a HTML form, and you can rightly conclude that the only way to cause a database access to occur on a server is from a CGI program that is initiated from a form that appears on a Web page sent by a user.

The examples presented in the remainder of this chapter are created using the HAHTsite IDE, by Haht Software. The purpose here is not to teach you how to use this tool. Rather, it is to demonstrate how a set of HTML pages can be written to:

* Connect to a database
* Query the database
* Format and display the result set

In this section the intent is not to show you HOW to use this tool, but to show you WHAT it is and WHAT it can do to provide the critical element of database access from within a Web application. The ways in which the HAHTsite IDE software accomplish this are quite similar to other Web database application development tool suites. Understanding this is a necessary element to understanding how Web applications accomplish database access.

Connect to a Database

The HAHTsite IDE, as is the case with most tools of this type, provide a GUI-based mechanism to connect an application to a database. The facility to accomplish connecting to a database is seen in Figure 13–12.

The Connection Manager is a tool that is accessed from the main toolbar within the HAHTsite IDE. Its purpose is to identify the database that the Web pages in the application are to connect with and to initiate the connection to that database. This database could be an ORACLE, or it could be Access 97, SYBASE, Informix, or any other ODBC compliant database. When configured properly, this connection becomes an attribute of the project—or in our case, the database application. It defines the name of the connection, the data source name, and an optional connect string that is passed automatically to the DBMS when a database connection is made.

Once the Connection Manager is configured correctly to a data source either directly or through ODBC, all the tables in that database are accessible by HTML pages. In HAHTsite IDE, as is the case with other Web database application development suites, the connection to a database is identified in the additional and proprietary HTML code

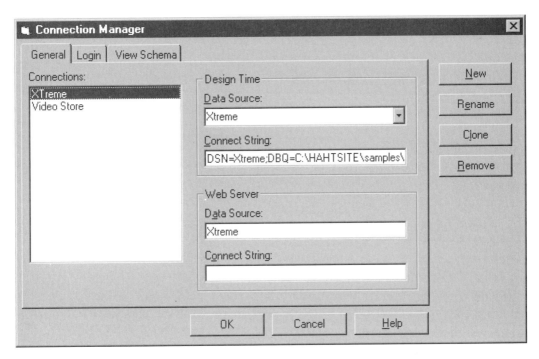

Figure 13-12   The Connection Manager dialog box.

that the tool adds to the HTML form that you create. The user doesn't see this additional HTML code when viewing the page in their browser, but the Web server and CGI programs running on the Web server receive, interpret, and act on the additional HTML code to provide the necessary database access.

Query the Database

The DB Table Widget, in HAHTsite IDE, is an object placed on a HTML page that is not viewable in a users browser but which accomplishes the actual format of the database query and display of the result set. To use the DB Table Widget on an HTML page, you simply drag the DB Table Widget icon as seen in Figure 13–13 and drop it on the HTML page where you want the result set of the query to be placed.

Once this object is placed on an HTML page, you can modify the attributes of the query in the Database Table Properties dialog box. As seen in Figure 13–14, you can identify the table in the database to be queried. You can also do table joins.

There are four tabs on this dialog box that define the type of query and the way the result set will display. The SQL tab is where you'd go to specify the exact nature of the query and result set. If you know and like to code SQL you can write it directly into the SQL dialog box, as seen in Figure 13–15. If you'd prefer to use a GUI interface, an SQL Assistant feature will guide you through the process in a friendlier environment.

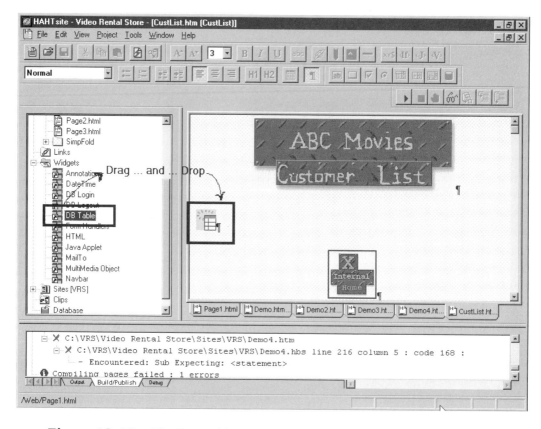

Figure 13–13 The DB Table Widget icon and the HTML page painter.

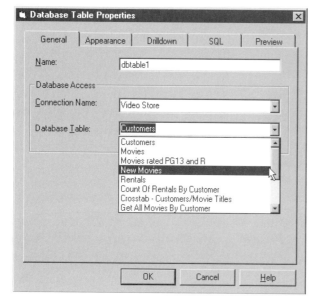

Figure 13–14 Select a table to query.

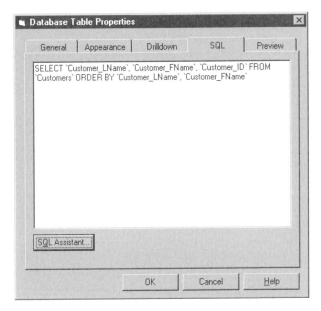

Figure 13–15 Describe the exact nature of the query.

Now, when you click on <OK>, the query will have been defined via SQL, and the query will execute when needed against the Oracle database table identified in the previous section titled: Connect to a Database.

I know the discussion in this section is very specific to HAHTsite IDE, and you must understand that the intent here is not to teach you how to use this tool. Rather, to show

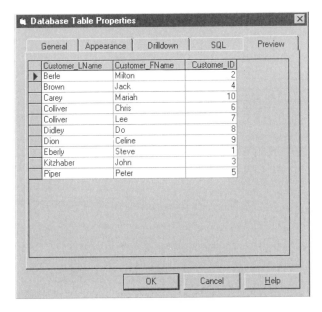

Figure 13–16 The Preview tab look at a defined query.

you the capabilities that exist in tools of this type and to also give you a sense of their ease-of-use. All the tools that I am aware of that fall into the category of Web database application development suites accomplish the same steps in a similar manner. Please refer back to Chapter 5 to learn more about some of the other tools in this category.

Format and Display the Result Set

Once you have defined the query, you can click on the Preview tab in the Database Properties dialog box (Figure 13–14) to see what your data will look like in the HTML form. An example of what the Preview tab looks like for a defined query is seen in Figure 13–16.

There are a number of ways in which you can modify the look of the result set. The one I use the most is to adjust the width of each column. Especially in a result set that contains a large number of columns, you want to be as careful as possible to include as little white space as possible. There is a nice and easy-to-use facility in HAHTsite IDE to do this, as is the case with the other tools that fall into the category of Web database application development suites.

Once you have adjusted the way the result set will look, click on <OK> to accept the definition.

At this point in the process, you have identified the database the application is to connect with, identified the table(s) to attach to, created the SQL to perform the query, and formatted the layout of the result set. All is done except for running the application.

As seen in Figure 13–17 from a Netscape browser, the result set formats and displays beautifully. Because of the definition of the DB Table Widget within HAHTsite, you should notice a few navigation prompts at the top of the table. These are placed automatically by the DB Table Widget.

The screen print in Figure 13–17 is the result set generated from a query against an Oracle 8 table. Oracle manages and stores the data that is accessed from the Web database application. However, once the data exists, Oracle 8 does not need to be running or active for the data that resides in its database tables to be accessed from the Web database application. That is the purpose of ODBC as discussed in multiple locations in previous chapters.

Drilling Down in a Web Database Application

Most Web database application development suites offer a capability commonly referred to as "drilling down" in their tools. What this means is that if you, as a user, click on a particular cell in the display of a database query, another query based on the values of the clicked cell will initiate and display in a subsequent HTML page.

You'll notice in Figure 13–17 that each cell in the column headed Customer_Id is underlined. This is the universally accepted format for a hot-link or hypertext link. If a user clicked on one of the values in any row underneath the column heading Customer_Id, she or he'd trigger a subsequent query to display a detail record of the customer whose ID had been selected (clicked).

I'll show you how easy this is to define using HAHTsite IDE. Again, the intent here is not to teach you how to use HAHTsite IDE. Rather, I do want you to get a sense of what tools of this type can do and the ease with which tasks such as this are accomplished. Whatever development tool you're using, as long as it supports database drill-downs, should be as easy.

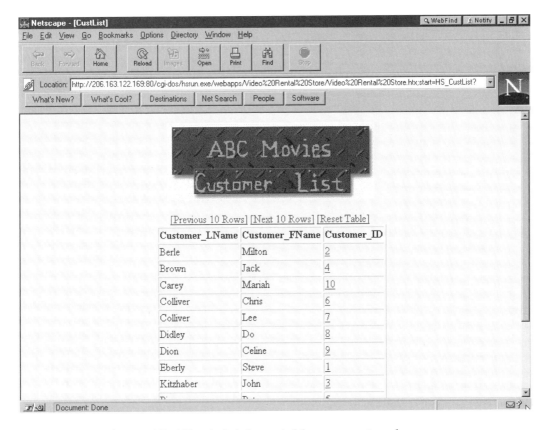

Figure 13–17 A database table as seen in a browser.

Notice in Figure 13–14 that one of the tabs in the Database Table properties dialog box is labeled Drilldown. This is where you'd go as the first step. The Drilldown window, which appears in Figure 13–18, allows you to specify what column in the result set is the drilldown column.

You'll also notice that an item labeled "Destination Page" in the Drill To section has a HTML page identified in it. This instructs HAHTsite IDE that when a user clicks in a cell that allows a drilldown, the results of the query are to display in an HTML page with an identifier of: HS_Page_3.

> HS_Page_3 is the internal identifier for Page_3. The HTML filename is Page_3.html, but HAHTSite (HS) precedes the page name with HS_.

Figure 13–19 shows what HS_Page_3 looks like inside the HAHTsite IDE. You'll notice in the painter window (middle right-side of the screen image) there are some fields

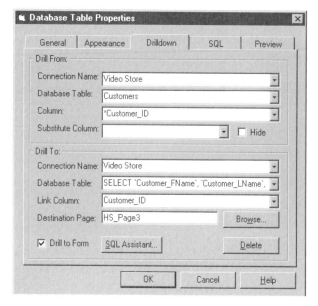

Figure 13–18   The drilldown
tab.

defined for each of the fields in the row selected. Specifically, for each field there is a text
identifier describing the field and a text box that will hold the actual database field.

At this point, we're almost done defining the drilldown function. What is left is a
process of identifying the source of the data for each of the display items on the HTML
page. Since all of the display items originate from the same database row, I'll show you
how to do this for the first field—First Name.

Double-click on the text box and you will see a Text Box Properties dialog box, as
seen in Figure 13–20. One of the tabs is labeled Database. If you click on this tab, there are
just two fields you need to specify. The first is the Data Set name and the second is the
Data Field name.

Provide these two values and click <OK>. That's it! That's all there is to it. Now, do
you want to see how it all works?

Let's say you click on the Customer_ID for a row in the Customer List window, as
seen in Figure 13–17. Assume that you click on Customer_Id = 9, which happens to be Ce-
line Dion, who happens to be my favorite singing artist. You will go to the Customer Update screen, known as Page_3.html, with the contents of the row in the database for Ce-
line Dion displayed on the page! The results of this drilldown are shown in Figure 13–21.
Pretty cool, isn't it?

Of course you know that the magic to all this is the interface between the HTML
page and the extensions provided to HTML by HAHTsite and the interpretation of those
extensions by a CGI program running on the server. To the user of this application, however, it looks like a very interactive and useful capability of an Oracle application.

HAHTsite IDE is one of a growing number of tools that fall into the category of Web
database application development suites that provide proprietary extensions to HTML
that accomplish the steps necessary to connect to a database, format and execute the

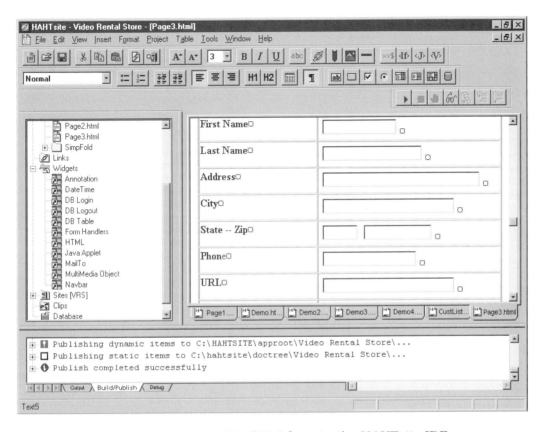

Figure 13–19   The "Drill To" form in the HAHTsite IDE.

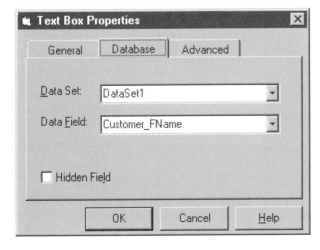

Figure 13–20   The Text Box properties dialog box.

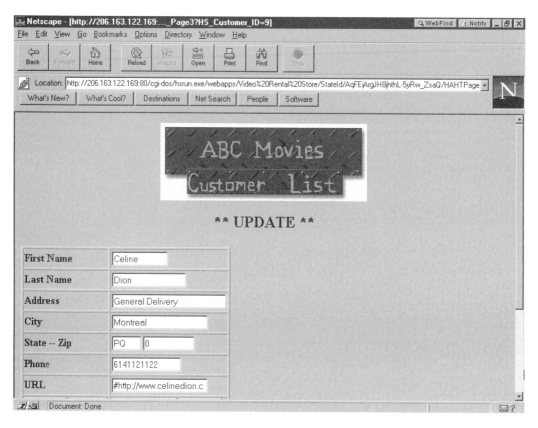

Figure 13–21   The effects of doing a drill-down operation.

query, and format and display the results on a Web page. If at this stage in the chapter you don't think you can use the HAHTsite IDE tool, this is good. The intent has not been to teach you this. If, however, you have a sense of how Web database application development tool suites work, then that is the intent here.

In the following section, I'll take the information presented so far one step further. Whereas you saw the mechanism that exists in Web database application development tool suites to perform database queries, the following section will show you the facilities that exist in tools of this type to perform database updates and how these facilities are incorporated in HTML.

Database Updates and HTML

So far you've seen how easy it is to structure and execute a query against a database from within a HTML form using HAHTsite IDE and the extensions it provides to the HTML specifications. Hopefully you recognize that other tools of this type perform the same functions in similar ways. Querying databases is fine, but what do you do if you want to insert rows, update existing information, or delete rows of information? No problem.

Figure 13–21 shows you the form that displays when you do a drilldown operation on a selected customer. At the bottom of the screen are a number of buttons that are of interest. These are seen in Figure 13–22.

Note: Oracle does not provide the same functionality as HAHTsite. Oracle provides the database, and HAHTsite supplied the capability to interface CGI programs to that database.

Looking at the bottom of the form, enclosed in a black rectangular box, are three database update buttons:

- Update
- Delete
- Insert

You should also notice two database movement buttons that are labeled:

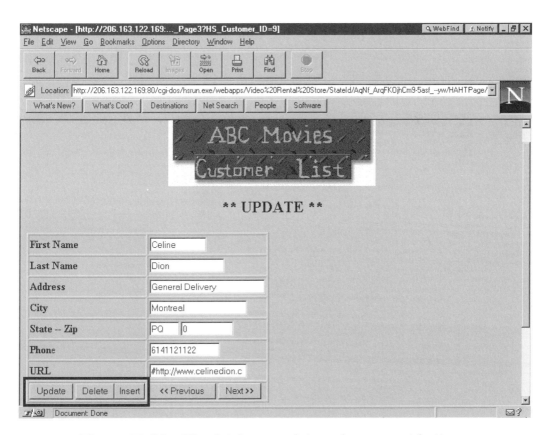

Figure 13–22   The database update and movement buttons.

- << Previous
- Next >>

Because of the point-and-click, graphical interface built into the current generation of Web database application development tool suites, adding these buttons into your forms and causing them to perform the database functions required is very easy. The buttons, and their functions as discussed in this section, need not appear on every Web form. In fact, very few of the Web pages you create will include forms that provide buttons that initiate database update actions. But, as the industry begins to grow more comfortable with the concept of allowing database update access from Web applications, the demand to include this capability in the applications that you design and write will increase.

I'll show you how easy it is.

Step 1: Place control on the form. There are three simple activities to this step, as seen in Figure 13–23. These are described as:

1. Position your cursor in the form where you want to add the control. You do this by right clicking at the correct position.

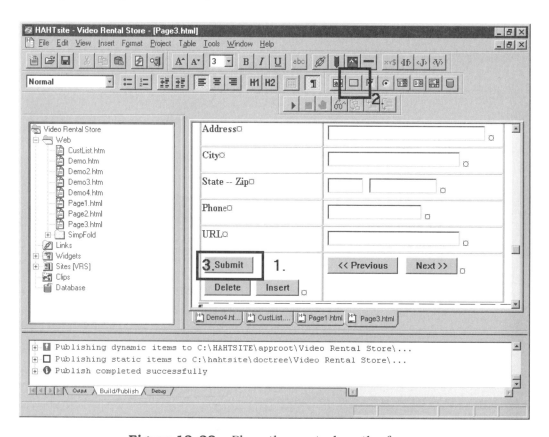

Figure 13–23   Place the control on the form.

2. On the toolbar you'll see a command button icon. Right click one time on this control.

3. When you do step 2, the command button control will be placed into your form at the position indicated. You'll notice that the name of the button is SUBMIT. This is ok for now—we will change it in the next step.

Step 2: Assign caption and action to the button. If you double-click on the button just placed on the form, you will see the Button Properties dialog box, as seen in Figure 13–24. There are two tabs in this window, the first is labeled General. There are two actions needed on this tab, as described below.

A. Supply a caption to the control. The caption is what will appear as a name for the control when it is displayed. Above the caption text box is a text box titled: Name. This is the internal name assigned to this control for use by some extended HAHT-site IDE functions.

B. Click on a radio button to indicate the type of action this button is to have. Since this is an <Update> button, click on the Button radio button.

Step 3: Select the type of database action. When you click on the Database tab in the Button Properties dialog box, you'll see two areas needing information from you, as seen in Figure 13–25. These are specifications of a Dataset that the database action is performed against and the type of action to perform. These are described below:

A. In the Dataset drop down list box, select the dataset that the intended action is performed against.

B. In the Action drop down list box, select the type of action that the button is to perform against the dataset identified above. Notice in Figure 13–25 that there are a number of different actions you can specify, such as:
   • Insert
   • Update

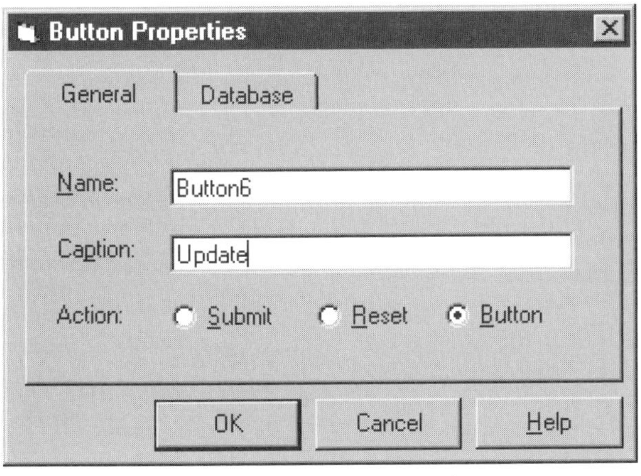

Figure 13–24 Button Properties look at the General tab.

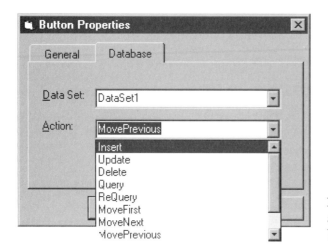

Figure 13–25 Supply dataset and action information to the button.

- Delete
- MovePrevious
- MoveNext

C. When done specifying the button properties, click the `<OK>` button.

You've seen how to create an UPDATE button. In the Action drop down list box in Figure 13–25 you'll see the MovePrevious and MoveNext actions. These are the actions you would select for a `<Previous>` and a `<Next>` button on an HTML form.

That's it! I said it was easy, didn't I? You've just seen how to place a control on a form that causes an update operation to be applied to the database when it is clicked. The CGI program running on the server is the component that does all the work for you—and you don't even have to write it! This is a supplied program by the software tool vendor.

Form Design Tips

The majority of this chapter deals with using HTML objects and HTML extensions to build forms that access databases. Although this chapter does not have a purpose of presenting GUI design principles, there are some form design tips and considerations that you should be aware of.

- Group input objects together on a form. You can do this by theme, function, data type, etc. This becomes an especially critical item as the length of the form increases.

- Columns that users will want to perform a drill-down query have to first display on the parent form. This may seem obvious, but is sometimes left off when the forms are initially designed.

- Consistent looks to your forms will help users become comfortable with them sooner. This means:
  - Use consistent fonts, colors, backgrounds, and graphics.
  - Place labels for objects on a page in a consistent manner. Make a decision and stick with it to either place your text describing the control to the left or to the right of the control.
  - Orient controls in a consistent manner. Your radio buttons and check boxes should all appear vertically or horizontally oriented.
  - Be consistent in where you place button bars. It is customary to place these at the bottom of the form, but if you deviate from this custom, be a consistent deviate.

- Pick meaningful, concise descriptions for controls. A text box labeled "TIN" is much less meaningful that one labeled "Social Security Number."

- Consider the tab order of the text-input objects when placing them. It is cumbersome and awkward for a user to have a tab order on text-input be: Name, City, State, Zip, Address. It is much better that the tab order be: Name, Address, City, State, Zip.

- Limit the size of the text box and text area controls on the form to the size of the data they will contain. It is a waste and is not very pleasing to look at when a text-input box that allows for 80 characters of input is placed on a form when the text-input box can only hold 8 characters—such as what you'd have for a password.

- Use the various methods described in this chapter to control the position of the controls on the form. You can really dress the form up if you take some time to lay out the objects well.

- Decide what objects to use based on the type of data. It is much better to use Male | Female radio buttons than Male | Female check boxes. A person can be either male or female, but never both or never neither. They have to be one or the other. A group of radio buttons serves this purpose nicely while check boxes would be confusing and could render erroneous data being sent.

- When a form requires data input from the user, this should be clearly indicated on the form. It is very aggravating to complete a multi-page form, press the `<Submit>` button, and then be informed that some needed pieces of information were not supplied.

In the Fall of 1996 I decided to renew my subscription to Info World magazine by using their Web input form. For those of you that receive complimentary subscriptions to magazines, you know there is a lengthy questionnaire that is required of you to be completed before you begin receiving the magazine. The publisher then uses this data to sell to advertisers. After taking about 15 minutes to complete Info World's online input form, I pressed the SUBMIT button, being quite proud of myself for being able to use their technological efforts. About 10 seconds later a page displayed that I had not input one or more required pieces of information. This would have been fine, but not only was I not informed what those critical pieces of information were but the HTML input form was re-presented—EMPTY!!! I had to reinput the entire form. This is an example of what you don't want to do.

- If you're writing your own CGI programs for database interactions, be aware of the naming limitations of the language being used to write those CGI programs. You can assign a name to an object on an HTML form that will not be acceptable to certain languages.

- Whenever possible, present defaults in controls such as buttons, check boxes, and lists. Be careful though, you could overdo this.

- Involve users in the design of the HTML forms. With HTML and some of the HTML editors and development tools available, you can very rapidly prototype pages. Take advantage of this capability by involving users to aid in designing an effective user interface. Remember, what looks good to you, the developer, may not look as good to the person using it.

There are a number of books available that will help you design effective Web forms. The list below is a great start.

Title:	Hybrid HTML Design : A Multi-Browser HTML Reference
Author:	Kevin Ready, Janine Warner
Publisher:	New Riders Publishing
ISBN:	1-56-205617-4

Title:	Mastering Web Design
Author:	John McCoyx
Publisher:	Sybex Press
ISBN:	0-78-211911-5

Title:	Creative HTML Design
Author:	Lynda Weinman, Bill Weinman
Publisher:	New Riders Publishing
ISBN:	1-56-205704-9

Moving On

This chapter focused on designing HTML forms that access databases. You know that HTML specifications provide no direct capability to access databases—that this capability is provided by one of three ways that were presented in the section titled Database Queries and HTML. This chapter used a hybrid of two of these methods: Code-less interfaces and HTML embedded SQL extensions. Toward this end you saw how the use of a tool like HAHTsite IDE facilitates this.

Chapter 14 presents material on the third way that you can incorporate database queries in HTML—by using a Custom CGI program.

CHAPTER 14

Accessing Oracle Databases Using CGI Programs

The material in the chapters leading up to this chapter all helped to lay the foundation to this, what may be the most significant chapter in the book to you. All the information in the preceding chapters flows into this chapter—Accessing Oracle Databases Using CGI Programs.

This chapter begins with a review of CGI basics you learned in previous chapters in this book. You will learn about CGI input and output processing, and some of the different ways that exist in which a client can make a request to the server when an HTML form is submitted. Then, you will see how CGI programs can be used to generate HTML.

Later in this chapter you will learn, among other things, how to write a CGI program to perform whatever type of database access is required by your Web database application. You will see examples of pseudocode written to perform the following functions:

- Query (select) records from an Oracle database
- Insert records in an Oracle database
- Update records in an Oracle database
- Modify records in an Oracle database

Basics Review

Recall what you learned in Chapters 5 and 12—that is, that Web application development suites allow you to create applications with full database access capabilities without having to write CGI programs that accomplish this back-end processing. These development tools usually include a CGI program that is already written and supplied with the product that does this database processing. If you are using one of these tools, then you will still find value in this chapter. The reason is that even though the CGI database access programs are already written and supplied for you, you may still find value in writing your own CGI programs, a few types of which are listed below:

- You will be able to create non-database query/update processes, such as:
  - Randomly modify the wallpaper that your application uses
  - Create a registry of people that have visited your site
  - Keep a count of the hits your Web site has had
- Provide financial transaction processing to your applications
- Provide statistics functionality in your application
- Supply documents stored in a document repository to the user

---

Tip: Even though I am not including specific code samples that show you how to perform the above, I would like to point you to a very useful URL for this type of CGI program. The URL is: `http:\\www.worldwidemart.com\scripts\`. The name of this site is Matt's Script Archive, and it is run by a CGI wire head named Matt Wright and is the home of a bevy of well-written free CGI scripts, including the ones listed above.

If you are not using a Web application development suite, then this chapter will be one that you refer to often. You will see specific examples of code that perform a number of different types of database access. Before we proceed into the actual code used to accomplish various types of database processing, let's review some of the things you learned about CGI in previous chapters to this book.

What Is CGI?

CGI is best described as the means by which a Web server communicates with applications that are external to the Web server and thereby have those programs perform some predefined process for it. CGI programs, CGI scripts, and gateway programs are synonymous—different names for the same thing. They are the programs that accept a request initiated by a browser and interpreted by a Web server, accept passed data from the Web server, and take an action predefined and described by the programmer in the CGI program. This action can be any of the following individually or a combination of two or more:

- Accessing of data either locally or remotely
- Processing of data
- Access available resources that are either local or remotely attached
- Create output

Because of CGI, the Web database application has the ability to extend its reach beyond the confines of the HTTP server. A user in Bangkok, Thailand, could provide input on an HTML form that is transmitted from his or her browser to your company's server in New York, where that server processes the HTML code and the request to initiate an external program. That external program could access a regional database located in Charlotte, North Carolina, receive the result set, and format that result set into an HTML form that is then transmitted back to the HTTP browser that initiated the request in Thailand.

The CGI Process

Figure 14–1 displays the normal CGI process flow. This process is described below.

1. A user, accessing a Web browser, sends a request to a Web server via HTML. This HTML includes a request to execute a CGI program, as well as any parameters the CGI program might need.

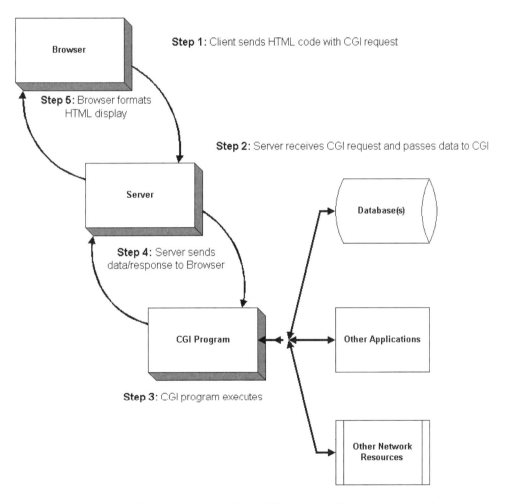

Figure 14–1 The CGI process flow.

2. The Web server receives the request from the browser, processes the HTML, and encounters the request to execute a CGI program. The Web server initiates the CGI program's execution by calling it and passing it any parameters that were received from the HTTP browser.

3. The CGI program executes. In its execution, it may:
   - Access no other resources
   - Access databases either locally or remotely
   - Access other applications or initiate the execution of other programs
   - Access other network resources

4. The Web server receives a result set from the CGI program if one is returned, and sends the data and/or response back to the browser via HTML.

5. The browser receives the HTML sent to it from the Web server and formats and displays the data received.

CGI Data Input and Output

CGI input data is data that is passed to the Web server from the user's browser, with the intent that the Web server will pass it to the CGI program. The CGI program uses this data to determine its logical execution path and to (potentially) format a query to a database.

Additionally, the Web server can format and pass information to the CGI program that describes the type of data that was passed. This is what happens when data is passed to a CGI program via standard input. By providing this type of information, the CGI program can determine how to process the data it receives.

There is one, and only one, way that CGI programs return output. That is, by standard output. Even in the rare situation when a CGI program returns no data, it still formats and generates a response via standard output that indicates there was no data sent.

CGI standard output data is returned in one of two formats: *parsed header output* and *non-parsed header output*. With parsed header output, the data created by the CGI program is received and interpreted by the Web server and then sent to the user's browser. With non-parsed header output, the Web server has the responsibility (and overhead) of generating the header information and sending it, along with the rest of the response, to the user's browser.

CGI Environmental Variables

Environmental variables are data that are passed from one program or process to another program or process. In Windows applications, environmental variables are passed in *.INI files. CGI scripts use environmental variables for a number of reasons—not the least of which is to pass data between the Web server and the CGI program. There are two types of CGI environmental variables: *request-specific* and *not request-specific* variables.

Request-specific variables are those environmental variables that are specific to the client request that the CGI program is fulfilling. Not request-specific variables are those environmental variables that are set during all client requests. Request-specific variables are those that are very specific to the type of request received from the user's browser while not request-specific are those that are very generic to any or all types of requests received from the user's browser.

CGI environmental variables, regardless of their type, are used by CGI programs to:

- Specify the type of processing and database request the CGI program must perform
- Indicate the type of browser the client is using
- Maintain and pass state information

For a listing of these environmental variables and the type of information contained in each, refer to Chapter 7, which gives a thorough description and explanation.

Passing CGI Data Streams

There are several ways that a Web client can transmit data strings to a CGI program—with three being the post popular. These are:

- GET
- ISINDEX
- POST

These are described in this section.

GET Method to Transmit CGI Data Streams. You use the GET method when passing data provided by users via HTML forms to CGI programs. Because of the limitation on the amount of data that can be passed (usually 256 characters) to a CGI program using the GET method, it is the least desirable way (of the three listed) to transfer data to the CGI program. Its strength is in its ease-of-use when passing only a few data fields.

The GET method causes a query string to append to the action URL when the user presses the <Submit> button on a form. A complete string passed to the Web server may look like:

```
GET /cgi-bin/processform.pl?action=READ&screen=QUERY HTTP/1.1
```

ISINDEX Method to Transmit CGI Data Streams. You use the ISINDEX method when the need exists to perform database queries. The latest HTML specifications allow for the addition of the <ISINDEX> tag to your HTML code. This tag allows the HREF URL to perform a query based on data input by a user. The syntax for this is:

```
<HEAD>
<ISINDEX HREF="URL-CGI Program">
</HEAD>
```

In this example, URL-CGI Program is the URL for the CGI program to execute. Therefore, assuming an URL for a CGI executable as: http://teleport.com/cgi-bin/processit.exe and passed parameters to this program of:

```
?lastname+taxyear
```

The HTML code would look as follows:

```
<HEAD>
<ISINDEX HREF="http://teleport.com/cgi-
bin/processit.exe?lastname+taxyear">
</HEAD>
```

Following this example, the Web browser would pass the following string to the Web server:

```
http://teleport.com/cgi-bin/processit.exe?lastname+taxyear
```

The Web server receives this string, and causes the `processit.exe` CGI program to begin executing with a passed command string of: `lastname+taxyear`.

POST Method to Transmit CGI Data Streams.   The POST Method is conceptually similar to the GET Method, with much broader application. Whereas the GET method appends the user supplied data to the ACTION URL, the POST Method is formatted and sent to the server in a stream of data of varying length which is passed to the CGI program.

A specific example of using the POST method to receive CGI data streams follows.

```
POST /cgi-bin/processit.exe HTTP/1.1
Accept: text/plain
Accept: text/html
Accept: */*
Content-type: application/x-www-form-urlencoded
Content-length: 42
state=OR&politics=Republican&Minimum=25000
```

When this data stream is received by the Web server, it passes it directly to the CGI program named: `processit.exe`.

Tip: The Content-Length environmental variable is not required, but it is a very good idea to include it—and to be accurate when using it. The reason you should use it is that some servers do not send an end of file marker to CGI programs. Without the Content-Length variable, the CGI program may not receive the correct data. The reason it is important to establish the correct parameter to signify the passed string length is that you may end up truncating or sending extraneous data to the CGI program in the passed string.

Reading User Data into CGI Programs

You've seen in the previous section three ways to get user-supplied data streams to a CGI program. In this section you'll see how to read and process that data in a CGI program.

As you know, CGI programs can be written in a number of different languages. You have your favorite one, which may not be mine. Therefore, the basic steps to read user data into a CGI program are described below in *pseudo-code*:

```
Determine the method used to transmit the data by querying the
REQUEST_METHOD and QUERY-STRING environmental variables
```

```
IF the GET method was used to transmit data THEN
  Parse the QUERY_STRING environmental variable name-value pairs into
  their respective components

ELSEIF the ISINDEX method was used to transmit data THEN
  Parse the QUERY_STRING environmental variable into its component parts

ELSE
  Read the value of the passed string from the CONTENT_LENGTH environmen-
  tal variable and parse this number of characters from the string in the
  QUERY_STRING environmental variable.

END
```

Once the passed string is either separated into its component parts or parsed appropriately, it can be processed by the CGI program accordingly.

Now that you've reviewed the basics of what CGI is and how data is received into, processed from, and output by a CGI program, it's time to see how a Web server uses the power of a CGI program to access databases by submitting and processing queries on behalf of a Web client.

Summary of Common Web Database Access Methods

HTML specifications provide no direct method for querying a database. There are a number of different methods you can use to build database connectivity into your HTML form. These are:

Code-less Interfaces

These are software toolsets that work in tandem with developer defined template files. The purpose of the templates is to define various views into the database and describe how data is to be displayed once it is retrieved. When these forms are incorporated into an HTML page and sent to the Web server for processing, they are processed by CGI programs that perform the actual querying and formatting of the data.

Custom CGI Program

These are "gateway" programs that are specifically written to accept and process SQL queries. These programs receive the user's request for DBMS data, parse the user inputs and create a query to accommodate the user request, and dynamically create a HTML document that transmits the result set back to the user. This method of database access is what is presented in this chapter.

HTML Embedded SQL Extensions

These are special HTML extensions supplied by RDBMS and other tool vendors that provide a mechanism to embed SQL statements directly into the body of the HTML file that is passed from the user to the Web server. When received at the server, this HTML file is parsed to pull out the SQL statements that are subsequently passed to a CGI program.

Why Use Custom CGI Programs for Database Access

Custom CGI programs are the most common method of accessing corporate databases, far eclipsing the other two methods described above. Code-less interfaces and HTML embedded SQL extensions may someday catch up and surpass the popularity of custom CGI programs. And, when that time does come, the need and use for custom CGI programs will continue—in fact, it may never end. There will always be an inherent limit to the power and flexibility of code-less interfaces and HTML-embedded SQL extensions that custom CGI programs will exceed. This is why all the major development toolkits provide API interfaces to more powerful languages.

Ways CGI Programs Access Corporate Databases

The following are some of the ways that custom CGI programs access corporate databases:

SQL Queries. These are the most common way, as well as the way used to access Oracle databases.

Non-SQL Queries. These are used to access non-RDBMS databases, including network databases, and hierarchical databases such as IMS.

ODBC/JDBC. These are APIs made available by the RDBMS vendor and CGI programming tool vendor to act as an interface between the front-end development tool and the back-end database.

Stored Procedures. Stored procedures are RDBMS-specific database instructions that are executed either on a predefined schedule or at will by a calling (accessing) program.

Ways CGI Programs Provide Advantages Over Other Methods

CGI programs give you, the developer, several advantages over other back-end programs. Some of these are described below.

Choice. There are a wide number of languages (more than 15) which you can choose from to write your CGI programs. These are broken into the following categories:

Compiled Languages—These are languages in which the original code syntax must be translated to a platform-specific set of binary executable code before it can be processed on a given platform. Examples of these are; C, C++, Fortran.

Interpreted Languages—These are languages where the original code syntax is read by, translated, and executed by the target machine at run time. Examples of these are; Perl, Visual Basic, Java.

Complexity. Because of the power and control the developer has in most CGI programming languages, custom CGI programs can be written to accomplish very complex tasks. This could include validation of user input before posting to a database, integration of the Web database application with other non-Web applications, and generation of dynamic HTML data presentations.

Control. CGI programs give you total control over the data input to your database, how that data is processed, how it is extracted from the database, and how it is presented to the user.

Exploit. Because of the API interfaces provided by most CGI programming-language tool vendors, you can exploit the power of other tools that interface with the CGI programming language to extend the functionality of the CGI program.

Flexibility. CGI programs give you the ability to access a wide variety of databases. Additionally, you can access more than one type of a database, from more than one database vendor, from within a single CGI program.

Choosing a CGI Programming Language

Choosing a CGI programming language is not much different from choosing a programming language for any other type of application. In fact, many of the factors discussed below are the same.

Code Libraries. Unless you are using a really obscure CGI programming language, have unlimited time, or have a very simple CGI program to write, you will probably need to make use of code libraries. The general rule of thumb is: Don't reinvent the code if you can get it already written!

Cost. The amount of money available in the project budget for support tools, development tools, testing tools, etc. should all be considered when evaluating CGI programming languages.

Function. Your CGI program will require that certain functionality be provided from the language that program is developed in.

Integration. If your CGI program will not interface with any other applications, then this is a non-issue. However, if this is not the case, you should consider the integration afforded by candidate languages with other applications and the languages used by those other applications.

Learning Curve. In addition to the current skill set of the present development team being a consideration factor, the amount of time in the project schedule to develop adequate skills in the proposed CGI programming language is a decision factor when choosing the language.

Life Cycle. The amount of rework that the CGI program is expected to endure during its life cycle is a decision factor in choosing the language it is written in. Very rarely are programs of any sort, including CGI programs, written and placed into production that never require any type of maintenance.

Present Skills. The skillset that exists in the development team should be considered carefully when choosing a CGI programming language. For example, a skilled Visual Basic programmer does not possess the skills needed to master the PERL language nearly as well as a skilled C++ programmer.

RDBMS Interfaces. Certainly one of the most significant (if not the most significant) consideration of a person writing a CGI program to access a Web database is the RDBMS interfaces provided by the candidate CGI programming languages. I generally choose C or C++ (using the Pro*C precompiler) to write CGI programs that access Oracle databases due to the direct interface that is supplied and the speed of data access thus afforded.

Schedules. The amount of time available to write the CGI program is critical to choosing a CGI programming language. C programs are generally more efficient than Visual Basic programs, although Visual Basic is generally a more productive programming language.

Speed. Certain types of processing are more intensive than others. Different programming languages handle certain functions with different efficiencies. For example, C++ offers more efficient string handling capabilities than does Visual Basic.

Accessing Web Database Using CGI Programs

Figure 14–2 is a generalized flowchart of the data and logic flows through a CGI program. What is not shown is the supplemental program logic that you would write to support whatever processing is required of the application to support business rules. This you'd add when it was required, based on the unique considerations of your application.

Note that once the CGI program determines the FORM method used to place user-supplied data in a place accessible by the CGI program, the program flow is not too dissimilar from what you may expect, nor what it might be for a simple database query program that is not accessed from the Web.

Tip: In reality, you will probably know what FORM method is used by your application to place user-supplied data in a place and format in which the CGI program can access it. You will know this because you probably will be the one to write it! The first decision branch is therefore included for documentation purposes to show you the two different types of ways in which you could retrieve the data into your CGI program—each based on the FORM method used.

Contents of the CGI Profile File

There are seven sections in a CGI profile file, but not all are required. The sections contained in a CGI profile file for your application are dependent on the CGI programming language and your architectural and operating environments. The seven sections are:

- Accept
- CGI
- Extra Headers
- Form External
- Form Huge

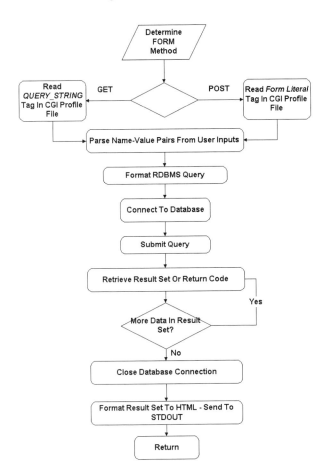

Figure 14–2   CGI database program flow.

- Form Literal
- System

Each of these are shown below as they might appear in a CGI profile file.

```
[Accept]
xxx/yyy=zzz…              If the MIME types found in the request header
as:
  Accept: xxx/yyy; zzzz...
xxx/yyy=Yes               If only the MIME type appears in the request
header

[CGI]
Authentication Method=    Method used for authentication (e.g., "Basic")
Authenticated Password=   If present is the Password in the request
Authentication Realm=     Name of realm for users/groups
Authenticated Username=   If present is the username in the request
```

CGI Version=	The version of CGI running and recognized by the server
Content Length=	Length specified in bytes of information supplied with the request
Content Type=	MIME content type of info supplied with request
Executable Path=	Physical pathname of the back-end cgi directory
From=	E-Mail of client user
Logical Path=	Extra path info in logical space
Physical Path=	Extra path info in local physical space
Query String=	String following the "?" in the request URL sent by the browser
Referer=	URL of referring document
Remote Address=	The remote client's network address
Remote Host=	The remote client's network hostname
Request Method=	The method specified in the request (e.g., "GET", "POST")
Request Keep-Alive=	Does the client request connection be re-used?
(Yes|No)	
Request Protocol=	The server's request protocol (e.g., HTTP/1.0)
Request Range=	Byte-range specified with the request
Server Admin=	E-Mail address of server's administrator
Server Name=	Server's network hostname (or alias from config)
Server Port=	Server's network port assignment
Server Software=	Version of the Web server software
User Agent=	String describing client/browser software/version

[Extra Headers]
; These are any "extra" headers that may be
; found in the request that initates the CGI
; program. They are listed in "key=value"
; form.

[Form External]
; If the decoded value string is more than 254
; characters long, or if the decoded value
; string contains any special control
; characters or quote marks the server puts
; the decoded value into an external tempfile
; and lists the field in this section as:
;   key=<pathname> <length>
;   where <pathname> is the path and name of
;   the tempfile containing the decoded
;   value string.
;   <length> is the length in bytes of the
;   decoded value string.

[Form File]
; If the form data contained any uploaded
; files, they are described in this section

```
; as:
;   key=[<pathname>] <length> <type>
;        <encoding> [<name>]
;        where <pathname> is the path and name
;        of the tempfile containing the
;        uploaded file,
;        <length> is the length in bytes of
;        the uploaded file,
;        <type> is the content type of the
;        uploaded file as sent by the browser
;        <encoding> is the content-transfer
;        encoding of the uploaded file,
;        <name> is the original file name of
;        the uploaded file.
```

[Form Huge]
```
; If the raw value string is more than 65,536
; bytes long, the server does no decoding. In
; this case, the server lists the field in
; this section as:
;   key=<offset> <length>
;        where <offset> is the offset from the
;        beginning of the Content File at which
;        the raw value string for this key is
;        located
;        <length> is the length in bytes of the
;        raw value string. You can use the
;        <offset> to perform a "Seek" to the
;        start of the raw value string, and
;        use the length to know when you have
;        read the entire raw string into your
;        decoder.
```

[Form Literal]
```
; If the request was a POST from a Mosaic form ; (with content type of
"application/x-www-
; form-urlencoded"), the server will decode
; the form data. Raw form input is of the form
; "key=value&key=value&...", with the value
; parts "URL-encoded." The server splits the
; key=value pairs at the '&', then splits the
; key and value at the '=', URL-decodes the
; value string and puts the result into
; key=value (decoded) form in the [Form
; Literal] section of the INI.
```

[System]
```
Content File=            Pathname of file containing raw request content
input to CGI processing
```

Debug Mode= (Yes|No)	Indicates if the server's CGI debug flag is set
GMT Offset=	Offset of local timezone from GMT, seconds
Output File= cessing	Pathname of file to receive results of CGI pro-

The information in the following sections showed you how to select, add, delete, and modify rows in a database from a Web database application. You will notice as you go through these pages that these four functions are accomplished using four different HTML pages, and four different CGI programs. Although upon cursory review the material in each of the following four sections might appear to be redundant, there are significant differences that you should note as they are presented.

Querying a Database

Let's take a look at an example of an HTML form querying a database. Each step in this process is described in detail. For the sake of clarity, all extraneous images, text, controls, and other objects that would ordinarily appear on a Web page are removed from this and the other examples in this section.

The Web Database Query Page

The HTML code below is used to generate the Web page as seen in Figure 14–3. The purpose of this Web page is to have the user select a movie rating to use in the WHERE clause of a SELECT statement.

```
<HTML>
<HEAD>
<TITLE>This is a SELECT Query Example</TITLE>
</HEAD>
<BODY>
</BODY>
<FORM METHOD=POST ACTION="http://teleport.com/cgi-bin/query.exe">
<P>Rating: <SELECT MULTIPLE RATING=Movie_Rating SIZE=3>
<OPTION VALUE="PG">PG</OPTION>
<OPTION VALUE="PG 13">PG13</OPTION>
<OPTION VALUE="R">R</OPTION>
<OPTION VALUE="NR">NR</OPTION>
</SELECT></P>
<P><INPUT NAME=Sub_button TYPE=SUBMIT VALUE="SUBMIT"></P>
</FORM>
</HTML>
```

Web Server Action on Receiving the Query Request

In the HTML code, you'll notice a few items and controls that are significant to the execution of this process. First is the <FORM METHOD> tag, that appears as follows:

```
<FORM METHOD=POST ACTION="http://teleport.com/cgi-bin/query.exe">
```

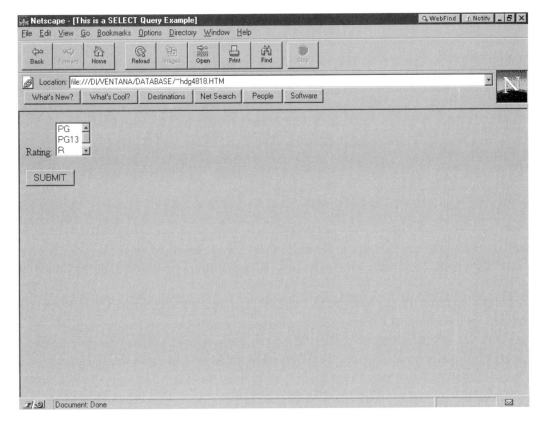

Figure 14–3 The Web page initiating a database query.

When the request, which is initiated from the browser is received at the Web server, the Web server places data passed to it in various sections of the CGI profile file, and then begins the execution of the `query.exe` program. This program is located in the `cgi-bin` directory on the Web server identified by `http://teleport.com`. Note that this is an example of URL addressing.

Some of the information placed in the CGI profile file by the Web server upon receiving this request is identified below:

```
[CGI]
Authentication Method=    Basic
CGI Version=              2.0
Content Type=             MIME content type of info supplied with
request
Executable Path=          d:\webpage\cgi-bin\query.exe
Request Method=           POST
Request Keep-Alive=       NO
Request Protocol=         HTTP/1.1
Server Name=              teleport
```

```
Server Port=                  126.160.112.50
Server Software=              WebSTAR 2.1
```

[Extra Headers]

[Form External]

[Form File]

[Form Huge]

[Form Literal]
```
MOVIE_RATING=PG 13
```

[System]

Take note that because the Web page uses the POST method, the passed data to the CGI program is achieved by using the FORM LITERAL section of the CGI profile file. If, on the other hand, the GET method had been used, then the Web server would have placed the passed information it received from the client browser into the QUERY STRING tag in the CGI section of the CGI profile file, and calculated and placed the length of the passed string in the CONTENT LENGTH tag, which is also in the CGI section of the CGI profile file.

Execution of the CGI Program for a Database Query

Referring back to Figure 14–2, you see that the first action performed by the CGI program is to determine the FORM method used. Also note that, in most cases, the person writing the CGI program will know which FORM method was used to pass information to the program. However, to determine the type of FORM method used is a simple process of querying the value of the Request Method tag in the CGI section of the CGI profile file. In this example, the value is POST.

Once the FORM method is determined, the server has only to parse the name-value pairs before it can get down to the actual database query. Depending on the FORM method, the parsing is different. If the FORM method is POST, then the name-value pairs are stored in the CGI profile file, in the Form Literal section. In our example, and since we are using the POST method, the following lines appear in the CGI profile file:

[Form Literal]
```
MOVIE_RATING=PG 13
```

If you are using the GET method, then the process is a bit more complicated, but not too difficult for most programming languages. It is a simple process of the following:

- Retrieve the contents of the Query String line in the CGI section of the CGI profile file

- Iteratively extract the name-value pairs, recognizing that each is separated by an ampersand (&).

Therefore, the following value in the Query String would extract to the associated name-value pairs:

```
CompanyName=ABC Systems Computers&Street=&URL=http:\\teleport.com
```

Name-value pairs ...

```
CompanyName=ABC Systems
Street=
URL=http:\\teleport.com
```

Referring back to Figure 14–2, you see that once the name-value pairs are parsed, the next steps are to:

- Format the Oracle query
- Connect to the database
- Submit query
- Retrieve result set
- Close database connection

At this point in the process, there is nothing special about this program and the fact that it originated from a Web initiated request—the program logic and process flow are *exactly* the same as if the program was *not* part of a Web database application. Because I want to keep the presentation of the material in this section as language-independent as possible, you'll see no sample code here. You would accomplish all of the above steps exactly the same as you would if this were not a Web-initiated program. Once the database connection is closed, however, it is time to format the result set to HTML and send it to the standard output device.

Types of CGI Output Responses

There are two ways to package a response to a Web client from a CGI program—*direct* and *indirect*. In the *direct* method, the CGI program bypasses the Web server and sends its output to the Web client directly. The Web server is involved only as a transport mechanism. The following is a code example of what a CGI program might produce if it is using the *direct* method.

```
HTTP/1.1 200 OK
Date: Tuesday, 22-Apr-97 16:02:10 GMT
Server: WebSTAR 1.0
MIME-version: 1.0
Content-type: text/html
Content-length: 1096
Last-modified: Tuesday, 22-Apr-97 16:02:10 GMT
<HTML>
</HTML>
```

Notice the existence of the HTTP/ character string in the first line of the sample code. To know what type of output processing a CGI program is using, the Web server inspects the first line of the CGI output file. If the first line starts with the character string "HTTP/," the Web server knows that this is a direct response. If this text string is missing, the Web server assumes the CGI program is using the indirect response.

In the *indirect* method, the Web server takes a more proactive role in the communication between the CGI program and the Web client by packaging the CGI response with header information. The following is a code example of what a CGI program might produce if it is using the *indirect* method.

```
Content-type: text/html

<HTML>
. . .
</HTML>
```

Notice the lack of existence of the HTTP/ character string in the first line of the sample code. This tells the Web server that the CGI program has generated output using the *indirect* method.

Output from a CGI Program Doing a SELECT Query

Once you determine what type of CGI output processing you want to use, the process of creating the HTML code to send back to the browser is a relatively simple process. The key is to realize that the CGI program creates and outputs the HTML code necessary to format an HTML page.

The listing below is a partial example of the HTML code needed to generate the Web page as seen in Figure 14–4.

```
Content-type: text/html

<HTML>
<HEAD>
<TITLE>Output From SELECT Query</TITLE>
</HEAD>
<BODY>
<TABLE BORDER=1>
<TR><TD><STRONG><CENTER>Title</CENTER></STRONG></TD>
<TD><STRONG><CENTER>Type</CENTER></STRONG></TD>
<TD><STRONG><CENTER>Rating</CENTER></STRONG></TD>
<TD><STRONG><CENTER>Male_Star</CENTER></STRONG></TD>
<TD><STRONG><CENTER>Female_Star</CENTER></STRONG></TD>
<TD><STRONG><CENTER>Qty</CENTER></STRONG></TD></TR>
<TR><TD>Best Of The WWF</TD>
<TD>Action</TD>
<TD>PG 13</TD>
<TD>Hogan</TD>
<TD></TD>
<TD>10</TD></TR>
<TR><TD>Tornado</TD>
<TD>Action</TD>
<TD>PG 13</TD>
<TD></TD>
<TD>Hunt</TD>
<TD>4</TD></TR>
<TR><TD>Somewhere In Time</TD>
<TD>Romance</TD>
<TD>PG 13</TD>
<TD>Reeves</TD>
```

```
<TD>Seymour</TD>
<TD>9</TD></TR>
</TABLE>
</BODY>
</HTML>
```

You should note a couple of things from this code sample. First, the very first line of code reads:

```
Content-type: text/html
```

As you know, this tells the Web server that receives this CGI output that the developer of the program is using the indirect method. Second, the HTML code is exactly the same as you would write if you wanted to write an HTML page.

The key to this process of having the CGI program generate the HTML code for the result page of the database query is this: Format the display of the result set in your CGI program exactly as you would format report lines of the query, with the exception that you have to include embedded HTML tags and tag pairs around the data.

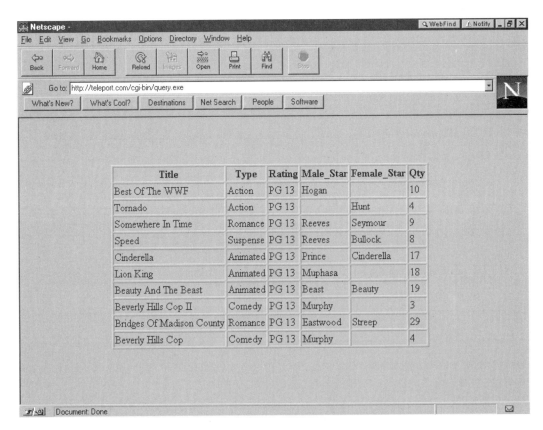

Figure 14–4   The output from the CGI program as seen in a browser.

Redirecting CGI Output

It is sometimes necessary to redirect the output from your CGI program to another information resource as its response. This is possible by generating a Location or an URL header line as the first line of the CGI output. The syntax of these header lines is:

```
Location: absolute or relative URL
URL: absolute or relative URL
```

Therefore, the following one line of code could be generated from your CGI program:

```
Location: /teleport.com/cgi-bin/redir.out
```

The contents of the `redir.out` file would then contain the HTML code that formats and displays the result set of the query in the user's browser.

There are a number of advantages to redirecting output from your CGI program. These are:

- When the CGI program needs to generate a static HTML page instead of a dynamic page of the query results, it is best to have these types of pages pre-defined. An example of this is if the result set of the query contained zero rows, you'd want to send a message to the user indicating this.

- If you are not sure of the format or layout of a result set, you could have the CGI program format a redirected output line, referencing a dataset that contains HTML code that indicates this.

- If another program besides the CGI program creates the result set, you would want to reference this "other programs'" output file from the CGI program so it can be seen in the clients browser.

Returning an Error Code

A Windows CGI program might need to send a status code and message to the user to indicate that there was something wrong when trying to process the SELECT query. This is accomplished using a special Status header line. The format for this line is:

```
Status: code description
```

The `code` is an HTTP status code and `description` is an explanation of the status code. Therefore, the following is a sample of some HTML code that could be generated from the CGI program to return an error code to the Web client.

```
Status: 400 Bad Request
Content-type: text/html
<HTML>
<TITLE>400—Bad Request</TITLE>
<BODY><H1>Bad request—error code 400</H1></BODY>
</HTML>
```

When seen in a browser, this CGI output would appear as shown in Figure 14–5.

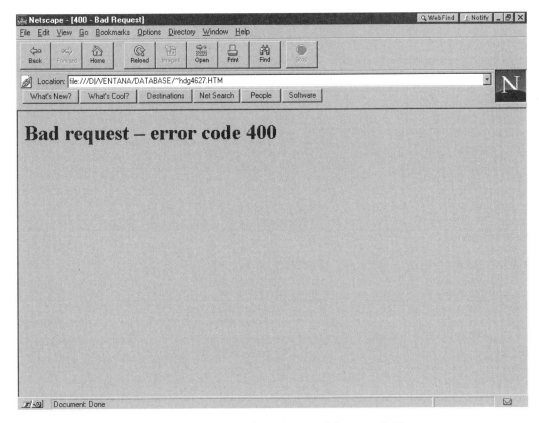

Figure 14-5   An error code generated from a CGI program.

Inserting Rows in a Database from a Web Application

Let's now see how you'd place functionality in your Web database application to add rows of data to your database from the Web front-end. As before, each step in this process is described in detail. Also, as before, and for the sake of clarity, all extraneous images, text, controls, and other objects that would ordinarily appear on a Web page are removed from this and the other examples in this section.

The Web Database Insert Row Page

The HTML code below is used to generate the Web page as seen in Figure 14-6. The purpose of this Web page is to have the user provide the information that will be used to create a new row in the database.

```
<HTML>
<HEAD>
<TITLE>Add a Record</TITLE>
</HEAD>
<BODY>
```

```
</BODY>
<FORM METHOD=GET ACTION="http://teleport.com/cgi-bin/addrec.exe">
<TABLE BORDER=4>
<TR><TD>TITLE:</TD><TD>
<INPUT NAME="M_Title" TYPE="TEXT" COLS=30 SIZE="30">
</TD></TR>
<TR><TD>TYPE:</TD><TD>
<INPUT NAME="m_type" TYPE="RADIO" VALUE="Action"> Action
<INPUT NAME="m_type" TYPE="RADIO" VALUE="Drama"> Drama
<INPUT NAME="m_type" TYPE="RADIO" VALUE="Mystery"> Mystery
<INPUT NAME="m_type" TYPE="RADIO" VALUE="Romance"> Romance
<INPUT NAME="m_type" TYPE="RADIO" VALUE="Comedy"> Comedy
<INPUT NAME="m_type" TYPE="RADIO" VALUE="Animated"> Animated
<INPUT NAME="m_type" TYPE="RADIO" VALUE="SPORTS"> Sports
<INPUT NAME="m_type" TYPE="RADIO" VALUE="RL"> Real Life
</TD></TR>
<TR><TD>RATING:</TD><TD>
<INPUT NAME="m_rating" TYPE="RADIO" VALUE="PG"> PG
<INPUT NAME="m_rating" TYPE="RADIO" VALUE="PG 13"> PG 13
<INPUT NAME="m_rating" TYPE="RADIO" VALUE="R"> R
<INPUT NAME="m_rating" TYPE="RADIO" VALUE="NR"> NR
</TD></TR>
<TR><TD>MALE STAR:</TD><TD><INPUT NAME="Male_Star" TYPE="TEXT" COLS=20
SIZE="20">
</TD></TR>
<TR><TD>FEMALE STAR:</TD><TD><INPUT NAME="FEMALE_STAR" TYPE="TEXT"
COLS=30 SIZE="30">
</TD></TR>
<TR><TD>QTY:</TD><TD><INPUT NAME="Qty" TYPE="TEXT" COLS=3 SIZE="3">
</TD></TR>
</TABLE>
<INPUT NAME="Submit" TYPE="SUBMIT" VALUE="ADD RECORD">
<INPUT NAME="Clear" TYPE="RESET" VALUE="CLEAR">
</FORM>
</HTML>
```

Web Server Action on Receiving the Add Row Request

In the HTML code snippet above, you'll notice a few items and controls that are significant to the execution of this process. First is the <FORM METHOD> tag, that appears as follows:

```
<FORM METHOD=GET ACTION="http://teleport.com/cgi-bin/addrec.exe">
```

You remember that the database query example in the previous section used the FORM METHOD=POST, while this example uses FORM METHOD=GET. In the section below, you'll see how the Web server treats this type of request.

When the request, which is initiated from the browser is received at the Web server, the Web server places data passed to it in various sections of the CGI profile file, and then begins the execution of the addrec.exe program. This program is located in the cgi-bin directory on the Web server identified by http://teleport.com.

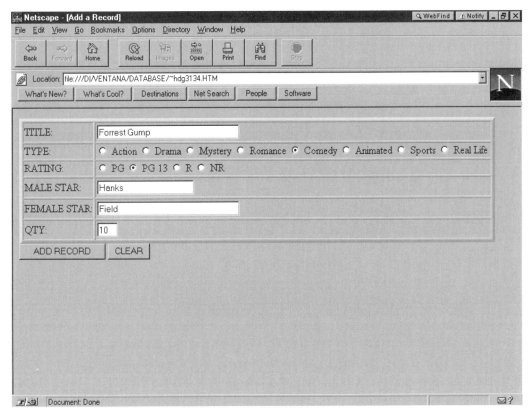

Figure 14–6   The Web page adding a row to a database.

Some of the information placed in the CGI profile file by the Web server upon receiving this request is identified below:

```
[CGI]
Authentication Method=   Basic
CGI Version=              2.0
Content Type=            MIME content type of info supplied with request
Executable Path=         d:\webpage\cgi-bin\addrec.exe
Query String=            m_title=Forrest Gump&m_type=comedy&m_rating=PG
13&male_star=Hanks&female_star=Field&qty=10
Request Method=          GET
Request Keep-Alive=      NO
Request Protocol=        HTTP/1.1
Server Name=             teleport
Server Port=             126.160.112.50
Server Software=         WebSTAR 2.1

[Extra Headers]
```

[Form External]

[Form File]

[Form Huge]

[Form Literal]

[System]

Take note that because the Web page uses the GET method, the passed data is sent to the CGI program in the Query String tag of the CGI profile file.

Execution of the CGI Program to Add a Database Record

Once the FORM method is determined, you have only to parse the name-value pairs before you can get down to the actual database query. Depending on the FORM method, the parsing is different. If the FORM method is POST, then the name-value pairs are stored in the CGI profile file, in the Form Literal section. In our example, and since we are using the GET method, the following lines appear in the CGI profile file:

Query String=   m_title=Forrest Gump&m_type=comedy&m_rating=PG 13&male_star=Hanks&female_star=Field&qty=10

Since this example used the GET method, then the process is a bit more complicated than using the POST method, but not too difficult for most programming languages. It is a simple process of the following:

1. Retrieve the contents of the Query String line in the CGI section of the CGI profile file

2. Iteratively extract the name-value pairs, recognizing that each is separated by an ampersand (&).

Therefore, the following value in the Query String would extract to the associated name-value pairs:

```
m_title=Forrest Gump&m_type=comedy&m_rating=PG 13&male_star=Hanks&fe-
male_star=Field&qty=10
```

Here are the name-value pairs...

```
m_title=Forrest Gump
m_type=comedy
m_rating=PG 13
male_star=Hanks
female_star=Field
qty=10
```

Referring back to Figure 14–2, you see that once the name-value pairs are parsed, the next steps are to:

• Format the Oracle query
• Connect to the database

- Submit SQL to add the record
- Close the database connection

With the before mentioned processing complete, there is nothing special about this program and the fact that it originated from a Web initiated request—the program logic and process flow are *exactly* the same as if the program was *not* part of a Web database application. You'll see no sample code here. You would accomplish all of the above steps exactly the same as you would if this were not a Web-initiated program in the CGI programming language of your choice. Once the database connection is closed, however, it is time to format the result set to HTML and send it to the standard output device.

Output from a CGI Program Doing an INSERT Row

Typically, there are two types of responses that you want to send from the CGI program when it processes an INSERT row request. First, assuming there were errors in the input data provided, you'll want to inform the user of the error and give her or him a chance to correct the error. Second, assuming there were no errors in the input data and the new row was successfully added to the database, you'll want to inform the user of this. In this section, you'll see how each of these two scenarios are accomplished.

Error on Input.   Figure 14–7 shows what a screen might look like right before the user clicked on the <Add Record> button. You'll notice that this should cause an error—there is nothing input for the movie title.

The Web Server would receive the request from the client's browser and place the following string in the `Query String` tag in the `CGI` section of the CGI profile file.

```
m_title=&m_type=comedy&m_rating=PG
13&male_star=Hanks&female_star=Field&qty=10
```

When the CGI program executes, it would do its normal initialization activities as seen in Figure 14–2, such as determine the FORM method and parse the name-value pairs. Before formatting the RDBMS query (in this case an INSERT), the program should do some edits to make sure the data it received was substantial enough and of the correct format to be able to use.

In this example, the CGI program would find that the user had provided no data for the m_title field. An obvious mistake. The most common process at this point is for the CGI program to format an HTML page and form that looks very similar to the one the user just saw, with the addition of a notification of the error. The HTML code below is an example of this, and Figure 14–8 shows what this HTML code looks like in a browser, including the error message.

```
Content-type: text/html
<HTML>
<HEAD>
<TITLE>Add a Record</TITLE>
</HEAD>
<BODY>
</BODY>
<FORM METHOD=GET ACTION="http://teleport.com/cgi-bin/addrec.exe">
```

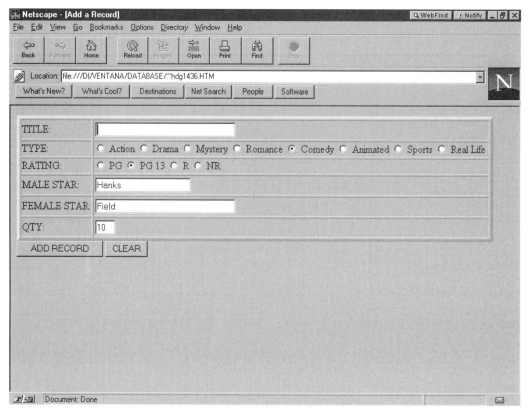

Figure 14–7   Oops, an error on input.

```
<TABLE BORDER=4>
<TR><TD>TITLE:</TD><TD>
<INPUT NAME="M_Title" TYPE="TEXT" COLS=30 SIZE="30">
</TD></TR>
<TR><TD>TYPE:</TD><TD>
<INPUT NAME="m_type" TYPE="RADIO" VALUE="Action"> Action
<INPUT NAME="m_type" TYPE="RADIO" VALUE="Drama"> Drama
<INPUT NAME="m_type" TYPE="RADIO" VALUE="Mystery"> Mystery
<INPUT NAME="m_type" TYPE="RADIO" VALUE="Romance"> Romance
<INPUT NAME="m_type" TYPE="RADIO" VALUE="Comedy"> Comedy
<INPUT NAME="m_type" TYPE="RADIO" VALUE="Animated"> Animated
<INPUT NAME="m_type" TYPE="RADIO" VALUE="SPORTS"> Sports
<INPUT NAME="m_type" TYPE="RADIO" VALUE="RL"> Real Life
</TD></TR>
<TR><TD>RATING:</TD><TD>
<INPUT NAME="m_rating" TYPE="RADIO" VALUE="PG"> PG
<INPUT NAME="m_rating" TYPE="RADIO" VALUE="PG 13"> PG 13
<INPUT NAME="m_rating" TYPE="RADIO" VALUE="R"> R
```

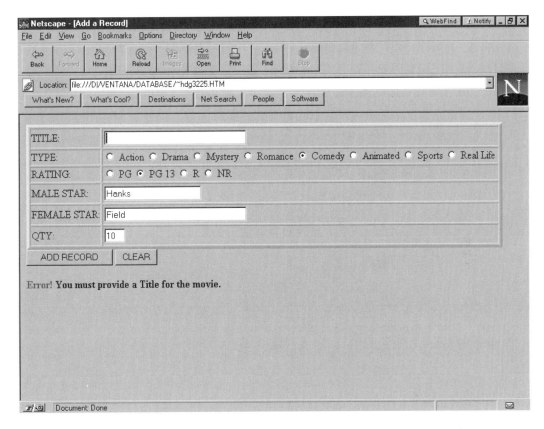

Figure 14–8   An error message displayed on the HTML input form.

```
<INPUT NAME="m_rating" TYPE="RADIO" VALUE="NR"> NR
</TD></TR>
<TR><TD>MALE STAR:</TD><TD><INPUT NAME="Male_Star" TYPE="TEXT" COLS=20
SIZE="20">
</TD></TR>
<TR><TD>FEMALE STAR:</TD><TD><INPUT NAME="FEMALE_STAR" TYPE="TEXT"
COLS=30 SIZE="30">
</TD></TR>
<TR><TD>QTY:</TD><TD><INPUT NAME="Qty" TYPE="TEXT" COLS=3 SIZE="3">
</TD></TR>
</TABLE>
<INPUT NAME="Submit" TYPE="SUBMIT" VALUE="ADD RECORD">
<INPUT NAME="Clear" TYPE="RESET" VALUE="CLEAR">
<P>
<STRONG><FONT COLOR=#FF0000>Error!</FONT> You must provide a Title for
the movie.</STRONG>
</FORM>
</HTML>
```

The HTML code that makes this Web page special is described as:

- The first line of code is using the indirect method of response to communicate with a Web server from a CGI program. This code is: `Content-type: text/html`

- The majority of the HTML code is exactly what the user last saw, with the exception of the error message. The lines of HTML code that accomplish the display of this are: `<P><STRONG><FONT COLOR=#FF0000>Error!</FONT> You must pro-vide a Title for the movie.</STRONG>`

Also notice in the last bulleted item above the use of the COLOR= attribute. This is an HTML level 2 specification that you've not seen yet. In this case, I decided to have the word "`Error!`" display in bright red so that it is more pronounced when the user views it.

Once the user views this Web page, provides a title for the movie and presses the `<Add Record>` button, the Web server and CGI program would process this request exactly as has been described previously.

Tip: The processing described in this section could easily apply to a variety of errors that might be encountered. For example, if the user provides data to be inserted into a database that would cause an invalid duplicate situation, you can simply modify the error message that displays at the bottom of their browser to inform them of this situation.

Add Record Was Successful.   Assuming the data provided by the user was successfully added to the database, you'll probably want to inform them of this fact. This is easily accomplished.

The process is to simply format a CGI response from your CGI program in the form of an HTML page and then send that response to the standard output from your CGI program. An example of what this HTML code might look like is seen in the code sample below.

```
Content-type: text/html
<HTML>
<HEAD>
<TITLE>Add Record Was Successful</TITLE>
</HEAD>
<BODY>
You successfully added the movie titled: Forrest Gump to the database.
Press the <IMG SRC="file:///d|/ventana/images/ch13-18/backbutt.gif"> to
continue.
</BODY>
</HTML>
```

Assuming the HTML code above was generated from a CGI program, this code would appear in a browser as seen in Figure 14–9.

At this point, the user could press the `<Back>` button on their browser and go back to the last viewed Web page.

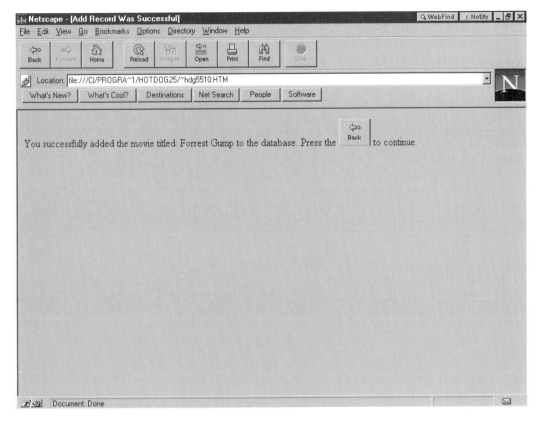

Figure 14–9   Notify the user that the "add record" was successful.

Deleting a Row from a Database Using a Web Application

Let's now see how you'd place functionality in your Web database application to delete rows of data from your database. As before, each step in this process is described in detail. Also, as before, and for the sake of clarity, all extraneous images, text, controls, and other objects that would ordinarily appear on a Web page are removed from this and the other examples in this section.

The Web Database Delete Row Page

The HTML code below is used to generate the Web page as seen in Figure 14–10. The purpose of this Web page is to have the user provide the information that will be used to delete a row in the database.

```
<HTML>
<HEAD>
<TITLE>Delete a Record</TITLE>
</HEAD>
<BODY>
```

```
</BODY>
<FORM METHOD=GET ACTION="http://teleport.com/cgi-bin/delrec.exe">
<TABLE BORDER=4>
<TR><TD>TITLE:</TD><TD>
<INPUT NAME="M_Title" TYPE="TEXT" COLS=30 SIZE="30">
</TD></TR>
<TR><TD>TYPE:</TD><TD>
<INPUT NAME="m_type" TYPE="RADIO" VALUE="Action"> Action
<INPUT NAME="m_type" TYPE="RADIO" VALUE="Drama"> Drama
<INPUT NAME="m_type" TYPE="RADIO" VALUE="Mystery"> Mystery
<INPUT NAME="m_type" TYPE="RADIO" VALUE="Romance"> Romance
<INPUT NAME="m_type" TYPE="RADIO" VALUE="Comedy"> Comedy
<INPUT NAME="m_type" TYPE="RADIO" VALUE="Animated"> Animated
<INPUT NAME="m_type" TYPE="RADIO" VALUE="SPORTS"> Sports
<INPUT NAME="m_type" TYPE="RADIO" VALUE="RL"> Real Life
</TD></TR>
<TR><TD>RATING:</TD><TD>
<INPUT NAME="m_rating" TYPE="RADIO" VALUE="PG"> PG
<INPUT NAME="m_rating" TYPE="RADIO" VALUE="PG 13"> PG 13
<INPUT NAME="m_rating" TYPE="RADIO" VALUE="R"> R
<INPUT NAME="m_rating" TYPE="RADIO" VALUE="NR"> NR
</TD></TR>
<TR><TD>MALE STAR:</TD><TD><INPUT NAME="Male_Star" TYPE="TEXT" COLS=20
SIZE="20">
</TD></TR>
<TR><TD>FEMALE STAR:</TD><TD><INPUT NAME="FEMALE_STAR" TYPE="TEXT"
COLS=30 SIZE="30">
</TD></TR>
<TR><TD>QTY:</TD><TD><INPUT NAME="Qty" TYPE="TEXT" COLS=3 SIZE="3">
</TD></TR>
</TABLE>
<INPUT NAME="Submit" TYPE="SUBMIT" VALUE="DELETE RECORD">
<INPUT NAME="Clear" TYPE="RESET" VALUE="CLEAR">
<P>
<STRONG><FONT COLOR=#FF0000>Warning!</FONT> Clicking on the *DELETE
RECORD* button will remove this record from the Database. If this is not
what you want to do, either click on the *CLEAR* button or on the *BACK*
menu bar item.</STRONG>
</FORM>
</HTML>
```

Web Server Action on Receiving the Delete Row Request

In the HTML code above, you'll notice a few items and controls that are significant to the execution of this process. First is the <FORM METHOD> tag, that appears as follows:

```
<FORM METHOD=GET ACTION="http://teleport.com/cgi-bin/delrec.exe">
```

You know by now that when the request is by the Web server, it places data passed to it in various sections of the CGI profile file, and then begins the execution of the del-

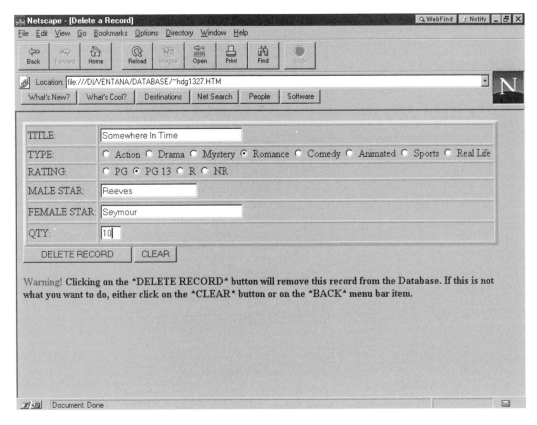

Figure 14–10 The Web page deleting a row from a database.

rec.exe program. This program is located in the cgi-bin directory on the Web server identified by http://teleport.com.

Some of the information placed in the CGI profile file by the Web server upon receiving this request is identified below:

```
[CGI]
Authentication Method=   Basic
CGI Version=                2.0
Content Type=            MIME content type of info supplied with request
Executable Path=         d:\webpage\cgi-bin\addrec.exe
Query String=            m_title=Somewhere In Time&m_type=Romance&m_rat-
ing=PG 13&male_star=Reeves&female_star=Seymour&qty=10
Request Method=          GET
Request Keep-Alive=      NO
Request Protocol=        HTTP/1.1
Server Name=             teleport
Server Port=             126.160.112.50
Server Software=         WebSTAR 2.1
```

```
[Extra Headers]

[Form External]

[Form File]

[Form Huge]

[Form Literal]

[System]
```

Take note that because the Web page uses the GET method, the passed data is sent to the CGI program in the Query String tag of the CGI profile file.

Execution of the CGI Program to Delete a Database Record

Once the FORM method is determined, you have only to parse the name-value pairs before you can get down to the actual database query. In previous sections, you've seen how this is done. When the parsing is complete, you would have the following name-value pairs defined.

Here are the name-value pairs...

```
m_title=Somewhere in Time
m_type=Romance
m_rating=PG 13
male_star=Reeves
female_star=Seymour
qty=10
```

Referring back to Figure 14–2, you see that once the name-value pairs are parsed, the next steps are to:

- Format the Oracle query
- Connect to the database
- Submit SQL delete request
- Close database connection

With the before-mentioned processing complete, there is nothing special about this program and the fact that it originated from a Web initiated request—the program logic and process flow are *exactly* the same as if the program was *not* part of a Web database application. You'll see no sample code here. You would accomplish all of the above steps exactly the same as you would if this were not a Web-initiated program in the CGI programming language of your choice. Once the database connection is closed, however, it is time to format the result set to HTML and send it to the standard output device.

Output from a CGI Program Doing a DELETE Row

Typically, there are two types of responses that you want to send from the CGI program when it processes a DELETE row request. First, assuming there were errors in the input data provided, you'll want to inform the user of the error and give her/him a chance to correct the error. Second, assuming there were no errors in the input data and the row was successfully deleted from the database, you'll want to inform the user of this. In the section titled "Output from a CGI Program Doing an INSERT Row," you saw examples of how to accomplish both of these types of responses.

Updating a Database Row from a Web Application

By now you should have a pretty clear idea of what needs to be done to update a row of data in a database from a Web application. Just to make sure, this section will show you.

The Web Database Update Row Page

The HTML code below is used to generate the Web page as seen in Figure 14–11. The purpose of this Web page is to have the user provide the information that will be used to update an existing row in the database.

```
<HTML>
<HEAD>
<TITLE>Update a Record</TITLE>
</HEAD>
<BODY>
</BODY>
<FORM METHOD=GET ACTION="http://teleport.com/cgi-bin/updrec.exe">
<TABLE BORDER=4>
<TR><TD>TITLE:</TD><TD>
<INPUT NAME="M_Title" TYPE="TEXT" COLS=30 SIZE="30">
</TD></TR>
<TR><TD>TYPE:</TD><TD>
<INPUT NAME="m_type" TYPE="RADIO" VALUE="Action"> Action
<INPUT NAME="m_type" TYPE="RADIO" VALUE="Drama"> Drama
<INPUT NAME="m_type" TYPE="RADIO" VALUE="Mystery"> Mystery
<INPUT NAME="m_type" TYPE="RADIO" VALUE="Romance"> Romance
<INPUT NAME="m_type" TYPE="RADIO" VALUE="Comedy"> Comedy
<INPUT NAME="m_type" TYPE="RADIO" VALUE="Animated"> Animated
<INPUT NAME="m_type" TYPE="RADIO" VALUE="SPORTS"> Sports
<INPUT NAME="m_type" TYPE="RADIO" VALUE="RL"> Real Life
</TD></TR>
<TR><TD>RATING:</TD><TD>
<INPUT NAME="m_rating" TYPE="RADIO" VALUE="PG"> PG
<INPUT NAME="m_rating" TYPE="RADIO" VALUE="PG 13"> PG 13
<INPUT NAME="m_rating" TYPE="RADIO" VALUE="R"> R
<INPUT NAME="m_rating" TYPE="RADIO" VALUE="NR"> NR
</TD></TR>
<TR><TD>MALE STAR:</TD><TD><INPUT NAME="Male_Star" TYPE="TEXT" COLS=20
SIZE="20">
</TD></TR>
<TR><TD>FEMALE STAR:</TD><TD><INPUT NAME="FEMALE_STAR" TYPE="TEXT"
COLS=30 SIZE="30">
</TD></TR>
<TR><TD>QTY:</TD><TD><INPUT NAME="Qty" TYPE="TEXT" COLS=3 SIZE="3">
</TD></TR>
```

```
</TABLE>
<INPUT NAME="Submit" TYPE="SUBMIT" VALUE="UPDATE RECORD">
<INPUT NAME="Clear" TYPE="RESET" VALUE="CLEAR">
<P>
<STRONG><FONT COLOR=#FF0000>Warning!</FONT> Clicking on the *UPDATE
RECORD* button will PERMANENTLY update this record inthe Database. If
this is not what you want to do, either click on the *CLEAR* button or on
the *BACK* menu bar item.</STRONG>
</FORM>
</HTML>
```

Web Server Action on Receiving the Update Row Request

In the HTML code above, you'll notice a few items and controls that are significant to the execution of this process. First is the <FORM METHOD> tag, that appears as follows:

```
<FORM METHOD=GET ACTION="http://teleport.com/cgi-bin/updrec.exe">
```

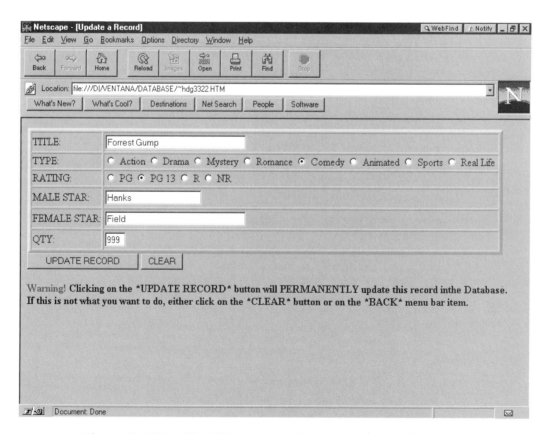

Figure 14–11   The Web page updating a row in a database.

You know by now that when the request to update a row is received by the Web server, it places data passed to it in various sections of the CGI profile file. It is after this occurs that the server begins the execution of the updrec.exe program. This program is located in the cgi-bin directory on the Web server identified by http://teleport.com.

Some of the information placed in the CGI profile file by the Web server upon receiving this request is identified below:

```
[CGI]
Authentication Method=      Basic
CGI Version=                 2.0
Content Type=               MIME content type of info supplied with re-
quest
Executable Path=            d:\webpage\cgi-bin\addrec.exe
Query String=                m_title=Forrest Gump&m_type=Comedy&m_rat-
ing=PG 13&male_star=Hanks&female_star=Field&qty=999
Request Method=             GET
Request Keep-Alive=         NO
Request Protocol=           HTTP/1.1
Server Name=                teleport
Server Port=                126.160.112.50
Server Software=            WebSTAR 2.1

[Extra Headers]

[Form External]

[Form File]

[Form Huge]

[Form Literal]

[System]
```

Take note that because the Web page uses the GET method, the passed data is sent to the CGI program in the Query String tag of the CGI profile file.

Execution of the CGI Program to Update a Database Record

Once the FORM method is determined, you have only to parse the name-value pairs before you can get down to the actual database update operation. In previous sections, you've seen how this is done. When the parsing is complete, you would have the following name-value pairs defined.

Here are the name-value pairs…

```
m_title=Forrest Gump
m_type=Comedy
m_rating=PG 13
male_star=Hanks
female_star=Field
qty=999
```

Referring back to Figure 14–2, you see that once the name-value pairs are parsed, the next steps are to:

- Format the Oracle query
- Connect to the database
- Submit SQL to update the row
- Close database connection

With the before-mentioned processing complete, there is nothing special about this program and the fact that it originated from a Web-initiated request—the program logic and process flow are *exactly* the same as if the program was *not* part of a Web database application. You'll see no sample code here. You would accomplish all of the above steps exactly the same as you would if this were not a Web-initiated program in the CGI programming language of your choice. Once the database connection is closed, however, it is time to format the result set to HTML and send it to the standard output device.

Output from a CGI Program Doing an Update Row

As you've seen, there are typically two types of responses that you would possibly send from the CGI program when it processes an UPDATE row request. The first is used if there were errors in the actual update process. In this case, you'll want to inform the user of the error and give her/him a chance to correct the error. Second, assuming there were no errors in the input data and the database row was updated successfully, you'll want to inform the user of this. In the section titled "Output from a CGI Program Doing an INSERT Row," you saw examples of how to accomplish both of these types of responses.

Tip: In most cases, you do not want to give the user the ability to modify the keys of the data in the database via your Web database application. If you do though, you can provide for this programmatically. If you do not, either place the key data on the form in a hidden field that is not modifiable, or place a warning message on the screen telling the user which field(s) they should not modify.

The information in the previous sections showed you how to select, add, delete, and modify rows in a database from a Web database application. Did you notice that these four functions were fulfilled using four different HTML pages, and four different CGI programs? This may be sufficient, but what if you want to provide these four functions in one HTML page, using one CGI program? The following section shows you how to accomplish this.

Providing Full Database Access from Your Web Application

With the understanding you've acquired so far about how to incorporate database access into your Web applications via CGI programs, the information in this section should come fairly easy to you. You will note that in the previous chapters a specific type of database access (query, insert, update, and delete) was accomplished with four separate Web pages accessing four separate CGI programs. In this section, I will show you how to provide full database access via one HTML page and one CGI program.

The Web Database Full-Access Page

The HTML code below is used to generate the Web page as seen in Figure 14–12. You'll notice from this figure that a new row is added to the bottom of the table. This new row of four radio buttons is used to indicate to the CGI program what type of database action the user intends.

```
<HTML>
<HEAD>
<TITLE>Full function DB access</TITLE>
</HEAD>
<BODY>
</BODY>
<FORM METHOD=GET ACTION="http://teleport.com/cgi-bin/procrec.exe">
<TABLE BORDER=4>
<TR><TD>TITLE:</TD><TD>
<INPUT NAME="M_Title" TYPE="TEXT" COLS=30 SIZE="30">
</TD></TR>
<TR><TD>TYPE:</TD><TD>
<INPUT NAME="m_type" TYPE="RADIO" VALUE="Action"> Action
<INPUT NAME="m_type" TYPE="RADIO" VALUE="Drama"> Drama
<INPUT NAME="m_type" TYPE="RADIO" VALUE="Mystery"> Mystery
<INPUT NAME="m_type" TYPE="RADIO" VALUE="Romance"> Romance
<INPUT NAME="m_type" TYPE="RADIO" VALUE="Comedy"> Comedy
<INPUT NAME="m_type" TYPE="RADIO" VALUE="Animated"> Animated
<INPUT NAME="m_type" TYPE="RADIO" VALUE="SPORTS"> Sports
<INPUT NAME="m_type" TYPE="RADIO" VALUE="RL"> Real Life
</TD></TR>
<TR><TD>RATING:</TD><TD>
<INPUT NAME="m_rating" TYPE="RADIO" VALUE="PG"> PG
<INPUT NAME="m_rating" TYPE="RADIO" VALUE="PG 13"> PG 13
<INPUT NAME="m_rating" TYPE="RADIO" VALUE="R"> R
<INPUT NAME="m_rating" TYPE="RADIO" VALUE="NR"> NR
</TD></TR>
<TR><TD>MALE STAR:</TD><TD><INPUT NAME="Male_Star" TYPE="TEXT" COLS=20
SIZE="20">
</TD></TR>
<TR><TD>FEMALE STAR:</TD><TD><INPUT NAME="FEMALE_STAR" TYPE="TEXT"
COLS=30 SIZE="30">
</TD></TR>
<TR><TD>QTY:</TD><TD><INPUT NAME="Qty" TYPE="TEXT" COLS=3 SIZE="3">
</TD></TR>
<TR><TD>PROCESSING REQUEST:</TD><TD>
<INPUT NAME="p_type" TYPE="RADIO" VALUE="QUERY"> Query
<INPUT NAME="p_type" TYPE="RADIO" VALUE="ADD"> Add
<INPUT NAME="p_type" TYPE="RADIO" VALUE="DELETE"> Delete
<INPUT NAME="p_type" TYPE="RADIO" VALUE="UPDATE"> Update
</TD></TR>
</TABLE>
<INPUT NAME="Submit" TYPE="SUBMIT" VALUE="PROCESS REQUEST">
```

```
<INPUT NAME="Clear" TYPE="RESET" VALUE="CLEAR">
<P>
<STRONG><FONT COLOR=#FF0000>Warning!</FONT> Clicking on the *PROCESS RE-
QUEST* button will PERMANENTLY affect the Database. If this is not what
you want to do, either click on the *CLEAR* button or on the *BACK* menu
bar item.</STRONG>
</FORM>
</HTML>
```

In Figure 14–12, you see what this HTML code looks like in a browser. Take note of the ability we are providing to the user to perform either a query, insert, update, or delete process against the database—all from this one HTML page.

Web Server Action on Receiving the Database Request

In the HTML code above, you'll notice a few items and controls that are significant to the execution of this process. First is the `<FORM METHOD>` tag, that appears as follows:

```
<FORM METHOD=GET ACTION="http://teleport.com/cgi-bin/procrec.exe">
```

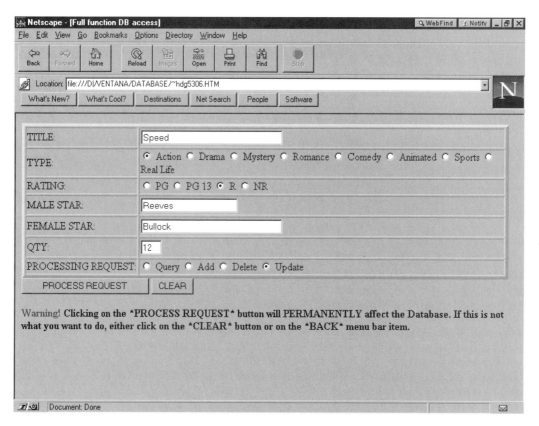

Figure 14–12   The Web page providing full database access.

You know by now that when the request is received by the Web server, the server places data passed to it in various sections of the CGI profile file. The server then begins the execution of the `updrec.exe` program. This program is located in the `cgi-bin` directory on the Web server identified by `http://teleport.com`.

Some of the information placed in the CGI profile file by the Web server upon receiving this request is identified below:

```
[CGI]
Authentication Method=    Basic
CGI Version=               2.0
Content Type=             MIME content type of info supplied with request
Executable Path=          d:\webpage\cgi-bin\updrec.exe
Query String=             m_title=Speed&m_type=Action&m_rating=R&male_
star=Reeves&female_star=Bullock&qty=12&p_type=Update
Request Method=           GET
Request Keep-Alive=       NO
Request Protocol=         HTTP/1.1
Server Name=              teleport
Server Port=              126.160.112.50
Server Software=          WebSTAR 2.1

[Extra Headers]

[Form External]

[Form File]

[Form Huge]

[Form Literal]

[System]
```

Take note that because the Web page uses the GET method, the passed data is sent to the CGI program in the `Query String` tag of the CGI profile file. Also note the addition of one extra parameter in the `Query String` tag of the CGI section. This extra parameter is: `&p_type=Update`. The other options that this field could be are: Query, Add, Delete, depending on which radio button the user selected.

Execution of the CGI Program to Take Action on a Database Record

Once the FORM method is determined, you have only to parse the name-value pairs before you can get down to the actual database update operation. In previous sections, you've seen how this is done. When the parsing is complete, you would have the following name-value pairs defined.

Here are the name-value pairs...

```
m_title=Speed
m_type=Action
m_rating=R
male_star=Reeves
female_star=Bullock
qty=12
p_type=Update
```

Referring back to Figure 14–2, you see that once the name-value pairs are parsed, the next steps are to:

- Format the Oracle query
- Connect to the database
- *Submit SQL to cause desired action to take place*
- Retrieve result set (if the process was a query)
- Close database connection

The critical step in this process is the one labeled *"Submit SQL to cause desired action to take place."* How do you know what the desired action is anyway? The answer is that it is given to you in the Query String that you parsed from within your CGI program. Recalling that the last name-value pair passed in this example is `p_type=Update`, this is how you know.

Interrogate the value of p_type and depending on the value of this field, your CGI program would either query a row on the database, add a row to the database, delete a record on the database, or update an existing record on the database. You could provide these four functions within the one CGI program, or you could accommodate the required processing by calling subroutines. Either option will work. The program logic and process flow, regardless of the method used, are *exactly* the same as if the program was *not* part of a Web database application. Once the database connection is closed, however, it is time to format the result set to HTML and send it to the standard output device.

Output from a CGI Program Performing an Unspecified Action on a Database

As you've seen in a number of previous examples, there are typically two types of responses that you would possibly send from the CGI program when it processes a database request of some sort. The first is used if there were errors in the actual database access processing. In this case, you'll want to inform the user of the error and give her/him a chance to correct the error. Second, assuming there were no errors in the input data and the desired database action was accomplished as desired, you'll want to inform the user of this. In the section titled "Output from a CGI Program Doing an INSERT Row," you saw examples of how to accomplish both of these types of responses.

Moving On

This long chapter should have provided you with the information needed to give you a very clear understanding of the role of all the components in a Web database application, and how they work together. Particularly, you learned how the CGI program is used to accomplish the actual database processing as requested by the user via HTML forms.

The next chapter introduces you to MIME, which is the set of agreed-upon formats that enable you to send binary files via e-mail, as e-mail attachments, or other methods besides e-mail. As you grow in your comfort level with building Web database applications, you will undoubtedly find this a very valuable addition to the scope of your applications.

CHAPTER 15

MIME
and Advanced
Data
Presentation

The earlier chapters in this book presented material on the tools available for Web database application development, Oracle database products, using the Oracle to build database components, Web database application architecture, and HTML and CGI programming and processing. You've seen a number of examples of how data can be formatted and displayed throughout many of these chapters. In this chapter, you'll learn how to incorporate multimedia components in your Web database applications. This certainly includes Oracle Web database applications where you want to incorporate audio, visual, or other non-HTML components on the Web pages seen by users.

What Is MIME?

MIME stands for Multipurpose Internet Mail Extension. It is a set of standards that specify both the type of file being sent from a Web component (either a Web server or browser) to another Web component as well as the method that should be used to turn that message back into its original form.

MIME standards are evolving. They define a growing set of data types that give you the ability to create Web applications that incorporate either new data types or objects such as audio, video, or three-dimensional virtual reality graphics, etc. For example, HTML is a MIME data type. So, too, is a JPEG graphics file and an audio (WAV) file. In fact, any type of information or file that can be stored electronically could be, and probably already is, a MIME data type.

MIME is bi-directional. It is the primary way that a Web server tells a Web client about the document that it's sending. MIME is also the way that a Web client tells a Web server the types of documents that it can receive and process. Some of the new capabilities provided by MIME standards and data types include:

- Inclusion of multiple objects within a single page
- Messages with multiple fonts
- Sending audio, video, graphics, multimedia files
- Sending text messages without regard to length
- Tagging messages with information so browsers know how best to handle them
- Transmitting character sets besides ASCII

Before MIME, the process of sending non-text and non-HTML files from one Web component (Web server, browser, or FTP site) to another was a complicated process. This process included the following steps:

1. The sender had to translate (uuencode) the source data and save it to disk in a place that could be retrieved by the recipient.
2. The receiver had to initiate the request to transfer the uuencoded file to their machine.
3. The receiver, once the file was transferred, had to decode the file back into its original format. An example of one of the screens used to identify some of the different types of file formats available for UUDECODEing is seen in Figure 15–1.

Then, the recipient could use or view the file.

Definition: UUENCODE Unix to Unix ENCODEing is a predecessor method to MIME for converting files from one format to another to allow transmission over the Web.

Uses for MIME on the Web

You've already seen MIME used in this book, although you may not know it. Remember from the previous chapter, when you saw how to create a Web page from within a CGI program to transmit back to the user, you saw the following code?

```
Content-type: text/html

<HTML>
. . .
</HTML>
```

The first line of code (`Content-type: text/html`) is what is referred to as a MIME header. Although you'll learn about MIME headers later in this chapter, for now you should understand that this line of code instructs the receiving browser that the rest of the page contains HTML text data. This is one example of MIME.

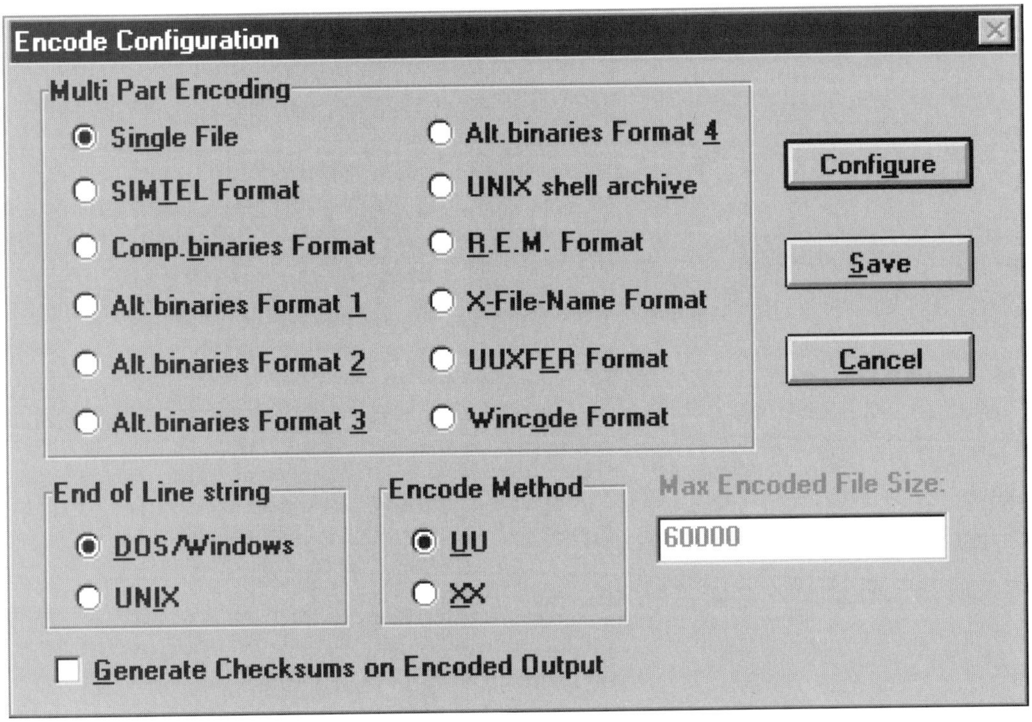

Figure 15–1 An example of an earlier uuencoding method.

MIME is also used to add multimedia, audio, video, and graphic elements to your application. In addition to making your pages more presentable, it also makes them more useful. Consider the following examples.

Example 1

- *Scenario #1*—You go to a Web site and can read the 1963 inaugural address from President John F. Kennedy, in which he spoke the infamous line: "Ask not what your country can do for you, ask what you can do for your country."

- *Scenario #2*—You go to a Web site and see a picture of President John F. Kennedy standing at the podium in his black tuxedo and hat during his 1963 inaugural address. When you click on his picture, a window pops up and you see a streaming audio/video recording of the actual address.

Which of the above two scenarios do you think carries with it more punch and has a more significant impact to the user? Let's take a look at another example that is perhaps more aligned with the type of application you might write some day.

Example 2

- *Scenario #1*—You work for a real estate firm and have been asked to place the listing your company manages on a Web page. So, you create a Web page with text descriptions of all the properties.

- *Scenario #2*—You work for a real estate firm and have been asked to place the listing your company manages on a Web page. So, you create a Web page that shows a picture of each property. When a user clicks on a picture for the property he or she is interested in, a multimedia player pops up and displays a walking tour of the house.

I think you'd agree that in both examples, scenario #2 carries more pizzazz, and has a greater impact than scenario #1. Do you want to see an example of what I'm referring to? Look at Figure 15–2 below.

You'll notice a couple of things here. First, next to the picture of actor Charlie Sheen you'll see two graphics—the first is highlighted with a square box around it and is the image of a microphone while the second is an image of a movie camera. Next, notice at

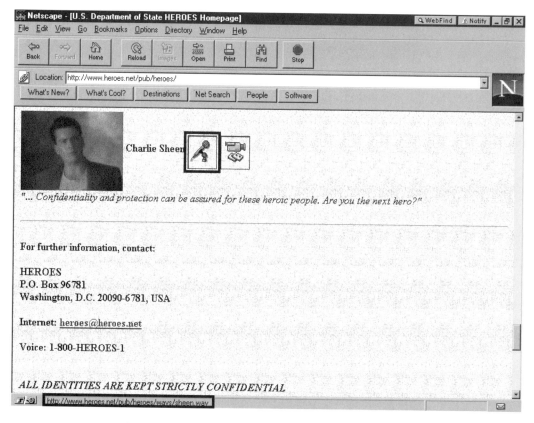

Figure 15–2   A Web page with extra "punch."

the bottom of the figure I've placed a black rectangle around what appears as an URL, specifically it is: `http://www.heroes.net/pub/heroes/avis/aviviv.html`.

If you click on this URL, the Web server at the United States Department of State, which is where the page seen in Figure 15–2 originates, will attempt to send a HTML file that contains a streaming video/audio image of Charlie Sheen speaking about the merits of patriotism. The HTML code to accomplish this is seen below:

```
<IMG SRC="http://www.heroes.net/pub/heroes/gifs/sheen.gif" ALIGN="MID-
DLE"></>Charlie Sheen </B>
<A HREF="http://www.heroes.net/pub/heroes/wavs/sheen.wav">
<IMG SRC="http://www.heroes.net/pub/heroes/gifs/audio.gif" ALIGN="MID-
DLE"></A>
<A HREF="http://www.heroes.net/pub/heroes/wavs/sheen.avi">
<IMG SRC="http://www.heroes.net/pub/heroes/gifs/video.gif" ALIGN="MID-
DLE"></A>
```

Assuming you clicked on the graphic of the movie camera, the file named: `http://www.heroes.net/pub/heroes/wavs/sheen.avi` would begin playing in your browser (after you waited for it to transfer from the Web server to your machine.) Your browser would know that it was receiving an audio/video file that it needed to play inside the browser by the MIME header. In this case, the MIME header for this file is:

```
Content-type: video/x-msvideo
```

MIME Headers

The code example above for the Charlie Sheen audio/video file is one of several types of MIME headers. MIME headers appear at the very beginning of the file being transferred. Although there are several more MIME header types required and available for e-mail transmission and receipt, the number of headers used for Web non-e-mail transfers is limited. In fact, you might be surprised to learn that *no* MIME headers are required to transfer a file, and in most cases only one will do.

The following is a snippet of HTML code in which a MIME header appears:

```
Content-type: text/html
<HTML>
<TITLE>No MIME Header</TITLE>
<HEAD></HEAD>
<BODY><H1>This is a test.</H1></BODY>
</HTML>
```

Figure 15–3 shows what this code looks like in a browser. Notice that this appears as you'd expect.

Now, consider the following snippet of HTML code and notice the absence of a MIME header.

```
<HTML>
<TITLE>No MIME Header</TITLE>
<HEAD></HEAD>
<BODY><H1>This is a test.</H1></BODY>
</HTML>
```

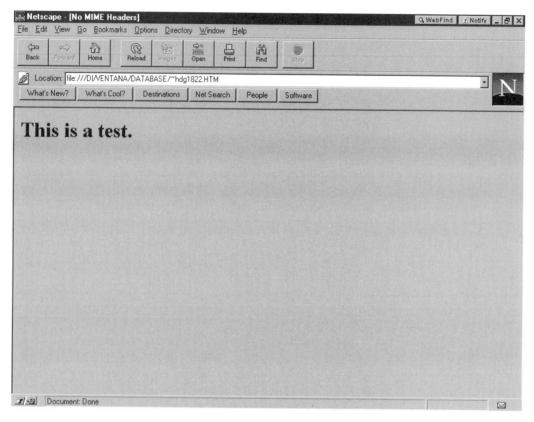

Figure 15–3   A little bit of HTML code with a MIME header.

When a browser receives this file, because there is no MIME header present, it treats the HTML code as regular non-HTML text. It will not apply any formatting to the character strings. This is seen in Figure 15–4.

Tip: The lack of HTML formatting and use of a MIME header could be advantageous to you. If you had some ASCII text files that you wanted to make available for viewing, without special HTML formatting tags, simply place them on a Web server as ASCII text files, without a MIME header. When a user's browser points to these files, they can view them as straight text files. Although they won't appear elegant in a browser, the purpose is still served.

MIME Types and Subtypes

The MIME specifications are evolving. They are submitted to and approved by the Internet Assigned Numbers Authority (IANA). Presently, there are 7 recognized MIME types, with hundreds of subtypes recognized by the IANA.

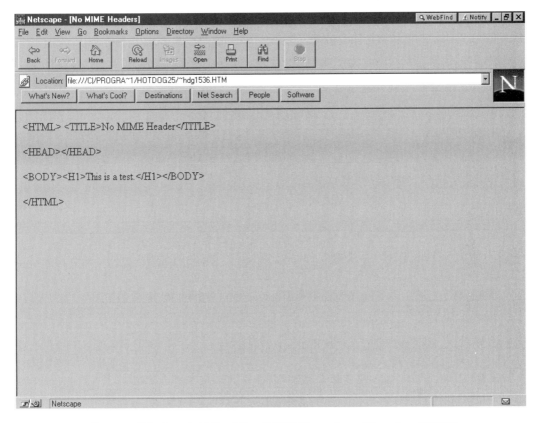

Figure 15-4   A little bit of HTML code without a MIME header as seen in a browser.

The following table describes the approved MIME types, as well as a *partial* sub-list of the approved subtypes.

Type	Description	Subtypes
Application	Message is data that does not fit into any of the other MIME types	cybercash, msword, postscript, rtf
Audio	Message is an audio file	32kadpcm, basic, wav
Image	Message is an image	cgm, gif, jpeg, tiff
Message	Message is an encapsulated e-mail message	external-body, news, partial, rfc822
Multipart	Message consists of multiple body parts	alternative, formdata, mixed, report
Text	Message is primarily ASCII text	html, plain, richtext, sgml, tab-separated-values
Video	Message is a video file	avi, quicktime, vnd.vivo

MIME Type/Subtype Examples

The following examples demonstrate the use of a combination of each of these types, along with a selected subtype.

Application Type: *Definition:*	Content-type: application/msword The body of the enclosed message is a MS Word document.
Audio Type: *Definition:*	Content-type: audio/wav The body of the enclosed message is an audio file saved in the WAV format.
Image Type: *Definition:*	Content-type: image/gif The body of the enclosed message is a graphics file saved in the GIF format.
Message Type: *Definition:*	Content-type: message/RFC822 The body of the enclosed message is encapsulated as an RFC822 message.
Text Type: *Definition:*	Content-type: text/html The body of the enclosed message is HTML code.
Video Type: *Definition:*	Content-type: video/mpeg The body of the enclosed message is an audio/video file saved in the MPG format.
Multipart Type: *Definition:*	Content-type: multipart/mixed; boundary=" @@@@@@@" The body of the enclosed message consists of file elements of different types and/or subtypes.

Multipart Type Example. With the exception of the ***multipart*** type, the use of the other six MIME types is self-evident. Specifically, the type/subtype MIME header appears before the body of the message. With the ***multipart*** type, MIME headers can appear throughout the message body. The following code snippet is an example of this.

```
Content-type: multipart/mixed; boundary="@@@@@@@"
—@@@@@@@
Content-type: text/html
<HTML>
<HEAD>Multipart MIME Example</HEAD>
<BODY>
—@@@@@@@
Content-type: text/plain
Now is the time for all good men to come to the aid of their country.
To be or not to be, that is the question.
Four score and seven years ago.
—@@@@@@@
Content-type: image/jpeg
… JPEG IMAGE DATA …
—@@@@@@@—
```

Tip: The beginning of an encapsulated boundary consists of two hyphens (--) followed by the boundary string. The end of an encapsulated boundary consists of two hyphens (--) followed by the boundary string followed by two more hyphens (--).

Custom MIME Types

If you have a need in an application to create and use a MIME type and/or subtype combination that does not exist, you have the ability to do this. For example, you may have need to define and use a MIME type/subtype combination that does not currently exist in an intranet application. This could be to allow an Adobe Acrobat file to be transmitted and viewed by a browser in a usable format. To define and use a customized type/subtype, you'd have to perform the following steps:

- Identify the type/subtype combination, and making sure it does not exist in the approved list of the IANA
- Configure the Web server to recognize the new type/subtype
- Make sure the browsers accessing the Adobe Acrobat file are configured to use a plug-in that formats and displays the file correctly
- Find or build a plug-in to display the file in the correct format

---

Definition: A plug-in is a reusable program that dynamically extends the base function of a Web page by adding features such as audio and video playback.

As you can imagine, this is not an easy process. You are much better off contacting the IANA to see if they have an approved type/subtype combination that you can use. Hopefully you can find a plug-in that you could use since these are usually quite difficult to write from scratch.

MIME Perspectives

Depending on your perspective, MIME means different things. As a developer, you need to understand MIME not only from your perspective but from the user's perspective. You need the user's understanding to design and build an application that is not only easy to use and functional, but fun.

MIME from a Developer's Perspective

Although it sometimes makes good sense to display text or straight HTML pages to your users, you will probably want to frequently include audio/video/graphics capabilities in your Web applications. To do this, you must maintain a keen awareness of available MIME types and subtypes. CGI applications are increasingly incorporating newer media types, such as: graphics, server-push animation, 2D and 3D charts, Virtual Reality Modeling Language (VRML), and plots and graphs. The following URLs will help you to keep up with evolving MIME types/subtypes.

```
ftp://ds.internic.net/rfc/
http://www.cis.ohio.state.edu/hypertext/faq/usenet/mail/mime-faq/top.html
http://www.cs.indiana.edu/docproject/mail/mime.html
http://www.netscape.com/assist/helper_apps/media-types.html
http://www.netscape.com/assist/helper_apps/what-is-mime.html
```

As you design and develop your Web database applications, be aware of the available MIME types/subtypes. Employ all available resources to make your Web pages as functional *and* attractive as possible.

A common sense design tip when using a MIME type that requires a plug-in is to provide a convenient way for the user to acquire the plug-in if it doesn't exist on their machine. You can easily do this with a text or icon hyperlink to a site that contains the needed plug-in.

MIME from a User's Perspective

Your users are becoming increasingly aware of and comfortable with multimedia Web applications. The application(s) you build for them should not only address the business needs, but be as enjoyable to use as other Web applications they might use. Therefore, your Web database application will probably need to support at the very least some sort of audio output and graphics/video display.

If you limit the design of your application to use only standard types and subtypes, the need for plug-ins should be minimal—at best. In most cases, you will probably be able to design and deliver a very useful and enjoyable Web database application by using nothing other than the standard types and subtypes. If you find the need to build an application that requires the use of a non-standard type or subtype, make it easy for the user to acquire and use the necessary plug-in(s).

As discussed in the previous section, you can do this by providing a hyperlink to a site that contains the plug-in from the Web page that requires its use. Be aware though that downloading and installing a plug-in does not always ensure that it is configured to be used automatically by the user's browser. Not all plug-ins automatically configure the browser. For example, the plug-ins seen in Figure 15–2 automatically configure themselves, but they require the user to completely close out of the browser they are using and restart it.

Figure 15–5 shows the screen the user would use to manually configure a plug-in to work with various MIME types and subtypes. Under the column heading File Type is listed the MIME type/subtype combination. The column heading Action lists the application that executes or action that takes place when the MIME type/subtype is encountered. Finally, the column heading Extension lists the various file extensions that would trigger the action specified.

In Figure 15–5, you see that a MIME type/subtype combination of `audio/x-pn-realaudio` will cause a plug-in program named `raplayer.exe` that is in the `c:\windows\system` directory to execute whenever a file with the extension of `ra` or `ram` is encountered in a Web message. With this definition, this machine is fully configured to automatically recognize and play the necessary plug-in whenever a real audio file is received in a Web message.

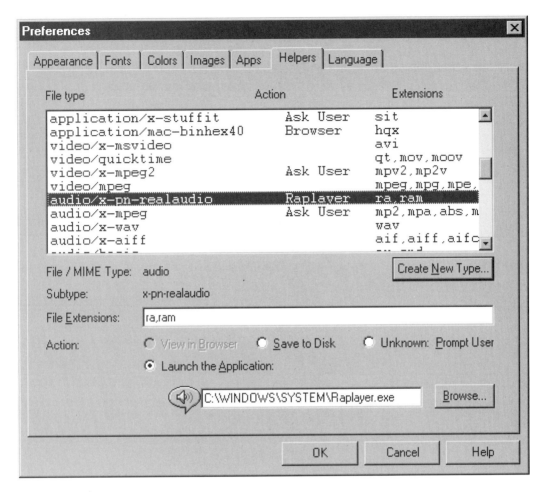

Figure 15–5   Configuring a plug-in for Netscape Navigator.

Tip: To get to the Preferences screen as seen in Figure 15–5, do the following in Netscape Navigator:
    On the main menu, click on the Options menu item
    Click on the General Preferences menu item
    Click on the Helper's tab

Moving On

This chapter presented foundation information that you can use to incorporate MIME in your Web database applications to add powerful and attractive multimedia components. You saw how easy MIME is to use, provided that you adhere to a few requirements—specifically use the `Content-type`: line and approved types and subtypes.

Chapter 16 shows you how to manage Web database access and the application state. As you know, the Web is inherently non-conversational in nature. Making a follow-up query based on the results of an initial database request is something that non-Web database applications handle with ease. You will learn how managing the application state gives you the ability to build pseudo-conversational applications.

CHAPTER 16

Managing Web Database Access and the Application State

As you know by now, the Web is an inherently "stateless" environment—it is non-conversational in nature. From one transaction to the next, unless you specifically build a mechanism to allow the application to keep track of where it is in a series of processes, it will lose track of where it's been. Often times, when an application loses track of where it's been, it doesn't know where it needs to go.

This chapter describes three different techniques that you could use to keep track of where an application is at any point in a series of steps that comprise a process—the application state. Those three techniques are:

- Hidden fields on forms
- Using database tables
- Cookies

You should notice that using HTML is not one of these techniques. This is because the current specifications for HTML do not specifically address support for managing state data. However, as you will see, you can use some of the features of HTML to incorporate the management of application state.

Tip: There has been much discussion lately about expanding HTML specifications to include managing of application state. Netscape Communications seems to be leading this initiative. You should expect to see this added to HTML specifications by the end of 1998.

What Is Application State?

"Application state" means the ability to keep track of what step an application is in, including providing access to all relevant data that step needs, at any point in a series of steps. Application state information therefore is the information that is maintained and transferred from one Web page or form or program to another for subsequent processing. To illustrate what I mean by "application state," consider the following example.

I've used a VCR Rental application in previous chapters to illustrate certain points. Assume that a clerk working for the video rental store wants to query all the movies that are rated PG 13, and from that list wants to perform a "drilldown" query to produce a list of all the movies that are cartoons, and of course are also rated PG 13. One solution to accomplish this would be to build a HTML form similar to the one seen in Figure 16–1, where the clerk is able to specify both the movie rating and the category on a single form.

As before, I have stripped out the unnecessary objects, graphics, and controls from the HTML forms used in this chapter for readability.

The HTML code used to create the form seen in the screen print in Figure 16–1 is shown below. Note the existence of two drop down list boxes that the user would use to make their selection.

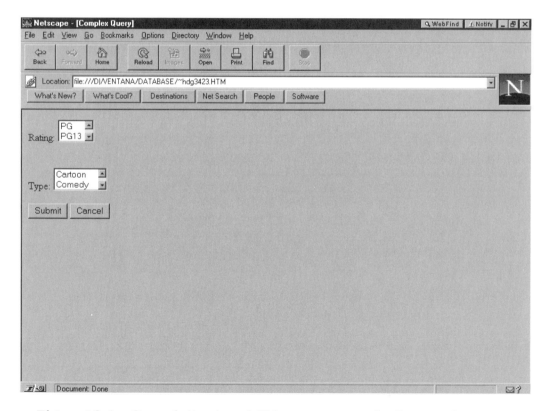

Figure 16–1   One solution to a drilldown query—make it a complex query.

```
<HTML>
<HEAD>
<TITLE>Complex Query</TITLE>
</HEAD>
<BODY>
<FORM METHOD=POST ACTION="http://teleport.com/cgi-bin/query.exe">
<P>Rating: <SELECT RATING=Movie_Rating SIZE=2>
<OPTION VALUE="PG">PG</OPTION>
<OPTION VALUE="PG 13">PG13</OPTION>
<OPTION VALUE="R">R</OPTION>
<OPTION VALUE="NR">NR</OPTION>
</SELECT></P>
<BR>
<P>Type: <SELECT TYPE=Movie_Type SIZE=2>
<OPTION VALUE="Cartoon">Cartoon</OPTION>
<OPTION VALUE="Comedy">Comedy</OPTION>
<OPTION VALUE="Drama">Drama</OPTION>
<OPTION VALUE="Mystery">Mystery</OPTION>
<OPTION VALUE="Romance">Romance</OPTION>
<OPTION VALUE="Suspense">Suspense</OPTION>
</SELECT>
<P>
<INPUT NAME="Submit" TYPE="SUBMIT" VALUE="Submit">
<INPUT NAME="Cancel" TYPE="RESET" VALUE="Cancel">
</FORM>
</BODY>
</HTML>
```

In the scenario as seen in Figure 16–1 and the HTML code above, there is no need to maintain the application state as the user is given the option of supplying enough information to the CGI program running on the Web server so that it can format and execute a complex query. In other words, all the activity required to accomplish a given task is incorporated on and provided for on one Web page, running one CGI program. But, this approach is limiting, because:

- It does not allow for the dynamic "building" of the Type list box. For example, the Types that list in the drop down list box are: Cartoon, Comedy, Drama, Mystery, Romance, Suspense. But, what if there were no movies rated PG *and* of the type Romance? Although this option is selectable in the two drop down list boxes, it is an invalid combination.

- The value in the two drop down list boxes are hard coded and so modifications require changes to the HTML code. Therefore, if a new movie of type "Action" were to become available, someone would need to make changes to the HTML code to accommodate this new movie type.

If an application could be built so that the results of the first query (the movie rating) are used to construct the second query (the movie type) in a second Web page running a second CGI program, then both of the above considerations are addressed. This means that the application is more flexible to change and requires less maintenance over time. Being able to keep track of the application state will allow us to build such an application.

Now, consider an example where you want to give the user accurate information to make a selection. You want to build an application that walks him or her through the following steps:

1. The user completes and submits a form specifying the rating of movies the customer wants to see. These ratings are supplied dynamically by performing a query against the database, extracting all the unique movie ratings.

2. From the result set above, the user selects and submits a second form where the type of movie the customer wants to see is indicated.

3. The result set from the second step will be a list of all movies that have the rating as specified in Step 1 and are in the category as specified in Step 2.

Given this architecture for the application, a movie rating could be added to or deleted from the database without any coding changes in the drop down list boxes. Such an architecture, requiring multiple steps, could never be accommodated without being able to keep track of where the application is in the series of steps.

A Web database application designed as described above is dynamic, accurate, and does not require modification as new ratings or movie types appear. This reduction in application maintenance increases the life of the application and keeps you spending more of your time writing new applications and less of it maintaining existing applications. All of this is because you have designed and constructed the application to maintain and recognize "state" information.

> Little attention has been paid to date in the media about the time and cost involved in maintaining Web database applications. This is because the technology is so new that very few (if any) companies have applications that are old enough to require maintenance. However, within 2 years you will see this become an area in Web application development that garners a tremendous amount of attention.

Authentication and Application State

Authentication means making sure that the person that is accessing all of the Web pages in your Web database application has permission to do so. If your application involves just one Web page, then this is not a problem—you simply provide for the entry and processing of a user ID and password on the one Web page.

But, what if your application involves 20 Web pages? As you know, each Web page has a unique URL, and any URL can be entered at any time from any machine in the world that is connected to the Internet. Just because someone entered a user ID and password on the first Web page of the application, which was subsequently authenticated, doesn't mean that they have the authority to see or process any of the other pages in the application—unless you somehow record in the other pages in the application that the person transmitting the Web page has previously passed a security process.

As a Web database application designer, you must consider the question: Do you want to make your Web database application accessible to anyone with a browser? If the answer to the question is "no," then you must build an ability into the application that allows for user authentication and restricted access. This requires the use of application state.

Assume you build a login screen that looks similar to Figure 16–2, with the HTML code necessary to create such a screen as shown next:

```
<HTML>
<HEAD>
<TITLE>User Id And Password</TITLE>
</HEAD>
<BODY>
<FORM METHOD=POST ACTION="www.teleport.com\cgi-bin\pass_ver.exe">
User ID:
<INPUT NAME="User_ID" TYPE="" COLS=8 SIZE="8"><P>
Password:
<INPUT NAME="passwrd" TYPE="PASSWORD" COLS=8 SIZE="8"><P>
Email Id: <INPUT NAME="email_id" TYPE="" COLS=40 SIZE="40"><P>
<INPUT NAME="Submit" TYPE="SUBMIT" VALUE="Submit">
<INPUT NAME="Reset" TYPE="RESET" VALUE="Reset">
</FORM>
</BODY>
</HTML>
```

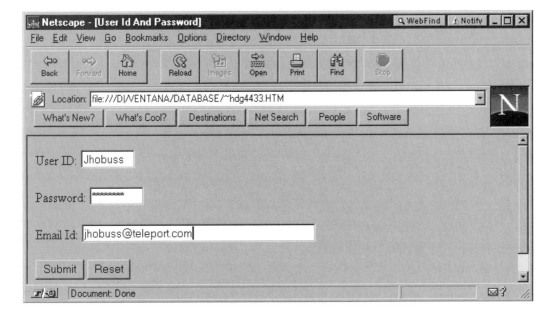

Figure 16–2 An example of a user authentication screen.

In the HTML code, you'll notice a special "TYPE" for the INPUT tag—PASSWORD. This type causes asterisks (*) to display to the user as they enter data in this field. Also notice that the name of the CGI program that executes on the Web server is pass_ver.exe. Presumably this CGI program would perform some sort of verification of the user_id/password combination that was entered by the user before access is provided to other system components.

OK, so the person that input the user_id/password passes your security check. If the user had not passed your security routine then you'd display a message back that tells them so. If the user did pass the security routine, then the pass_ver.exe CGI program would format and send a Web page back to the user that gives them access to sensitive information in your database. Is this the right thing to do? The answer is: Yes and no.

Yes, you want to give the authorized user access to the information they want and have authority to access, but you still want to keep the unauthorized user out. What if the URL of the Web page that you display to the user, the one that gives them access to sensitive information after they passed your security routines, somehow falls into the hands of someone that shouldn't have access to your system. That person could circumvent your security front-end by merely using the URL of the Web page that follows the security routines. Remember: every Web page has a unique URL. Any URL can be typed into a browser at any time by any machine that is connected to the Internet, thus potentially giving the user the ability to view the Web page associated with the URL. Not a good situation, agreed?

Consider the Web page seen in Figure 16–3. This is an example of a Web page that could be generated from your `pass_ver.exe` CGI program when the user passes the security check.

The HTML code used to generate this screen is seen below. You should notice nothing particularly intriguing about this code.

```
<HTML>
<HEAD>
<TITLE>Access To Sensitive Information</TITLE>
</HEAD>
<BODY>
<FORM METHOD=POST ACTION="www.teleport.com\cgi-bin\empl_adj.exe">
ID Of Employee Whose Salary You Are Adjusting:
<INPUT NAME="empl_id" TYPE="" COLS=8 SIZE="8"><P>
Percentage Change In Monthly Pay:
<INPUT NAME="change_rate" TYPE="TEXT" COLS=6 SIZE="6"><P>
Increase <INPUT NAME="up_down" TYPE="RADIO">
Decrease <INPUT NAME="up_down" TYPE="RADIO"><P>
<INPUT NAME="Submit" TYPE="SUBMIT" VALUE="Submit">
<INPUT NAME="Reset" TYPE="RESET" VALUE="Reset">
</FORM>
</BODY>
</HTML>
```

The VCR scenario in Figure 16–1 and the Employee Salary Adjustment Web page in Figure 16–3 are both excellent examples of situations where you would benefit from maintaining application state. Without the ability to transfer information from the sign-on

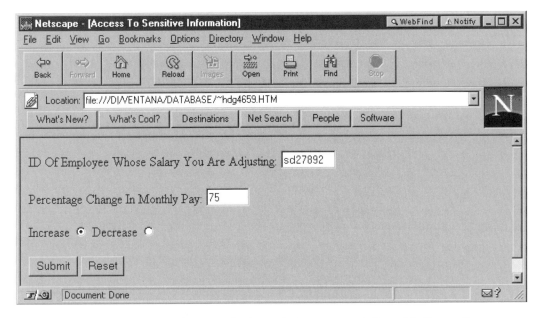

Figure 16-3   A Web page that contains very privileged information.

page to the data manipulation pages that a user has passed security, anyone that knows the URL of the data manipulation pages could access them and manipulate the data that those pages affect. In the following sections of this chapter you'll see a number of different ways to accommodate this.

Using Forms to Maintain State

Recall in Figure 16–2 that there were three pieces of information required to be input on this screen. These were:

- User ID
- Password
- E-mail ID

Once the user pressed the `<Submit>` button and sent this transaction to the Web server which in turn initiated the `pass_ver.exe` CGI program, it is the responsibility of the `pass_ver.exe` program to perform whatever security validation routines are required. However, it is also the responsibility of the `pass_ver.exe` program to format and send the HTML code as seen in Figure 16–3 back to the user.

What if instead of sending the form that looks like Figure 16–3, the `pass_ver.exe` program formats and sends the form that looks like Figure 16–4? Take a close look at these two figures. Go ahead, look at them again and think about what you see that's different about them.

You should see that there's nothing visibly different about these two Web pages. This is what you'd want both the authorized and the unauthorized user to see as well.

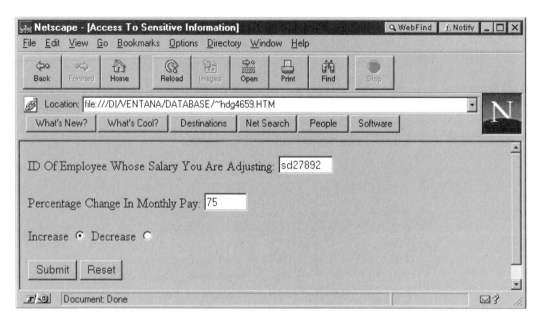

Figure 16–4   A Web page that contains very privileged information—with a hidden field.

Nothing visible. However, there is a lot going on in this Web page that is unseen—the critical data passing mechanism to maintain application state. And the catalyst to this is the use of hidden fields on forms.

In other words, information gathered on Web page 1 which is sent to and processed by the CGI program `pass_ver.exe` is placed in hidden fields that the CGI program `pass_ver.exe` places on Web page 2 that is then sent back to the user. When the user provides information on Web page 2 and presses the `<Submit>` button, the information that is contained in the hidden fields is returned to the `pass_ver.exe` CGI program and the CGI program recognizes the existence and verifies the contents of the hidden fields before continuing on with the required processing.

Contrast the scenario described above with one where a hacker attempts to gain access to your system by typing in the URL of Web page 2 from their browser. They would click on the `<Submit>` button to send the Web page to the `pass_ver.exe` CGI program. But, the `pass_ver.exe` CGI program would interrogate the contents of the hidden fields contained on this form and determine that there was nothing in them. Alas, it would then be able to rightfully conclude that the page was submitted by someone that had not initially logged onto the system via Web page 1.

Take a look at the sample HTML code below that was used to create the Web page seen in Figure 16–4.

```
<HTML>
<HEAD>
<TITLE>Access To Sensitive Information</TITLE>
```

```
</HEAD>
<BODY>
<FORM METHOD=POST ACTION="www.teleport.com\cgi-bin\empl_adj.exe">
ID Of Employee Whose Salary You Are Adjusting:
<INPUT NAME="empl_id" TYPE="" COLS=8 SIZE="8"><P>
Percentage Change In Monthly Pay:
<INPUT NAME="change_rate" TYPE="TEXT" COLS=6 SIZE="6"><P>
Increase <INPUT NAME="up_down" TYPE="RADIO">
Decrease <INPUT NAME="up_down" TYPE="RADIO"><P>
<INPUT NAME="Submit" TYPE="SUBMIT" VALUE="Submit">
<INPUT NAME="Reset" TYPE="RESET" VALUE="Reset">
<INPUT NAME="user_id" TYPE="HIDDEN">
<INPUT NAME="password" TYPE="HIDDEN">
</FORM>
</BODY>
</HTML>
```

You'll notice that what makes this snippet of HTML code different from the code used to generate Figure 16–2 is the following two lines:

```
<INPUT NAME="user_id" TYPE="HIDDEN">
<INPUT NAME="password" TYPE="HIDDEN">
```

These are hidden fields which, as the name implies, contain the user ID and password that are subsequently used to verify and determine the application state. Because these are protected fields, they can not be overtyped or modified by the user. The idea here is that the pass_ver.exe CGI program would transfer the values the user supplied in Figure 16–2 into the two hidden fields that are transmitted back to the user and as seen in Figure 16–4. When the user completes this Web page and presses the <Submit> button which in turn causes the empl_adj.exe CGI program to begin execution on the Web server, this program can retrieve, interrogate, and validate the values it receives in the user_id and password hidden fields, thus determining the application state. In this example, the application state is that the user had successfully entered required information as seen in Figure 16–2 so they are authorized to view and submit the screen seen in Figure 16–4.

This is all well and good, but what if an unauthorized person input the URL for the Web page that adjusts an employee's salary? The answer is that they would see the Web page exactly as you see it in Figure 16–4, and they may even try to input some values and press the <Submit> button. The problem for them will be when the empl_adj.exe CGI program executes this data and determines that there is nothing in the user_id and password hidden fields. It should be written to reject the transaction and log the user ID of the offending intruder.

Tip: As you know the contents of HTML pages, including hidden fields, can be seen in most commercial browsers. This could lead to a compromise of your carefully crafted application. To circumvent would-be intruders you could build or acquire an encryption/decryption interface to your CGI programs that keeps the data in the hidden fields safe.

Using Database Tables to Maintain State

Using Oracle 8 database tables to maintain state information has its advantages and disadvantages. One of the advantages is that a user's session activity information is maintained from one session to the next. By using hidden fields and not database tables, when the user disconnects from the Internet they lose their tracking capabilities. However, by using fields stored in an Oracle 8 database the information can be saved for later reuse.

An easily understood application of this is in an online shopping application where the user might be called away from their computer mid-way through the shopping activities. When they log on later it would be nice (and easy if you are using database tables to maintain state information) if you could display a partially completed order form on a Web page and ask them if they want to continue shopping or discard and start over. Such a screen is seen in Figure 16–5.

There is another advantage to using tables in an Oracle 8 database to maintain state information. That is by preprocessing user selections. For example, consider our online shopping catalog example. Wouldn't it be beneficial to the user to maintain a running tally of their purchases, as they select items and put them in their virtual shopping cart? You can do this easily using database tables to maintain state information—it is quite a bit more complex to do this using hidden fields.

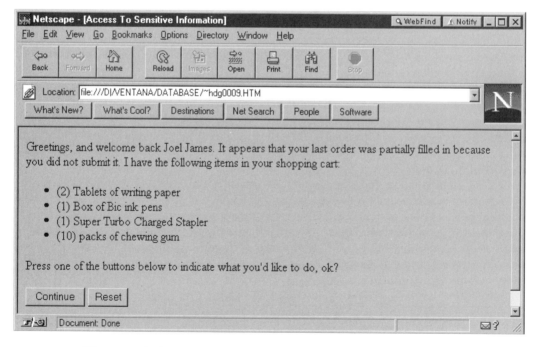

Figure 16–5   An example of a benefit of using database tables to maintain state.

Such advantages are not without disadvantages. One of the most significant is what to do with partial information that is left in your database tables. You could find your Oracle 8 tables quickly filling up with partial data that will never be completed.

Consider again the online shopping catalog example. What if the user browses through your catalog, selects a number of different items (which causes rows to be inserted in an Oracle 8 database table that keeps track of such things), and then exits your catalog without ever placing and finalizing the order? How do you know when they did this whether they intend not to finalize the order for the items or perhaps had their internet connection inadvertently terminated by their service provider? How long do you keep this information in your tables before a stored procedure deletes it? All of these questions need to be answered when you use database tables in this type of an application to maintain state information.

To maintain state information in an Oracle 8 database table is a relatively simple process. It is a process of determining what information needs to be retained to be able to provide adequate security while at the same time providing suitable functionality in your application. This may sound complex, but it is not. It is a simple process:

1. Design your Web pages to gather the information necessary to determine your applications state.

2. Build your CGI program to receive this information from the Web page and store it in an Oracle 8 database table in a format and manner that satisfies the business need.

3. Build a mechanism in your Web pages and CGI program to delete information stored in the Oracle 8 database when it is no longer needed to maintain state information.

4. Repeat from step 1 until the application is complete.

Using Persistent Cookies to Maintain State

Cookies are yet another mechanism that is used to maintain an application's state. A cookie is a small packet of data that a Web server stores on a Web client machine to keep track of certain application-specific information. There is a tremendous amount of hard disk space currently being taken up on Web servers with discussion groups dealing with the issue of "cookies." In this section, you'll learn about cookies, how they are used, and how they can be used to maintain an application's state. You can decide for yourself whether the use of cookies makes sense for your application.

What Is a Cookie?

As you can see in the definition above, a cookie is a small piece of data that is sent to your browser from a Web server. This data is accepted by your browser, checked for proper length, expiration date, path and domain, and then saved. A popular misconception is that cookies can contain viruses or executable computer code. This is untrue. A cookie can contain whatever data you want—but it cannot contain programs or viruses (which are actually programs). For example, in an application you could create a unique user ID for a visitor, save it as a cookie to that person's hard drive, and then that user would never have to enter his or her user ID again. Instead, his or her browser would read it from the cookie file and ship it to the Web server along with the requested URL.

Additionally, in a virtual mall environment as you've read about earlier in this chapter, virtual shopping carts can be created that will allow the browser to quit and 12 months later come back and still have the same products in their cart. Although you've seen how this is done with database tables, it could also be done (albeit less glamorously and less sophisticated) with cookies.

Tip: A cookie can be no more than 4,000 characters in length, which is certainly more than most applications require.

How Do Cookies Work?

If an application uses cookies, the use of those cookies is mostly accomplished by routines built into the user's browser by the developer of the browser. You, the developer, must add some components to your application that complete the cookie environment, but for the most part the necessary features are already present. Netscape Communications Corp. is the leading proponent for the use of cookies and has built superior functionality into its Navigator browser to handle cookies.

When a user clicks a link to a page, his or her browser checks the URL of the link against information that is in its cookie database. On a non-Macintosh machine, the name of this file is COOKIES.TXT. On a Macintosh machine, the name of this file is Magic-Cookie. An example of what the contents of this file looks like is seen in Figure 16–6.

If it has a cookie that matches the domain and path of the link that was requested, it will send the cookie to the server along with the request for the page. If it has no cookie for the requested URL, then processing continues as you've already learned by the server receiving the URL request. If no cookie exists for the requested URL but the Web page referenced by the URL needs to insert one in your cookie file, an entry in your cookie file will be created automatically for you.

Using the information seen in Figure 16–6, let's say that I request the URL `www.ma-tisse.net:80`. My browser would search the `cookies.txt` or `MagicCookie` file (if I had a Macintosh machine) and find an entry that matches this URL. So, along with the request for the page it would send the rest of the information that is in the `cookies.txt` or `MagicCookie` file for this URL.

Tip: You should know that when a Web server sends a cookie to a browser (translated: adds a line to the `cookies.txt` or `MagicCookie` file) no other browser can read the cookie other than the one that placed it.

How Can You Use Cookies?

Cookies can be used for a number of things. The three uses listed here are not meant to be conclusive. They may, however, give you some ideas on how you can use them in your applications.

Maintain Application State.   When a user logs in to your Web database application, and that application needs to verify the users login identification and password in a

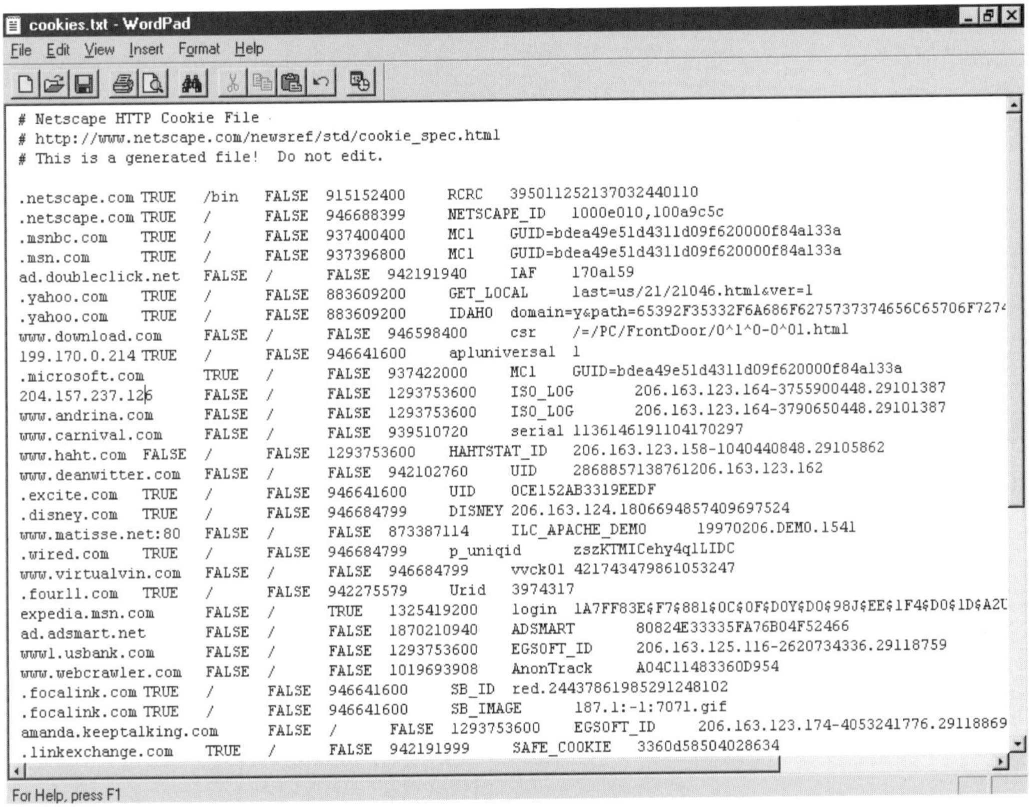

```
 cookies.txt - WordPad                                                    _ 8 X
File  Edit  View  Insert  Format  Help

  D  |ᵇ 🖫 | 🖨 🔍 | 🏚 | ¼ | 🖹 🖺 ⟲ | 🖳 |

# Netscape HTTP Cookie File
# http://www.netscape.com/newsref/std/cookie_spec.html
# This is a generated file!  Do not edit.

.netscape.com TRUE    /bin   FALSE  915152400    RCRC      395011252137032440110
.netscape.com TRUE    /      FALSE  946688399    NETSCAPE_ID  1000e010,100a9c5c
.msnbc.com    TRUE    /      FALSE  937400400    MC1       GUID=bdea49e51d4311d09f620000f84a133a
.msn.com      TRUE    /      FALSE  937396800    MC1       GUID=bdea49e51d4311d09f620000f84a133a
ad.doubleclick.net  FALSE  /      FALSE  942191940    IAF       170a159
.yahoo.com    TRUE    /      FALSE  883609200    GET_LOCAL  last=us/21/21046.html&ver=1
.yahoo.com    TRUE    /      FALSE  883609200    IDAHO     domain=y&path=65392F35332F6A686F6275737374656C65706F7272⟨
www.download.com    FALSE  /      FALSE  946598400    csr       /=/PC/FrontDoor/0^1^0-0^01.html
199.170.0.214 TRUE    /      FALSE  946641600    apluniversal 1
.microsoft.com        TRUE   /      FALSE  937422000    MC1       GUID=bdea49e51d4311d09f620000f84a133a
204.157.237.126      FALSE  /      FALSE  1293753600   ISO_LOG       206.163.123.164-3755900448.29101387
www.andrina.com      FALSE  /      FALSE  1293753600   ISO_LOG       206.163.123.164-3790650448.29101387
www.carnival.com      FALSE  /      FALSE  939510720    serial 1136146191104170297
www.haht.com  FALSE   /      FALSE  1293753600   HAHTSTAT_ID  206.163.123.158-1040440848.29105862
www.deanwitter.com   FALSE  /      FALSE  942102760    UID       2868857138761206.163.123.162
.excite.com   TRUE    /      FALSE  946641600    UID       0CE152AB3319EEDF
.disney.com   TRUE    /      FALSE  946684799    DISNEY 206.163.124.1806694857409697524
www.matisse.net:80   FALSE  /      FALSE  873387114    ILC_APACHE_DEMO     19970206.DEMO.1541
.wired.com    TRUE    /      FALSE  946684799    p_uniqid     zszKTMICehy4qlLIDC
www.virtualvin.com   FALSE  /      FALSE  946684799    vvck01 421743479861053247
.fourll.com   TRUE    /      FALSE  942275579    Urid      3974317
expedia.msn.com      FALSE  /      TRUE   1325419200   login  1A7FF83E$F7$881$0C$0F$D0Y$D0$98J$EE$1F4$D0$1D$A2U
ad.adsmart.net       FALSE  /      FALSE  1870210940   ADSMART       80824E33335FA76B04F52466
www1.usbank.com      FALSE  /      FALSE  1293753600   EGSOFT_ID     206.163.125.116-2620734336.29118759
www.webcrawler.com   FALSE  /      FALSE  1019693908   AnonTrack     A04C11483360D954
.focalink.com TRUE    /      FALSE  946641600    SB_ID  red.24437861985291248102
.focalink.com TRUE    /      FALSE  946641600    SB_IMAGE      187.1:-1:7071.gif
amanda.keeptalking.com         FALSE  /      FALSE  1293753600   EGSOFT_ID     206.163.123.174-4053241776.29118869
.linkexchange.com    TRUE    /      FALSE  942191999    SAFE_COOKIE  3360d58504028634

For Help, press F1
```

Figure 16–6   The contents of a COOKIES.TXT file.

CGI program, upon verification you could send a cookie to that machine indicating acceptance into your application. Then, and every time thereafter that that user accesses your site, when a secured URL is requested, the cookie data for your site as maintained in the `cookies.txt` or `MagicCookie` file will be sent to your Web server at the same time the URL request is sent. The CGI program executing on the Web server will verify the data passed to it from the cookie file for validity, accuracy, and currency.

Virtual Shopping Mall.   A virtual shopping mall system could be developed using cookies. These cookies would "remember" what a person wants to buy by recording what was placed in his or her virtual shopping carts. By doing this, if a person spends three hours ordering books at your site and suddenly has to get off the net, that person could quit the browser and return later (weeks, months, or even years if you're so bold!) and still have those items in a shopping basket—because they've been in that user's `cookies.txt` or `MagicCookie` file all along.

Site Personalization.   This is fast becoming one of the most frequently used ways that people are finding to employ the functionality of cookies. By using cookies to personalize a site, the information a user sees is tailored to that person's interests. Perhaps the best use of this that I've seen is what the folks at Yahoo have done. They have published a site where a user can request a slew of different types of information. Every time the user accesses that site again, a tailored virtual newspaper is displayed. As seen in Figure 16–7, the information is laid out nicely and the best part is it is tailored to what I want to read.

I can click on the bookmark to this site any time during the day and get up-to-date weather on the cities of my choosing, I can find out what the current price is on investments I'm tracking, and I can find out what the latest news is in the world of medicine, technology, or any of a number of other fields.

Additional Information on Cookies

You've read earlier in this section that most of the logistical work necessary to use cookies is provided for in the current implementation of the most popular browsers, namely Netscape Navigator, Mosaic, and Microsoft Internet Explorer. What is not discussed in this section is the actual syntax of the `cookies.txt` or `MagicCookie` file, nor the commands necessary to place or extract information into or from these files. This is an advanced component to CGI programs and therefore is not covered in detail in this chapter.

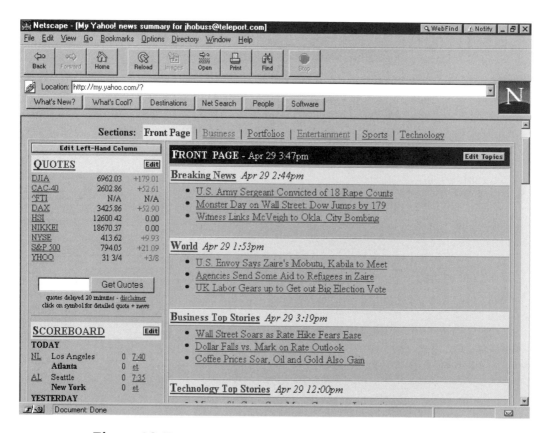

Figure 16–7   A personalized Web site that uses cookies.

There are, however, a number of books available that provide good coverage of this topic. The following are a few.

Title:	CGI Developer's Guide
Publisher:	Macmillan Computer Publishing
Author:	Eugene Kim
ISBN:	1-57-521087-8

Title:	CGI Programming Unleashed, 2nd edition
Publisher:	Macmillan Computer Publishing
Author:	Berlin
ISBN:	1-57-521151-3

Title:	CGI Programming in C & Perl
Publisher:	Addison Wesley Publishing Company
Author:	Thomas Boutell
ISBN:	0-20-142219-0

Moving On

In this chapter you learned how to manage Web database access and the application state by reading about and seeing the three most popular methods available for this, namely hidden fields on forms, database tables, and cookies.

In the next chapter you will read about some of the tips and tricks available to improve the performance of Web applications that use HTML to access databases. Additionally, you will read about some key topics to building maintainable Web database applications and actually doing maintenance on those applications.

CHAPTER 17

Improving Performance of Web Database Applications

I t is no longer enough to merely build a Web application that has database access that satisfies a business need. With ODBC and the tools available to integrate Web and database technologies, the "art" in Web database application development is no longer in marrying the two toolsets. Rather, the "art" lies in crafting an application that not only meets the business needs *but* is efficient as well.

This chapter describes some techniques you can use to build efficiency in your Web database applications. It is segmented into two major sections: Application Optimization and Database Optimization.

Application Optimization

In previous chapters you've read how Web database application, in many ways, is similar to a client/server application. I trust you've developed a sense and appreciation of this as you've read along. Hopefully you have enough information now to defend this position in a discussion with someone less enlightened than you who argues that they are two different things. If you're a believer in what I've said on this subject, then it may throw you for a loop, but one of the ways that a Web database application is *dissimilar* from a client/server application is in the way you can do many things to optimize the application components.

Optimizing a Web database application encompasses more things than just optimizing queries or indexing tables. There are a number of application-specific issues that directly affect the overall performance of your delivered application. In this section you'll learn about most of these.

Access Speeds

The speed in which users connect to your Web database application has a tremendous impact on the performance of that application. For example, suppose a page in your Web database application displays the results of a database query in which 72,000 bytes of information are transmitted. Recognizing that it doesn't matter that the percentage that these 72k bytes are data versus HTML code, you should know that a 72k byte return set is not a large amount of data for some queries.

Now, assume a user accessing this Web page is using a 14.4 kbps (kilo bits per second) modem. It will take approximately 40 seconds to transfer this data from your Web server to the user's browser. Assume another user accessing this page is using an ISDN line that is comprised of dual 64 kbps channels. It will take approximately 9 seconds to transfer the same amount of data from your Web server to this user's browser.

In the current environment of ISDN and T1 data lines, you should not assume that every person accessing your Web pages has access to high speed data lines and modems. If you build your application assuming the worst, then the people accessing your application at higher speeds than the worst scenario will be pleased with its performance.

CGI Programs

CGI programs cause a performance degradation in your application—there is no doubt about this. However, in many cases this is a degradation that you will just have to accept due to the functions you want to build into your application that can not be accomplished in HTML code. The amount of that degradation is very much dependent on the following items specific to CGI programs:

The language the CGI program is written in

The number of functions performed by the CGI program

The types of database access performed in the CGI program

The number of CGI programs

Recognizing that CGI programs have the potential of seriously degrading the overall performance of your application, you should design these with *at least as much* forethought and consideration as you would to the database access modules in a non-Web database application. I have emphasized the phrase *at least as much* because of the number of other issues that contribute to the performance (or lack thereof) of your application besides CGI programs. Fortunately, this is one of the things that you do have some control over.

Change

A Web site that changes is usually a Web site that enjoys repeat visitors. A number of tools are available now that automatically notify users when a Web site they are interested in changes so they can make a more informed decision about whether or not to revisit the site. It behooves you to consider this aspect when designing your Web site.

Occasionally a Web site designer will lose site of performance issues when designing how to integrate change into the Web site. This causes a degradation in the performance of the completed application as well as an impact in the productivity of the developer of the Web pages. Therefore, when designing a Web site and the pages on that site, consider the degree and frequency of change to the site after it goes online.

Tip: Most of the tools that scour the Web and report on changes to Web sites of interest do little more than read the contents of the <TITLE> . . . </TITLE> tag pair on the site's home page. Therefore, if you want to build what appears as a frequently changing site you may get away with doing little more than changing the contents of the <TITLE> . . . </TITLE> tag pair.

Development Suites

Development suites are highly productive tools to help you build Web database applications. Although I have not been able to dig up any sound and valid statistics (other than those provided by software vendors—but then again I did write "...sound and valid...") I believe there is about as much productivity improvement in using a development suite to build a Web database application as there is in using a development suite to build a non-Web database application.

Consider the time it takes to build a non-Web database application with a development suite tool like PowerBuilder versus the same application with a tool like C. In other than the rarest of circumstances a developer can build an application with PowerBuilder much quicker than the same application with C. So, too, can a Web database application developer create an application quicker using a development suite than if that person was using a straight programming language.

Having written the above, you should also know that an application written using a development suite may suffer negative performance impacts when it executes because of the nature of the development suite. For example, in the previous paragraph I compared writing an application in PowerBuilder versus C, noting that in most cases an application can be written quicker using PowerBuilder than C. However, in most cases the application written in C will execute quicker and be more responsive than the PowerBuilder application. Although there are many reasons for this that are outside of the scope of this book, you should understand that your use of a development suite to develop a Web database application may negatively affect the performance of that application when it is in production.

Functions in Web Pages

The number and types of functions you place in your Web pages directly affect their performance. For example, an HTML page that displays static text information performs much quicker than a dynamic HTML page that contains several complex operations to format and display a page.

In Chapter 13 you saw how you can retrieve the values that display in a dropdown list box on an HTML page from a database query. Although this type of function will result in an always-correct and current representation of the data in the dropdown list box, your application will perform much better if the values in the dropdown list box are static HTML values.

The trade-off in this example is how important is it to always retrieve the values that display in a dropdown list box from a database query and thus suffer the negative performance impact? If the information is very dynamic in nature and contains a small result set, then go ahead and populate the dropdown list box with a database query. However, if the information is a parts list that never changes (or is a 100 row result set—who wants to scroll through a 100 item list in a dropdown list box?), then save the CPU cycles and format the dropdown list box using static value.

Java Applets

There is no doubt about it—Java applets are wonderful additions to a Web database application that needs the functions supplied by them. However, you also know that it takes time to transfer the applet to the user's machine—and the larger the applet, the longer it takes to transfer. Therefore, use this feature sparingly if you are not sure the user has the applet on their machine.

Module Size

With the following exceptions, all the components of your Web database application must be downloaded to the user's machine *before* they can be viewed:

Web pages

Audio/visual/graphic components

Some components in an intranet application

Cookies (after the initial creation)

Result sets of database queries

Since very few people (and possibly even fewer of your users) have access to dedicated T1 or ISDN lines, the amount of time it takes to download the various application components should be evaluated carefully when designing the application. This is not to say that you should make no use of graphical elements in your application. On the contrary, as you've read in previous chapters, the effective use of multimedia components in your Web database application is very important to the acceptance of the application. However, you need to carefully balance the size of the modules that you create against their value once viewed in a user's browser.

Take the Web page viewed in Figure 17–1 as an example. This one page is 192,000 bytes. The majority of this space is taken by a Java applet and graphic *.GIF file that are both downloaded so that the flag seen in the middle of the page appears to be waving in the wind. With no intended lack of respect to the author of this page, this is an example of a module size that is unnecessarily large due to a graphic and applet that are not needed.

I would rather have seen a flag waving and would have preferred to have this page display in my browser in 15% of the time that it took than to have to wait 53 seconds for a graphic and an applet to download. This is especially true in that the page that this graphic appears on is a junction page—that is, it contains very little useful information other than to act as a router to other, more meaningful pages.

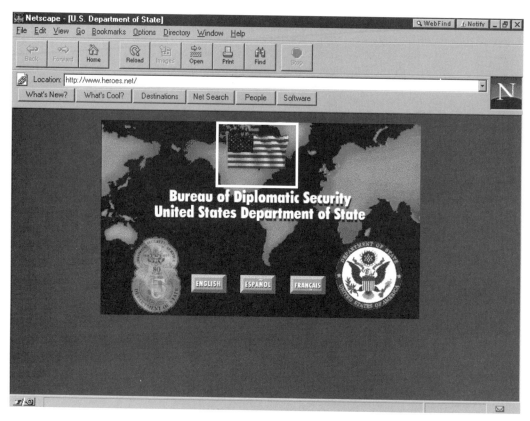

Figure 17-1   A very large module with very little added benefit.

Multimedia Components

As you know, multimedia application components such as *.AVI (movies), *.WAV (sounds), and *.JPG (graphic images) files take a very long time to transfer to a user's machine. For example, a 60-second *.AVI file that displays something like an interview with the company's CEO takes about 6,340,000 bytes. Over a 28.8 kbps modem this file would take about 29 minutes to download! That means the user would be waiting almost a half hour for a file to download to a machine so it could be viewed in a browser. This is the bad news.

The good news is that via MIME header types and companion applications that you learned about in Chapter 16, you do have the ability to embed multimedia components in your Web database applications. However, use this capability sparingly as the performance impacts are significant.

Number and Types of Graphics

For the same reason that you should limit the use of multimedia components in your Web database application, you should also limit the number of graphics. It is a conundrum that one of the things that transformed the Internet to the Web (graphics) is also one of the things that is contributing to the increasing negative performance on the Web.

Use graphics in your Web database applications enough as is necessary to communicate the message you want to send and make the pages appealing. But, use them frugally. At the same time you are weighing the value of placing graphics on your Web pages, consider the file type of the graphics you use.

For example, an image saved in *.GIF format occupies about ½ as much disk space (and therefore transfers to a user's browser about twice as fast) as the same image saved in *.PCX format. Although it is true that a file saved in *.PCX format will render crisper in a browser than the same file saved in *.GIF format, in most cases the difference is negligible. Consequently, consider the performance impacts associated with the time it takes to transfer a graphic image when deciding the type of graphics to use in your Web database application.

Searchability

Providing an appropriate search facility in your Web database application is almost a necessity—this is especially true as the number of pages in your Web site increases. You owe it to the people browsing your site to make as much information about your site available to them in as convenient a manner as possible. Searchability provides this.

In a Web database application, searchability takes on different proportions than in a non-Web database application. In addition to providing the ability to flexibly and efficiently find information contained in the Web pages on your site, you may also want to provide the ability to develop a custom search mechanism into your database. In either case, providing search engines in your Web application could negatively impact the performance of that application and therefore needs to be designed carefully.

Figure 17–2 is an example of how one company, Powell's Bookstore in Portland, Oregon, has built an efficient and effective search capability into its site. This company has tens of thousands of titles cross indexed and categorized in a number of different ways, yet, a search of all of the titles is very efficient. Take a look at that site and try out the search engine.

If you don't have a book or author to look for, use this book as a search target. But, don't be surprised if Powell's lists none available on their shelves as this book no doubt is a best seller.

Security

If your application requires the use of some sort of security mechanism (these are discussed in detail in Chapter 20), this ultimately adds an additional component to the application and therefore probably impacts the performance of the application. However, this does not *have* to be the case.

Even in applications where sensitive information such as social security numbers, phone numbers, e-mail addresses, credit card numbers, or phone numbers are transferred through Web pages, a well-designed application that uses a commercial product for handling of this information will have a negligible overall performance impact. Figure 17–3 shows how a Netscape browser informs users that it is handling a secure transaction—with a key in the lower left corner of the browser. If a transaction were not secure, the key would appear broken.

In addition to protecting the types of information described above, you will probably want to protect all the information contained in your databases from prying eyes.

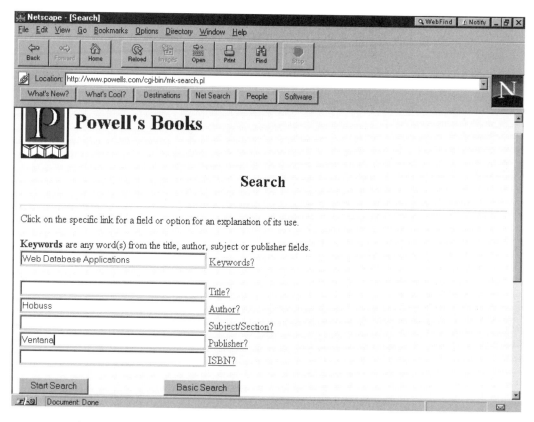

Figure 17-2   An example of a very efficient search capability.

Consult with your corporate auditors about this. However, the integrity of your database information is an important issue that may require varying levels of security built in the application and this may impact the overall performance of that application.

User-Input Validation

If your applications call for users inputting data on forms, you ought to provide at least the same level of on-the-fly input validation in your Web database applications as you would in a non-Web database application. As you know, HTML specifications provide for limited editing capabilities on user input. Therefore, you have a choice to make when it comes to user-input validation:

> Create your HTML pages using a scripting language that allows for user-input validation when the data is entered. Examples of these are JavaScript, Visual Basic, etc.

> Provide this capability via a CGI program running on the Web server and transmit any/all error back to the user to correct.

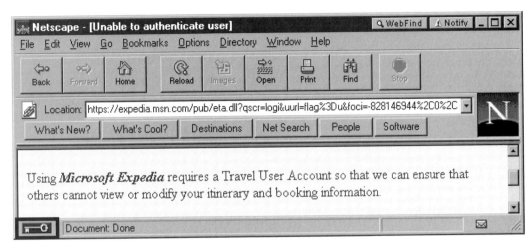

Figure 17-3   Security in an application does not have to impact performance.

The first choice provides for more direct user-input validation as it is done on the user's machine. However, it usually requires more of the developer's time to write the code to create the Web pages. The second choice allows you to create your Web pages quicker, but requires a CGI program for user-input validation. And, this validation is being done on the Web server. This means that in cases of error, the Web page must be transmitted from the user's machine to the Web server and back again for the user to correct errors.

Tip: If you decide to use a CGI program for user-input validation, make sure that every field that can accept user input is edited in one iteration of the CGI program. Very little is more irritating to a user than completing a lengthy form, pressing the <Submit> button, and then going through a series of iterations while the CGI program notifies them of one error at a time. If there are multiple errors on a form, show the user all the errors at one time.

Database Optimization

In the previous section you read about many of the things you can do at an application level to improve the performance of your Web application. In this section you'll read about ways that you can improve the performance of your Web database application that pertain specifically to the data and databases.

Ask Only for What You Need

On a database query, only fetch the rows and columns that you need to satisfy the intent of the query. Extracting unnecessary information negatively affects the performance of your application by:

The time it takes your RDBMS to extract the unnecessary data

The time it takes your CGI program to format the unnecessary data

The time it takes to transmit the unnecessary data from the Web server to your browser

The time it takes your user to search through the unnecessary data to view the relevant data

Create Temporary Tables for Users

If the data the users will be accessing from your Web database application supports it, you could create a temporary database accessed only by the Web database application. This makes sure that no other access will be made to the database that Web users are accessing and therefore maximizes its throughput.

Create Views on the Server and Link to Them

A view that your Web application links to gives you a powerful mechanism for controlling access to specified rows and columns. In this way you can control exactly what and how much information a Web database application can access.

Criteria Should Match Server Data Structure

The criteria you specify in a query should match the data structure on the server. This improves the efficiency of the query as Oracle does not need to translate the requested data structure into the actual data structure.

Consider the following query, where the rating type requested by the user is in a local variable rating_requested, and the movie's rating is stored in the table as movie_rating:

```
select * from movies
where :rating_requested =
  decode(movie_rating, 1, 'PG',
                       2, 'PG 13',
                       3, 'R',
                       4, 'NR')
```

The above is a badly written query because the query must check each row in the movies table to see if the requested rating matches. The following is an example of a correctly written query that extracts the same result set:

```
select * from movies
where movie_rating =
  decode(:rating_requested, 'PG', 1,
                            'PG 13', 2,
                            'R', 3,
                            'NR', 4)
```

Here the conversion of the movie rating is performed once, and assuming that the movie_rating column is properly indexed, will return the result set quickly.

Distributed Databases

An environment where the databases that a Web application uses are distributed provides the application developer with the opportunity to take advantage of a secure and accessible pool of data. It is relatively easy for a DBA to replicate a database from production databases and then use the replicated database for Web database application access. The replicated data can then be held in a secure location away from the production data that was used to create it.

Distributed databases also give the developer the ability of creating an environment where the location of the data is completely transparent to the user. As is the case in a client/server environment, where the users of data should have no knowledge or consideration to the actual location of data being accessed, so is the case with the user of a Web database application.

Do As Much Work on the Server as Possible

Just as most large client/server implementations have separate machines for database servers, print servers, file servers, etc., so should you consider having separate machines for your database server from what you are using for a Web server. The probability is that your Web server is much more powerful than the machines being used by the people accessing your application. Therefore, you will achieve increased performance in your application if you have the server do as much work as possible. This means, among other things, that you should consider formatting and laying out the result set of a database query in a CGI program running on the server as opposed to a Java program running on the client machine.

Taking this thought one step further, consider locating your Web server on a different machine than your database server. This will also cause an increase in the performance of your application as you can tune the Web server for handling Web requests and CGI processing while tuning your database server for handling data requests.

Do Not Use Dropdown List Boxes Based on Large Number of Records

Dropdown list boxes are wonderful additions to HTML forms and can really be a productivity aid in helping your users access pertinent information. A dropdown list box that includes 4 different movie ratings to choose from (PG, PG 13, R, NR) is a lot more useful and productive than a dropdown list box with the names of 10,000 movies that you might own.

In a situation where you really think it would aid the usefulness of your application to have a large result set display in a dropdown list box, it is better to replace this with a dialog box. In the dialog box the user can enter selection criteria (i.e., All movies that begin with the word "Beverly") and click on a `<Submit>` button which would then return a greatly reduced result set in the dropdown list box (i.e., Beverly Hills Cop, Beverly Hills Cop II, Beverly: The Maiden of Green Acres, etc.).

Error Handling

Should handling database errors in a Web database application be any different than how you'd handle database errors in a non-Web database application? The answer to this question is—probably not!

For example, attempting to insert a duplicate row should result in the same type of error message for both Web and non-Web applications. However, it is important to recognize that handling a duplicate row situation in a Web database application takes a lot longer to communicate to a user than in a non-Web database application. Therefore you should attempt to programmatically avoid error situations in a Web database application before encountering them when at all possible. It is frequently not good enough to trap the error and report it to the user in a Web database application—the objective should be to avoid the error in the first place.

Open Web Pages Without Retrieving Data

When you display a Web page, in other than the rarest of circumstances, you should have the user provide some sort of selection criteria prior to clicking on the <Submit> button. This accomplishes two objectives to improve the performance of your application:

It displays the original selection page quicker as this is frequently a static HTML page

It allows the user to specify selection criteria that improves the performance of the selection query and display of the result set from that query

State Data Stored in a Database

As you read in Chapter 17, it is possible (and sometimes desirable) to store state information about an application in a database. Although in most cases you can either use cookies or simply pass application information from Web page to Web page, it is sometimes necessary to use the database method to maintain information over multiple application sessions.

Because this state information is maintained in database, many more calls to a database are generated to retrieve and store this information. This causes incrementally increased application execution times. Therefore, use this technique sparingly and only when necessary.

Stored Procedures

Stored procedures are precompiled SQL programs that execute much quicker than native SQL and can be executed at any time. They are much the same in concept as subroutines. As discussed in Chapter 13, stored procedures add efficiency to your application in several ways.

Complex logic can be executed directly in the database, thereby reducing data transferred to the clients. Code is in parsed form decreasing execution time. Stored procedures exploit tight integration with the database engine, making references to data with less overhead. And, perhaps best of all, you can build a library of routine tasks that you can reuse in many applications.

Stored procedures also allow you to pass argument data to them. So, this means that you could have a stored procedure that is a query and you pass to it from your CGI program (that is accessed from a Web page) the selection criteria to use during the query.

This technique not only does the database query much quicker than a native SQL call but keeps you from having to write the actual query—you are executing it in the form of a stored procedure.

Moving On

In this chapter you learned some techniques that can be used to build efficiency in your Web database applications. These were categorized by Application Optimization and Database Optimization issues.

In Chapter 18 you will learn about some of the techniques useful in migrating data from enterprise data stores to server-based databases. Specifically you'll learn about the features in Oracle that facilitate this process, such as replication and synchronization. These are two components that are very important in a Web database application that accesses Oracle databases.

Section IV: Advanced Topics in Internet Database Publishing

CHAPTER 18

Migrating Data from Enterprise Data Stores to Server-Based Databases

In this chapter you will learn about some of the techniques used to migrate data from enterprise data stores to server-based Web databases. By migrate, I mean the process of moving data from one machine or Oracle 8 database to another machine or Oracle 8 database. Specifically you'll learn about the features in Oracle 8 that facilitate this process, such as replication.

You'll first read about how to determine what to migrate from your corporate databases to Web servers. This is not simply a process of "copying" a database from one location to another. Next, you'll learn about some of the features in Oracle 8 that you can incorporate in your overall data strategy that facilitate deployment of corporate databases to be accessed by Web applications. Finally, you will read about backup and recovery principles that you can apply to your Web databases.

What to Migrate

Before you decide what database objects to migrate (in the event some or all of the data used by your Web database application is currently available), you must decide whether or not you *should* migrate data. In other words, just because data that could be used by your Web database application currently exists doesn't mean that you *must* use it.

The following are some factors you should consider when deciding whether or not to use existing data within your Web database application:

- Access
- Location
- Response Time
- Security

The following sections explore each of these four items in detail.

Access

In this context the word access refers to the ways in which the data contained in the database is used. For example, if your Web database is to have read-only access, and if the data used by the Web database application currently exists in another Oracle 8 database that provides full read/write access, then it may be a wise decision to replicate the existing full-access database and create the read-only Web database. This approach yields the following advantages:

Separation of Data—Your Web Oracle 8 database is a separate file from the production database

Safety—Your production Oracle 8 database is isolated and unknown (to Web browsers) and therefore is in a safer environment

Response Time—Your production Oracle 8 database response time is not impacted by the hits required to support the Web application

Additionally, if your Web database application only requires a much smaller subset of a production database, then it may make better sense to extract and create the Web database on a pre-determined basis from the production database. If you decide to do this, there are a number of ways you can accomplish this, such as: Replication, Stored Procedures, and Scheduled Programs. Each of these techniques is accomplished in a different way, and you can learn how to do each of these actions in one of the book references I listed in Chapter 9.

Location

Because the Internet is global, the word location in this context means the location of the Oracle 8 database that is accessed by the Web application. The location of the Web server in relation to the database server is a much more important factor than the relation of the user to the Web server.

Therefore, in most cases a Web database is better located if it is geographically close to the Web server. This is because the time it takes to transmit data from the Web database server to the Web server sometimes is a function of the distance between the two devices. Certainly high-speed digital and satellite communications mitigate the effects of long-distance communications between a Web server and database. However, you should consider the physical location of the database accessed by a Web server when deciding whether or not to migrate data from a production database. If your production database is geographically distant from your Web server, this would favor the decision to migrate the production database to a Web database.

Response Time

The quality of the response time currently existing with your production database, coupled with the degradation added to this due to the hits it will take if it becomes a Web database, may result in a response time for all users that is not acceptable. If this is the case, you should consider migrating data off the production database to the Web server.

At the same time you're considering the impact of Web access on your production database, you should also consider the impact that the Web server software has on your production database server if you choose to have both the Web server and database server on the same physical machine. Most commercial Web servers require at least 16 MB of dedicated memory while 32 MB is preferred and 64 MB is ideal. If your production database server does not have these resources to spare and you don't want to or can't upgrade the machine, then you have little choice but to make another machine the Web server. Of course this Web server could access a production database on a different physical machine, and this is an option you should consider.

Security

Security is a significant consideration in the design of your Web database application. In fact, this is such a significant concern that Chapter 19 in this book is dedicated to this topic. To summarize Chapter 19 though and place it in the context of this section, the location of the database accessed by your Web application in relation to your production database is a serious matter. Although the current batch of security and firewall products offer adequate security for your data, you may nonetheless be uncomfortable deploying an application that offers access to corporate data from anyone with a Web browser.

If this describes your comfort level, then migrating the data used by the Web database application from a production database should make good sense to you. However, if you are comfortable with the protection offered by security routines and firewalls, then you should not let this consideration alone stop you from deciding to access your production databases from your Web application(s).

Determine What to Migrate

All right, you've read and understood the previous sections, and for whatever reason(s) you've decided to migrate data from production databases to create your Web databases. How do you decide what to migrate? That's the subject of this section.

ONLY MIGRATE THOSE DATABASE COMPONENTS NEEDED BY YOUR WEB APPLICATION. I've capitalized this point to highlight its significance. If you apply (and you should!) standard data modeling techniques to your Web application, and remove all redundant data in the tables and design the database with efficiency in mind, you should be assured of accomplishing this objective.

The application of data modeling processes is outside the scope of this book. However, there are many books currently available that will help you develop your skills in this area. Some of these are:

Title:	Conceptual Modeling Databases & Case Studies
Author:	P. Loucopoulos
Publisher:	John Wiley & Sons
ISBN:	6-00-084490-5

Title:	Database Modeling & Design, 2nd edition
Author:	T. Teorey
Publisher:	Morgan Kaufmann Publishers Inc
ISBN:	1-55-860294-1

Replication

Centrally stored databases are a thing of the past in corporate IS departments. No longer can most companies depend on one database or database-site to keep up with the high volume of database requests. With the advent of RDBMS products that support replication and continuing with the need for databases to support Web applications, more and more computer systems are becoming decentralized. The method most often used to accomplish this decentralization is replication. Database replication is defined as the method of creating synchronized copies of databases for use by different groups of users or over the Internet.

Replication allows you to centrally control access to your database while allowing free exchange of data between the components in the replicated databases. It also improves the accessibility of the data by bringing it closer to the user. By placing replicated databases on or near a Web server you can create a distributed environment with much less associated network traffic than if your Web database were located on a network server.

The Oracle 8 product includes some very nice features for replicating databases. The biggest advantage that I see with the replication facilities in Oracle 8 are that synchronization of the replicated databases is an automatic process—it occurs in the background without you having to do anything but set it up.

Unfortunately, the decision to replicate or not to replicate a database is rarely a clear and decisive issue. In most cases you will need to weigh the factors most important to you to make the correct decision. The following sections describe some of the situations that exist which would lead you to one decision over another.

When to Use Replication

Replication of corporate databases should be used in the following circumstances:

- When users are located in geographically different offices and they have need to access similar information.
- When a business need exists to provide 24-hour-per-day, 7-day-per-week access to database data. Such is certainly the case with a Web database application because of the perpetual nature of the Internet.

When Replication Should Not Be Used

There are a number of situations when replication should not be used. These are listed below.

- When the replicated database processes a large number of update transactions. Certainly a replicated database that processes more update transactions than the source database is not a practical use of replication. This is because as the transaction volume on a replicated database increases, so do the data conflicts increase between the source and replicated databases.

- When it is absolutely crucial that the data in the replicated database is current and up-to-date. Replicated database are current and up-to-date only when they are created and updated. As time progresses and update transactions are applied to the source database, the replicated database becomes increasingly out-of-date until the target database is automatically synchronized.

As I wrote earlier, the decision to use or not to use replication is rarely an easy one. My general inclination is to use replicated databases except when the data being accessed in the replicated database is required to be current.

Objects That Are Replicatable

All the following objects in an Oracle 8 database are replicatable:

- Tables
- Queries
- Forms
- Reports
- Macros
- Modules
- Stored Procedures

System objects are not replicatable. But, this should not be a consideration of yours in the design of a Web database application as you would probably never have the need to replicate system objects.

A good book that thoroughly covers database replication strategies and techniques in Oracle 8 is:

Title:	Oracle Unleashed
Author:	Numerous
Publisher:	Sam's Publishing
ISBN:	0-67-23087-2

Backup and Recovery

As you have read many times in previous chapters, a Web database is not much different from a non-Web database. The major distinction between the two is that a Web database is accessed from a CGI program that is executed from an HTML page. One of the areas where a Web database has a great deal in common with a non-Web database is in Backup and Recovery.

In this section you'll learn about the techniques and procedures you can use to back up a Web database and subsequently restore a backed up database. I think by the time you finish this section you'll agree that there is a lot of similarity here.

Backing Up a Web Database

The considerations that determine the frequency that a Web Oracle 8 database is backed up are the same as those that determine the frequency of non-Web Oracle 8 database backups. The one factor that most uniquely identifies a backup procedure for a Web Oracle 8 database is the need to keep that database available 24 hours per day, seven days per week.

If you are backing up a read-only Web Oracle 8 database, then the possibility of losing changes made to the database after the backup begins and before it finishes is inconsequential. However, if your Web application allows updates to a database, then the availability of the database while it is being backed up is an issue to be addressed. Fortunately, most of the backup and archival tools available, including the backup facility that ships with the Oracle 8 product, handle concurrent access of the database while it is being backed up. A concurrent access to a Web Oracle 8 database while it is being backed up is the same type of issue and is handled in the same way by commercial backup utilities.

Designing a Backup Strategy

How you design your backup strategy is largely a function of how often the data changes, how quickly you want to be able to recover in the case of a database failure, and how much risk you are willing to take to lose changes made to the database.

I recommend doing backups of the transaction log twice daily, with full backups once a week. The advantage to this strategy is that it allows you to recover quickly in the event of a failure while keeping the negative impacts caused by the backup processes to a minimum. The disadvantage to using this type of transaction log strategy is that it is more difficult to restore the server in the event of a failure.

Restoring a Web Database

Like Sybase System 11 and many other RDBMS products, Oracle 8 does not allow you to restore a database while the database is available to Web applications. This means that there's just no way around it—whenever you restore a Web database from a backup that database is unavailable to your Web application until the restore finishes.

If your Web application is accessing a database that is replicated, you are already familiar with the issue of availability while the databases are being synchronized. Whatever your synchronization frequency is, you are familiar with the issue of availability.

It's a hushed little secret on the Web, but Webmasters very rarely publish or disclose when their site is scheduled to be unavailable. I'm not really sure why it is, perhaps it has to do with the nature of the type of person that excels at being a Webmaster, but this is a guarded secret. When a Web site is unavailable and you receive a message similar to the one in Figure 18–1, you have no way of knowing for sure if the reason is because you've entered an invalid URL or that the Web site is currently unavailable.

What this means to you is that when you design your site's backup and restore procedures, recognize and accept that it is acceptable on the Web to have your site unavailable for short periods of time spaced quite a period of time apart, so long as the frequency or duration of these outages does not become excessive. Be careful though! I am not advocating that it is ok or acceptable to pull your Web databases off-line with no notification

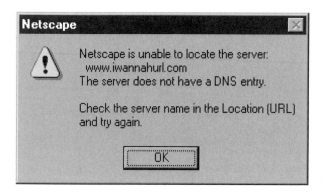

Figure 18–1   A Web site that
is unknown, or unavailable?

to your users. I am merely suggesting that current Net etiquette allows your site to be off-line a certain small percentage of time.

When you think about when to restore a Web Oracle 8 database, the considerations you'd apply to this decision are the same as you'd apply when determining whether or not to restore a non-Web Oracle 8 database. For example:

- Is the data corrupt, and if so, how corrupt is it? In other words, could the problem that makes you think about restoring the database be solved by deleting some records or perhaps re-indexing tables?

- What is the impact to the user of restoring a database? Unlike a backup which can be done while the database is being used, a restore makes the database unavailable while it is being restored.

- How much recovery work needs to be done once the database is restored? This has a lot to do with when the database was last backed up and how volatile the data in the database really is. Generally, the more volatile the data is that resides in a data-base, the more frequent the backups should be.

Tip: If a database that needs to be restored is replicated, you may be better off by simply deleting the old database and synchronizing it with the replicated database. This technique has the potential of supplying you with a current database without having to restore from a backup.

Moving On

This chapter presented some ideas and techniques you can use to migrate data from enterprise data stores to server-based Oracle 8 Web databases. You also learned about replication and the backup/restore processes.

In Chapter 19 you will learn about how you can implement security modules and procedures in your Web database application to safeguard your data. Hopefully, this material will give you the information you need to gain a level of comfort in the design and implementation of your Web database application.

CHAPTER 19

Using Firewalls and Security Components to Protect Your Data

If your Web application involved no interface whatsoever with your corporate data-bases, the security of your Web site and information in your Web server would be of high significance to you. If it is not, it should be. Now, add to this the capability that you build in to your application to access (and possibly update) your databases, and you have an issue that should get the hairs on the back of your neck bristling.

This chapter introduces you to the issues of Web-based security and describes some of the things that you can do to secure your Web applications, including your Web-accessible Oracle databases. It is not intended to be a primer on the subject. It is intended to introduce you to the issues and components that you need to be aware of to safeguard your investment in your Web site and your data.

Oracle Security

A good place to start this chapter is a quick review of the security available within Oracle. Then you can see how these security features can be applied in a Web database applica-tion.

There are two methods of security available in Oracle: database security that re-quires a password to access a database and user-level security that can be applied to data-base objects.

Your first line of defense for an Oracle database is a well-thought out password scheme. All the fine tuning you do to hone your security will be for naught if you neglect the following pointers.

- Tell the users that their passwords are secret. It is amazing to see how many users tape their passwords to their computer monitor for all to see. Stress that no one else should use the login with that user ID and password.

- Make sure that the passwords you set up aren't obvious. "PASSWORD" and the user ID aren't good choices for passwords.

- Consider having your Web front end encrypt the Oracle password so that it doesn't travel the Internet free for hackers to read.

- If you're using Oracle 8, check out the new password-aging feature. This will allow you to have the database automatically force the user to change her password at specified intervals.

Before going much further, this is a good point to learn the parts of Oracle's security scheme. In Oracle, the end users who log into the database are, amazingly enough known as *users*. Actions that a user can take in the database are called *privileges*. Privileges come in two types: *system* and *object*. System privileges give superuser-like capabilities (such as UPDATE ANY TABLE). You probably won't be using them in your Web application much. Object privileges give the ability to manipulate database objects (such as updating the data in a table). You'll be working most frequently with these privileges. Oracle provides five basic types of privileges for database objects, described in this table:

Privilege	Objects	Description
SELECT	tables, views	view all rows
INSERT	tables, views	add new rows
UPDATE	tables, views	change values in existing rows
DELETE	tables, views	remove rows
EXECUTE	stored procedures	run the stored procedure

Note that stored procedures only have one privilege associated with them: EXECUTE. If a user is granted EXECUTE privileges for a stored procedure, all the DML statements within the procedure are run with the privileges of the owner of that stored procedure. Explicit privileges for objects within the stored procedure are not necessary.

Roles are collections of privileges (either system or object or both) that define a particular function, or role. These roles are then assigned to users, who pick up the role's privileges. Roles can also be assigned to other roles, thereby making modular privilege definitions easier.

Assigning privileges to a role or user or giving a user a role's privileges is known as *granting*. Often, you'll hear of a user's or role's privileges referred to as *grants*. Just know that grants are the same thing as *privileges*.

In the following sections I'll show you how to:

- Add a new role via Oracle Security Manager
- Grant object privileges to a role
- Adjust the permissions for a user or role to Oracle database objects

Connecting to Security Manager

In Chapter 9, you learned how to use Security Manager to create a new user and how to give a password to that user. Recall that Security Manager can either be started in two ways:

From the Start Menu, click on Security Manager in the Enterprise Manager program group in your Start Menu

or

Select Security Manager from the Tools | Applications menu in the Enterprise Manager console.

Remember as well that using Security Manager requires logging in as a user with DBA privileges (such as SYSTEM). Since we granted DBA privileges to our WEBDEVEL user created in Chapter 8, we'll use WEBDEVEL in the examples here.

Once you've logged in, you're greeted with the main Security Manager screen: Adding a New Role

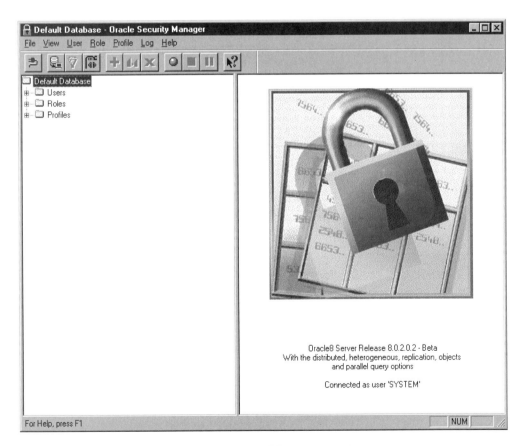

Figure 19–1 Security Manager main screen.

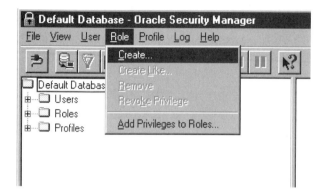

Figure 19–2 Creating a new role.

Creating a New Role Using Security Manager

It's quite simple to create a new role. To do so, click on `Role | Create . . . .`

Type in the role name and leave the Authentication type set to None. (The other authentication types are for more advanced security than is needed here.) Click on the `<Create>` button.

To see the role you just created, double-click on the `<Roles>` node, on the left side of the screen.

The `<Roles>` node expands to show all roles currently existing in the database, listed alphabetically. Note the new WEB_ORDER listed after the system-defined roles.

Figure 19–3 Naming a role.

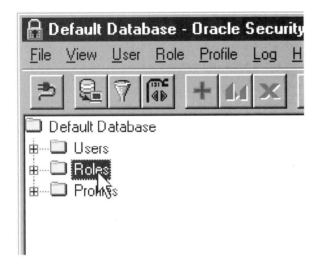

Figure 19–4   Expanding the Roles node.

Granting Object Privileges to a Role

Let's grant SELECT and UPDATE privilege on the table WEBDEVEL.PRICES for this example. First, click on Roles | Add Privileges to Roles.

Choose "Object Privileges" the Privilege Type dropdown box.

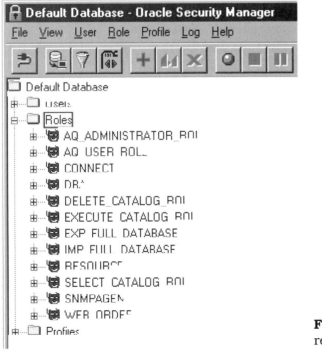

Figure 19–5   Displaying current roles.

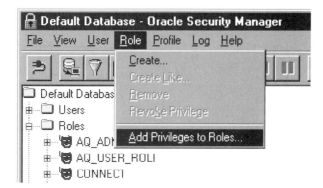

Figure 19–6 Adding Privileges to a Role.

The lower box will bring up a schema hierarchy. Double-click on the user WEB-DEVEL to expand the available objects.

Next, double-click on the Tables node to show WEBDEVEL's current list of tables.

Highlight the PRICES table and the desired object privileges, here SELECT and UP-DATE.

Now to apply this privilege, click on the Apply button.

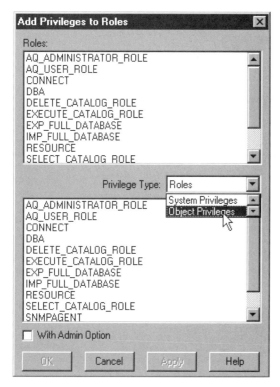

Figure 19–7 Choosing Object Privileges.

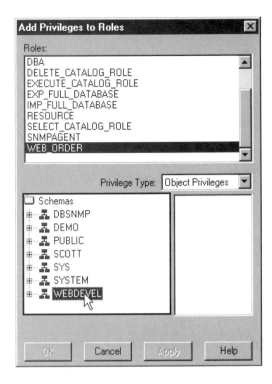

Figure 19–8 Expanding the WEB-DEVEL schema.

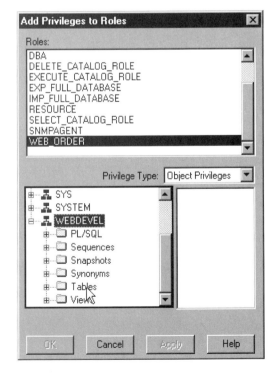

Figure 19–9 Expanding the Table node.

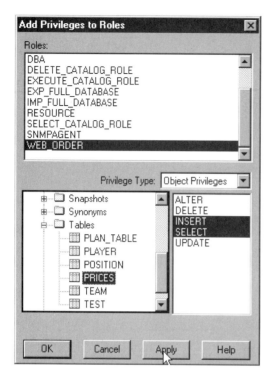

Figure 19–10 Choosing the Object and Object Privileges.

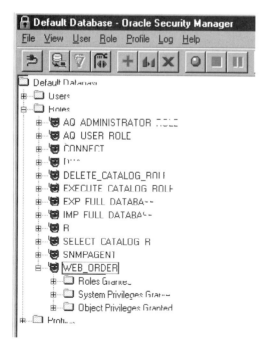

Figure 19–11 Applying the Object Privilege.

Viewing Privileges for a Role

We can now view the privileges we just granted using the Role hierarchy. If the Roles hierarchy is not expanded, double-click on the Roles node as shown in Figure 19–4. Then double-click on WEB_ORDER to expand its node. You'll see a list of three types of privileges: roles granted, system privileges granted, and object privileges granted to this role.

We want to see the object privileges granted to this role. Double-click on the "Object Privileges Granted" node. The two privileges we just granted appear.

Granting a Role to a User

Although you can grant object privileges directly to a user, granting privileges to a role makes a lot of sense. You can define the type of users of your application, create a role for each type of user, and then grant these roles to the end user IDs. This makes security maintenance a lot easier when it's time to add a new user. All you need to do is grant the appropriate role to the user. This section shows how to accomplish this task.

Let's suppose that you have a new user of your application, Joe Smith who will entry order through your Web application. You've already created a user ID JSMITH. To grant the WEB_ORDER role to Joe, follow these steps:

Choose the Users | Add Privileges to Users menu item.

Click on JSMITH in the upper window, and WEB_ORDER in the lower window. Then click on the <Apply> button. The role is now granted.

Don't click on the "With Admin Option" check box. This option not only grants Joe the WEB_ORDER role, but gives him the permission to grant it to other users.

Viewing Roles Granted to a User

Checking which roles are assigned to a user is similar to viewing privileges that have been granted to role.

To see Joe's roles, navigate down the User's hierarchy, first expanding the User's node, then the JSMITH node, and finally the Roles Granted node. Here we see that Joe has the CONNECT role, which allows him to log into the database and the WEB_ORDER role that we just granted to him.

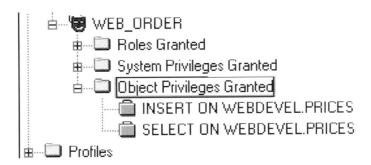

Figure 19–12   The Role WEB_ORDER's Privilege Nodes.

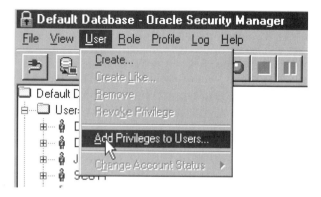

Figure 19–13 WEB_ORDER's Object Privileges.

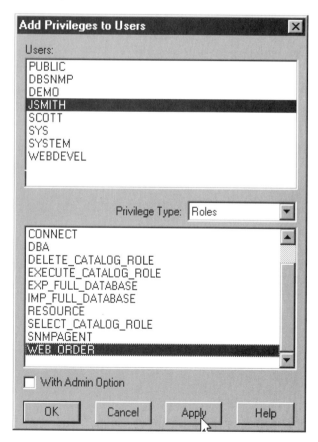

Figure 19–14 Adding a Privilege to a User.

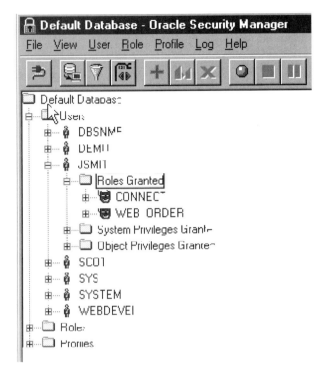

Figure 19–15   Viewing a User's Granted Roles.

Using SQL to Administer Database Security

Security Manager provides a useful interface for granting and viewing users and privileges. As you become more savvy with Oracle, however, you'll find that using SQL is more convenient for setting up your security system.

The actions in Security Manager above can also be accomplished with the following SQL statements:

```
CREATE ROLE role_name;
```
Create a role.

```
GRANT SELECT, INSERT, UPDATE, DELETE ON
table/view_name TO user/role_name;
```

Grant object privileges (choose one or several of the privileges) to a particular user or role.

```
GRANT EXECUTE ON stored_procedure_name TO user/role_name;
```
Grant permission to execute a stored procedure to a particular user or role.

```
GRANT role_name TO user_name/role_name;
```
Grant a role (and all of its privileges) to a user or another role.

You can also take away privileges using SQL:

```
DROP ROLE role_name;
```
Get rid of a role and all of its associated privileges. Any users who have this role granted to them will lose the role's privileges.

```
REVOKE SELECT, INSERT, UPDATE, DELETE ON table/view_name FROM
user_role_name;
```
Take away one or several object privileges from a user or role.

```
REVOKE EXECUTE ON stored_procedure_name FROM user_role_name;
```
Take away execute privileges on a stored procedure from a user or role.

```
REVOKE role_name FROM user/role_name;
```
Unassign a role and its associated privileges from a user or another role.

Using SQL to administer security allows you to create scripts that can be modified and rerun time and again. You can also use Security Manager to view any privilege you've assigned using a GRANT statement—a privilege is a privilege to Oracle no matter how it's created.

For more information on these statements, refer to the *Oracle Server SQL Reference* and the *Oracle Server Administrator's Guide*.

Oracle Security and Web Database Applications

You may be thinking to yourself that the discussion in the previous sections is pretty cool (hopefully), but are left wondering how this applies to you—a person needing to use Oracle databases in Web applications. I'll explain that now, and you'll be surprised how transparent the folks at Microsoft have made this.

As you may already know, whenever you access a database either directly or via ODBC, you must log-in to the database. Oracle is no different.

Depending on the programming language you use to build the CGI program that reads the Oracle database, the syntax for the connection parameters varies. However, and this is a universal truth, you must provide at least the following parameters when connecting to this type of database:

- Database Name
- Database Type
- Database Location
- User Name
- Password

With the first four items the Operating System can locate and find the correct database that the CGI program needs to access. With the last two items, the program gains whatever types of security access has been granted to the user that is attempting to log in.

Given this background, the scenario you could use to provide secure access to your Oracle databases from Web applications is as follows:

The database objects are created for the database that is accessed from the Web database application.

Roles are defined for the Oracle database that are specific to the privileges you wish to give to different levels of user.

Users are defined and assigned certain roles based on the types of access they need.

A translation database Table is written that is used to correlate a user name/password combination that someone enters on a Web page with a User ID/password combination as recorded in the Oracle database. The reason you do this and don't give Web users their User IDs and passwords as recorded in Oracle is the potential for a serious breach of security. It is always a good idea to implement a translation process as described here.

Write your HTML pages for your application, including the one that a user supplies their user ID and password on.

Write your CGI program that is called from the HTML page identified above. This CGI program will perform a user ID/password translation as identified two steps above, and then attempt to log in to the Oracle database needed for the application, based on the Oracle user ID and password.

If the log in to the Oracle database is successful, the application continues and the application state (the fact that this user has successfully logged in to the Oracle database) is maintained using one of the methods described in Chapter 16. If the log in was unsuccessful, a message is formatted and sent back to the user from the CGI program notifying the user of this.

Web Site Security—The Problem

Robert T. Morris. Do you remember his name? He's the Ivy league student who is best known as being the creator of the infamous Internet Worm that brought down about half of all the Internet servers in 1988. He was able to do this by making a small change in a C-based `sendmail` program that overflowed an internal buffer and altered a pointer stack to gain unauthorized access to the servers.

Hackers, denizens, thieves, scoundrels. Whatever you choose to call them, they are out there, right now, thousands of them. Their objective ranges from harmless access of unauthorized sites to blatant and catastrophic destruction of data files and, potentially, hardware. Looking at pictures of Robert T. Morris shortly after his arrest would not give you any indication of his actions. He looked (at least to me) like a typical college student. Robert T. Morris didn't look like a hacker, and chances are the one that breaches your security won't look like one either.

So, what can you do to prevent unauthorized access to your Web site? First, you should understand how all the components in a Web application fit together. Second, you should know what facilities are available to help to prevent unauthorized access to your site. Third, you should build a site that is as difficult to circumvent as possible. Fourth, trust no one.

The remaining sections in this chapter cover the first two items listed in the previous paragraph. How you build your site to be as difficult to circumvent as possible is largely dependent on what components you choose to buy and develop.

Security of Your Web Server

Most modern Web server software systems provide facilities for automatic directory listings. There are many benefits to this capability, but one of the problems with it is that users have free access to view all the documents in the Web document domain. In most situations, this is not a problem as most of the time you place documents in the domain directories so they can be accessed. But, what about files that are placed in these directories that don't have a specific URL that references them? Or, how about files that used to be accessed by Web pages but for whatever reason the links to them have been broken? You may think they are safe, but they are not. Anyone with access to the directories these files are in has the potential to access the files directly.

As a Webmaster, if this is included in your job description, you should monitor access to the various directories in your domain as well as where documents are located within the domain. Many companies go so far as to restrict who places files in domain directories to *only* the Webmaster to prevent the kind of situation described here.

Server-Side Includes

As you learned in Chapter 6, Server-Side Includes (SSIs) are HTML commands that reside on the Web server that are included in Web pages when they are constructed. They are typically used to hold HTML tag pairs that are common among a group of Web pages. Think of them as the HTML equivalent of subroutines. The upside of SSIs is that they save a lot of time coding HTML and offer you the ability to standardize the look and feel of certain components of Web pages. The downside risk of SSIs is the ability they give to hackers to cause an unwanted program to execute.

Consider the following SSI entry:

```
<STRONG><!-#exec cgi="/../cgi-bin/getURL"-></STRONG>
```

As you know, this code causes a server-based CGI program named getURL to execute. However, what if a hacker was able to gain access to the domain directory that contained this SSI and change it to read?

```
<STRONG><!-#exec cmd="rm -rf /"-></STRONG>
```

The result of this changed command executing would be that almost everything on your server's hard disk would be deleted. And, the damage would be done (potentially) long after the hacker made the change and left your site.

The solution to this occurring is to turn off the Web server's ability to process an "exec" form in an SSI. But, if you do this you also lose the potentially beneficial aspects of being able to do this. Unfortunately, this is not the only example of a difficult decision you'll have to make when you design the security components in your Web site.

Child Execution Privileges

It's possible to configure your Web server so that child processes are started as the user `root`. This, in most cases, is a good thing as it makes program component location simplified. However, it also presents a security problem. The problem is that a CGI program that executes with `root` privileges could effectively change the user ID of the user to another user ID, thus giving the changed-to user ID (i.e., a system administrator) access to your entire Web site. The solution to this is to ensure that your server configuration file is not configured to execute child processes as `root`.

Secure Sockets Layer (SSL)

SSL is a security protocol that provides Web applications with the ability to communicate with a user in a secure session. The SSL protocol resides between the HTTP and TCP/IP layers, thus providing a shield between the user and TCP/IP. SSL is a protocol that is currently in transition as different groups attempt to define how it should be implemented. It is not a standardized protocol as of this writing, although by year's-end 1997 it should be. Then you will see products introduced that give you the ability of handling the secure transmission of server authentication, data encryption, and message safeguarding.

CGI Security

CGI scripts are an especially dangerous Web application component in terms of security. Regardless of the quality of the code written in the CGI program, there exists the potential of hacker subversion of the CGI program. For example, consider the CGI program that sends a HTML form that includes an area for the user to enter text information. If the user enters text information as she or he should, then all is well. But, what if the user enters the following in this text box instead of text data?

```
<IMG SRC="/hidden/badimage.gif">
```

The result would create havoc on your Web server.

Another problem with CGI scripts is that sometimes they (or the libraries that are referenced from within the CGI scripts) contain code that is unwanted at least, and devastating in the extreme. There are many libraries and routines available off the Internet of common CGI routines. A large number of developers download and use these routines in the construction of their CGI programs or Web sites. In most cases, there's no problem with this. However, consider the following one line of code that could be embedded in a UNIX-based CGI script that is hundreds or even thousands of lines long:

```
rm -rf
```

This line of code (which incidentally would delete the files from your server's hard disk if it executed) sticks out here, because there is no code surrounding it. But, would you be able to spot it so easily if it were in the middle of a 5,000 line CGI script? This is an issue you need to consider when you download code and libraries from the Internet. It is also an issue to be considered when you are deciding to whom within your company you give access to the cgi-bin directory.

Tip: Never, never, never download and execute object code from the Internet or any source unless you are 100% sure that the code is stable and contains nothing it shouldn't.

Firewalls

Take a look at Figure 19–16. It shows a typical Web site architecture that uses a component called a "firewall" to provide another layer of security for your Web database applications. A firewall is a combination of hardware and/or software that only allows messages to pass through it that are recognized.

Firewalls are user-configurable components that separate a corporation's data from users accessing its Web pages in a Web application. An example of how a firewall could be used is to allow all outgoing communications (Web pages) but only allow incoming Internet e-mail communications. Or, in an example a little closer to the subject of this book, the firewall could be configured so that only a set of pre-authorized user IDs are allowed access to data within the firewall while screening out all others.

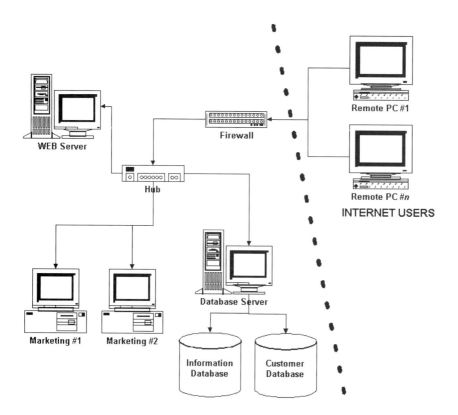

Figure 19–16   Web site architecture with firewall.

Other Resources

The following sections contain additional resources available to you if you want to learn more about Internet security.

Books on Security

Title: Intranet Firewalls: Planning & Implementing Your
              Network Security System
Author: Scott Fuller, Kevin Pagan
Publisher: Ventana
ISBN: 1-56-604506-1

Title: Net Security: Your Digital Doberman
Author: Michael Alexander
Publisher: Ventana
ISBN: 1-56-604518-5

Title: Internet Commerce
Author: Andrew Dahl and Leslie Lesnick
Publisher: Simon & Schuster
ISBN: 1-56-205496-1

Title: Special Edition Using Microsoft Commercial Internet System
Author: Peter Butler, Roy Cales, and Judy Petersen
Publisher: Que Books
ISBN: 0-78-971016-1

Title: Web Site Administrator's Survival Guide
Author: Jerry Ablan
Publisher: Sam's Net Publishing
ISBN: 1-57-521018-5

Title: Special Edition Using CGI
Author: Jeffry Dwight, Michael Erwin
Publisher: Que Books
ISBN: 0-78-970740-3

Useful URLs

A FAQ presented by Oxford University on firewalls and their use in Internet security

```
http://www.lib.ox.ac.uk/internet/news/faq/archive/firewalls-
faq.html
```

A WWW security FAQ presented by Compuserv

```
http://ourworld.compuserve.com/homepages/perthes/wwwsecur.
htm
```

Final Quarterly Report of the UKERNA Secure E-mail Project

```
http://www. tech.ukerna.ac.uk/pgp/secemail/q4.html
```

Internet Firewalls Frequently Asked Questions from the V-One Company.

```
http://www.v-one.com/pubs/fw-faq/faq.html
```

One of the places where hackers meet that contains a huge collection of hacking and related links.

```
http://incyberspace.com/woodstok/hack/
```

Moving On

This chapter introduced you to the features built in Oracle that allow you to add security to your database objects. You then learned how to use these features in conjunction with a Web deployment of your Oracle database application. This was followed with a description of some of the things you should be careful of with CGI programs. Finally, you read about the components of a secure Web database application.

In Chapter 20 you will see how to build a simple class registration Web database application. This chapter pulls together the preceding chapters and shows you how to build the class registration application, from start to finish.

CHAPTER 20

Designing an Internet Course Delivery System

The following text is set with a decorative drop cap "T".

This is the first of two "summation" chapters. It is a chapter that deals specifically with the issues relating to the analysis and design of a Web database application. In this chapter, you will take what was learned in the previous chapters and see how it is applied to the analysis and design of a Web database application.

There is very little information in this chapter that is specific to the actual construction of an Oracle 8 Web database application. That is saved for Chapter 21. I want to include a complete chapter on analysis and design issues for a couple of reasons:

- Without a solid effort in the analysis and design of an application, even a Web database application, the construction efforts and completed application will be at best minimally effective and at worst a disaster.

- Too often Web application developers forego effective analysis and design steps in favor of delivering the application quickly. This is a grave mistake. I want to show you how much critical and valuable information is acquired by performing analysis and design processes.

Recall that in Chapter 8 you learned how to design a Web database application. You will see how the information contained in that chapter, plus various other pieces of information from the other chapters in this book, are applied to the actual design of a Web database application. Then, in Chapter 21, this will be taken to the next logical step, which is the actual construction of a Web database application.

The material for this chapter first appeared as a series of articles in the May 1997 through August 1997 issues of "Exploring Sybase SQL Server." As a contributing editor for this magazine, I wrote these articles and they are condensed and reprinted here with permission by The Cobb Group.

Background

XYZ Systems, Inc. (a fictitious name for a real company and not to be confused with ABC Company, the fictitious organization profiled in Chapter 21) is a software vendor with 10 products in its inventory. Its education and training curriculum consists of more than 40 instructor-led courses. These courses cover XYZ's products, as well as other companies' products that complement its own. XYZ decided to adapt some of its existing instructor-led courses for delivery in a multimedia format over the Internet.

Management at XYZ had two principal objectives in mind when they funded this project. First, they wanted to give their customers Web access to high-quality training on some of XYZ's core technologies. Second, XYZ must be able to easily and cost-effectively administer the system by having the course administration system interface to existing customer and accounting information. This objective included the desire to build a system that was easy and inexpensive to maintain from a programming standpoint. Management didn't want to spend large amounts of money whenever its Web page changed.

The major architectural components and tools were

- *Oracle 8*—This is the DBMS for the existing customer and accounting systems.
- *PowerBuilder v5.0*—This tool is used to build the customer and accounting system. XYZ had the highest staff proficiency using this tool.
- *Macromedia Authorware*—The training coordinator saw this product demonstrated at a conference he attended and felt it held the potential to fill XYZ's need for a tool to develop training materials for delivery over the Net.
- *Existing Web Site*—XYZ had an existing Web site that was built and supported by a Web master. He believed that this would make an excellent platform from which to deliver the training courses.

The members of the project team felt that although it was not chic to do so, what they were building was a client/server system. Most of the characteristics of a client/server system were in place for the course-delivery system, namely:

- *Shared Resources*—The application would take advantage of shared resources.
- *Platform Independence*—Because of the Net delivery of the courses, it certainly was platform independent.
- *Message-Based Interface*—The system had to include a message-based interface.
- *Server Transparency*—Certainly the takers of the courses would have no need to know the location of the server; they only needed to know the URL (Universal Resource Locator) for XYZ.
- *Scalability*—Certainly the delivery of the courses would be scalable.

XYZ's Existing Environment

XYZ's architectural computing environment, including its Web site, looked similar to the diagram in Figure 20–1 at the beginning of the project. XYZ had just implemented an Ethernet 100 mbps network with NetBios communications. The database servers were on Pentium 200 MHz processor machines with 128 MB of EDO memory running Windows NT version 4.0. The prime DB server was located in the company headquarters in California and was replicated at six sites—three in the United States and three in other countries.

Here's the basic architecture of the client workstation side as well as XYZ's server side. The Web server was also a Pentium 200 MHz processor with 64 MB of EDO memory running Windows NT version 4.0. The server was also located in the company's headquarters. Each client machine attached to the network was configured with a Pentium 75 MHz processor with 16 MB of EDO memory running Windows 95.

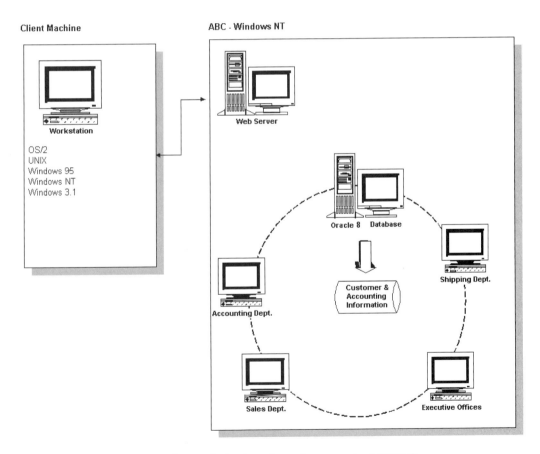

Figure 20–1   The architectural environment at XYZ Company.

Project Analysis

XYZ decided to initiate the project with a four-person project assessment team. The initial four-person team was comprised of

- Project leader
- Database administrator
- Training coordinator
- Webmaster

This group was responsible for developing a Joint Requirements Planning (JRP) document. The JRP's purpose would be to:

- Identify the team members and their responsibilities
- Establish the business objectives of the project
- Establish the Rapid Application Development (RAD) approach to be used

JRP Documents

The JRP team published the JRP-Phase I document, which was used to build the project team and to document the developers' perspective of management's expectations for the project. In the JRP-Phase II document, the deliverable would be the primary source document used for the design of the system.

JRP-Phase I.   For the sake of brevity, I've paraphrased the JRP-Phase I document here. The following are the major sections in this document.

Defining Roles and Responsibilities.   Project team members' roles and responsibilities were identified as follows:

- *Project leader*—Leads the project through completion and resolves any issues arising that may impede the team's progress. The PL had first-line responsibility for the success of the project.
- *Database administrator*—Identifies and resolves any database-dependent issues.
- *Training coordinator*—Determines which courses will be delivered over the Net and represents the Training Department's interests.
- *Webmaster*—Designs and builds the Web pages that facilitate the course delivery.
- *Curricula developer*—Designs and builds the actual courses to be delivered over the Net.
- *Network engineer*—Identifies and resolves any network-dependent issues.

Establishing Business Objectives.   JRP identified the business objectives of the system to be:

- Achieve profitability within nine months after going online.
- Identify four products initially on which to develop courses, followed by four more products within six months.

- Use as much of XYZ's existing architecture and toolset as possible to build this system.
- Design and build the system to require little effort and expense to maintain.

Establishing the RAD Approach. The RAD approach means the definition of the specific method used to conduct a Rapid Application Development activity in connection with the analysis and design phases of a project. JRP established the RAD approach as follows:

- Use the existing Data Dictionary for the tables in the customer and accounting database.
- The project probably wouldn't require data modeling as the data could be used as is. However, XYZ wouldn't know this for sure until later in the project.
- Use PowerBuilder as the GUI painter, application development tool, and prototyping tool.
- Wouldn't use an automated testing tool. XYZ didn't have one and didn't feel one was justified for this project.

Trouble with the JRP Phase I. Upon submission of the JRP Phase I document, management agreed to all of the items in the three major sections, with one exception. They wanted to develop and deliver Internet courses on all 10 of the company's products when the system went online; they didn't want to take the phased approach. In addition, they didn't want to extend the delivery date of the system.

When the Project Leader met with management to resolve this matter, she learned that management had a false expectation for the system. Management believed that if they made the system available only in the western region HQ, and not the rest of the United States or the world, that the time saved could be spent writing the additional course materials. Although the Project Leader didn't correlate the two activities (replication of data with the writing of course materials), she did get management to agree to reconsider this position until after the JRP Phase II document was produced. Her thinking was that the various matrices produced in Phase II would disclose the data dependencies and could be used to either support or refute management's expectations.

JRP-Phase II. The second phase of the JRP activity took three weeks to accomplish and was much more complex than Phase I. Whereas Phase I was accomplished in a couple of meetings, Phase II required a more thorough analysis of the existing network and data structures, as well as the proposed network and data structures.

Experienced in the analysis, design, and construction of client/server applications, the Project Leader determined that the deliverables from the JRP Phase II would be:

- CRUD diagram—CRUD stands for Create, Read, Update, Delete
- Entity/Location matrix
- Entity/Volume matrix
- Action/Frequency matrix

For the sake of brevity, I won't include in this chapter the pre-existing matrices (from the original customer and accounting database creation project) the project team referenced. However, I will discuss the similarities and discrepancies between the existing and new matrices in the following sections.

CRUD diagram. The CRUD (Create, Read, Update, Delete) diagram needed considerable modification from what had been created when the customer and accounting database was first built. Although the CRUD created (and referenced during this project) when the database was first built was specific to accounting and customer information only, the PL believed that a CRUD specific to the new functions would be more beneficial and less disruptive to their short project time frames.

The CRUD diagram that was created is shown in the table below. It included functions that people accessing the system would use, regardless of whether the action touched on the existing database.

Entity —-> Function V	Web Master	Student	Training Manager	Training Devlpr	Sales	Shipping	Execs
Register/ Take Course		C					
Sell/Record Learning Credits					CRUD	CRUD	
Ship Learning Credit Coupons					CRUD	CRUD	
Adjust Course List	CRUD		CRUD	CRU			
Produce/ View Status		C	R	R	CR	CRU	R
Adjust Learn- ing Credits			CRUD		CRUD	CRU	
Build/Update Web Pages	CRUD						

C = Create, R = Read, U = Update, D = Delete

The CRUD diagram includes functions that all people accessing the system would use.

Entity/Location Matrix. The purpose of the Entity/Location matrix (shown in the table below) is to determine, at a very early stage, the consequences and impacts of the application distribution. Because this project entailed adding functions to an existing database, the project team created their Entity/Location matrix ignoring the fact that current data is accessed in the customer and accounting database. They wanted to make sure that what was already developed wouldn't prejudice their thoughts on what needed to be developed.

Location--> Entity V	Western Region HQ	Northern Region	Southern Region	Eastern Region	Europe	Asia	South America
Web Master	AU	AU	AU	AU	AU	AU	AU
Student	SU	SU	SU	SU	SU	SU	SU
Training Manager	SU	SR	SR	SR	SR	SR	SR
Training Developer	SU	AU	AU	AU	AU	AU	AU
Sales	AU	AU	AU	AU	AU	AU	AU
Shipping	AU	AU	AU	AU	AU	AU	AU
Executives	AR	AR	AR	AR	AR	AR	AR

A = Access ALL Occurrences of Data, R = Read, S = Access SAME Occurrences of Data, U = Update, D = Access DIFFERENT Subset of Data

This Entity/Location matrix developed by the XYZ project team proved that the type of access needed in each location was identical.

What the project team discovered when comparing this matrix against the in-place matrix for the existing customer and accounting database is that, although some of the entities accessing the data are different, the type of access needed in each location was identical. This was a crucial finding in terms of project deadlines and management's expectations for the scope of the project. It meant that XYZ wouldn't need to add any data elements.

Entity/Volume Matrix.   The purpose of the Entity/Volume matrix is to determine the data distribution and server sizing issues. The project team discovered several key items when they plotted their data on the Entity/Volume matrix, which is shown in the table below.

First, servers in the western, northern, and southern regions would experience the greatest volume and growth impacts. Second, sales and shipping would be the two entities in the company that had the greatest volume. Third, student access and need for data would be somewhat consistent across all sites. The project team would use this information in the next phase of the project to make some recommendations regarding architectural modifications.

Location -> Entity V	Western Region HQ		Northern Region		Southern Region		Eastern Region		Europe		Asia		South America	
Volume/ Growth -->	V	G	V	G	V	G	V	G	V	G	V	G	V	G
Web Master	5	80	5	80	10	40	5	10	5	10	5	10	5	10
Student	30	75	45	90	50	30	40	20	40	10	40	5	45	5
Training Manager	10	10	15	20	25	10	35	5	35	0	35	0	20	5
Training Developer	10	5	10	5	10	5	10	5	10	5	10	5	10	5
Sales	80	40	90	40	20	5	20	3	5	10	25	30	10	15
Shipping	90	30	30	30	25	30	10	25	5	5	25	20	20	5
Executives	1	0	0	0	0	0	0	0	0	0	0	0	0	0

V = Volume in 1,000s, G = Growth in %/Qtr

Action/Frequency Matrix. The Action/Frequency matrix is used to determine the network loading considerations. XYZ used this matrix, as seen in the table below, to help determine the type of processing demand the new system will make on the network.

The data in the Action/Frequency matrix correlated with the data in the Entity/Volume matrix. Additionally, the project team was pleased to see that the data in the Action/Frequency matrix correlated with the data in the Entity/Volume matrix. Whereas the Entity/Volume matrix showed that the western, northern, and southern regions had the greatest projected volume of data for each entity, these same regions also had the greatest projected frequency for certain actions.

Management on Track

Do you recall the wrench that management threw in the works at the end of Phase I, when they wanted to implement the delivered system with all the courses at once? Their thinking was that the time saved in not promoting the data to all database server locations could be used to write course materials. With the Entity/Location and Entity/Volume matrices, management saw that data replication and synchronization was already occurring in the regional offices and that very little (if any) time could be shaved from the project by implementing in the HQ offices initially. Having reconciled this difficulty, the project leader secured approval from management to proceed into the next phase of the project, the design of the new system.

Location -> Action V	Western Region HQ		Northern Region		Southern Region		Eastern Region		Europe		Asia		South America	
Volume/ Growth —>	F	G	F	G	F	G	F	G	F	G	F	G	F	G
Register/ Take Course	80	80	40	80	50	40	25	20	15	10	15	10	15	10
Sell/Record Learning Credits	80	75	50	75	50	60	45	50	50	10	5	10	5	10
Ship Learning Credit Coupons	80	10	0	0	0	0	0	0	0	0	0	0	0	0
Adjust Course List	20	50	0	0	0	0	0	0	0	0	0	0	0	0
Product/ View Status	30	30	30	20	30	20	15	10	10	5	10	5	10	5
Adjust Learning Credits	5	30	30	30	10	40	5	20	10	30	15	10	25	10
Build/ Update Web Pages	80	80	10	10	0	0	0	0	0	0	0	0	0	0

F = Frequency in 1,000s, G = Growth in %/Qtr

The Design Process Described

The Project Team quickly determined that the normal System Development Life Cycle that some members of the team were quite comfortable with would not work for this project. The reason was that they believed that although there would be a clearly recognizable date at which the system would be made available to users (aka "put in to production"), that this would be little more than a phase that immediately preceded another development phase. This "iterative" aspect to the application led them to believe that a more refined development methodology was required. What they decided on was a hybrid development process.

With this release cycle as a model, the Project Team determined the following about the Design steps in their project:

Release Cycle

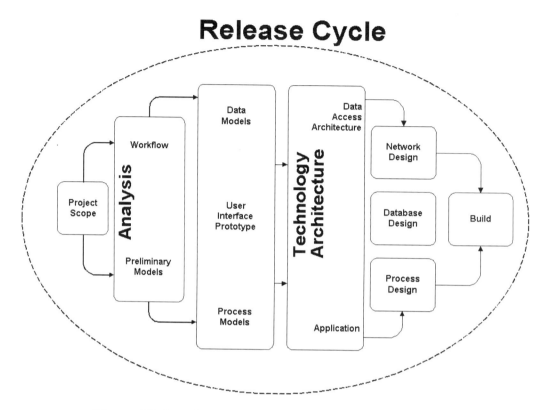

Figure 20–2   The design process used by XYZ Software.

- Between the data models developed when the Customer and Accounting database was initially built and the various matrices developed during the analysis phase of the project, they had all the data models they needed to continue with the design and construction of the application

- They would forego the User Interface Prototype step due to the simple fact that the interface requirements were known at the time

- The Data Access Architecture and Application Architecture were both already known due to the existing Web presence that XYZ had and the Customer and Accounting database

- The Network Engineer, who was a member of the Project Team, determined that there was no need to perform a rigorous Network Design due to the results of the Entity/Location and Entity/Volume matrices that were produced during the analysis phase

- The Database Administrator concluded what had been suspected from the beginning of this project—there was no need to perform a Database Design process in the

Design phase of the project because the existing Customer and Accounting database met the needs of the training application

What was remaining to be done in the Design phase of the project was to do a Process Design. The results of the Project Team's efforts in this regard are described in the following section.

Process Design

The project team used, as a starting point, the functions listed in the CRUD diagram to develop their process design. The CRUD diagram produced during the analysis phase of the project is shown below.

Entity --> Function V	Web Master	Student	Training Manager	Training Devlpr	Sales	Shipping	Execs
Register/ Take Course		C					
Sell/Record Learning Credits					CRUD	CRUD	
Ship Learning Credit Coupons					CRUD	CRUD	
Adjust Course List	CRUD		CRUD	CRU			
Produce/ View Status		C	R	R	CR	CRU	R
Adjust Learning Credits			CRUD		CRUD	CRU	
Build/ Update Web Pages	CRUD						

C = Create, R=Read, U=Update, D=Delete

What the Project Team decided in terms of the design of their application is described below in a manner specific to each function.

Register for Course. A User accesses the company's Uniform Resource Locator (URL) for the online course registration system. This was called the *Account Sign-On Screen*. They input their company name, their name, and their company's confidential support number into the *Account Sign-On* Web page—and press <Enter> to transmit the request. The request is received by the server at company headquarters and a query is made to the database to perform the following:

- Verify that the Company name and support number entered are valid

- Extract and display in a Web page sent back to the student the number of credits available (these are the number of credits purchased by the company, less any credits that may have already been used)

- Assuming the user input a valid company name/support number combination and the company has support credits available, the Web page displayed to the user lists the number of credits available for use and the courses available to take. This is called the *Support Credit Confirmation Screen*. The course list also lists the number of credits that will be charged to the company's account if the user follows through and begins a course. If the user input an invalid company name/support number combination, or if there were no support credits available to the company, the server will format and transmit an *Invalid Company/Support Number screen*.

- The user selects a course from the list and presses `<Enter>`. The server receives this Web page and sends back to the user a *Course Request Confirmation Screen* (Web page), which informs the user that if they press `<Proceed>` their company's account will be decremented the number of support credits the requested course costs. The user can either press `<Proceed>` at this point or `<Cancel>`. If they press `<Cancel>`, the Server will display the *Support Credit Confirmation Screen*. If they press `<Proceed>`, the company's support credits are decremented by the number of credits the student has just registered for costs, and the course registration process is considered complete.

Take Course.   When a student begins taking a course, the server will copy two entities to the student's machine:

- A "cookie" to help keep track of the progress the student makes through the course

- A Java applet that will actually play the multimedia files that constitute the training course

---

As you know, a "cookie" is a mechanism for maintaining application information across multiple sessions. The Web is a "stateless" environment, which means from the transmission of one Web page to the next, each is considered discrete and totally independent actions. This non-conversational nature of the Web means that programmers must manually build a mechanism to keep track of what actions were performed in a series of user-initiated activities to be able to determine what action is yet to be performed. "Cookies," or small files that record the stage of execution of an application, are that mechanism.

Once these two files are copied to the student's machine, the server sends a Web page named *Course Delivery Screen* to the student's machine. The purpose of this HTML page is to do the following:

- Receive the multimedia file that contains the actual course the student requested to take
- Initiate the execution of the Java applet that plays the multimedia course

The architecture of the courses is not described here, but are exactly the same as a multimedia course that would be taken from a CD-ROM with one exception—the courses developed by XYZ were very small in comparison to allow quick transmission to the student's machine. Once the course is completed, the Java applet transmits a HTML page to the server indicating that the course is complete. The server recognizes this HTML page and formats and transmits a *Course Completion screen* to the user. At the bottom of this screen the student is given a choice to either sign-off or register to take another course. If they click on the <Sign-Off> button, the server will format and send a *Have a Good Day* screen. If they press the <Re-register> button, the server will format and retransmit the *Support Credit Confirmation Screen*. This completes the process of taking a course.

Sell/Record Learning Support Credits. A Learning Support Credit (LSC) is a prepaid educational credit which, when redeemed, allows someone to take a specified number of hours of training. Product Support Credits (PSC) are prepaid technical supports which, when redeemed, allow the caller to receive technical support on the products they have purchased from XYZ. When a sales person sells LSCs, they input this information in exactly the same manner they have been using to input PSCs. This is an existing process that requires no modification in terms of application or architecture components.

XYZ sells PSCs at a predetermined rate. These PSCs are redeemed at a given ratio each time an employee from a customer calls the Product Support department for help with a problem. XYZ had a task of determining the ratio of PSCs to LSCs. Once this was done, the project team was able to fully utilize the application components already in existence.

Ship LSCs. Again, because of XYZ's already existing PSC processes, the shipping of LSCs was a very simple process to design. At XYZ, a Visual Basic program scheduled to run nightly produced a report that was routed to the printer in the Shipping Department. The Visual Basic program queried the database and extracted the number of credits added during the day, and placed this information on the report in the form of a confirmation certificate. This report was formatted in such a way that it could be folded, inserted into an envelope, and mailed to the addressee, who was the purchaser of the PSCs.

The only change required in this process was in the way the Visual Basic program formatted the report. A code on the database would provide a legend that could be interpreted to indicate whether the credits purchased during the day were for LSCs or PSCs. The Visual Basic program would place the correct verbiage on the report.

Adjust Course List. XYZ had been offering instructor led training courses for a long time before they decided to begin offering Web-delivered courses. To support the administration of their instructor-led courses, XYZ had built a couple of tables in their Customer and Accounting database. These are seen in Figure 20–3 as the ORDER_DE-TAIL and COURSE tables.

As you can see from this structure, all the information necessary to accommodate Web initiated account verification and delivery of training exists in the four tables. The "Course_ID" column in the COURSE table is coded to reflect whether or not the course is an instructor-led or Web-delivered course.

With this existing database structure, there was no modification required to handle the adjustment of course lists that would occur from time to time specific to Web-delivered courses.

Produce/View Status. This is yet another process that required very little modification to accommodate Web-delivered training courses. The Project Team identified two areas that required slight modification:

- A Customer Account status report, which was executed on a nightly basis via a scheduled procedure, required an additional detail line to show the number of LSCs purchased, used, and available, in addition to the detail line that showed the number of PSCs purchased, used, and available.
- A Customer Account status window needed modification to show the number of LSCs purchased, used, and available, in addition to the detail line that showed the number of PSCs purchased, used, and available.

Other than these two modifications, there was nothing else identified by the Project Team that needed to be addressed to handle this function.

Adjust Learning Credits. This was a function that the Project Team identified would require a lot of "procedural" change and a little bit of coding.

There was very little need to ever adjust PSCs once they were entered into the database, so there was not an identified process that the Project Team could utilize. But, they

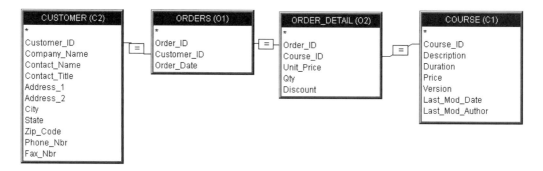

Figure 20–3 The customer and accounting information database.

did recognize that because of the unstable nature of the Web, a student might find their connection to XYZ's server would break after they started taking a course and before they were finished. This would create a situation where the student's employer would have already had their LSCs decremented and the student would not have finished taking the course.

The procedural change involved receiving notification from the student or his/her employer that an adjustment was necessary and verifying the validity of the assertion. Once the claim was substantiated, the sales person fielding the call would use a new window that would be developed to adjust LSCs. This would be a PowerBuilder window that would allow the sales person to manually adjust the number of LSCs available to a client company.

By designing such a process, the Project Team felt that this action should initiate two processes:

- An audit record of the transaction so that accountability for adjusting a customer's LSCs could be maintained.
- A confirmation certificate would be automatically generated from a Visual Basic program and mailed to the customer notifying them of this adjustment. The Project Team identified that this would entail a minor adjustment to the Visual Basic program that was already written to produce PSC and LSC confirmation certificates.

Although management at XYZ recognized the validity of these actions, they rejected including both of them in the initial construction of the Web application. Their thought was that this could be a "Phase II" activity.

Build/Update Web Pages.   This was a process that required no changes to the existing architecture, but would constitute the majority of the development work to build this application. To highlight the development activities, the following work was identified by the Project Team:

- Create the Web Pages Used to Support the Delivery of Training
- Account Sign-On Screen
- Support Credit Confirmation Screen
- Invalid Company/Support Number Screen
- Course Request Confirmation Screen
- Support Credit Confirmation Screen
- Course Delivery Screen
- Course Completion Screen
- Have a Good Day Screen
- Other Development Efforts
- Use of "cookie" to keep track of course registration and delivery process
- Java applet to play the multimedia course on the client machine

- Modify Visual Basic program to recognize the sale of LSCs and format a confirmation report accordingly

- Modify the Customer Account Status Report and Customer Account Status Window to add a line showing the number of LSCs purchased, used, and available in addition to the detail line that showed the number of PSCs purchased, used, and available

- Create PowerBuilder window to allow a sales person to manually adjust the number of LSCs available to a client company

A Slight Change in Toolset

During the Design Phase of the project, the Web Master received an evaluation copy of a Web development tool called HAHTsite IDE. This is a new breed of tool that includes most of the utilities needed to completely build a Web application, including:

- HTML Editor

- GUI Web page construction

- ODBC interface to RDBMS products

- HTML extensions to allow database updates from the HTML

- Sophisticated testing and Web page publication interface

After playing with this tool and getting familiar with it, it was decided that the Web pages should be developed using HAHTsite IDE—not in PowerBuilder. It was determined that PowerBuilder would remain XYZs tool-of-choice to build Windows-based applications. It was also decided that HAHTsite IDE would be used in this development effort and if proven to work as expected, would become XYZ's tool-of-choice to build and maintain its Web site and Web-delivered applications.

The Development Process

The PowerBuilder developer had 80 hours worth of work on this project. The developer had modified an existing Customer Account Status report and window. He had also written a new window to manually adjust a client company's purchased learning credits should a system fail while a student was in the middle of a course.

The DBAs modifications of the stored procedures to accommodate the selling and shipping of learning credits was quite rudimentary. It involved the following:

- Modified the Visual Basic program that runs nightly to produce a confirmation certificate showing the number of credits purchased during the previous business day, which is subsequently mailed to the customer.

- Modified the Visual Basic program that ran nightly and produced the Customer Account status report to show the number of Learning Credits purchased during the day.

- Tested the entire process. This activity took most of the time allocated to the DBA for this phase of the project.

With 152 hours of development work ahead, spanning five calendar weeks, the Web master's development tasks were the most significant development activity in the development phase of the project. Her work is described in detail in the following sections.

Mirrored Sites

Because XYZ's Web site would be used in new ways (i.e., the number of hits would increase substantially, and the length of time people would be connected to the site would increase dramatically while they were taking a course), the project team decided that XYZ needed a mirrored Web site.

A mirrored Web site works in many ways like a replicated database. That is, the Web site objects accessible over the Internet are duplicated in two different locations and are kept in sync. A mirrored Web site is different in that it's rarely accessed from an external user's browser. Rather, a mirrored Web site exists so that the objects that comprise a Web site can be built and tested without affecting the production Web site. Then, when the objects have been satisfactorily tested, they're moved from the mirrored site to the production site.

So, the Web master's first action was to create a mirrored Web site, placing all existing database and Web objects inside it. In this way, when a set of components was tested, it could easily be published into the production site.

Development Approach

The Web master looked at the development activities that were part of this project, as summarized below, and saw marginal value in placing a priority of one task over another.

- Find and employ a Java applet to play the courses.
- Build the "cookie" mechanism to keep track of a lesson's progress.
- Develop seven new Web pages.

Because of the reliance on an externally developed tool used to play the courses to the students (the Java applet), the Web master decided that this activity should commence immediately and could occur in tandem with the development of Web pages. Other than this, the project team identified no contingencies between the tasks in the project plan.

The Hunt for a Java Applet.   After an exhaustive search of the tools available on the Net, the project team decided that XYZ would use the *Shockwave Flash* applet, from Macromedia Incorporated. Since the actual courses would be written using Macromedia products, the team believed that the greatest degree of reliability could be achieved by using its Java applet to play files created using Macromedia products. In addition, XYZ's Web page development tool would incorporate the transfer and playing of Java applets to a user's machine quite nicely.

If you'd like to see this applet in action, visit the Macromedia Incorporated Web site at `http://www.macromedia.com`.

Cookies.   As you've already seen, a *cookie* is a mechanism for maintaining application information across multiple sessions.

Once the Web master spent a little more time with the Web page development tool of choice, the HAHTsite IDE, the team pleasantly discovered that writing a cookie into the application was unnecessary. This is because some of the HTML extensions built into the tool automatically maintain state information, eliminating much of the need for cookies to handle state information.

However, in designing the system, the architects also recognized that a connection might break before the user was finished with a course. Cookies were originally planned to address this situation. But, since the team had decided that cookies were unnecessary, the Webmaster decided to change the system's design slightly, thus eliminating the need for a cookie.

The change involved the point of time at which the system would decrement the client company's account balance of learning credits. Under the original design, the system charges the company's balance of learning credits before the student began the course. However, if the course credits weren't charged against a client company's balance until after the course was completed, no adjustment was necessary in the event of a broken connection. The user would simply reinitiate the connection and continue the course. When the course was completed and the student saw the Course Completion page, the actual adjustment to the purchased and unused learning credits would occur.

However, this plan contained a security risk: Someone could take a course for free by starting and taking a course but terminating the connection right before finishing the course and being presented with the Course Completion page. To shore up this potential breach, the company decided on the following approach:

- Notify the students early in the course registration process that as soon as the course began, their employer's account balance would be decreased by the number of credits the course costs.

- In a follow-up development activity, build a mechanism to create course completion certificates, which are automatically triggered after the student completes the course and progresses through the Course Completion page. This is where, among other things, their employer's account balance of learning credits would then be decreased.

Develop the Web Pages

Figure 20–4 shows the first screen developed by the Webmaster, which is the first screen in the process a user would follow to sign-up and take a Web course.

What isn't shown on this graphic or included in this chapter is the actual coding and development of each of these Web pages. The intent of this chapter isn't to teach HTML or how to use the HAHTsite IDE, but rather to discuss how to design an application that uses an Oracle 8 database as the back-end RDBMS to a Web-delivered application.

The process of accomplishing a database connection to an Oracle 8 database and execution of a query against a table is a graphical process involving just a few steps that has been discussed previously in this book and is presented again in detail in Chapter 21. Since Oracle 8 tables are ODBC-compliant and the development tool used by XYZ was

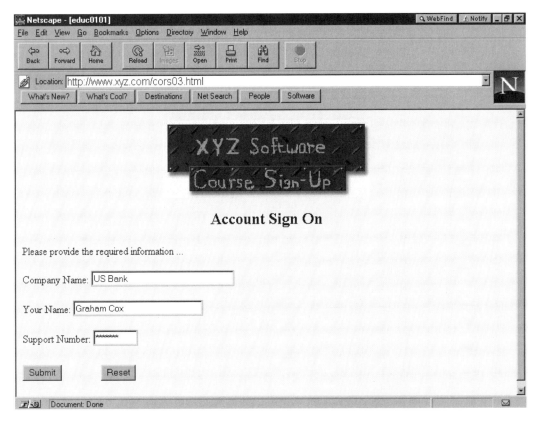

Figure 20–4   The account sign-on screen.

ODBC-enabled, the actual database connection and query construction were greatly simplified.

Figure 20–5 shows the Support Credit Confirmation screen, which is the next screen displayed to the user once the information supplied on the account sign-up screen is validated against the Customer and Accounting information database. Note that this screen dynamically displays the results of a query extracting the names of the courses that can be taken given the number of learning credits available.

Once this page is displayed, and the user has selected the course to take, the user clicks the <Take Course> button to display the Course Request Confirmation screen. This is the last chance to bail out of the process before the course actually begins. This is also the screen where, when the user clicks the <Proceed> button, the Shockwave Flash Java applet is downloaded to the student's machine.

The Webmaster quickly developed the remaining screens, completing them within the project time frames. XYZ's home page required one last change: Adding a button for the user to click on to initiate the whole Internet-delivered course process. The Webmaster added the highlighted graphical bar element in Figure 20–6 to accomplish this task.

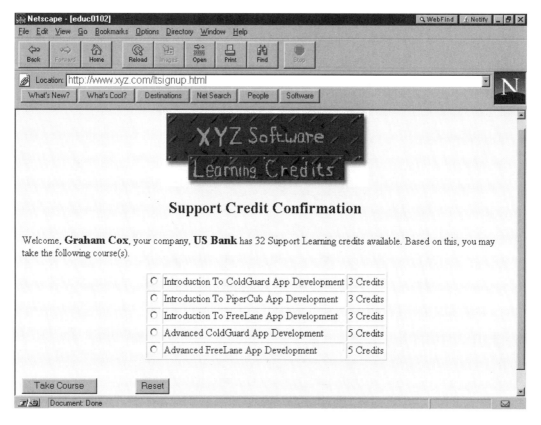

Figure 20–5   The Support Credit Confirmation screen.

Adding this graphical bar (which in HTML terminology is called a hypergraphics link) involved the Webmaster writing four lines of HTML code.

I'm not including in this section the other three screens (Invalid Company/Support Number screen, Course Completion screen, and Have a Good Day screen) the Webmaster developed as these are static HTML pages that have no database access.

Implementation

The one problem XYZ encountered during the construction process wasn't in the database or Web page development but in the creation of the actual courses. The curricula developers had a difficult time keeping the course length down to the original mandate of 256,000 bytes. After a couple of meetings between all project team members, management relented and compromised by allowing a maximum course length of 750,000 bytes. Between this and breaking up the courses into more finite and discrete (smaller) components, the curricula developers were able to stay within the appointed guidelines.

XYZ implemented its new system on schedule and within budget following a short beta-testing period. Amazingly (to the management of XYZ) and pleasingly (to the project

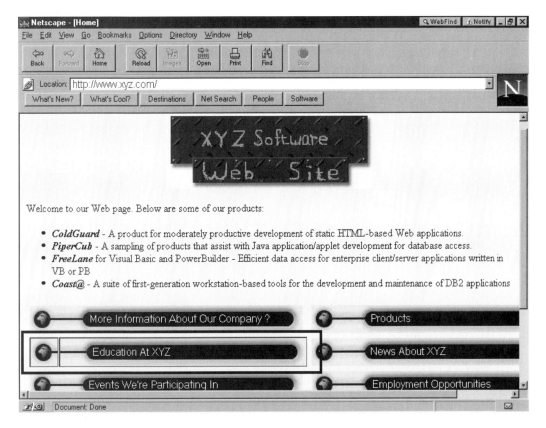

Figure 20–6 XYZ's home page with a link added to the education department's pages and the Web-delivered courses.

team), no major modifications were found necessary during beta testing. Therefore, XYZ implemented its new Internet course-delivery system with the following:

- A direct mail campaign to existing customers notifying them of the new service.
- A training session in which XYZ's sales force learned how to sell the new service.
- A splash page on XYZ's Web site describing the new service. A *splash page* is a temporary Web page that displays prior to the display of a company's home page and is usually reserved for late-breaking or highly interesting information.

Post-Implementation Analysis

XYZ implemented its system at the end of 1996. In the months since implementation, the company has seen better-than-expected response to the system, with revenues from this service 32 percent greater than anticipated. Because of this high demand, XYZ had to install three additional modems at its server, but XYZ considered it a small price to pay for the extra success.

XYZ recognizes that much of its ability to build and implement this system so successfully came from the exceptional design and configuration of its customer and accounting information database. Without the ability to easily build a Web-based front-end interface to a substantially existing database, XYZ knows that developing this application would have required much more time. Once again, the success of an application, in this case a state-of-the-art Web database application, is highly affected by the design and construction of the database.

Moving On

This chapter presented a case study of the actual analysis, design and construction phases of the Web database application. Emphasis was placed throughout the chapter on the analysis and design component of this application.

In Chapter 21, you'll focus on the actual construction and implementation activities revolving around the development of a Web database Internet and intranet application.

CHAPTER 21

Building a Simple Class Registration System

T

his chapter focuses on how to use HTML and a Web database application development suite to construct a Web database application that includes both Internet and intranet access. The company profiled in this chapter is A Better Computer (ABC) Company, a fictitious corporation that provides, among other things, computer training. The Web application profiled in this chapter contains, among other things, a query facility so that Web visitors can see what training classes are held in cities near them. This is the Internet component to the database that is profiled in this chapter. The intranet component presented in this chapter is the facility used by ABC employees to update the Oracle 8 database that maintains the data that describes the course offerings and availability of ABC Company.

In this chapter I will show you the various components of this application, and describe how it was constructed. You will understand the various components and how they interrelate and interoperate. You will see how the application and application components are constructed. That is the intent of this chapter. Although the source code and database for this application are included on the CD-ROM, the approach taken here will not be to lead you through the process of installing and executing the application on your hard drive from the CD-ROM. To me, those types of examples, the ones where you install a semi-working application on your hard drive, are never nearly as meaningful as a clear description of how something was constructed so that you can take that description and apply it to your unique circumstances.

Application Configuration

The configuration of this application is based upon several key factors. First, to provide Web access to the inventory of courses that ABC Company has, as well as their availability. Second, to provide in-house access to this data for administrative purposes. Although this application provides no capability to actually register for a course online, this capability could be easily added.

The basic configuration of this application is as follows:

- Oracle 8 database with four tables
- HAHTsite IDE used as the application development tool
- Global front-end to the application that provides both Inter- and intranet access
- Security login screen to protect from unauthorized access to the intranet components on the site

Structure of the Database

As seen in Figure 21–1, there are four tables in this database. These are:

Available Courses. This Table is accessed only by ABC employees over the intranet who need to maintain the information contained in it by either Inserting, Updating, or Deleting rows. The table contains the following columns:

- *Course_Id*—*Datatype: Number.* This contains a unique identifier for each course. This column is joined automatically to the column of the same name in the `Class_Registration` table whenever both tables are open at the same time.
- *Course_Name*—*Datatype: Text.* Contains the name of the course.
- *Course_Duration*—*Datatype: Number.* Contains the number of days in duration for the course.

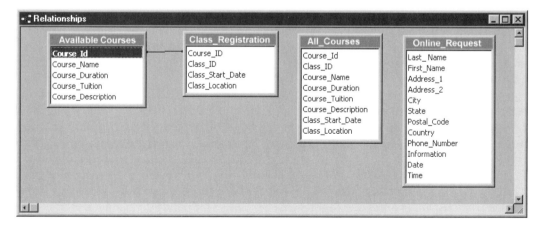

Figure 21–1 The database structure.

- *Course_Tuition*—*Datatype: Currency*. Contains the cost to attend the course.
- *Course_Description*—*Datatype: Text*. Contains up to 255 characters of description text for the course.

Class_Registration.   This table is accessed only by ABC employees over the intranet who need to maintain the information contained in it by either Inserting, Updating, or Deleting rows. The table contains the following columns:

- *Course_Id*—*Datatype: Number*. Contains a unique identifier for each course. This column is joined automatically to the column of the same name in the `Available_Courses` table whenever both tables are open at the same time.
- *Class_Id*—*Datatype: Text*. Contains a unique identifier for each time the course is offered. In other words, a given course may be offered five times. In such a case, there would be five rows in this table, and the `Course_Id` column would be identical for each row because the course being offered is the same. The `Class_Id` column would have a unique value for each row to identify that row.
- *Class_Start_Date*—*Datatype: Date/Time*. Contains the date that the class starts.
- *Class_Location*—*Datatype: Text*. Contains the city/state that the class identified by the row is to be held.

All_Courses.   This table is accessed by users over the Internet who want to gather information on when and where specific courses are to be offered. The table is created from a Join Query that takes the contents of the `Available_Courses` table and joins it to the `Class_Registration` table on the `Course_Id` column. The table contains the following columns:

- *Course_Id*—*Datatype: Number*. Contains a unique identifier for each course. This column is joined automatically to the column of the same name in the `Available_Courses` table whenever both tables are open at the same time.
- *Class_Id*—*Datatype: Text*. Contains a unique identifier for each time the course is offered. In other words, a given course may be offered five times. In such a case, there would be five rows in this table, and the `Course_Id` column would be identical for each row because the course being offered is the same. The `Class_Id` column would have a unique value for each row to identify that row.
- *Course_Name*—*Datatype: Text*. Contains the name of the course.
- *Course_Duration*—*Datatype: Number*. Contains the number of days in duration for the course.
- *Course_Tuition*—*Datatype: Currency*. Contains the cost to attend the course.
- *Course_Description*—*Datatype: Text*. Contains up to 255 characters of description text for the course.
- *Class_Start_Date*—*Datatype: Date/Time*. Contains the date that the class that this record represents starts.
- *Class_Location*—*Datatype: Text*. Contains the city/state that the class identified by the row is to be held.

HAHTsite IDE, the tool used to build this application, does not provide a convenient mechanism to Join and access two or more tables from a Web page. Therefore, the `All_Courses` table was created to satisfy Web requests where information from both tables is needed. The `All_Courses` table is either created manually from within Oracle 8 by someone executing the Join Query or automatically in a prescheduled Visual Basic program that automatically executes the Join Query.

OnLine_Request. This table is accessed by users over the Internet who want to provide input of any type to ABC Company. This input could be a comment on the Web site, a request for product information, or a request to have someone call. The table contains the following columns:

- *Last_Name*—*Datatype: text.* Contains the last name of the person completing the Feedback form.

- *First_Name*—*Datatype: text.* Contains the first name of the person completing the Feedback form.

- *Address_1*—*Datatype: text.* Contains the first address line of the person completing the Feedback form.

- *Address_2*—*Datatype: text.* Contains the second address line of the person completing the Feedback form.

- *City*—*Datatype: text.* Contains the city of the person completing the Feedback form.

- *State*—*Datatype: text.* Contains the state of the person completing the Feedback form.

- *Postal_Code*—*Datatype: text.* Contains the postal code of the person completing the Feedback form.

- *Country*—*Datatype: text.* Contains the country of the person completing the Feedback form.

- *Phone_Number*—*Datatype: text.* Contains the phone number of the person completing the Feedback form.

- *Information*—*Datatype: text.* Contains up to 255 characters of free form text data supplied by the person completing the Feedback form.

- *Date*—*Datatype: date/time.* Contains the date when the person completing this form pressed `<Submit>`.

- *Time*—*Datatype: date/time.* Contains the time when the person completing this form pressed `<Submit>`.

HAHTsite IDE Development Tool

The HAHTsite Integrated Internet Development System merges content creation, client- and server-side logic development, data access (ODBC or native API), automated distributed deployment to multiple sites, team development, and application life cycle management into one seamlessly integrated software system.

HAHTsite IDE uses a proprietary CGI program interface, coupled with proprietary HTML extensions, to free the developer from having to write CGI programs. Here is an example of how helpful a development tool can be to place the Update button (which causes the Oracle 8 database to be updated with whatever values appear on the screen) as seen in Figure 21–2 and then to make it functional against an Oracle 8 database is a simple process of:

1. Identifying the connection to the Oracle 8 database
2. Pasting the controls (including the `<Update>` button) and objects on the Web page where you want them to appear
3. Double-click on the `<Update>` button to change its properties
4. Select (Update) as being the database action that occurs when the user clicks the `<Update>` button

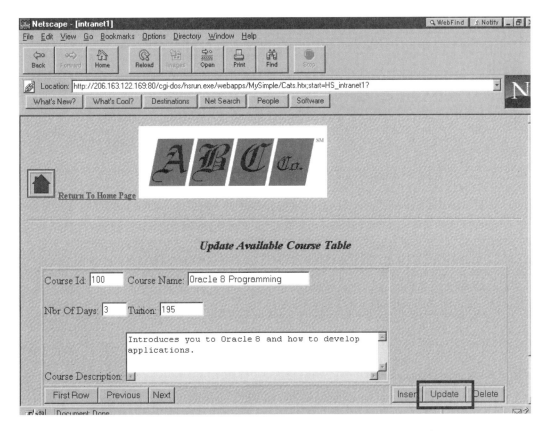

Figure 21–2 A Web page in our application with an `<Update>` database button.

That's it—there's nothing more to it. When a user accesses this Web page, makes changes to the data appearing on it, and then clicks the <Update> button, the interaction between the extensions to HTML that are included on the Web page and the CGI program (supplied by HAHT with the HAHTsite IDE toolkit) running on the Web server causes the Oracle 8 database to be updated. As you're probably curious as to what these extensions are, I want to show you what the HTML code looks like that the HAHTsite IDE creates *just for* the <Update> button on the Web page as seen in Figure 21–2. This is shown below.

```
NAME=Button5
 TYPE=Button
 VERSION="2.0"
 HAHTVERSION="2.0"
 SAVECONTENTS=True
 IGNORECONTENTS=False
 DISPLAYONLOAD=True
 KEEPCONTENTSONPUBLISH=0
 DYNAMICCONTENT=1
 SetTrace=False
 UseMethod=False
 UserMethod=""
 DataSource=DataSet1
 Action=2
 —><INPUT NAME=Button5 TYPE=SUBMIT VALUE=Update><!—HAHT-Extension
/HAHTCHARWIDGET —><!—HAHT-Extension HAHTCHARWIDGET
```

Global Front-End

This Web database application incorporates a front-end that is accessible by both Internet and Intranet users. This is seen in Figures 21–3 and 21–4.

In Figure 21–3 and Figure 21–4, there are four areas on the screen of particular interest to understanding how the front-end to this application works. These are:

1. Toolbar for quick navigation to other Web pages
2. Company logo on every page
3. Hot-links to other Web sites of interest
4. Easy navigation to other Web pages

The following sections describe each of these.

Toolbar for Quick Navigation to Other Web Pages. A toolbar at the top of the home page is a fairly consistent element on most Web sites. Although one of the purposes of the home page is to inform the user what site they're at, the primary purpose is to provide a central navigation point to other key sections on the Web site as well as other areas of interest to the person looking at your Web page.

On ABC's Web site home page, the following hypergraphic links are supplied on the toolbar:

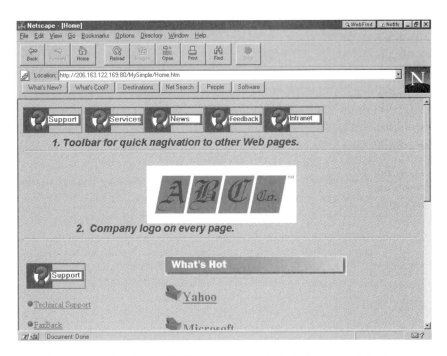

Figure 21–3 The ABC Company global front-end to their Internet and intranet site.

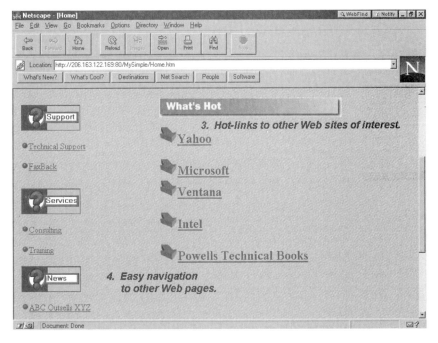

Figure 21–4 Bottom half of the ABC Company global front-end to their Internet and intranet site.

- *Support*—Provides access to the various pages that describe the support phone numbers that are offered by ABC Company. Figure 21–5 shows what the user would see if they clicked on the `<Support>` icon. This is a Web page that includes two hypertext links to other Web pages that provide contact information.

- *Services*—Provides access to the various pages that describe the types of services offered by ABC Company, namely Consulting and Training. Figure 21–6 shows what the user would see if they clicked on the `<Services>` icon, which is a Web page that includes two hypertext links to other Web pages that provide information on Consulting and Training services. The hypertext link to the Training services page is discussed in detail in a later section as this page performs database access and format of the result set on a Web page.

- *News*—Provides access to the various pages that list the Press Releases issued by ABC Company. This is also another fairly typical item on a corporate Web site.

- *Feedback*—Provides access to a customer feedback form. Although this is described in detail later in this chapter, feedback forms are a quite common item on corporate Web sites. What makes this feedback form unique in that not only is it able to accept new input and then post that input to an Oracle 8 database, but the Feedback form is also used to browse and/or update and/or delete existing comments supplied by previous users.

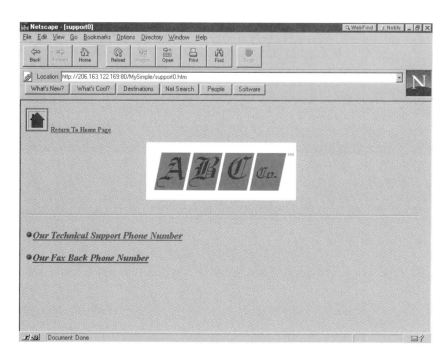

Figure 21–5   What the users see when they click on the `<Support>` icon.

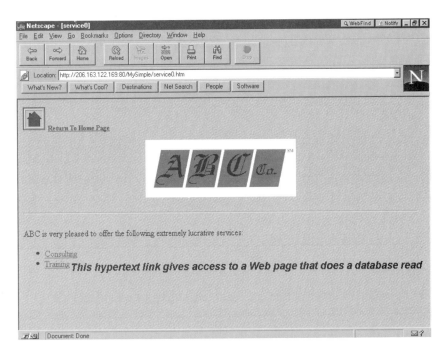

Figure 21-6   What the users see when they click on the <Services> icon.

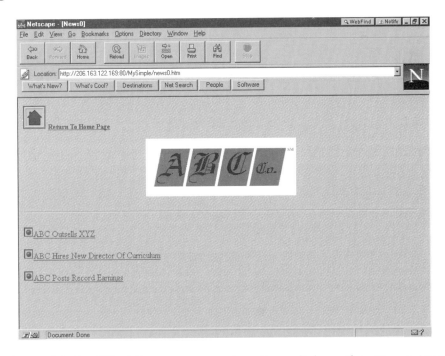

Figure 21-7   What the users see when they click on the <News> icon.

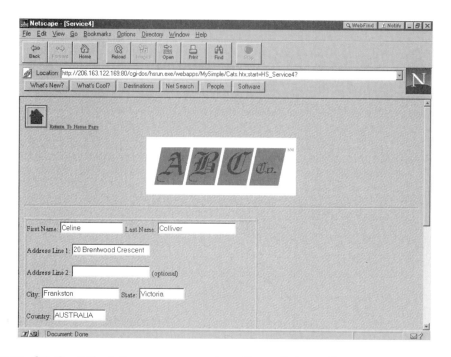

Figure 21–8   What the users see when they click on the `<Feedback>` icon.

- *Intranet*—Provides access to the company's intranet site. This is described in detail later in this chapter. For now, you should know that the Web pages accessed from here allow ABC Company employees to update the Oracle 8 tables on their machines. Employees use these to keep track of the names of courses offered by ABC Company as well as the dates and locations that those courses are offered. The results of this data entry and update is then viewed externally by users accessing the `Services | Training Services` Web pages.

Company Logo on Every Page.   You'll notice that every page in the ABC Company Web site has a consistent look to it. This look is achieved by the following:

- The background for each page is identical
- Each page has a Return to Home icon and hypertext link at the top
- Each page has a company logo on it

In other than a rare circumstance, you should strive for a consistent look to the Web pages in your application. You want to affirm in a very passive way that the page the user is viewing in their browser belongs to your site, and that they have not linked out of your site to another companies site.

Hot-Links to Other Web Sites of Interest.   Another common item appearing on corporate Web site home pages are hypertext or hypergraphic links to the Web sites of affiliate companies. This is an aid to people that are browsing your site and wish to go to

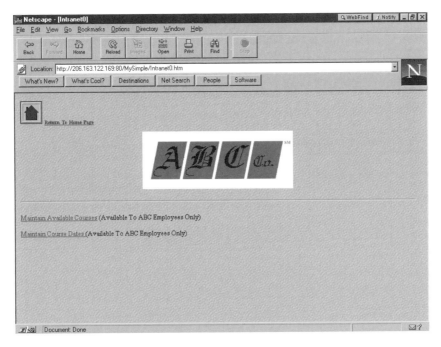

Figure 21–9   What the users see when they click on the `<Intranet>` icon and after they log in to the database.

another site of a related company. Some companies are finding it lucrative to place references to other organizations' Web sites on their own Web site by charging those other companies a preset fee to do so. This makes sense and helps all parties concerned.

- The person browsing the Internet is given a convenient way to move from site to related site.

- Your company receives revenue from the organizations that are listed on your Web site.

- The organizations that are listed on your Web site have the hits on their own Web sites increase as more people link to them from your site.

Easy Navigation to Other Web Pages.   Along the left border of the home page you'll see a series of icons that also appear in the toolbar, followed by the hypertext links to the pages that are contained in those sections. This gives the user the ability to easily and quickly navigate to the page of their choice while avoiding using the toolbar. Let me give you an example.

Refer back to Figure 21–3, where you'll see the toolbar at the top of the ABC Company home page. Let's say that someone wanted to find out the telephone number for the FaxBack service. They would have to do the following:

- Click on the icon on the toolbar that says `<Support>`.
- Wait for the page, as seen in Figure 21–5 to display in their browser.
- Click on the hypertext link that references the FaxBack telephone number.
- Wait for the page to display in their browser.

This four step process can be expedited by using the hypertext and hypergraphic links that appear on the left side of the ABC Company home page. To get the FaxBack telephone number using the links on the left side of the home page, the user would simply do the following:

- Look down the left column of the ABC Company home page, as seen in Figure 21–4 until he or she found the hypertext link to the companies FaxBack telephone number and click on the link.
- Wait for the page requested to display in their browser.

That's all their is to it, and the user is pleased to have had his/her time respected by building into the application this time-saving aid.

Security Login Screen

On the ABC Company home page, as seen in Figure 21–3, access to the company intranet site is indicated. Although many companies that have Internet and intranet sites have them separated, a growing trend as organizations become more comfortable with security over the Internet is to allow access to an intranet site from the Internet site's Web pages.

Obviously you don't want to allow access to the intranet pages by an unauthorized person. So, you need to build security into your Web database application to keep the unauthorized people out of the pages you don't want them in. You can accomplish this, as seen in the Web database application profiled in this chapter, by providing access to all restricted Web pages from one Web page. In that one Web page you'd require the user to complete a security login process. If they fail security, they are now allowed to view any of the pages that follow. If they pass security, they have whatever access you wish to give by the way you develop the application.

HAHTsite has a very nice implementation of the security login process. Basically, it allows you to place what they call a Database Login Widget on any Web page that is contained in an application. When a user accesses a Web page that contains this invisible Database Login Widget (the Web page seen in Figure 21–9 contains one of these) they are first presented with a Database Login screen, as seen in Figure 21–10.

Once they supply the needed information, it is automatically verified against an Oracle 8 table of authorized users. If the information supplied by the user does not match what is stored in the Oracle 8 table, a message displays and the user is not allowed to view the Web page. If the information supplied is validated, then the user would see the desired page, in this case that would be the page seen in Figure 21–9.

The following sections describe the components in this Web application that provide database access to an Oracle 8 database. These include both Internet application components and intranet application components.

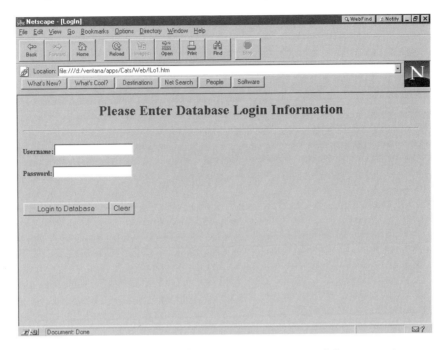

Figure 21–10 The database login screen as part of the security process.

Web Database Internet Components in the Application

There are three Web pages that comprise the Internet accessible components in this application. These are:

- Training Course Listing Page
- Course Date/Location Page
- Feedback Page

Each of these are discussed in detail in the following sections.

Training Course Listing Page

From the ABC Company home page, the Training Course Listing page is accessed by one of the following:

- Clicking on the Services icon in the toolbar and then on the Training hypertext link, or,
- Clicking on the Training hypertext link that is directly below the Services icon that appears along the left side of the home page

When one of the above is done, the page seen in Figure 21–11 displays.

What is wonderful about the HAHTsite IDE as a tool to develop Web database applications is the ease in which the page seen in Figure 21–11 was created. Again, I don't

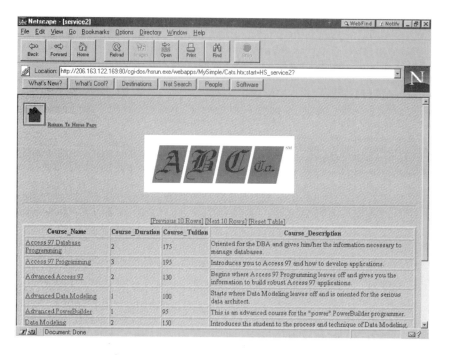

Figure 21–11   The course list page.

want to teach you how to use this tool, but I do want to give you an idea of how easy it is to use development tool suites in the construction of a Web database application. So, the process of creating the page seen in Figure 21–11 is:

- From within the HAHTsite IDE, open the application object
- Click on `File`, then `New`, then `Page` to create a new page
- Place the graphics on the page where you want them. For Figure 21–11, this is the house that appears in the upper left corner, the hypertext link to return to the home page, and the corporate logo.
- Click on the Widgets icon, then on the Database Table icon, and drag the icon over and drop it on the new page where you want it to appear.
- Double-click on the Database Table icon just placed on the page, and then on the Database connections tab.
- Click on the Database Connection drop down list box and select the database connection that you want to access in this Web page.
- Click on the Tables drop down list box and then select the Table that you want to access in this Web page.
- Click on <OK>.

That's it. When this page is viewed in a browser, the HAHTsite extensions to HTML and their interactions with the CGI program supplied by the product take care of establishing a connection to the database, accessing the desired records in the database, formatting the result set onto a Web page, and then transmitting the Web page back to the user.

Do you see the hypertext links at the top of the table in Figure 21–11? These are navigation aids that are automatically supplied by HAHTsite IDE because of the use of the Database Table widget. I did nothing to create these navigation aids that wasn't already provided for in the tool.

The purpose of this page is to list a few pieces of information available for each of the course titles offered by ABC Company, specifically,

- Course Name
- Course Duration
- Course Tuition
- Course Description

You'll notice that each of the items listed under the column heading Course Name is a hypertext link. In HAHTsite IDE, this is termed a *database drilldown*. What it means is that if a user clicked on any of the items listed in the Course Name column, a follow-up query is generated to retrieve additional information I specify that is based on the course the user selected.

In other words, it doesn't make a whole lot of sense to show all of the course dates and locations for every course on the page seen in Figure 21–11, does it? It's best to give as little information as necessary to allow users to select the course information they need. Then, when they have selected a specific course, give them more detailed information.

Assuming a user clicks on one of the courses listed under the Course Name column, thus triggering a database drilldown, the Course Date/Location page as discussed in the next section will display.

Course Date/Location Page

The Course Date/Location page is only displayed if the user selected a specific course to view additional information from the Training Course Listing Page. The Course Date/Location page, as seen in Figure 21–12, contains the following button controls that appear at the bottom of the page:

- *Clear*—Causes all the fields on the form to appear empty
- *MoveFirst*—Causes the records that display one-at-a-time on the page to cycle back to the first retrieved row for the course
- *MoveNext*—Causes the next record retrieved for the requested course to display on the page
- *MovePrevious*—Causes the previous record displayed and retrieved for the requested course to display on the page

A user would automatically access this Web page after they had indicated a particular and singular course preference by clicking on a specific item that appears under the Course Name column on the Training Course Listing page. Once on this page, they could

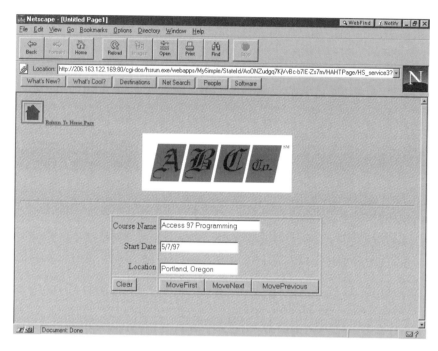

Figure 21–12   The Course Date/Location page.

view the dates and locations for all the times that this course was taught, conceptually to pick a date and location nearest to them and fulfilling their needs.

Because of the interaction between the extensions to HTML provided by HAHTsite IDE and the CGI program supplied with the HAHTsite product, a person developing this Web page would find it a very easy process to place the buttons on the page that control the movement through the result set. Once placed on the page, causing them to take the action described above is a very simple four-step process. Again for the sake of understanding the power of Web development suites without trying to teach you how to use the HAHTsite product, the process of creating database functionality in a button is described as:

- Double-click on the button to which you want to establish database access while in the HAHTsite IDE
- On the Button Properties window, click on the Database tab
- On the Action drop down list box, select one of the listed database actions (i.e., Clear, MoveFirst, MoveNext, MovePrevious, Insert, Update, Delete, etc.)
- Click <OK>

Once the above is done by a user, whenever that user clicks on one of the database-update buttons, the action specified for that button will automatically occur—with no additional programming required on your part.

Feedback Page

From the ABC Company home page, the Feedback page is accessed by one of the following:

- Clicking on the Feedback icon in the toolbar, or,
- Clicking on the Feedback icon that appears along the left side of the home page

When one of the above is done, the pages seen in Figure 21–13 and Figure 21–14 displays.

The Feedback page is quite similar to the other pages you have seen in this application that accept user input and display the results of database queries. The page consists of a form that has various controls on it that accept user input and display the results of queries. What is different about this page is the types of buttons at the bottom of the form. These, and the descriptions of their actions are:

- *Submit*—Once the Feedback form is completed by the user, they would click on the `<Submit>` button that causes the information supplied by the user to be transmitted to the CGI program running on the server. The CGI program would format and insert the data into the Oracle 8 table named: `OnLine_Request`.

- *Reset*—The `<Reset>` button, when clicked, causes all the data that is currently displayed on the form to be cleared from the form. It does not cause the data to be deleted from the database.

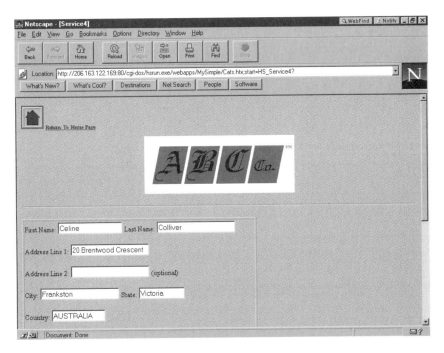

Figure 21–13   The top half of the Feedback page.

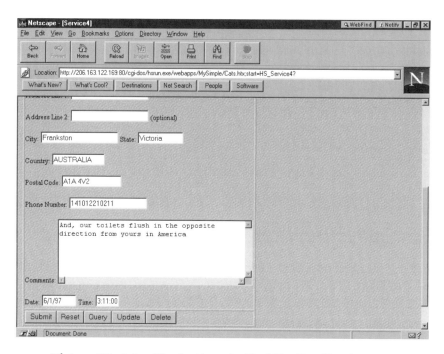

Figure 21–14 The bottom half of the Feedback page.

- *Query*—A user could enter his or her first and last name in the appropriate form fields, press the <Query> button, and the CGI program running on the server would retrieve the record that exists in the OnLine_Request table that is a match on the first and last name and display the results on this form. The user could then either modify some of the data and press the <Update> button or simply press the <Delete> button to remove these records from the database.

- *Update*—As described above, the <Update> button causes the record that exists in the OnLine_Request table that is a match on the first and last name entered on this form to be updated with the values as they exist on the form in the various fields.

- *Delete*—As described above, the <Delete> button causes the record from the On-Line_Request table that matches on the first and last name entered on this form to be deleted from the table.

As you learned in the previous section named Course Date/Location Page, the actual process to add the database access functionality described here is a very simple process. The code that actually accomplishes the desired database action is contained in the CGI program running on the server as supplied with the HAHTsite IDE tool.

Web Database Intranet Components in the Application

There are two Web pages that comprise the intranet accessible components in this application. These are:

- Maintain Available Courses
- Maintain Course Dates

Each of these are discussed in detail in the following sections.

Maintain Available Courses Page

From the ABC Company home page, the Maintain Available Courses page is accessed by one of the following:

- Click on the `<Intranet>` icon that is in the toolbar, or,
- Click on the `<Intranet>` icon that appears along the left side of the home page

From here, you will see the Database Login screen as seen in Figure 21–10. Complete this screen with your User Name and Password, and click `<Submit>`. If the information supplied is incorrect, you'll receive an error message. If it is correct, you are allowed access to the intranet site whose first page is what appears in Figure 21–9. Click on the hypertext link that says `Maintain Available Courses` and the Web page as seen in Figure 21–15 will display.

The purpose of this page is to allow authorized ABC Company employees access to update the contents of the Oracle 8 database table named `Available_Courses`. This Web page is quite similar to the other Web pages that allow database access, with the dif-

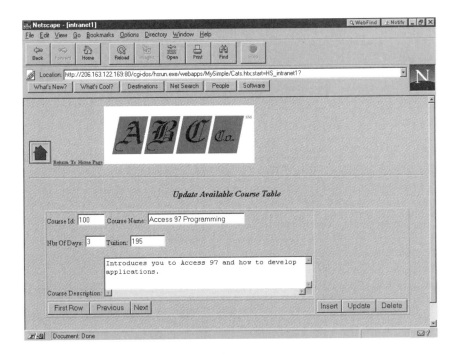

Figure 21–15 The Maintain Available Courses intranet page.

ference being that this page provides update access to Oracle 8 tables that ABC Company wants to restrict to authorized users.

The buttons that appear at the bottom of this page perform the following functions:

- *First Row*—Re-query the `Available_Courses` table and display the first record retrieved on this Web page.

- *Previous*—Re-query the `Available_Courses` table but position the record displayed on the row immediately prior to the currently displayed record.

- *Next*—Re-query the `Available_Courses` table but position the record displayed on the row immediately following the currently displayed record.

- *Insert*—Insert the data that appears on the form into the `Available_Courses` table.

- *Update*—Update the data that is in the `Available_Courses` table with the data that currently appears on the form.

- *Delete*—Delete the row in the `Available_Courses` table that currently appears in the form.

As you learned in previous sections, to cause the actions described above to be assigned to the various buttons is a very simple process. The code that actually accomplishes the desired database action is contained in the CGI program running on the server as supplied with the HAHTsite IDE tool.

Maintain Course Dates Page

From the ABC Company home page, the Maintain Course Dates page is accessed by one of the following:

- Click on the `<Intranet>` icon that is in the toolbar, or,
- Click on the `<Intranet>` icon that appears along the left side of the home page.

From here, you will see the Database Login screen as seen in Figure 21–10. Complete this screen with your User Name and Password, and click `<Submit>`. If the information supplied is incorrect, you'll receive an error message. If it is correct, you are allowed access to the intranet site whose first page is what appears in Figure 21–9. Click on the hypertext link that says `Maintain Course Dates` and the Web page as seen in Figure 21–16 will display.

The purpose of this page is to allow authorized ABC Company employees access to update the contents of the Oracle 8 database table named `Class_Registration`. This Web page is quite similar to the other Web pages that allow database access, with the difference being that this page provides update access to Oracle 8 tables that ABC Company wants to restrict to authorized users.

The buttons that appear at the bottom of this page perform the following functions:

- *First Row*—Re-query the `Class_Registration` table and display the first record retrieved on this Web page.

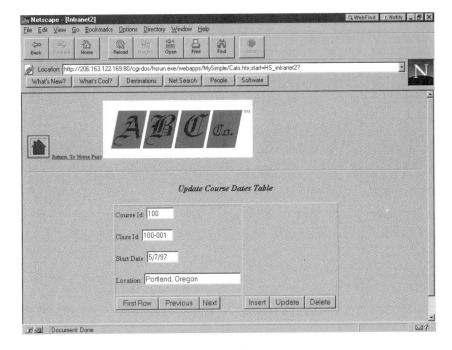

Figure 21–16 The Maintain Course Dates intranet page.

- *Previous*—Re-query the `Class_Registration` table but position the record displayed on the row that is immediately prior to the currently displayed record.
- *Next*—Re-query the `Class_Registration` table but position the record displayed on the row that is immediately after the currently displayed record.
- *Insert*—Insert the data that appears on the form into the `Class_Registration` table.
- *Update*—Update the data that is in the `Class_Registration` table with the data that currently appears on the form.
- *Delete*—Delete the row in the `Class_Registration` table that currently appears in the form.

As you learned in previous sections, to cause the actions described above to be assigned to the various buttons is a very simple process. The code that actually accomplishes the desired database action is contained in the CGI program running on the server as supplied with the HAHTsite IDE tool.

Moving On

This chapter examined the Web database application that a fictitious company named ABC Company developed for both Internet and intranet access. Each of the Web pages that provided access to Oracle 8 database tables was described in detail as well as how the actual database table access is accomplished.

In Chapter 6 and 13 you learned how to write HTML code to construct attractive Web pages that could display database data. In Chapters 7 and 14 you learned how CGI programs accomplish the actual database access and function as an interface between the user's request for data and the actual access of the data. In Chapters 8 and 20 you learned how to design a Web database application to take into account the unique considerations of a Web-based database application. In Chapters 9, 10, and 11 you learned how to use the facilities in Oracle 8 to construct the database objects that would be accessed by a Web database application. And in the other chapters in this book you learned about the other issues to be concerned with when you are tasked with designing and building a Web database application.

APPENDIX A

CD-ROM
Contents

About the Companion CD-ROM

The CD-ROM included with your copy of this book contains valuable software for the design and development of Web database applications that use an Oracle 8 database.

Navigating the CD-ROM

The folders on the CD contain demo and evaluation copies of a wide variety of products you could use to help build an Oracle 8 Web database application.

CD-ROM Contents

Software Folder

HAHTsite. The product name is: HAHTsite IDE. HAHTsite IDE is a Web database application development suite with a full complement of tools to help you build Web applications with or without database access. This is the tool that was used in the development of the applications profiled in Chapters 20 and 21 of this book. For more product information, visit HAHT Software's Web site at: http://www.haht.com/.

Web_Wiz. The product name is: WEB Wizard. Web Wizard: The Duke of URL is a Windows program designed to help you create homepages for the World Wide Web. With WEB Wizard you can create your own customized homepage in just a matter of minutes—guaranteed. The file on the disk is a self-extracting ZIP file. If you execute it and ther result is Web Wiz 32.EXE, the software should load successfully.

WEB Wizard: The Duke of URL offers these features:

- Quick and easy homepage creation
- Ability to specify homepage title and subtitle
- Links and bullet lists
- Specify background colors and bitmaps
- Automatically creates a mailto: reference for your e-mail address
- Easily add text to your homepage

For more product information, visit ARTA Media Groups Web site at: `http://www.halcyon.com/artamedia/webwizard`.

GIFCLIB. The product name is: gd GIF C Library. gd GIF C Library is a graphics library. It allows your code to quickly draw images complete with lines, arcs, text, multiple colors, cut and paste from other images, and flood fills, and write out the result as a .GIF file. This is particularly useful in World Wide Web applications, where .GIF is the format used for inline images. For more product information, visit Boutell.Com's Web site at: `http://www.boutell.com/`.

MapEdit. The product name is: MapEdit. Mapedit is a WYSIWYG editor for imagemaps, available for Microsoft Windows and X Window Systems. Version 2.24 for Windows 3.1, 95 and NT, as well as 10 variations of Unix, is now available. All these versions support client-side imagemaps, targeting of individual frames, and more. For more product information, visit Boutell.Com's Web site at: `http://www.boutell.com/`.

WebLater. The product name is WebLater. WebLater remembers every URL you copy to your Windows clipboard. Do people mention URLs to you constantly in e-mail and newsgroups and IRC? Would you rather look at them later instead of interrupting your work? That's what WebLater is there for. For Windows 3.1, 95, and NT. For more product information, visit Boutell.Com's Web site at: `http://www.boutell.com/`.

Wusage. The product name is: Wusage. Wusage is a statistics program that helps you determine the true impact of your web server. It provides valuable marketing information with solid numbers about your web site's popularity. For more product information, visit Boutell.Com's Web site at: `http://www.boutell.com/`.

PerlMUD. The product name is: PerlMUD. For real-time, interactive teleconferencing, this suite is a complete Internet Multi-User Dimension system written in Perl. The shareware file on the disk is a TAR file for UNIX platforms running PERL 5. Establish your own electronic speakeasy, on-line chat, software support area, or corporate conference call environment. Cross-platform, and now with both "vanilla web" and Java clients. For more product information, visit Boutell.Com's Web site at: `http://www.boutell.com/`.

cgicLibr. The product name is: cgic CGI Library. cgic CGI Library and it is an ANSI C-language library for the creation of CGI-based World Wide Web applications. cgic CGI Library should be compatible with any CGI-compliant server environment. For more product information, visit Boutell.Com's Web site at: `http://www.boutell.com/`.

Baklava.   The product name is: Baklava. Baklava is Boutell.Com's sprite graphics library for Java programmers. Baklava, a free software product, makes it easy to create animated objects in your Java programs. Give a sprite an image to display and a direction to move in; it'll let you know when it collides with another sprite, right down to the pixel. Many other conveniences for sprite programming are provided. High-level, powerful, fast. For more product information, visit Boutell.Com's Web site at: `http://www.boutell.com/`.

HTMLPro3.   The product name is: HTML Assistant Pro 3. It is a "point and click" editor for making World Wide Web pages. It runs under MS Windows (Version 3.x or Windows 95 and not on Windows NT). Making a Web page is easy with HTML Assistant Pro 3. You begin with a blank screen and an idea and start typing. Mark up your page using push button tools so you don't have to remember complicated codes. Including hypertext links (highlighted words that link your page to other Web pages), is simply a matter of copying and pasting the URL (Uniform Resource Locator) for the page you want to point to. Whatever you want to do—share interests or research, advertise your product or service, or publish your ideas, HTML Assistant Pro 3 gets you on the Web easily and quickly. For more product information, visit Brooklyn North Software's Web site at: `http://www. brooknorth.com/`.

HTML_97.   The product name is: HTML Assistant Pro 97. HTML Assistant Pro 97 is the "point and click" editor for making World Wide Web Pages. It runs under Microsoft's Windows 95/NT 4.0. You begin with a blank screen and an idea and then start typing. Or convert your existing word processor document to HTML in seconds using the powerful RTF-HTML Instant Converter. Mark up your page using push button tools so you don't have to remember complicated codes. Add Java, Image Maps, Frames, Multimedia, Active X, Tables, Forms, Fonts, the latest and greatest web page enhancements—the customizable Multiple User Tool Bars mean that the program will never be out of date! Whatever you want to do—share interests or research, advertise your product or service, or publish your ideas, HTML Assistant Pro 97 will get you on the Web easier and faster than you ever thought possible! For more product information, visit Brooklyn North Software's Web site at: `http://www.brooknorth.com/`.

URL_Grab.   The product name is: URL Grabber 95. URL Grabber 95 is a small floating tool bar that resides on your MS Windows 95 desktop. With URL Grabber 95 it's easy to "grab" and file URLs from news groups, e-mail messages and other sources, as you are reading them. With a "click" of a mouse, URL Grabber 95 will automatically convert a collection of URLs to active WWW links on an HTML page. For more product information, visit Brooklyn North Software's Web site at: `http://www.brooknorth.com/`.

JDPro.   The product name is: JDesignerPro. Use JDesignerPro to create intranet and Internet Java database applications. Run a live demo, view screen shots, learn about its exciting features and more. JDesignerPro is the Java system which combines both the development environment and deployment system in a single, integrated package. For more product information, visit Bulletproof Software's Web site at: `http://www.bulletproof.com/`.

Alibaba. The product name is: Alibaba. Alibaba is a Web server product for Windows 95 and WIndows NT sold and supported by Computer Software Manufaktur. This is only a short list of Alibaba features available, please look through their manual (also on this CD-ROM) for a complete description of all available features.

- Multithreaded High Performance WWW Server
- Implemented as NT system service
- HTTP 1.0 protocol
- SSL Security
- Directory listings
- CGI (DOS-CGI, WINCGI 1.3, 32bit CGI, DLL interface and ISAPI)
- GET, POST and HEAD commands
- Configurable network port
- Multiple server addresses (Multihoming) (only under NT)
- Directory ignores
- Aliases
- Icon extensions for directory listings
- Definable MIMEtypes
- Access logging (Common Logformat 1.2)
- Error logging with selectable levels
- Extended logfiles
- Configurable error messages
- ImageMaps (NCSA including points and CERN format)
- Integrated or external image mapper
- HTTP access control (by Users, Groups and Sites)
- Disallow clients
- AliAdmin for easy server administration
- Remote administration (via NT and via TCP)
- AliAuth for access and general document administration
- File redirection
- ISINDEX support
- Automatic start of a command script at server startup
- Footer and Header (appends automatically a footer to every HTML page)
- Online statistic, used together with footers

- Built-in Server Side Includes with many extensions (like page counters)
- Server PUSH
- Connection Keep-Alive support
- Internal and external redirections
- Netscape Cookie support
- Uninstaller

For more product information, visit Computer Software Manufaktur's Web site at: `http://www.csm-usa.com/`.

EMWAC.   The product name is EMWAC. EMWAC is a Web server product for Windows NT developed and supported by the Edinburg University, in Edinburg, England. For more product information, visit Edinburg University's Web site at: `http://www.ed.ac.uk/`.

ER/Studio.   The product name is: ER/Studio. ER/Studio is an Entity Relationship (E-R) Diagramming tool that allows you to design logical and physical data models for client/server and web applications as well as create star-schema models for data marts and enterprise-wide data warehouses.

ER/Studio can generate physical schemas for all major databases as well as reverse engineer existing database schemas into E-R diagrams. ER/Studio data models are database independent. They can be converted automatically from one database platform to another using ER/Studio's powerful data type mapping facilities. The result is faster application development, better data integrity, and high performance database designs. For more product information, visit Embarcadero Technologies Web site at: `http://www.embarcadero.com/`.

INET_Creatr.   The product name is: Internet Creator. Internet Creator was developed with the small- to medium-sized business in mind. The trial version on the CD is a Windows 95 version. It is capable of producing any type of Web site, but has special tools that allow businesses to setup an online catalog or store quickly and easily. The program includes powerful site setup wizards that can collect information about your business, then setup business tools like e-mail based ordering, a shopping basket ordering module, payment and shipping choices, and a sophisticated searching capability. For more product information, visit Forman Interactive's Web site at: `http://www.formaninteractive.com/`.

FolkWeb.   The product name is: FolkWeb Server. FolkWeb Server is shareware that you can try for 30 days but must then register. It is a Web server that has the following features:

- Supports Windows NT 3.5 or Windows 95.
- WIN 32 multithreading where each connection has a dedicated thread.
- HTTP 1.0 protocol compliant.
- Supports GET, HEAD, and POST request methods.

- Supports Content negotiation.
- Uses built-in NCSA compatible clickable Image-Maps.
- Uses built-in database connectivity. Now you can publish your databases without writing a single line of CGI code.
- Supports Windows CGI/1.2 protocol.
- Supports ISAPI protocol.
- Uses GUI based control application for server settings with online help.
- Supports URL to path mapping (aliasing).
- Supports extension to MIME type mapping.
- Supports document to URL redirection.
- Access logging.
- Error logging.
- Access authentication by users or groups.
- Can change access realms without restarting server.
- Supports IP filtering.
- Built-in and configured URLs.
- Uses built-in directory listing with image and header extensions.
- Automatic backing of log files
- Database connectivity extensions: adding new records
- Change all settings without reloading the server
- Capability to run FolkWeb Control Panel from the server.
- Customized DB reports (background, headnote, footnote, logo)
- Customized directory listing (background, headnote, footnote, logo)
- CGI 1.1 support (not to be confused with Windows CGI/1.1 and 1.2 which already supported)
- Perl CGI 1.1 support.
- Fully NCSA compliant log files
- Improved documentation

For more product information, visit ILAR Concepts Web site at: `http://www.ilar.com/`.

WebMania.   The product name is: WebMania! WebMania! is a full-featured shareware HTML editor which includes unparalleled support for Frames, Forms, and Client-Side Image Maps! It also includes 60 user-programmable toolbar buttons which allow you to add new HTML tags as you learn them, and/or as HTML standards evolve. For this reason alone, WebMania! will NEVER become obsolete! ***New for version 2.0— Spell Checker, generate CGI forms and PERL scripts, as well as mailto forms, open and edit multiple documents!! Much, much more! You must have VBRUN 300.DLL to run the program. For more product information, visit Q&D Software Developments Web site at: `http://www.q-d.com/`.

WebForms. The product name is: WebForms. The WebForms shareware lets you create your own forms which you can link to your home page, allowing you to conduct surveys, collect orders for your products, anything you can think of! Responses are automatically sent to your mailbox, then read by WebFormsTM and collected in a Response Database! It's all controlled by YOU, and all you need is an e-mail address! No CGI?? No problem!! WebForms can handle your forms with or without CGI!! This new version of WebFormsTM contains some fantastic new features, including CGI form and Perl script generation! You must have VBRUN 300.DLL to run this program. For more product information, visit Q&D Software Developments Web site at: `http://www. q-d.com/`.

ShowBase. The product name is: ShowBase. Showbase lets you put your database on the Web without programming, you can use ShowBase to index your data and create an interface that provides keyword searching as well as hypertext browsing. The search interface is simple, easy to use, and customizable. As well, you can customize the output to suit your needs. ShowBase supports ODBC compliant databases as well as multimedia files, and is compatible with most Web servers and platforms. When you install the software, you will be prompted for a serial number. The serial number to use for this trial version of the product is: 153256235044582. For more product information, visit Show-Base Inc.'s Web site at: `http://www.showbase.com/`.

WebMedia. The product name is: Web Media Publisher Pro. It is a Web site development product that boasts the following features:

- 32Bit
- HTML 3.2, Netscape, and MSIE features
- Spell Checker
- FTP File Upload
- Preview images while adding to document
- Internal Web browser
- Easy tables creation
- Easy forms creation with preview
- Easy frames creation
- Full Java and Shockwave support
- User definable toolbars
- Multi-file search and replace
- WYSIWYG background text and background color selection
- Target Windows
- Default HTML template
- DDE control of Netscape and MS Explorer
- Import and Convert NCSA Image Maps in HTML

- Convert files between Macintosh, UNIX, and DOS formats
- Unlimited file size
- Extended character list
- Choose font colors, size, and face quickly and easily
- Drag-and-drop text editing
- Colored HTML tags
- Find and replace
- Relative path names
- Web timer
- Auto Convert types foreign characters into HTML character entities

For more product information, visit Web Media Incorporated's Web site at: `http://www.wbmedia.com/`.

CGILIB. The product is a PERL language library whose name is: cgi-lib.pl. The cgi-lib.pl library has become the de facto standard library for creating Common Gateway Interface (CGI) scripts in the PERL language. Go to the official Web site for cgi-lib.pl, with the most up-to-date releases of the library.

The cgi-lib.pl library makes CGI scripting in PERL easy enough for anyone to process forms and create dynamic Web content.

The library has the following features:

- Extremely simple to learn and easy to use
- Designed for operation under PERL5 and PERL4
- Very efficient
- Compatibility with all CGI interactions, including File Upload
- Convenient utility functions
- Compatible with PERL5 security features such as taint, warnings, (command line options -Tw) and use strict
- Debugging facilities
- A good starting point for migration to more sophisticated libraries

For more product information, visit Steven Brenner's Web site at: `http://www.bio.cam.ac.uk/cgi-lib/`.

CGIHTML. The product name is CGIHTML. Cgihtml is a set of CGI and HTML routines written for C written by Eugene Eric Kim, eekim@eekim.com. It was named one of the top 2 CGI tools in the August, 1996 issue of PC Computing. For more product information, visit E. E. Kims Web site at: `http://www.eekim/`.

SQL_NAV. The product name is: SQL Navigator. SQL Navigator is the revolutionary GUI tool for server-side database development and management. It provides an integrated environment for schema management and full life cycle support of stored procedure coding, testing and tuning. It was conceived, designed and developed by database developers and DBAs. This is a 30 day trial version. The installation script will prompt you for a password. You should use the password: **gallaxy**. Make sure you enter this password in lower-case characters. For more product information, visit Technosolutions Incorporated Web site at: `http://www.technosolutions.com/`.

Limits of Liability and Disclaimer of Warranty

The authors and publisher of this book have used their best efforts in preparing the CD-ROM and the programs contained in it. These efforts include the development, research, and testing of the theories and programs to determine their effectiveness. The authors and publisher make no warranty of any kind expressed or implied, with regard to these programs or the documentation contained in this book.

The authors and publisher shall not be liable in the event of incidental or consequential damages in connection with, or arising out of, the furnishing, performance, or use of the programs, associated instructions, and/or claims of productivity gains.

The programs on this CD and are presented "as-is." If you have problems running a program, you should contact the software manufacturer for help. Some of the software on this CD-ROM may be shareware; there may be additional charges (owed to the software authors/makers) incurred for the registration and continued use of the shareware. See individual program's README file for more information.

Frequently Asked Questions

This appendix contains answers to some of the most frequently asked questions about the process of Web database application development. Although these questions and answers will not address *all* of the issues that you may have, you'll find that they provide answers to most of the basic questions you'll encounter. Here are the questions that are answered in this appendix:

- What are Web applications?
- What are intranets?
- What is a Web database and why have one?
- What types of databases are accessible in a Web database application?
- What are the advantages of web database applications for the user?
- What are the advantages to a company from building a Web database application?
- What is the role of databases in web applications?
- What are the components in a Web database application?
- What should I consider when choosing a programming language?
- What are some of the languages available to help me build a Web database application?
- What are Web database application development suites?
- What are some of the benefits and limitations to HTML?

- What is a CGI program?
- How does a CGI program fit in the architecture of a Web database application?
- How does data get passed from a HTML page to a CGI program?
- Are there any programming principles that I should be aware of when writing CGI programs?
- Where should security exist in a Web database application?
- What types of join relationships are recognized in Oracle 8?
- What types of objects are allowed on HTML forms?
- How can I format and submit a database query from within a HTML page?
- Why should you use custom CGI programs for database access?
- What is MIME?

What Are Web Applications?

Web applications share some common characteristics:

They understand and use HTML as their display vehicle

They use the bi-directional client/server model of data communications and information collection

They provide facilities to access a variety of protocols, including HTTP, FTP, Telnet, and Gopher

They use Uniform Resource Locators (URLs) for document and resource addressing

What Are Intranets?

Recently a new word has become popular when describing a segment of the Internet—*intranet*. An intranet is a private network inside a company or organization that uses the same kinds of software that you'd find on the public Internet, that is targeted for internal use only. Because of their secure nature (they can usually only be accessed by employees of the company that have the intranet), intranets were the first vehicle for development and deployment of Web database applications.

Intranets, like Internets, are not defined by physical or geographical boundaries. Anyone with a Web browser can access a corporate intranet site from anywhere in the world—although only those people who have security permissions are allowed to enter. An intranet site is usually identified in the same way that an Internet site is identified—by an URL.

What Is a Web Database and Why Have One?

A Web database is not too much different from a non-Web database—the distinguishing characteristics are that Web databases are accessed from a Web browser and Web databases can have no data components that reside on the user's machine. A Web database is part of an application that is deployed over either the Internet (for external user's access) or a corporate intranet (for internal use only). Web databases come in many different varieties such as Oracle Corporation's Oracle 8, Access 97, Sybase, Informix, DB2, and many others.

What Types of Databases Are Accessible in a Web Database Application?

There are four types of database that are accessible from within a Web database application. These are:

1. *Flat-file database*—This is the oldest type of database, and is often referred to as a spreadsheet database. A distinguishing characteristic of a flat-file database is that columns and rows are used to collect and store small and discrete pieces of information into a table.

2. *Relational database*—These are databases that contain one or more database tables where one or more columns of information are related to one or more columns of information in another table. Relational databases hold great promise for Web database application development. They are fast, extremely efficient, and flexible. They are also able to be easily migrated from one physical location to the other and most of today's RDBMS vendors provide synchronization facilities in their products to ensure that data which resides in multiple locations is kept in sync automatically (well, pretty much automatically!).

3. *Object-oriented database*—An OO database consists of columns and rows, very similar to flat-file and relational databases. Each object in the database has one of three classes: number, text, date. There are processes (attributes) the database stores for each class of data. For example, it allows manipulation of data stored as dates (i.e., adding a month or subtracting 72 hours), but not data stored as text.

4. *Hybrid database*—A hybrid database is considered by many to be the aggregation of the best components and features of RDBMS and OODBMS products. Hybrid databases handle data that RDBMS products can use, as well as non-text items such as pictures, audio/video clips, etc. Hybrid databases allow you to process complex queries.

What Are the Advantages of Web Database Applications for the User?

There are two groups of users of Web database applications. These are people that access your Web database application over the Internet, and the employees of a corporation that have a Web database application accessed over their intranet.

The advantages of a Web database application deployed over the internet are:

- A broader reach than conventional advertising or marketing
- Automated sales force
- Access to company information from the comforts of home (or their workplace)

- Ability to interface with the company data without having to purchase expensive equipment or software

  The advantages of Web database applications to intranet users are summarized as:

- Graphical user interfaces to corporate data
- Access to up-to-date company information
- Greater opportunity to interact with other people, departments, and technologies within the company
- Ability to customize their browsers to meet their specific needs
- Integration of the Web database application with other applications running on their machines

What Are the Advantages to a Company from Building a Web Database Application?

The number one reason why a company should do business on the Web by building and deploying a Web database application is that if they don't, with all other competitive issues being equal, their competition will out-perform them. The following list describes some of the reasons why this is the case.

1. *Expand reach*—On the Web, you can make a sales presentation or put promotional material in the hands of interested people while all your sales people are sound asleep in their beds. Orders can be taken and product queued for shipment before your first cup of coffee in the morning. You no longer have to pony up the $3—$4k it costs to send a sales person around the world to meet with customers

2. *Corporate image enhancement*—In addition to the marketing and sales opportunities doing business on the Web presents, there is a lot of opportunity to conduct Public Relations activities on the Web—thereby performing image enhancement. This includes: corporate mission statement, goals, philosophies, charities it donates to, and testimonials of what a great company it is to do business with and work for.

3. *Improved customer service*—Customers are demanding more from the companies they do business with. This includes:
   - More product choices
   - Less expensive products and services
   - Increased customer service

   Regarding the last item, the Web provides a tremendous opportunity to provide customer service that is not only very responsive but one of the least expensive ways to implement.

4. *Lead generation*—When a person browses your Web site, you can track and extract their login ID. You know they are at least a candidate customer—and with their login ID you can send follow-up sales/marketing material. If a person downloads something from your Web site that they can access and retrieve for free, then you know you have a qualified lead. You can follow-up on that lead with whatever you decide. The point is that it has incrementally cost you very little to generate this lead.

5. *Product/service delivery channel*—The Web represents a new delivery channel for products and services. It is not the only one for most companies, but it is one that deserves attention. In the coming years, as companies become more astute at doing business on the Web, we will see the recognition that the Web is a viable and significant delivery channel of products and services.

6. *Reduce operating expenses*—Companies are operating with profit margins that are thinner today than ever before. Doing business on the Web allows companies to reduce their operating expenses by: maintaining current sales volumes while decreasing staff counts and expenses, reducing the number of people that work in support, reducing the cost of marketing and direct mail, reducing public relations costs, and by culling out unprofitable products and services due to the improved data on which products and services are profitable and which are not.

7. *Test marketing*—The Web is a great place for a company to "test market" a number of things. These include: new products, new services, and new marketing campaigns.

What Is the Role of Databases in Web Applications?

Although you can think of one or more ways that *your* company could make use of a database in its Web applications, the following list is a good introduction.

- Inter-business agreement and document processing, such as ordering, purchasing, invoicing, and automated payment processing.

- Demographics, such as customer, supplier, and business partner profiles that are accumulated and used to improve and customize customer services.

- Customer status and account management used to manage past purchase history, and predict future purchase patterns.

- Establishment and maintenance of customer profiles for use in finely tailored advertising and sales campaigns.

- Inventory management and status to reduce cash reserves held in inventory, to product online and interactive catalogs, to interface with inventory control systems, and to provide virtual shopping malls.

- Sales tracking and call management to monitor, track, and increase the effectiveness of the sales force and various marketing campaigns.

- Technical product specifications that are available by customers and field staff to search for product specifications, parts lists, troubleshooting information, and pricing.

What Are the Components in a Web Database Application?

There are five major components in a Web database application environment. These five components are:

1. *Web server*—The Web server is the software component that reacts to and interfaces with Web browser/client. It has no ability to create or update Web pages or documents. Rather, it reads a request for information coming to it from a Web browser,

usually in the form of an URL, locates the requested page, and sends the requested page back to the Web browser.

2. *Application server*—The role of the application server is to sit between the Web Server and RDBMS and is responsible for maintaining an open connection between the Web server and the RDBMS at all times.

3. *Web browser/client*—The Web browser/client is the software that runs on a client machine and performs necessary communication functions. The main functions performed by Web browsers/clients are to: establish and maintain communications with a Web server, pass user requests and data to the Web server, display information received from a Web server, and to view files not originating from a Web server.

4. *CGI program*—The CGI program, an optional component, is intended mainly to interact with the Web server by using one of a number of different standards. Its primary method of Web server interaction is to connect the Web server to external programs.

5. *Relational DataBase Management System (RDBMS)*—The purpose of the RDBMS package is to manage, safeguard, and control the data that is accessed by the Web database application.

What Should I Consider When Choosing a Programming Language?

The decision of which programming language to use to develop your Web application is not much different from the decision of which programming language to use to develop any other application. It helps to view a Web database application as just another application development project. It has its own unique set of factors that must be evaluated, but the same statement can be made about any development project.

There are a number of items to consider to determine which is the best programming language to use. These items are:

1. *Skillset of developers*—A knowledge of the skills required for the project and what skills exist in current staff.

2. *Scope of the project*—An awareness of the scope of the project and the range of functions and capabilities of the various programming languages.

3. *Application interfaces*—Web database applications will interface to either existing or newly created databases as well as potentially to other applications used by the company.

4. *Availability of support tools*—Regardless of the skills of your developers against the requirements of the task, it is a very valuable investment of time to address the issue of support tool requirements and availability.

5. *Database interfaces*—The type and number of databases your Web database application will access and interface with is an important factor in determining what language you select.

6. *Platforms application will run on*—If you are writing an application where components of that application are distributed to a client's machine, then you must be aware of the platforms that run on those machines.

What Are Some of the Languages Available to Help Me Build a Web Database Application?

Although this is not a comprehensive list (new tools and languages are being brought to market at a feverish pace) it is comprehensive in terms of the languages that comprise at least 98% of all the code written in programming languages to create Web database applications. The most popular languages are: C, C++, COBOL, Java, JavaScript, Perl, Power-Builder, Shell Script, Visual Basic, and Visual Basic Script.

What Are Web Database Application Development Suites?

Application development suites are one of the quickest growing segments in the Web market. Companies, both customers and suppliers alike, learned in the early 1990s that a development tool used in isolation and detached from other tools often becomes a little used tool. Application suites remedy this problem by offering a selection of tools used to develop Web applications. For example, most application development suites include the following integrated components; WYSIWYG development interface, an Image Map editor, the ability to write Visual Basic or JavaScript scripts, a basic compiler, a debugger, a Web publishing tool, an application server, and a freeware or evaluation copy of a Web server.

What Are Some of the Benefits and Limitations to HTML?

Although you really don't have much of a choice when deciding to build a Web database application (you *really should* use HTML), some of the benefits available by using HTML are: a rapid development environment, extensive cross-platform support, and support for multiple types of media included on the Web pages.

Like everything else in the world of computing, HTML is not free from limitations. Although the standard is rapidly evolving to remove many of these limitations, the day will probably never come when this tool is free from limitations. The limitations of HTML as a Web page development tool are: limited user-input capabilities, limited page layout capabilities, and limited programmatic capabilities.

What Is a CGI Program?

CGI programs, or scripts (the terms are used interchangeably) are executable files—programs written, compiled, and linked in one of a number of different languages. The most common language for a CGI program is Perl, but other languages include C, C++, Java, JavaScript, Visual Basic, PowerBuilder, etc. Perl's dominance as a CGI development language has recently been challenged by not only many of these other languages but also by Web development tools.

As you know, HTML has no facilities to directly query a database. Through CGI, this capability exists. By utilizing CGI scripts, a request can be sent from within HTML, and processed by the HTTP server, to query the database for specific information, and then display the result set in dynamically built HTML code. With this capability, there is no need to have to manually change a Web page whenever data on that page changes.

How Does a CGI Program Fit in the Architecture of a Web Database Application?

A CGI program is a major component in a Web database application. To understand how it fits in the architecture of the application you need to understand how all the pieces of a Web database application work together. This process is described below.

Step 1: A user, accessing a browser, sends a request to a server via HTML. This HTML includes a request to execute a CGI program, as well as any parameters the CGI program might need.

Step 2: The server receives the request from the browser, processes the HTML, and encounters the request to execute a CGI program. The server initiates the CGI program's execution by calling it and passing it any parameters that were received from the browser.

Step 3: The CGI program executes. In its execution, it may:
• Access no other resources
• Access databases either locally or remotely
• Access other applications or initiate the execution of other programs
• Access other network resources

Step 4: The server receives a result set from the CGI program if one is returned, and sends the data and/or response back to the browser via HTML

Step 5: The browser receives the HTML sent to it from the server and formats and displays the data received

How Does Data Get Passed from an HTML Page to a CGI Program?

There are a number of ways that a browser can transmit data strings to a CGI program—with the following three being the post popular. These are: GET, ISINDEX, and POST. Each of these are discussed in detail in Chapters 7 and 13 of this book.

Are There Any Programming Principles That I Should Be Aware of When Writing CGI Programs?

The short answer is: Yes. Assuming you are already a programmer, well schooled in sound programming techniques, there are a few issues unique to CGI programming you need to be aware of. The principles are: Application performance, the use of comments, the HTTP protocol and specifications you are supporting in the application, the choice of language and its particular syntax conventions, naming conventions that are standards for the language, the use of a separate development site from the production site, the standards that exist within your company for the development of applications, and the user of libraries as a productivity and system-quality aid.

Where Should Security Exist in a Web Database Application?

The perils of Web commerce have been discussed at length in the media. As a result of all the attention paid to the subject historically, the development and deployment of commercial Web sites is much less dangerous. There are four primary areas where you must ensure that proper security safeguards are in place to protect your data and resources. These four areas are:

1. *Physical*—This is perhaps the easiest component area to ensure safety in that the physical security of computers and computing devices has been an issue of concern to MIS managers for a number of years.

2. *Software*—Your software is much more vulnerable on a Web site than in almost any other type of delivery method. The Web is a very "open" environment. If you see a graphic on a Web page, or an applet that you'd like, it's easy (albeit illegal) to snag it. Because of this, you must be keenly aware of the security issues persistent as you design your application.

3. *System–Hacker!*—The meaning of this word is clearly understood by even the most neophyte computer user. The consequence of a hacker breaching your system and causing damage of some sort could range in severity from annoyance to catastrophic. Even the variety of breach that is more annoying than anything else will cause you great embarrassment when your boss asks you how someone was able to break through the security layers and gain access to your system. Be warned, making your system too secure from Hacker attack is something that would be very hard to do, provided you don't make it cumbersome or difficult for the good people to access.

4. *Data*—As much as "Protect Yourself" was a moniker for the 1980s and 1990s, "Protect Your Data" will become an identifying phrase for the 1990s and beyond. An easy argument could be made for paying more attention to protecting the integrity and confidentiality of the data accessed by your Web database application than to the security of the system as a whole.

What Types of Join Relationships Are Recognized in Oracle 8?

Oracle 8 recognizes three types of join relationships. These are:

1. *Inner join*—This is the default type of join. It joins the two tables *only* when the values in the two joined fields are equal.

2. *Left join*—This type of join takes all the records from the left-most table, regardless of the right-most table having any matching values in it.

3. *Right join*—This type of join takes all the records in the right-most table, regardless of the left-most table having any matching values in it.

What Types of Objects Are Allowed on HTML Forms?

There are seven basic objects on an HTML form that you have available to receive input from users. These are: checkbox, command buttons, list box, password, radio button, text, and text box.

How Can I Format and Submit a Database Query from Within an HTML Page?

HTML specifications provide no direct method for querying a database. There are three main methods you can use to build database connectivity into your HTML form. These are:

1. *Code-less interfaces*—These are software toolsets that work in tandem with developer defined template files. The purpose of the templates is to define various views into the database and describe how data is to be displayed once it is retrieved. When these forms are incorporated into an HTML page and sent to the HTTP Server for processing, they are processed by CGI programs that perform the actual querying and formatting of the data.

2. *Custom CGI program*—These are "gateway" programs that are specifically written to accept and process SQL queries. These programs receive the user's request for DBMS data, parse the user inputs and create a query to accommodate the user request, and dynamically create an HTML document that transmits the result set back to the user.

3. *HTML embedded SQL extensions*—These are special HTML extensions supplied by RDBMS and other tool vendors that provide a mechanism to embed SQL statements directly into the body of the HTML file that is passed from the user to the HTTP server. When received at the server, this HTML file is parsed to pull out the SQL statements that are subsequently passed to a CGI program.

Why Should You Use Custom CGI Programs for Database Access?

Custom CGI programs are the most common method of accessing corporate databases, far eclipsing the other two methods described above. Although code-less interfaces and HTML embedded SQL extensions may someday catch up and surpass the popularity of custom CGI programs, this is not expected for many years. And, when that time does come, the need and use for custom CGI programs will continue—in fact, it may never end. There will always be an inherent limit to the power and flexibility of code-less interfaces and HTML-embedded SQL extensions that custom CGI programs will exceed. This is why all the major development toolkits provide API interfaces to more powerful languages.

What Is MIME?

MIME stands for Multipurpose Internet Mail Extension. It is a set of standards that specify both the type of file being sent from a Web component (either a Web server or browser) to another Web component as well as the method that should be used to turn that message back into its original form. To you, the person designing or building a Web database application, MIME allows you to incorporate the inclusion of audio, video, and multimedia elements in your application.

APPENDIX C

WWW Database Development Resources

This appendix contains a list of the available resources accessible over the Internet that provides wonderful examples, documentation, freeware, demoware, or shareware, that will help you in the design and development of Web database applications. This is not an all inclusive list, but it is certainly substantial enough that you will get more than enough of what you need to get you moving nicely down the road.

The references are broken down into the following categories:

- Databases
- Programming languages
- Other
- Reference material
- Security
- Web servers

Databases

A site developed and maintained by David Muir Sharnoff that is devoted to being a repository of free Web databases and tools:

```
http://cuiww.unige.ch/~scg/freedb/freedb.list.html
```

A site developed and offered by Bristol Database Resources, Inc. that provides access to a large number of demo applications written for a variety of RDBMS products:

```
http://bristol.onramp.net/
```

A site where you can download a copy of the Postgres95 Web database software:

```
http://s2.ftp.cs.berkeley.edu:8000/postgres95
```

A site where you can download a free copy of the Experimental Multimedia Database— MMDB:

```
http://www.univ.triests.it/cgi-bin/wwwwais
```

A site devoted to disseminating information and links to other commercial sites specific to Web Database Gateway products:

```
http://cscsun1.larc.nasa.gov/~beowulf/db/existing_products.html
```

A site devoted to providing sample scripts and examples of using Oraperl as a CGI/RDBMS interface:

```
http://www.nofc.forestry.ca/features/script.html
```

The Microrim Corporation site that is specific to its R:WEB product:

```
http://www.microrim.com/
```

Oracle Corporation's Web site where you can find abundant and copious amounts of information on not only the Oracle RDBMS family of products but related products as well:

```
http://www.oracle.com/
```

The Sybase Corporation's Web site where you can find abundant information on Sybase SQL Server:

```
http://www.sybase.com/products/internet/websql
```

The IBM Corporation site that offers a Web interface for its DB2 database:

```
http://as400.rochester.ibm.com/qdls/400home/ncc/webconn/db2www.htm
```

The Informix Corporation's Web site that is specific to its flagship Informix RDBMS products:

```
http://www.informix.com/informix/dbweb/grail/freeware.htm
```

The Microsoft Corporation Web site that is specific to its Visual FoxPro product:

```
http://www.microsoft.com/vfoxpro/
```

The Borland International site that is specific to dBASE for Windows:

```
http://www.borland.com/product/db/dbase/windbase.html
```

Another site devoted to disseminating information and links to other sites of interest specific to DbPerl, which is a database access applications programming language:

```
http://www.hermetica.com/technologia/dbi/
```

Newsgroup devoted to problem resolution with IBM DB2 databases:

```
news:comp.databases.ibm-db2
```

Newsgroup devoted to Informix database issues:

```
news:comp.databases.informix
```

Newsgroup designed to address issues specific to Microsoft Access:

```
news:comp.databases.ms-access
```

Newsgroup designed to deal with issues specific to the Microsoft SQL Server product:

```
news:comp.databases.ms-sqlserver
```

Newsgroup dealing with topics relating to Oracle SQL database products:

```
news:comp.databases.oracle
```

Newsgroup that offers discussion on Sybase SQL Server:

```
news:comp.databases.sybase
```

Newsgroup that deals with issues specific to the database aspects of Visual Basic:

```
news:comp.lang.basic.visual.database
```

Other

To learn more about SQL and the history of SQL, try these two URLs:

```
http://www.bf.rmit.edu.au/oracle/docs.html#tinalondon
http://waltz.ncsl.nist.gov/~len/sql_info.html
```

A great location to review what some view as standards for developing and using image maps:

```
http://hway.com/ihip/cside.html
```

You can grab a free copy of WinZip, the world's leading file compression software from this site:

```
http://www.winzip.com/winzip/download.html
```

Macromedia Corporation's site that includes Director and Shockwave, two tools useful in developing multimedia applications that might be deployed over the Internet:

```
http://www.macromedia.com
```

The site listed here lists graphics software that is available for downloading:

```
http://sun1.bham.ac.uk/s.m.williams.bcm/images/viewers.html
```

The following URL contains lists of other links for tips on HTML and graphics:

```
http://maui.net/~mcculc/resource.htm
```

The newsgroup listed below can help to provide answers to questions about HTML:

```
news:com.infosystems.www.authoring.html
```

Browsers treat certain HTML tags and tag pairs differently. To see a list of the differences among the various browsers, look at:

```
http://www.colosys.net/~rscott/barb.htm
```

EDP Markets is a company that makes extensive use of a Web database application to provide its services, which are to find people to fill technical positions for companies willing to pay a fee for this service:

```
http://www.edpmarkets.com
```

A good example of the use of an image map in a Web application:

```
http://www.z100portland.com
```

A site sponsored by GNN, a subsidiary of America Online, that provides a set of tools for browsing, authoring, and Web publishing:

```
http://www.tools.gnn.com/download.html
```

A site put together by Spider Technologies where you can try out a copy of Art Gallery, a Web site development tool:

```
http://www.netdynamics.com/action
```

The home page for the Edify Electronic Workforce product that is sold and supported by Edify Corporation:

```
http://www.edify.com/
```

The home page for the IQ Live Web product that is sold and supported by IQ Software, Inc.

```
http://www.iqsc.com/
```

The home page for Krakatoa, a Web search tool developed and sold by CADIS, Incorporated:

```
http://www.cadis.com/
```

The web page for LivePAGE, an open, nonproprietary text and information management software product developed and sold by Netscape Communications:

```
http://www.netscape.com/comprod/products/tools/
```

The web page for Live Wire and Live Wire Pro, two products developed and sold by Netscape Communications to enable novice users to create and manage Web content, Web sites, and live online Web applications for intranets and the Internet:

```
http://www.netscape.com/comprod/products/tools/
```

The web page for FrontPage, Microsoft Corporations offering for a Web application development suite:

```
http://www.microsoft.com/frontpage/
```

The web pages for Oracle Designer 2000 and Oracle Developer 2000 Oracle Corporation's Web application development tool suite offerings:

```
http://www.oracle.com/products/tools/des2k/
http://www.oracle.com/products/tools/dev2k/
```

The web page for Tango, the web database application development suite from Everywhere Development Corporation:

```
http://www.everyware.com/products/tango/
```

The home page for Webdbc, from Stormcloud Development Corporation, which is a Web database application development suite:

```
http://www.ndev.com/
```

The home page for WebHub from HREF Tools Corporation, which is technology that provides a complete object-oriented framework for industrial strength web application development.

```
http://www.href.com/
```

The home page for Webinator, the product from Thunderstone Corporation that is billed as being a Web walking and indexing package that allows a Web site administrator to create and provide a high quality retrieval interface to collections of HTML documents.

```
http://www.thunderstone.com/
```

The home page for Web Objects, the development tool suite from NeXT Software that is an environment for developing and deploying World Wide Web applications:

```
http://www.next.com/webobjects/
```

Microsoft Corporation keeps a pretty comprehensive collection of ODBC drivers on their Web site at the following URL:

```
http://www.microsoft.com/odbc/
```

Programming Languages

A relatively new scripting language that is beginning to gain a loyal following is named Eva. You can find out all about this language and get a demo copy of the product from:

```
http://www.techware.com
```

Micro Focus LTD., a PC-based COBOL language tool developer with U.S. headquarters in Palo Alto, California:

```
http://www.microfocus.com
```

The site developed by Netscape Communications that provides a brief introduction to JavaScript and a number of examples and pointers to other relevant JavaScript sites:

```
http://home.netscape.com/comprod/products/navigator/version_3.0/script/in
dex.html
```

Netscape Communications site where you can find the official documentation and reference materials for JavaScript:

```
http://home.netscape.com/eng/mozilla/gold/handbook/javascript/index.html
```

A site where you can find a growing number of tutorials that help to learn JavaScript:

```
http://outworld.compuserve.com/homepages/vood/script.htm
```

Directory of Java-related products, objects, and sites:

```
http://www.gamelan.com/
```

A couple of newsgroups devoted to Java and JavaScript:

```
news:comp.lang.java
news:comp.lang.javascript
```

The home page for Information Analytics and their 4W Publisher and 4W Publisher Pro products:

```
http://www.4w.com/4wpublisher/
```

The home page for the Amazon product that is sold by Intelligent Environments:

```
http://www.ieinc.com/
```

The home page for the Speedware product that is sold by Speedware Toronto:

```
http://www.speedware.com/
```

The home page for the Centura Web Data Publisher product that is sold by Centura Software:

```
http://www.centurasoft.com/
```

The home page for the Delphi product that is sold and supported by Borland International:

```
http://www.borland.com/delphi/
```

The home page for the Foxweb product that is sold and supported by Eon Technologies:

```
http://www.foxweb.com/
```

To find out about the cgic programming language:

```
http://www.boutell.com/cgic/
```

A great place to try out and get resource information about CGI++ is:

```
http://sweetbay.will.uiuc.edu/cgi++
```

A great resource if you are planning on using Visual Basic as a CGI language is:

```
http://website.ora.com/devcorner/db-src/index.html
```

The home page for HAHT Software, the company that has developed and sells the HAHTsite IDE product:

```
http://www.haht.com/
```

Oracle Corporation's web page devoted to Oracle Power Objects, which is the development tool that facilitates Web application development:

```
http://www.oracle.com/products/tools/power_objects/
```

The home page for PowerBuilder, the product offering of Sybase Incorporated that is a programming tool that helps you build Web applications:

```
http://www.powersoft.com/products/devtools/pb50/
```

Newsgroup devoted to writing CGI scripts for the Web:

```
news:comp.infosystems.www.authoring.cgi
```

Newsgroup devoted to writing HTML:

```
news:comp.infosystems.www.authoring.html
```

Newsgroup devoted to using images and image maps on the Web:

```
news:comp.infosystems.www.authoring.images
```

The web page for Software Engine, the flagship product from Software Engines, Inc.:

```
http://www.engine.com/
```

Reference Material

The Web developer's virtual library:

```
http://www.stars.com/
```

A site maintained by Jeff Rowe that deals with Web database tools and techniques:

```
http://cscsun1.larc.nasa.gov/~beowulf/db/existing_products.html
```

A listing of the Internet Service Providers (ISPs) located around the world can be found at:

```
http://www.thelist.com/
```

Billed as the largest online source of books, both technical and non-technical, this is an URL that you'll want to bookmark:

```
http://www.amazon.com
```

This site gives information on how to register a domain name:

```
http://www.internic.net
```

The JAVA white paper: This site describes the underlying principles of Java's development and intended use:

```
http://www.javasoft.com/nav/read/whitepapers.
```

For those of you that are highly interested in the underpinnings of the Java language specification, you can find this at:

```
http://www.javasoft.com/nav/read/index.html
```

A site developed by Interface Technologies Corporation that is devoted to providing a series of articles and tutorial to help with the design and development of a Web site:

```
http://www.iftech.com/classes/webdev/webdev0.htm
```

A site devoted to image maps, how to create and use them in Web applications:

```
http://hoohoo.ncsa.uiuc.edu/docs/tutorials/imagemapping.html.
```

A Yahoo site developed and maintained exclusively for CGI programmers:

```
http://www.yahoo.com/computers_and_internet/internet/world_wide_web/cgi_c
ommon_gateway_interface/index.html
```

The URL for *Web Techniques* magazine:

```
http://webtechniques.com/
```

An electronic magazine for the Java community as published by IDG Communications:

```
http://www.javaworld.com/
```

A site that gives information about how to develop a searchable database site that also includes references to a number of other sites focused on providing information specific to Web database application development:

```
http://www2.ncsu.edu/bae/people/faculty/walker/hotlist/isindex.html
```

This is a tutorial made available by the same people that sell WebSite, a Web server product that is very popular in small to medium sized installations:

```
http://solo.dc3.com/db-src/index.html
```

A newsgroup devoted to the Perl CGI programming language:

```
news:comp.lang.perl
```

The *Web Manual of Style*, written by Patrick Lynch, can be found at:

```
http://info.med.yale.edu/caim/StyleManual_Top.html
```

A Web site sponsored by Ohio State University and dedicated to espousing information about MIME:

`http://www.cis.ohio.state.edu/hypertext/faq/usenet/mail/mime-faq/top.html`

A Web site developed by Indiana State University and dedicated to MIME:

`http://www.cs.indiana.edu/docproject/mail/mime.html`

A couple of areas on the Netscape Communications Corporation Web site devoted to MIME:

`http://www.netscape.com/assist/helper_apps/media-types.html`
`http://www.netscape.com/assist/helper_apps/what-is-mime.html`

Security

A site sponsored by Netscape Communications that deals specifically with Secure Sockets Layer (SSL):

`http://www.netscape.com/newsref/std/ssl.html`

Take a look at this URL if you are interested in web security:

`http://www.nortel.com/entrust/certificates/primer.html`

A site that is specific to CGI security:

`http://www.primus.com/staff/paulp/cgi_security`

A web site with a substantial amount of information on the subject of CGI security is available at:

`http://www.cerf.net/~paulp/cgi_security/`

A FAQ presented by Oxford University on firewalls and their use in Internet security:

`http://www.lib.ox.ac.uk/internet/news/faq/archive/firewalls-faq.html`

A WWW security FAQ presented by Compuserve:

`http://ourworld.compuserve.com/homepages/perthes/wwwsecur.htm`

Final Quarterly Report of the UKERNA Secure Email Project:

`http://www.tech.ukerna.ac.uk/pgp/secemail/q4.html`

Internet Firewalls Frequently Asked Questions from the V-One Company:

`http://www.v-one.com/pubs/fw-faq/faq.html`

One of the places where hackers meet that contains a huge collection of hacking and related links:

`http://incyberspace.com/woodstok/hack/`

Web Servers

The NCSA HTTP Server:

```
http://hoohoo.ncsa.uiuc.edu/
```

The home page for the A-XOrion Database Server product offered by Clark Internet Services:

```
http://www.clark.net/infouser/
```

The home page for the dbWeb product that is now sold and supported by Microsoft Corporation:

```
http://www.microsoft.com/intdev/dbweb/
```

Microsoft Corporation includes a copy of its Internet Information Server (IIS) in its Windows NT version 4.0. If you have an earlier version of Windows NT, you can download a copy of IIS from:

```
http://www.microsoft.com/infoserv
```

The home page for the DynaWeb product that is sold and supported by Inso Corporation:

```
http://dynabase.ebt.com/dbproduct/index.htm
```

The home page for the Personal Web Site Toolbox, a tool offered by W3.Com Incorporated:

```
http://www.w3.com/
```

The web page for Sapphire Web, the product offering from Bluestone Software that facilitates the creation and management of a Web site:

```
http://www.bluestone.com/
```

The following URLs list places where you can find out more and possibly download demoware versions of server logging tools:

```
http://www.eit.com/software/getstats/getstats.html
http://www.boutell.com/wusage
http://www.openmarket.com/products/webreport.html
```

A newsgroup devoted to issues specific to Web servers:

```
news:comp.infosystems.www.servers.misc
```

The web page for SiteBase, the Web server product offering from Cykic Software:

```
http://www.cykic.com/
```

Index

LICENSE AGREEMENT AND LIMITED WARRANTY

READ THE FOLLOWING TERMS AND CONDITIONS CAREFULLY BEFORE OPENING THIS DISK PACKAGE. THIS LEGAL DOCUMENT IS AN AGREEMENT BETWEEN YOU AND PRENTICE-HALL, INC. (THE "COMPANY"). BY OPENING THIS SEALED DISK PACKAGE, YOU ARE AGREEING TO BE BOUND BY THESE TERMS AND CONDITIONS. IF YOU DO NOT AGREE WITH THESE TERMS AND CONDITIONS, DO NOT OPEN THE DISK PACKAGE. PROMPTLY RE-TURN THE UNOPENED DISK PACKAGE AND ALL ACCOMPANYING ITEMS TO THE PLACE YOU OBTAINED THEM FOR A FULL REFUND OF ANY SUMS YOU HAVE PAID.

1. **GRANT OF LICENSE:** In consideration of your payment of the license fee, which is part of the price you paid for this product, and your agreement to abide by the terms and conditions of this Agreement, the Company grants to you a nonexclusive right to use and display the copy of the en-closed software program (hereinafter the "SOFTWARE") on a single computer (i.e., with a single CPU) at a single location so long as you comply with the terms of this Agreement. The Company re-serves all rights not expressly granted to you under this Agreement.

2. **OWNERSHIP OF SOFTWARE:** You own only the magnetic or physical media (the en-closed disks) on which the SOFTWARE is recorded or fixed, but the Company retains all the rights, title, and ownership to the SOFTWARE recorded on the original disk copy(ies) and all subsequent copies of the SOFTWARE, regardless of the form or media on which the original or other copies may exist. This license is not a sale of the original SOFTWARE or any copy to you.

3. **COPY RESTRICTIONS:** This SOFTWARE and the accompanying printed materials and user manual (the "Documentation") are the subject of copyright. You may not copy the Documenta-tion or the SOFTWARE, except that you may make a single copy of the SOFTWARE for backup or archival purposes only. You may be held legally responsible for any copying or copyright infringe-ment which is caused or encouraged by your failure to abide by the terms of this restriction.

4. **USE RESTRICTIONS:** You may not network the SOFTWARE or otherwise use it on more than one computer or computer terminal at the same time. You may physically transfer the SOFT-WARE from one computer to another provided that the SOFTWARE is used on only one computer at a time. You may not distribute copies of the SOFTWARE or Documentation to others. You may not re-verse engineer, disassemble, decompile, modify, adapt, translate, or create derivative works based on the SOFTWARE or the Documentation without the prior written consent of the Company.

5. **TRANSFER RESTRICTIONS:** The enclosed SOFTWARE is licensed only to you and may not be transferred to any one else without the prior written consent of the Company. Any unautho-rized transfer of the SOFTWARE shall result in the immediate termination of this Agreement.

6. **TERMINATION:** This license is effective until terminated. This license will terminate auto-matically without notice from the Company and become null and void if you fail to comply with any provisions or limitations of this license. Upon termination, you shall destroy the Documentation and all copies of the SOFTWARE. All provisions of this Agreement as to warranties, limitation of liability, remedies or damages, and our ownership rights shall survive termination.

7. **MISCELLANEOUS:** This Agreement shall be construed in accordance with the laws of the United States of America and the State of New York and shall benefit the Company, its affiliates, and assignees.

8. **LIMITED WARRANTY AND DISCLAIMER OF WARRANTY:** The Company warrants that the SOFTWARE, when properly used in accordance with the Documentation, will operate in sub-stantial conformity with the description of the SOFTWARE set forth in the Documentation. The Com-pany does not warrant that the SOFTWARE will meet your requirements or that the operation of the SOFTWARE will be uninterrupted or error-free. The Company warrants that the media on which the

SOFTWARE is delivered shall be free from defects in materials and workmanship under normal use for a period of thirty (30) days from the date of your purchase. Your only remedy and the Company's only obligation under these limited warranties is, at the Company's option, return of the warranted item for a refund of any amounts paid by you or replacement of the item. Any replacement of SOFTWARE or media under the warranties shall not extend the original warranty period. The limited warranty set forth above shall not apply to any SOFTWARE which the Company determines in good faith has been subject to misuse, neglect, improper installation, repair, alteration, or damage by you. EXCEPT FOR THE EXPRESSED WARRANTIES SET FORTH ABOVE, THE COMPANY DISCLAIMS ALL WARRANTIES, EXPRESS OR IMPLIED, INCLUDING WITHOUT LIMITATION, THE IMPLIED WARRANTIES OF MERCHANTABILITY AND FITNESS FOR A PARTICULAR PURPOSE. EXCEPT FOR THE EXPRESS WARRANTY SET FORTH ABOVE, THE COMPANY DOES NOT WARRANT, GUARANTEE, OR MAKE ANY REPRESENTATION REGARDING THE USE OR THE RESULTS OF THE USE OF THE SOFTWARE IN TERMS OF ITS CORRECTNESS, ACCURACY, RELIABILITY, CURRENTNESS, OR OTHERWISE.

IN NO EVENT, SHALL THE COMPANY OR ITS EMPLOYEES, AGENTS, SUPPLIERS, OR CONTRACTORS BE LIABLE FOR ANY INCIDENTAL, INDIRECT, SPECIAL, OR CONSEQUENTIAL DAMAGES ARISING OUT OF OR IN CONNECTION WITH THE LICENSE GRANTED UNDER THIS AGREEMENT, OR FOR LOSS OF USE, LOSS OF DATA, LOSS OF INCOME OR PROFIT, OR OTHER LOSSES, SUSTAINED AS A RESULT OF INJURY TO ANY PERSON, OR LOSS OF OR DAMAGE TO PROPERTY, OR CLAIMS OF THIRD PARTIES, EVEN IF THE COMPANY OR AN AUTHORIZED REPRESENTATIVE OF THE COMPANY HAS BEEN ADVISED OF THE POSSIBILITY OF SUCH DAMAGES. IN NO EVENT SHALL LIABILITY OF THE COMPANY FOR DAMAGES WITH RESPECT TO THE SOFTWARE EXCEED THE AMOUNTS ACTUALLY PAID BY YOU, IF ANY, FOR THE SOFTWARE.

SOME JURISDICTIONS DO NOT ALLOW THE LIMITATION OF IMPLIED WARRANTIES OR LIABILITY FOR INCIDENTAL, INDIRECT, SPECIAL, OR CONSEQUENTIAL DAMAGES, SO THE ABOVE LIMITATIONS MAY NOT ALWAYS APPLY. THE WARRANTIES IN THIS AGREEMENT GIVE YOU SPECIFIC LEGAL RIGHTS AND YOU MAY ALSO HAVE OTHER RIGHTS WHICH VARY IN ACCORDANCE WITH LOCAL LAW.

ACKNOWLEDGMENT

YOU ACKNOWLEDGE THAT YOU HAVE READ THIS AGREEMENT, UNDERSTAND IT, AND AGREE TO BE BOUND BY ITS TERMS AND CONDITIONS. YOU ALSO AGREE THAT THIS AGREEMENT IS THE COMPLETE AND EXCLUSIVE STATEMENT OF THE AGREEMENT BETWEEN YOU AND THE COMPANY AND SUPERSEDES ALL PROPOSALS OR PRIOR AGREEMENTS, ORAL, OR WRITTEN, AND ANY OTHER COMMUNICATIONS BETWEEN YOU AND THE COMPANY OR ANY REPRESENTATIVE OF THE COMPANY RELATING TO THE SUBJECT MATTER OF THIS AGREEMENT.

TECHNICAL SUPPORT

PRENTICE HALL DOES NOT OFFER TECHNICAL SUPPORT FOR THIS SOFTWARE. HOWEVER, IF THERE IS A PROBLEM WITH THE MEDIA, YOU MAY OBTAIN A REPLACEMENT COPY BY EMAILING US WITH YOUR PROBLEM AT: discexchange@phptr.com

Should you have any questions concerning this Agreement or if you wish to contact the Company for any reason, please contact in writing at the address below.

Robin Short
Prentice Hall PTR
One Lake Street
Upper Saddle River, New Jersey 07458